# Black Hands, White House

# Black Hands, White House

## Slave Labor and the Making of America

**Renee K. Harrison**

Fortress Press
Minneapolis

BLACK HANDS, WHITE HOUSE
Slave Labor and the Making of America

Copyright © 2021 Renee K. Harrison. Printed by Fortress Press, an imprint of 1517 Media. All rights reserved. Except for brief quotations in critical articles or reviews, no part of this book may be reproduced in any manner without prior written permission from the publisher. Email copyright@1517.media or write to Permissions, Fortress Press, PO Box 1209, Minneapolis, MN 55440-1209.

Cover image: *Monthly Payroll for Carpenters and Joiners at the President's House, February 1795.* National Archives, Records of the Commissioners of the City of Washington
Cover design: Savanah Landerholm

Print ISBN: 978-1-5064-7467-0
eBook ISBN: 978-1-5064-7468-7

*The bent backs straightened up. Old and young who were called slaves and could fly joined hands. . . . They rose on the air. They flew in a flock that was black against the heavenly blue. Black crows or Black shadows. It didn't matter, they went so high. Way above the plantation, way over the slavery land. Say they flew away to* Free-dom*. . . . They say that the children of the ones who could not fly told their children. And now, . . . I have told it to you.*

—VIRGINIA HAMILTON, *The People Could Fly*

*To Christopher,*
for inspiring me to turn my
lament into a manuscript;
*to Ron and Nick,*
for in your garden, this work has blossomed;
*and to the Ancestors,*
for which no monument rests
on the National Mall

# Contents

# Figures

# Acknowledgments

*Black Hands, White House* is a labor of ancestral love birthed into wholeness with the care of all the following conversation partners and supportive communities.

Sincere thanks to my colleagues who perfected this work: Veronice Miles: you nurtured this manuscript as though it was your own. Your support, collaborating spirit, and editorial discernment were invaluable. Ronald Hopson, my colleague and brother: your intellect, constructive feedback, and critical perspective sharpened this work. Yolanda Pierce: our soul talks and sisterhood and your life-giving prayers fueled me and this manuscript to completion. Angela D. Sims: our ancestral musings and sojourn into the horrid shepherded the contours and delivery of this work—#uralwaysrightontime. Velma E. Love: our sisterhood and ancestral journeying together have always been my soul comfort and compass. Pamela R. Lightsey: your advocacy for LGBTQIA+ persons is a reminder of why we must make visible the stories of those invisibilized. Stephanie Sears: our friendship and creative brainstorming inspired the creativity in this work. Allezo Nevell Owens: your well of support, edits, and friendship never runs dry.

Baba Awo Falokun Fasegun: thank you for your spiritual guidance and reading me home. Àṣẹ. Riggins R. Earl Jr., my mentor, gadfly, and Br'er Rabbit voice in my head: you have shaped and nurtured my mind and soul and provided me the tools to deconstruct the past with reverence to enslaved people. Amanda Hendler-Voss and Meg Maguire: may you continuously feel the blessings of those who labored because of your faithfulness to erect a national monument in their honor. Jennie S. Knight: your support with research at Monticello and the University of Virginia helped inform this work. Andrew McBride: our moments at the gate inspired chapter 7 and will stay with me for a lifetime. Michelle Vanheuckelom: our friendship and conversations over tea in Belgium helped me think clearer about the necessity of this work. Heartfelt thanks to my editor at Fortress Press, Carey C. Newman, a gem of a human being, the midwife of this work, and the master of metaphors. I am also grateful to Ulrike Guthrie, my editor who has carried my voice and work over the years. Equal gratitude to Richard Brown, director of the University of South Carolina Press, for initially seeing the potential of this work. *Black Hands, White House* is due in part to my Howard University School of Divinity (HUSD) graduate research assistants over the years: Cleon Huff, Crystal West, Rashid Hughes, David Belton II, and Nicole Marie Melton. I am profoundly impacted by my students at various institutions, past and present, especially those doctoral students in the history department at Howard who captivate my imagination, fuel my intellect, and nourish my soul.

There is no adequate language to articulate my mom and dad's love and support. Lloyd Preston Harrison Sr. (1924–2001), whose spirit lives with me daily, and my mom, Mary June Hamilton Harrison, my best friend and greatest inspiration (thank you, Mom, for listening to portions of my manuscript): I pray I have represented you both well. Warm thanks to family members who aided this project: Tiombe Wise, Natasha Hemmings, Linda Hemmings, Parlett Harrison, Thelonious Wise, and Amber Wise. Elaine Womack, my mom and "the author" who gets me without me uttering a word. And to Garrett Imahn Kynard, my godson, and Quiana Lewis Wallace and Marcia "Cia" Price, my mentees, for always challenging me to create, write, and live authentically.

Yolonda (YR) Summons, my love, my spouse, and North Star whose presence and *itutu* (coolness) stills me. Your insights streamlined this work, and your writing retreats carried me to publication. And to Satchmo, our pup: you are my most joyous melody. Finally, to the ancestors, my muse, my breath, and raison d'être: *Le egun a se de, and I pray I have represented you well. Àṣẹ.*

# Black Voices Calling

## The Vibrations, the Shoes, and the Native Son

*I got shoes, you got shoes*
*All o' God's chillun got shoes*
*When I get to heab'n I'm goin' to put on my shoes*
*I'm goin' to walk all ovah God's Heab'n*

*I got-a wings, you got-a wings*
*All o' God's chillun got-a wings*
*When I get to heab'n I'm goin' to put on my wings*
*I'm goin' to fly all ovah God's Heab'n*

—Negro spiritual, "All God's Chillun Got Wings"

In summer 2010, I arrived in the nation's capital and stood in the Yard of the university that I had dreamed of attending as a young teen. Decades earlier, my father's heart attack derailed my plans, causing me to stay closer to home and enroll in a local university in the San Fernando Valley, thirty miles from my childhood home in southern Los Angeles. Now the place I dreamed of attending as a student became the place I would later serve as an associate professor, The Mecca: Howard University in Washington, DC. My arrival in the nation's capital was filled with enthusiasm and hope. After all, America had elected its first Black president. I held no illusions that the election of the forty-fourth US president, Barack Hussein Obama, and the presence of the First Black Family in the house that enslaved laborers built would resolve racism in America. As James Baldwin describes, I have come to know, witness, and experience an America that is more violent than democratic toward Black, Indigenous, and other disenfranchised peoples.

My initial introduction to the city was marked by openness, hospitality, and kindness. Dr. Ron Hopson, a psychology professor at Howard and interim academic dean in the School of Divinity at the time, and his partner, Nicholas Manning, invited me to stay at their home while securing housing. A couple of weeks turned into five months filled with the aroma of Nick's cooking and the joy of their ethnically and socially diverse DC dinner parties, along with quiet moments with Lincoln, their pup. My Saturday morning ritual included bookstore browsing, museum visits, and walks to the National Mall just minutes away from their home.

During these Saturday morning walkabouts, I began to feel connected to something both unforeseen and yet familiar, something deep and unshakeable. I have come to recognize this feeling as a yearning, an urging and a passion that is at the heart of who I am and why I am and why I am here. I pose these themes—Who are you and why are you here?—to my students at the start of my classes, and they guide us through the semester as we delve into America's origins and past.

My vocational passion is grounded in history. I am driven by a deep yearning to connect with Black people, devalued and long forgotten during and since American slavery. I am drawn to communing with them, hearing their stories, and learning more about them—their contributions, spiritual strivings, rituals and rhythms, wit and wisdom, and how they negotiated spaces of white terror and whiteness. I am also inspired by thinkers like Frederick Douglass and those provocateurs, conjurers, artisans, and healers during this period who possessed a keen way of subverting the masters' tools.

Though important, I am not interested initially in stories about enslaved and free Black people's resilience and how they survived, overcame, and resisted. Black people *are* resilient—and they are also catching hell while living in America. I am also not interested in parading how America freed over four million Black people after a deadly Civil War or how Black people persevered or fought back against white supremacy and violence. I am interested in why America was built on white nationalist ideology and why Black people were held in bondage in the first place and how the weight and longevity of such harm and captivity continue to impact Black people's psyche, well-being, and spiritual and economic freedom. The enslaved past cannot be seen absent of American terrorism and the intentional construction and manipulation of whiteness, which created access and opportunity for white colonists at the expense of Black lives. For me, sitting with enslaved and free Black people's stories, particularly stories of loss, pain, displacement, and violence, is an act of compassion. By sitting, I find deeper meaning to their lives as well as my own and feel a profound commitment to honor them, their stories, and the truth of our past.

My vocational passion is also grounded in teaching. I love teaching history. I love how my students' eyes light up with recognition and their faces express "ah-ha," "no way," or some form of affirmation or exasperation. Teaching history fuels me. My most profound passion is those aspects of history that historian Barbara Brown Zikmund identifies as "hidden"—histories that we, as a human community, often overlook, malign, misrepresent, omit, or ignore. Yet while hidden histories fuel my passion, I also struggle with the normative gaze and a one-dimensional depiction of American history—a story of American exceptionalism, unity, freedom, justice for all, and patriotic white men.

On no occasion was this clearer to me than the autumn Saturday morning in 2010 that I took a walkabout with Ron's thirteen-year-old son, Christopher Hopson. As Christopher and I made our way through the National Mall to the United States Holocaust Memorial Museum, I was taken back by the long lines outside the museum waiting for entry. Americans and other visitors were eager to sit with and honor Holocaust stories. I remember vividly walking through the museum feeling that sense of something both unforeseen and familiar as we made our way around a corner, then straightway toward the end of the tour. Along the wall appeared thousands of shoes. We could not move once we saw them. The sight was sobering.

Soldiers took these four thousand shoes and other personal items from Jewish people as they were marched into killing fields. Shoes and other leather goods were often repaired by camp prisoners or broken down and recycled for other purposes. The poem in the photo (figure 1.1), written by Yiddish poet Moses Schulstein, reads, "We are the

**Figure I.1.** *Shoe Exhibit.* United States Holocaust Memorial Museum, Washington, DC.

shoes / We are the last witnesses / We are shoes from grandchildren and grandfathers / From Prague, Paris, and Amsterdam / And because we are only made of fabric and leather / And not of blood and flesh / Each one of us avoided the Hellfire."

I realized that when we, the human community, find the courage to uncover the hidden aspects of history, the shoes of history appear. Yet the irony of history and its scribes is their ability to suppress and regulate the dissemination of knowledge. What we know and how we come to know it depends mostly on the dominant voices at the center of the public square. There, the dominant voices shape a single universal narrative as though their whitewashing account of history is all there is to know. Without counternarratives, like the shoes of history and other material artifacts and personal stories and testimonies from those persecuted, devalued, and exploited by the dominant culture, we would never know the depths of human atrocity in America.

I left the museum that day with a heavy heart. I was also dismayed at how America has no problem pointing outward to the Holocaust, the persecution and genocide of European Jews during World War II, and fails to look inward to its primary role in American slavery and the crimes committed against Black and Indigenous peoples.

I thought about this all as I often do as Christopher and I continued walking that day to view the stand-alone monuments on the National Mall. Then came my self-revelation: Where is the stand-alone monument to which we, as Black people, can go? Where is the monument solely dedicated to American slavery—a monument that points to America's crimes against Black people and honors those Black people who built the nation's capital city and played a major role in building America's infrastructure and wealth? In exasperation, I finally said the thinking part out loud and asked Christopher, "Where is the stand-alone monument that speaks solely to the United States' role in slavery, its subjugation of over four million people by the end of the Civil War, and the contribution of these laborers to the production of the United States and its national city? Where is it?" Christopher turned to me and said, "You should write it, Renee. Since you are asking the question, maybe that means you should write about it."

I went home that night still heavy. I searched the internet hoping to find a stand-alone monument on American slavery, something that moved me like the shoes at the Holocaust museum or the grandeur of the Lincoln, Washington, and Jefferson memorials. But there was nothing close to what I imagined. I returned to the National Mall each weekend after that and searched and visited the shoes and other monuments. The closest I could find is Freedmen's Memorial, which I problematize in chapter 6 of this book. I wept when I saw Freedmen's Memorial. There were no words. As Toni Morrison describes in her Nobel Prize speech on her summation about language, "The silence [was] deep, deeper than the meaning available in words."[1] It was the kind of silence that had me dumbstruck and weeping without tears. Even in a monument paid for by formerly enslaved women and men, they had wronged us. Six years later, in 2016, came the Smithsonian National Museum of African American History and Culture, which I mention in chapter 8, a necessary, noteworthy, and timely museum. However, I was looking and am still looking for something in addition to a repository of artifacts and a place where objects of significant historical, scientific, artistic, and cultural interests are exhibited.

In the years since my arrival in the nation's capital, whenever I am invited to speak at different venues, I explore the city of slavery with listeners, asking them to imagine and ponder the presence of enslaved laborers scattered about the barren landscape before the emergence of iconic buildings and institutions. I would ask them, What once stood in this place that we now stand? Was it a slave pen that once held Black people? Or a slave market that sold them? Was it once a slave graveyard or a place where enslaved women and men were bred like cattle? Or a plantation and farm on which they served?

I spent days researching the city that was once the site of one of the largest slave markets in the country. Daily, white men herded enslaved women, men, and children across the National Mall to sell them at various markets and hold them in pens (makeshift cages). I studied what lay beneath the iconic federal buildings, museums, and other institutions and structures and uncovered a world built on top of another. Before the landscape became filled with grand buildings and avenues, enslaved Black people labored against their will in Virginia, Maryland, and the surrounding areas.

The glaring omission in our history now had a hold on me. Each week, young Christopher Hopson asked, "So, Renee, are you going to write about it?" One day, during early winter of 2011, when I could no longer venture into the cold to walk the National Mall, when I could hear the echoes of young Christopher and the vibrations of those enslaved Black people who had labored in these streets, on that day, I started mapping out this book. My deepest desire is to honor their stories and the work of their hands, those Black people who arrived in chains and built this nation brick by brick, soul by soul, generation after generation.

When the cold winter dissipated, I returned to the National Mall, giving much thought to the United States' ties to the transatlantic slave trade network and its connection to those European countries, namely Portugal, Spain, the Netherlands, Denmark, France, and Great Britain, involved in the displacement of millions of Black-bodied people. Throughout this work, I wondered about the presence or nonpresence of modern-day stand-alone monuments commissioned by the government of these respective countries. How many of these countries had erected monuments honoring enslaved laborers and placed the memorials in the heart of their capital cities or a prominent section of the city with ties to the trade? In what ways do those stand-alone monuments speak to the respective government's role in selling, trading, and enslaving for free labor, millions of Black-bodied people? Between 2016 and 2019, I traveled and spent time in each of these European countries' capital cities searching for answers.

In 2020, the increase in Black Lives Matter protests and discussions about monument removal and erection has led many countries to focus on their role in the slave trade and the contributions of enslaved laborers. As of 2020, three of the six European countries—the Netherlands, France, and Portugal—have commissioned and completed noteworthy stand-alone memorials in their capital cities. In 2002, the Dutch government commissioned Surinamese sculptor Erwin de Vries to design a memorial in Amsterdam, the Netherlands' capital. De Vries's National Slavery Monument, representing the past, present, and future, stands in Oosterpark, an area that harkens to the Dutch's involvement in the slave trade.

In 2012, France erected Mémorial de l'abolition de l'esclavage (the Memorial to the Abolition of Slavery), the world's largest slave trade memorial designed by visual artist Krzysztof Wodiczko and architect Julian Bonder. The two visionaries fashioned the country's memorial in Nantes, the site of the most active slave-trading port in eighteenth-century France. The monument rests on the water's edge and, after viewing, points visitors to a one-mile-radius walking tour to eleven touchpoints—information boards and markers—throughout the city to educate them on France's role in the trade and economic development. Recently, France's Ministry of Culture solicited design proposals for a monument to stand in its capital city, Paris, in the Tuileries Gardens near the Louvre.

In 2017, the Lisbon city government authorized a slavery memorial in the Portuguese capital city adjacent to the coast, next to Campo das Cebolas, a significant area of the trade. Angolan artist Kiluanji Kia Henda's design, entitled Plantation—Prosperity and Nightmare, symbolizes Portugal's enrichments from the slave trade at the cost of Black lives. Henda's 540 sugarcanes, representing Portugal's "white gold," are made of black aluminum and stand in view of the ocean. Visitors are invited to walk among the sugarcanes for quiet reflection. In the center of the memorial is a small amphitheater for further reflection and public discussions.

To date, the US joins the list of those European countries—Denmark, Spain, and Britain—that do not have a stand-alone monument in the heart or prominent section of their capital cities commissioned by their respective government or monarchy.

Though Denmark has no such monument, one noteworthy mention is the collaborative work of Danish artist Jeannette Ehlers and Virgin Islands artist La Vaughn Belle in their creation of I Am Queen Mary in 2018. The noncommissioned monument honors Mary Thomas, a nineteenth-century formerly enslaved Black woman known as "Queen," who led a fiery revolt in St. Croix against Danish in 1878. The monument rests on the banks of a port in Copenhagen, Denmark's capital city and the center of commerce and trade.

To date, Spain and Britain also have no commissioned monuments in their respective capitals of Madrid and London. In Britain, the Memorial 2007 Project set out to create a permanent memorial erected in London's Hyde Park in 2007, which pointed to Britain's role in the trade and subsequent economic prosperity and honors enslaved laborers and their descendants. In 2008 Boris Johnson, mayor of London at the time, endorsed the project. In 2016, the memorial project group founded by Oku Ekpenyon received authorization to place a memorial in Britain's capital city. But the British government refused to fund the project. According to an article printed in BBC News dated June 10, 2020, Ekpenyon noted, "The [British] government gave £1m for the maintenance of Auschwitz but has continued to tell me that no funds are available for our memorial. I find that insulting. They would rather acknowledge another's atrocity than one's own atrocities."[2]

In addition to the countries actively involved in the transatlantic slave trade, my travels also led me to Berlin, Germany's capital city, on three separate occasions in 2013, 2018, and 2019. Since my time at the US Holocaust Memorial Museum, I wondered what Germany's government had to say about its role in human persecution, servitude, and genocide. I spent time at the Memorial to the Murdered Jews of Europe, a memorial designed by architect Peter Eisenman, engineered by Buro Happold, and funded by the German government and private citizens in 2005. My time there moved me to reflect deeper about the importance and need for a commissioned monument in the United States. Though all memorials have their shortcomings, the memorials in Germany,

France, and Copenhagen struck me at my core and became the catalyst of this work and my call for a National Sanctuary Memorial to Enslaved Black Laborers on the National Mall. A National Slave Memorial is not a new conception to the United States government. In 2003, the 108th Congress introduced a bill (H.R. 196—National Slave Memorial Act) during its 2003 Congressional session for the erection of a National Slave Memorial in the nation's capital. The legislation was not adopted.

While writing this book, no day passed without me thinking about the Indigenous peoples who lived on the land before the formation of the nation's capital. Their presence before Europeans' arrival and their annihilation and displacement and broken treaties stayed with me throughout the writing process. My heart wept and filled with pride when the Standing Rock Sioux tribe and other tribal groups and their allies camped out for nearly six months between 2016 and 2017 to protest the construction of the North Dakota pipeline. Tribal leaders argued that the government was violating its treaty and the pipeline would disrupt sacred burial grounds and inevitably contaminate the nearby river, on which tribes relied for nourishment, cleansing, and spiritual practices. I thought about them daily though I knew deep down America would get its pipeline.

I wanted to say more about the Indigenous peoples of the United States in this book, especially the Anacostan (Nacotchtank), Piscataway, Pamunkey, and other Indigenous peoples living on the land before the emergence of the nation's capital. It became clear to me to produce two publications. Enslaved Black women, men, and children are the focus of this book. In my next work, tentatively entitled *Smudging Our Way Out of Darkness: Native American Spirituality and American Genocide*, I turn my attention to the plight of the Indigenous peoples—namely, those tribal groups who occupied lands within the nation's capital and beyond its borders and are still struggling with America's broken promises. I believe their spirituality has something unique to teach us about being American, civil, democratic, and human. Both groups' contributions to America are significant and deserve their own publication and equal treatment.

Important to note is my use of the terms *the Indigenous peoples, Native peoples, Native Americans*, and *the Indigenous peoples of the United States*. My use of these four terms is to signify the presence and agency of over 570 tribal groups before the conception of the Americas—namely, the United States of America—and before European arrival and disruption. In those cases where I have not identified a specific tribal group, clan, community, or band by name, I have chosen to use these four terms interchangeably to respect the preference of various tribal groups and to point the reader to these first inhabitants and their descendants before Europeans colonized the region.

Though this book has breathed in me for ten years, it has been with me, knowingly and unknowingly, for a lifetime. As I finish writing, I think about the shoes at the Holocaust Museum, about the insistence of young Christopher Hopson, who graduated with departmental distinction from Harvard University in 2019 with a double major in social studies and African American studies and is studying political theory at Oxford University by the time this book is released. I think about him and his urging in relation to the eruption of protests led by young people throughout the United States in response to the killing of unarmed Black men and women by police. I think about the public demonstrations against the detrimental policies set forth by the forty-fifth president's administration that adversely impact and disadvantage the poor and Black and Brown people. I think of the hundreds of migrant children separated from their parents and locked in cages at the close of this book in 2020. "This is who we are and who we have been," I think to myself, remembering the slave ships, slave pens, and slave patrols and the violent removal of the Indigenous peoples in the nation's capital to make way for a democratic government and new nation.

I close this book with eyes wide open and hopeful that the urgings and protests of our young will continue calling us each to a more perfect union, one that acknowledges that we are all God's children with a right to our shoes—and, most importantly, our wings.

\*   \*   \*

*Black Hands, White House* is not a comprehensive work. I admit there are some holes. But this much is clear: First, that enslaved and free Black people under the threat of harm and death helped built this nation, fiscally and physically. Second, that there are no federally funded monuments on the National Mall and in the epicenter of the nation's capital dedicated solely to these laborers and their families' sacrifices, no monuments that acknowledge, respect, or honor their contributions and America's role in the institution of slavery and the transatlantic slave trade. Third, that America has presented a one-dimensional story about its origins and patriotic white men—a story depicted in monuments and grounded in ideas of American exceptionalism, freedom, and valor. Once the hidden is made known, the challenge will be to come to grips with what we see and to reexamine who we are as a nation and how we will honor, through a national monument, those who built this country yet whom we have maligned for centuries. We learn from enslaved and free Black people's contributions to this nation that Black people were intelligent, hardworking, fair, ingenious, faithful, and forgiving people. Their sacrifice and labors underscore that what Black people lacked—and still lack—in the new country they built was the same access, freedoms, and entitlements as people of European descent.

I invite you to read this work as though you are on a journey, what I sometimes like to think of as a "walkabout." On this journey, there will be lots to see. The open road will feel bumpy, smooth, and long at times, with detours and reflection points along the way. You may wonder if I am straying from my subject and taking you off course through unnecessary canyons, scenic byways, and lookout points. But I am not. You see, on this journey, there are stories that simply need to be told so that the story I am telling can be seen in its full significance and light. Gas up.

# Part I

## Captured and Caged

---

*And Still They Built New Worlds*

---

# CHAPTER ONE

# Black Bodies
## *White Minds, and the Irony of Liberty*

### The Enslaved Community's Contribution
### to the American Economy

*WHEN in the Course of human Events, it becomes necessary for one People to dissolve the Political Bands which have connected them with another, and to assume among the Powers of the Earth, the separate and equal Station to which the Laws of Nature and of Nature's God entitle them, a decent Respect to the Opinions of Mankind requires that they should declare the causes which impel them to the Separation.*

—THE DECLARATION OF INDEPENDENCE

*This Fourth [of] July is yours, not mine. You may rejoice, I must mourn.*

—FREDERICK DOUGLASS, "WHAT TO THE
SLAVE IS THE FOURTH OF JULY?"

*But it is not permissible that the authors of devastation should also be innocent. It is the innocence which constitutes the crime.*

—JAMES BALDWIN, *The Fire Next Time*

When Thomas Jefferson, the youngest member of the Second Continental Congress, penned the iconic words "WE hold these Truths to be self-evident, that all Men are created equal," slavery was well underway in the mainland North American colonies. The first draft of Jefferson's

Declaration of Independence was written during the second meeting after members of the First Continental Congress, the governing body of the thirteen colonies, convened to discuss their rights as white men and their quest for independence from the tyrannies of Britain. Delegates from twelve of the thirteen colonies were present to take a stand against a British monarchy whose financial backing and signed decrees they once sought to bolster their acquisition of lands, ships, commodities, and humans. Georgia officials chose not to send delegates because of their reliance on Great Britain's militia to help them overtake the Muscogee Creek peoples.

The Muscogee Creek peoples were commonly referred to as the Creeks, a term created by Europeans to signify those Indigenous peoples (Native Americans) living at the time in river valleys throughout Tennessee, Alabama, Georgia, Florida, and North Carolina.[1] In the Georgia region, over 675,000 acres along the Ocmulgee River in Macon were at stake, and Georgians, in a battle against the Muscogee peoples, turned to Great Britain for support. Georgia's absence at the First Continental Congress did not impede the gathering of the delegates from Connecticut, Delaware, Maryland, Massachusetts, New Hampshire, New Jersey, New York, North Carolina, Pennsylvania, South Carolina, Rhode Island, and Virginia. The men representing these twelve colonies were resolute in freeing the colonies from Great Britain's control and forming an independent government.

During the Second Continental Congress meeting, five delegates—Thomas Jefferson (Virginia), John Adams (Massachusetts), Robert R. Livingston (New York), Roger Sherman (Connecticut), and Benjamin Franklin (Pennsylvania)—were selected to form a committee tasked with crafting a written response to King George's tyrannical behavior, especially that relating to the 1774 Coercive Acts (also called Intolerable Acts). These acts, imposed by Great Britain on the colonies, were designed to punish the colonists for capital offenses, such as the 1773 confrontation at Boston Harbor, often referred to as the Boston Tea Party.

On December 16, 1773, Samuel Adams and other colonists, known as the Sons of Liberty, disguised themselves as Native Americans (offensively described by Europeans as Mohawk Indians) and boarded three ships docked in Boston Harbor. Their mission was to conceal their identities while staging a protest against the British Parliament's levying of taxes against the colonies for commodities exported from Europe to the thirteen colonies. The colonists saw the taxation system as Britain's attempt to exert power and control over them, as was evident in Great Britain's passage of the 1773 Tea Act, which permitted Parliament to tax imported tea and also required colonists to purchase tea solely from British companies. Adams and the other protesters demanded that the ships and their cargo of tea return to Britain. The British refused, and in response, the Sons of Liberty threw overboard and destroyed 342 chests of tea owned by the East India Company, a powerful British trading corporation founded under Queen Elizabeth I by royal charter in 1600. As a result of these actions, the British Parliament closed the Boston port to trade and in 1744 imposed the Coercive Acts. The acts included the Boston Port Act (which outlawed trade in Boston Harbor), the Quartering Act (which mandated housing for British soldiers stationed in the colonies), the Administration of Justice Act (which sanctioned extradition to Europe of British officials charged in the colonies with capital crimes), and the Massachusetts Government Act (which repealed the 1691 Massachusetts Charter and granted a royally appointed governor power over the Province of Massachusetts Bay). The colonists' discontent with these and other punitive actions became the impetus for the Continental Congress's efforts to free themselves from Great Britain's tyrannical rule and the resultant Declaration of Independence. The European immigrants were essentially at war with their own government.

Jefferson, the most gifted writer among the five delegates, crafted a response with nearly twenty indictments against the British Crown, including charging King George with attempting "to establish 'a detestable & insupportable tyranny.'"[2] The king's actions, they declared, gave way to "the cause of America's separation from Britain."[3] The Declaration of Independence could be seen as a *freedom-by-war-if-necessary* manifesto. Yet the irony of the colonists' declaration was its patriotic tenor and legitimation of freedom from oppression for themselves without acknowledging their complicity in the oppression of others. The majority of the delegates were white Christian men who, despite their language of freedom, were actively engaged in massacring the Indigenous peoples of the Americas and dispossessing them of their occupied lands. They were also actively engaged in owning and selling Black-bodied people for the purpose of building and buttressing a New World infrastructure and economy in both the North and the South. At the time Jefferson penned the Declaration of Independence, slavery had been flourishing in the American colonies for nearly 155 years. Though omitted from historical narratives about America's greatness, Black people were foundational to European progress in the American colonies and throughout the New World.

In his speech "What to the Slave Is the Fourth of July?," Frederick Douglass highlights another paradox inherent in the Declaration of Independence, a document that espouses ideas of freedom for white colonists with capital and voting power. Douglass implies that the declaration's "one People" and "WE" clauses were inclusive only of its fifty-six white male signers and those Christian European immigrants, now self-made citizens, residing within the mainland North American colonies. At the time of its conception, the framers had the freedoms and privileges of themselves and their descendants in mind. Douglass makes this "WE" ("one People") onus clear when he writes, "The Fourth [of] July is yours, not mine. You may rejoice, I must mourn. . . . Is it not astonishing that, while we are ploughing, planting and reaping, using all kinds of mechanical tools, erecting houses, constructing bridges, building ships, working in metals of brass, iron, copper, silver and gold . . . we are called upon to prove that we are men!"[4] Douglass is clear the declaration was not written for those enslaved men, women, and children laboring against their will throughout the American colonies. The framers sought independence from British oppression while simultaneously "nationalizing slavery in its most horrible and revolting form."[5] Black people were not only laboring but also demeaned, beaten, and sexually violated while doing so.

Slave breeding, a practice where enslaved women, men, and children were forced to mate like cattle, was a direct assault against Black people and no doubt one of the most demoralizing practices during American slavery. Of the estimated 11.9 to 12.5+ million African people taken from Africa on ships by Europeans, an estimated 500,000 (5 percent or more) were exported directly from Africa to the mainland North American colonies. That number grew to over four million at the close of the Civil War, an increase, in large part, due to slave breeding, slave births on American soil, and trade deals between American and West Indies colonists. At the height of slavery in the American colonies, there were an estimated forty-seven breeding farms.[6] Slave breeding was so common that one former enslaved woman exclaimed, "We were nothing but cattle." Another stated, "Most slave owners did not care who fathered the children, as long as they kept on coming. They employed studs or forced couples to mate 'just like cattle.' . . . On the Blackshear place, slave owners took all the fine looking boys and girls that was thirteen years old or older and put them in a big barn. They used to strip them naked and put them in a big barn every Sunday and leave them there until Monday morning. Out of that came sixty babies."[7]

Colonists saw the practice as a viable means of increasing their workforce. Jefferson himself looked to childbearing Black women when exploring ways to increase the revenue needed to hire faculty and staff at the University of Virginia. In a letter to John Wayles Eppes, Jefferson writes,

> I know no error more consuming to an estate than that of stocking farms with men almost exclusively. I consider a woman who brings a child every two years as more profitable than the best man of the farm. What she produces is an addition to the capital, while his labors disappear in mere consumption. The agreement you propose therefore, with this modification would be really acceptable to me, and more salutary for my affairs than to sell land only. The selection of the individuals should be made with a fair and favorable eye to the interests of Francis [Jefferson's grandson], the valuation left to any good and unconnected judges.[8]

Ironically, while the colonists celebrated "unalienable and God-endowed rights" afforded to them by the Declaration of Independence, they were breeding Black bodies and instituting laws denying these very same rights to those they held in bondage. But why would the framers include Black people in their "unalienable God-endowed rights" clause? Why would they grant them "life, liberty, and the pursuit of happiness"? Their gaze on Black-bodied people was affixed not on Black peoples' humanity but rather on their utility value. Thus they made a calculated decision to see Black people first and foremost as property, not people and chattel, not individuals with destinies and dreams. They chose to see them as collective commodities, not children of God endowed with the same rights as them. The United States emerged from the commodification of Black people forced to produce commodities of other forms.

Black people were bought, sold, traded, inherited, punished, or injured at will. They were also often bartered as collateral or used as terms of condition for business transactions, such as securing loans and paying off debts. In some cases, local and state governments received huge tax revenues from the colonists' selling and trading of Black people. Black people were so essential to the expansion of the new European frontier that advertisements publicizing their sale filled the American landscape. The following represent a mere snapshot of the countless ads that ran in newspapers and pamphlets and were posted throughout the American colonies:[9]

---

## GREAT SALE OF NEGROES AND THE SALUDA FACTORY, BY J. & L. T. LEVIN.

On Thursday, December 30, at 11 o'clock, will be sold at the Court House in Columbia,

---

## ONE HUNDRED VALUABLE NEGROES.

It is seldom such an opportunity occurs as now offers. Among them are only four beyond 45 years old, and none above 50. There are twenty-five prime young men, between 16 and 30; forty of the most likely young women, and *as fine a set of children as can be shown!!*

Terms,&c. Dec. 18, '52.

---

## VALUABLE NEGROES AT AUCTION-

BY J. & L. 'T. LEVIN.

Will be Sold, on MONDAY, the 6th day of December-, the following valuable NEGROES:—

Andrew, 24 years of age, a bricklayer and plasterer, and thorough workman.

George, 22 years of age, one of the best barbers in the State.

James, 19 years of age, an excellent painter. These boys were raised in Columiba, and are exceptions to most of boys, and are sold for no fault whatever. The terms of sale are one-half cash, the balance on a credit of six months, with interet, for notes payable at bank, with two or more approved endorsers. Purchasers to pay for necessary papers

WILLIAM DOUGLASS.

November 27, 36. (28–29)

---

## NEGROES AT AUCTION.—BY J. & L. T. LEVIN.

Will be sold, on Monday, the 3rd January next, at the Court House at 10 o'clock,

22 LIKELY NEGROES, the larger number of which are young and desirable. Among them are Field Hands, Hostlers, and Carriage Drivers, House Servants,&c., and of the following ages: Robinson 40, Elsey 34, Yanky 13, Sylla 11, Anikee 8, Robinson 6, Candy 3, Infant 9, Thomas 35, Die 38, Amey 18, Eldridge 13, Charles 6, Sarah 60, Baket 50, Mary 18, Betty 16, Guy 12, Tilla 9, Lydia 24, Rachel 4, SCIPIO 2.

The above negroes are sold for the purpose of making some other investment of the proceeds; the sale, will, therefore, be positive.

Terms.—A credit of one, two, and three years, for notes payable at either of the Banks, with two or more approved endorsers, with interest from date. Purchasers to pay for papers.

Dec. 8, '43.

* *Black River Watchman* will copy the above, and forward bill to the auctioneers for payment.

## Poor little Scip!

LIKELY AND VALUABLE GIRL AT PRIVATE SALE.

A LIKELY GIRL, about seventeen years old (raised in the up-country), a good Nurse and House Servant, can wash and iron, and do plain cooking, and is warranted sound and healthy. She may be seen at our office, where she will remain until sold.

ALLEN & PHILLIPS, Auctioneers and Com. Agents.

*Dec.* 15, '49.

## PLANTATION AND NEGROES FOR SALE.

The subscriber, having located in Columbia, offers for sale his Plantation in St. Matthew's Parish, six miles from the Railroad, containing 1,500 acres, now in a high state of cultivation, with Dwelling House and all necessary Out-buildings.

ALSO,

50 LIKELY NEGROES, with provisions.

The terms will be accommodating. Persons desirous to purchase can call upon the subscriber in Columbia, or on his son at the Plantation.

T. J. GOODWYN.

*Dec.* 6, '41.

By the time the Founding Fathers signed the Declaration of Independence, the price of Black bodies was higher than any other time since Black people's arrival on American shores.[10] Decades before the First Continental Congress meeting in 1774, the average price of Black people fluctuated between $200 and $425. At the time of the declaration's signing and the years immediately following the American Revolution, the average price for an enslaved person rose to more than $525.

At the time of the signing, slavery was a dominant force that drove and sustained the mainland North American colonies' economic growth. This impacted the framers' desire to separate from Britain to establish a government, apart from the British Crown. For the Founding Fathers and early colonists, this period of independence, economic growth, land acquisition, and nation building was their moment, the launching pad toward America's greatness.

But for Douglass and other Black people, as well as white allies and abolitionists, slavery was a "peculiar institution," an intentional system of abusive labor practices that afforded European immigrants economic, political, and social advantages that would not have occurred without subjugation of Black people and the displacement of the Indigenous peoples from their homelands. The forced transplantation of women, men, and children out of Africa to toil in the American colonies was crucial to America's greatness. The young nation was dependent on the commodification of Black bodies and their dispersal throughout the New World (the Americas and the West Indies). The young nation was also reliant on the commodities they produced: tobacco, rice, cotton, sugar, indigo, wheat, rum, rubber, whale oil, fish, horses, lumber, wood, silks, furs, and even (as we just saw) humans for labor—all for European consumption and advancement. Both Black people and the commodities produced by their hands coupled with the indigenous minerals taken from their African homelands bolstered the economies of the mainland North American colonies, South America, the West Indies, and Europe.

Enslaved laborers' contribution to the mainland North American colonies went beyond agriculture. Many Black people worked as domestics, maids, cooks, seamstresses, midwives and nannies, launderers, carriage drivers, butlers, bakers, tailors, stable boys, and waiters. Some were blacksmiths, painters, carpenters, bricklayers, quilters, basket weavers, stonemasons, millers, fishermen, and so forth, working in both rural and urban areas as well as on small farms and lavish plantations. Black people were also "rented out" by their owners to help build the US Capitol, the White House, and other federal and private structures. These multiple spheres of labor contributed to the United States' economy and its growth during and beyond the colonial beginnings of the nation.

Just as the Declaration of Independence was written against the backdrop of the Boston Tea Party and other acts of patriotic protest against the British Crown, so was the declaration written against the backdrop of these same patriotic men and others exploiting Black people for labor. As historian Edward E. Baptist notes, the "commodification, suffering, and forced labor of African Americans is what made the United States powerful and rich."[11] Without a doubt, "millions of dollars were pocketed year-after-year from the trading of human beings," and "in several states, money from this industry was the 'chief source of wealth.'"[12] Enslaved labor was foundational to the mainland North American colonies, and the commodities Black people produced helped Europe's economic growth and presence in the world. Slave labor provided the capital, which in turn financed the Industrial Revolution in England.[13] The production of cotton and sugar alone served as the base of American capitalism and European economic growth.[14] The American dream did not begin in white colonists' quest for independence from Britain. It began when Black bodies were forced onto slave ships and made to labor on stolen lands in the New World.

Undeniable are the contributions the enslaved and later freed persons made to the United States and those countries—Portugal, Spain, the Netherlands, Denmark, France, Britain—involved in their violent removal from Africa and subsequent subjugation throughout the world. As an emerging young nation, it became clear to America's Founding Fathers and their European forebears that their economic growth and self-interests rested in the hands of Black-bodied people, skilled and unskilled African artisans who brought their crafts with them to the New World. These Black-bodied laborers and their descendants helped bring into existence regions that now make up the tapestry of the United States and other parts of the world.

## Chief Source of Wealth

> *I own I am shock'd at the purchase of slaves,*
> *And fear those who buy them and sell them are knaves;*
> *What I hear of their hardships, their tortures, and groans*
> *Is almost enough to draw pity from stones.*
> *I pity them greatly, but I must be mum,*
> *For how could we do without sugar and rum?*
> *Especially sugar, so needful we see?*
> *What? give up our desserts, our coffee, and tea!*

—WILLIAM COWPER, "PITY FOR POOR AFRICANS"

The institution of slavery was the backbone and lifeblood of the American economic system. Slave labor made possible the growth, production, and distribution of commodities at a fraction of the cost of production by paid laborers.[15] Tobacco, rice, cotton, flour, fish, wheat, indigo, corn, pine boards, staves and headings for building ships for the transport of goods, and horses were the top commodities that helped forge the United States' existence free of the British Crown. The production and trade of these commodities within the mainland colonies and throughout the Americas, West Indies, Europe, and Africa provided windows of wealth and investment opportunities for both the framers of the Declaration of Independence and other white colonists. Yet enslaved laborers received meager compensation, housing, clothing, shoes, and weekly or monthly food rations. It is also important to note that each colony's profits and sustainability depended upon its labor force and the size and composition of that labor force—poor white indentured laborers; enslaved and free Black women, men, and children; and later Black sharecroppers and tenant farmers.[16] Without this massive labor force, the evolution of tobacco, rice, cotton, and sugar would not have emerged on the world stage as essential staple crops that helped to line the pockets of the British Crown and other European countries and also solidify America's independence and presence as a major player in the slave trade.

## Prince Tobacco

In the late fifteenth century, the Indigenous peoples of the Americas introduced tobacco to Spanish immigrants from Spain who later introduced the herb to English immigrants from Great Britain. The Indigenous peoples used tobacco for medicinal and spiritual purposes. Thomas Harriot, an English mathematician and translator who helped design ships, made this observation after communing with the Indigenous peoples living in present-day Virginia:

> There is an herb called uppowoc, which sows itself. . . . It has several names . . . the Spaniards generally call it tobacco. Its leaves are dried, made into powder, and then smoked by being sucked through clay pipes into the stomach and head. The fumes purge superfluous phlegm

and gross humors from the body by opening all the pores and passages. Thus, its use not only preserves the body, but if there are any obstructions it breaks them up. By this means the natives keep in excellent health, without many of the grievous diseases which often afflict us in England. This uppowoc is so highly valued by them that they think their gods are delighted with it. Sometimes they make holy fires and cast the powder into them as a sacrifice. If there is a storm on the waters [or escape from danger], they throw it up into the air and into the water to pacify their gods. . . . This is always done with strange gestures and stamping, sometimes dancing, clapping of hands, holding hands up, and staring up into the heavens. During this performance, they chatter strange words and utter meaningless noises.[17]

By the late sixteenth century, tobacco had become popular throughout England among the middle and upper classes. In its early stages, the English promoted the herb's healing properties for treatment of diseases and other ailments. In the decades that followed, tobacco's medicinal properties became a stimulant in great demand throughout Europe.

In the early seventeenth century, John Rolfe and a group of European settlers left England and traveled to Jamestown, Virginia, planting sugar and searching for gold. After several unsuccessful attempts to find gold and grow sugarcane, the settlers discovered the lucrative possibilities of growing tobacco instead. Rolfe, who later "married" the Indigenous chief's daughter, Pocahontas, had a popular West Indies tobacco seed shipped to Jamestown and began cultivating the crop in the Virginia colony. Tobacco was in such high demand in Europe that the early English settlers, with backing from the British Crown and the London Company, a joint-stock company established by King James I, began recruiting English indentured servants to work the tobacco fields. These indentured servants were incentivized to leave Europe for work in the colonies, specifically Virginia; colonists were willing to pay for their travel across the Atlantic to the New World and provide a contract for service, which included housing and meal provisions.

In 1609, the London Company posted an advertisement in their pamphlet, the *Nova Britannia*, recruiting Englishmen to travel to America to work throughout the Virginia colony. The ad read as follows:

The London Company wants settlers to go to Virginia

Free Land!

Free ship fare!

Sign up now to work for a Virginia Planter

Work for 7 years to pay back the planter for your fare to Virginia. After 7 years you will receive Land, clothing, some livestock and tools.

Come! Be an indentured servant. Then start a life of your own.[18]

Colonists also benefited from this system of indentured servitude because the British Crown awarded colonists fifty acres of land in the New World for each recruited laborer. Upon expiration of the contract (normally between four and seven years), the indentured servant received "freedom dues," an agreed-upon end-of-term bonus. The bonus generally included a parcel of land (usually twenty-five to thirty acres), a cow or other livestock, money, new clothes, food rations for up to a year, and a gun.[19] Although some indentured servants were treated unfairly, most received their freedom and service benefits, and a small percentage became elites in the mainland North American colonies.[20] Both the indentured servants' contract for hire and their termination benefits signified their status as legally free people and showed some respect for their work and humanity.

By 1617, the Jamestown colony had sold and sent its first shipment of tobacco to England.[21] By 1624, that meager first shipment increased to two hundred thousand pounds.[22] The profitability of manufacturing tobacco became even more evident when the Virginia General Assembly mandated that colonists build port towns to prepare tobacco for shipment, including warehousing, inspecting, and storage. The development of port towns also led to the establishment of settlements in Virginia (Norfolk, Alexandria, and Richmond) and in Maryland (townships in Prince William County). Enslaved laborers along with white indentured servants "built a massive tobacco production complex along the Chesapeake Bay and its tributaries."[23] Both colonies within the middle (Delaware, New Jersey, and New York) and south-ern regions (Maryland, North Carolina, and Virginia) of the United States were deeply vested in growing, cultivating, and shipping tobacco, though some colonies were more successful and therefore prosperous than others.

The colonists' decision to use indentured and enslaved laborers for tobacco production was their second attempt to create a sustaining labor force. Their first attempt in using the Indigenous peoples failed, due in large part to native peoples' susceptibility to diseases, death, and absconding, given their familiarity with the terrain. Colonists who relied on the production of tobacco as a major cash crop and investment opportunity turned to slave labor when the indentured servant pool became scarce and too expensive. During slavery and Reconstruction, in some areas of the country, like North Carolina, cultivating one acre of tobacco required approximately nine hundred human labor hours.[24] The influx of enslaved laborers meant colonists in colonies like Virginia and Maryland could keep their labor costs down and profits up while also meeting the growing demands for this cash-producing crop. The growth of the crop from seed to full maturation was an arduous process for both indentured and enslaved laborers. Tobacco cultivation was a yearlong process. It involved preparing the seed beds (tilling/fertilizing); sowing the seeds; transplanting the seedlings to the fields; fertilizing and tend-ing to the growing plant; weeding, worming, and suckering the plant; harvesting, picking, curing, and sweating the tobacco; and finally laying the tobacco out to grade, bundle, and form into so-called hands to pack into hogsheads (wooden barrels) and store in warehouses in prepara-tion for exportation. Thus unlike indentured servants, enslaved laborers were forced to work year-round from sunup to sundown.

By 1638, three million pounds of tobacco were sold and shipped to Europe.[25] The trading of tobacco between the mainland North Amer-ican colonies and Europe and European countries with other nations resulted in the spread of the crop across the globe. In the 1680's, enslaved laborers in both the Virginia and Maryland colonies planted, cultivated, and harvested nearly twenty-five million pounds of tobacco per year for sale in Europe.[26] Though sale prices fluctuated causing profit loss at times, slaveowners still harvested the crop in mass numbers. The pro-duction number rose to nearly thirty million pounds in 1709, thirty-four million pounds in 1731, and fifty-five million pounds at the start of the American Revolution.[27] Tobacco emerged as the economic epicenter of Virginia and Maryland. At the time of the signing of the Declaration of Independence and shortly thereafter, Virginia and Maryland were exporting more than one hundred million pounds of tobacco. By the time colonists fought for their independence from Great Britain in the American Revolutionary War, tobacco accounted for 75–85 percent of the total value of all exports for Virginia and Maryland.[28] Colonists used the crop as collateral for loans from France to finance their war efforts.

Tobacco paved the way to economic growth and stability for both individuals and geographic regions within the mainland North American colonies and Europe. The declaration's principal framer, Thomas Jefferson owned an elaborate tobacco plantation in Virginia. Other politicians, merchants, and investors also benefited tremendously from the cultivation and harvesting of tobacco produced in the mainland North American colonies.

In 1760, a decade before the American Revolutionary War, Pierre Abraham Lorillard established a snuff-grinding factory in New York for processing tobacco, cigars, and snuff. The Lorillard Tobacco Company's original trademark displayed on the outside of the company's hogshead (barrel) is the insignia of a Native American man leaning on a hogshead, smoking a pipe, and pointing to an inscription on the barrel that reads, "Best Virginia," the colony wherein Lorillard purchased his tobacco. The Lorillard Company, which arose in the eighteenth century, is known for modern-day cigarette brands such as Newport, Maverick, Old Gold, Kent, Beech Nut, True, Satin, and Max.

In 2014, Reynolds American, a subsidiary of the British American Company (a multinational British company based in London), purchased Lorillard for 27.4 billion. Lorillard's founder, Pierre Abraham Lorillard, was killed by the British during the occupation of New York in the American Revolutionary War. At the end of the war, tobacco production began to dwindle in the colonies, leaving small and large farmers to turn their interest to other corps. In the mainland North American colonies, the tobacco industry birthed on the backs of indentured and enslaved Black women, men, and children enriched an economy and provided colonists and Europeans a so-called healing agent and recreational luxury for generations to come.

## Princess Rice

Although the commonwealth of Virginia led in tobacco production, rice cultivation in areas such as the Carolinas and Georgia was not far behind by the turn of the eighteenth century. The production and sale of rice put the Carolinas, specifically South Carolina and the Sea Islands, and Georgia on the map as major contenders in advancing the United Colonies' and Europe's capital. In particular, the cities of Georgetown and Charleston advanced the South Carolina region and made the colony the leading producer of rice in the northern latitudes from the seventeenth century to the end of the American Civil War. Rice production was so important to this region that in 1691, the South Carolina General Assembly passed a law allowing rice to serve as a form of currency with which colonists could pay their taxes and other debts.

Between 1698 and 1830, the amount of exported rice from the port of Charleston increased from ten thousand pounds to over twenty million pounds, most of it going to Great Britain, which packaged 85 percent of this cash crop for redistribution throughout Europe.[29] In terms of rice production, Georgia was not far behind South Carolina. When rice production reached the shores of Georgia's Lowcountry, the colonists who opposed slavery hoped to use indentured servants to work the rice fields. However, all that changed when the colonists realized that the success of this cash crop depended on a large involuntary workforce such as what South Carolina had. By 1750, Georgia colonists repealed their law against slavery, and a new institutional pro-slavery framework took hold, making Georgia a leading contender in the production of rice. By the early to mid-nineteenth century, Georgia was producing nearly 90 million pounds of rice—12.2 million in 1839, 24.7 million pounds in 1849, and 51.7 million pounds in 1859 (equivalent to filling in 1,323 football fields). Approximately 95 percent of these total estimates were exported to other regions.[30]

Although rice culture was particularly common and lucrative in South Carolina and Georgia, a small number of slave-owning agricultural territories such as Louisiana, Mississippi, Alabama, Florida, and North Carolina produced rice too. South Carolina, however, was the one colony that intentionally sought enslaved labor to advance the economic welfare of the colony and its individuals, families, and companies.

The toll of rice production on the souls and bodies of enslaved laborers is undeniable. The average life expectancy for enslaved laborers working in rice fields was sixteen years, and then they would die, illuminating the harsh and labor-intensive realities of rice production, realities worse than all the other cash crops in the mainland North American colonies. For a successful harvest, laborers had to work from sunrise to sundown and beyond in order to complete the long process of preparing the rice for sale. This included clearing, plowing, and tilling fields; building water canals; irrigating, weeding, and harvesting; then sheaving, threshing, cleaning, and winnowing; and finally packaging the rice for shipment to other regions.

Because rice cultivation was labor intensive, colonists in South Carolina, Georgia, and other areas argued that enslaved Black bodies were better suited to the challenge than indentured servants or free workers. The colonists felt this was due in large part to Black women, men, and children's adaptability to humid weather and the grueling work hours that rice cultivation required. Given this, enslaved laborers were forced to endure atrocious working conditions, working ten- to twelve-hour days in the ankle- to knee-deep mud swamps necessary for cultivating rice. This environment made them susceptible to illnesses or dangers: skin outbreaks and rashes; insect, mosquito, and snakebites; alligator attacks; heat exhaustion; and sicknesses from standing in polluted marshes all day. Plantation owners expected them to work long hours, and if they failed to do so, they were beaten, flogged, or otherwise severely punished.

Colonists also argued that enslaved Africans were particularly well suited to rice cultivation because of their familiarity with the crop. Many enslaved Africans had cultivated rice in Africa and brought a particular knowledge and skillset to the New World. Some of the early rice seeds planted in the New World came from African regions such as Senegal, Gambia, Ghana, Sierra Leone, West-Central Africa, and Madagascar. Enslaved laborers from these areas were often sold in "gangs" or masses, creating some of the largest auctions in the New World for planters seeking rice farmers. As a result, it was common for enslaved laborers from the same rice-producing African region to be transplanted to the same American colony.

On February 8, 1859, Joseph Bryan, one of Savannah's notorious slave dealers, placed an advertisement in the *Savannah Republican* for the sale of Africans from the Windward Coast. The advertisement of the "gang" sale was also placed in three other Georgia newspapers—the *Christian Index*, the *Albany Patriot*, and the *Augusta Constitutionalist*—as well as the *Charleston Courier* (South Carolina), the *Mobile Register* (Alabama), the *New Orleans Picayune* (Louisiana), the *Memphis Appeal* (Tennessee), the *Vicksburg Southern* (Mississippi), and the *Richmond Whig* (Virginia). The advertisement read as follows:

---

### FOR SALE. LONG COTTON AND RICE NEGROES.

A Gang of 460 Negroes, accustomed to the culture of Rice and Provisions; among whom are a number of good mechanics, and house servants. Will be sold on the 2d and 3d of March next, at Savannah, by JOSEPH BRYAN. Terms of Sale—One-third cash; remainder by bond, bearing interest from day of sale, payable in two equal annual instalments, to be secured by mortgage on the negroes, and approved personal security, or for approved city acceptance on Savannah or Charleston. Purchasers paying for papers. The Negroes will be sold in families, and can be seen on the premises of JOSEPH BRYAN, in Savannah. Three days prior to the day of sale, when catalogues will be furnished.[31]

South Carolina was home to some of the nation's most affluent plantation owners who made their fortunes from rice production. Twenty-one out of thirty-five rice-producing families in South Carolina owned at least five hundred enslaved Black people.[32] Nathaniel Heyward, a wealthy South Carolina plantation owner who served in the American Revolution, for example, is noted as one of the wealthiest rice planters in the New World. After inheriting land from his father, Heyward increased his wealth by acquiring additional land through grants and land deals. He owned more than 1,800 Black women, men, and children who worked his nineteen plantations spread across 25,000 acres from Beaufort to Colleton to Charleston, South Carolina. When he died in

1851, Heyward willed to his family his estate, which was worth more than $2 million, equivalent to $65+ million in 2018.

Likewise, Colonel Joshua John Ward, the forty-fourth Democratic lieutenant governor of South Carolina, was lauded as "the king of rice planters." Before his death in 1853, Ward held 1,092 Black bodies in bondage, and following the settlement of his estate, his heirs held approximately 1,130 enslaved Black people against their will on his estates throughout South Carolina (among them the Alderly, Brookgreen, Longwood, Oryantia, Prospect Hill, and Springfield plantations). Ward's plantations produced 3.9 million pounds of rice, which was exported to some of the most expensive world-trade markets, including European markets.

With time, South Carolina became known as one of the wealthiest regions in the New World. Although rice cultivation began its downward spiral at the close of the Civil War because colonists could no longer rely on enslaved labor to support their economic endeavors, the door of prosperity from the time of American slavery and into the future was opened for colonists like Heyward and Ward and their families for generations to come.

## King Cotton

The emergence of cotton in the mainland North American colonies likewise brought forth new wealth. By 1860, there were "more millionaires per capita in the Mississippi River Valley" than anywhere else in the New World.[33] Cotton was, in essence, king. As antebellum preacher and historian Abel Charles Thomas wrote,

> C Stands for Cotton. Its beautiful bolls.
> And bales of rich value, the Master controls.
> Of' "mud-sills" he prates, and would haughtily bring.
> The world to acknowledge that "Cotton is King."
> But "Democrat Coal" and "Republican Corn,"
> The locks of the monarch have latterly shorn;
> And Slaveocrats, living by clamorous fraud,
> By Freemen shall yet into learning be awed,
> That the sceptre is not in position nor gift,
> But only in honest, industrial thrift.[34]

The wealth of the Cotton Belt spread from Maryland on down to Florida, Georgia, Alabama, Tennessee, Mississippi, Louisiana, Arkansas, and Texas. The textile industry in the New World and abroad skyrocketed due to the production, sale, and trade of cotton in the mainland North American colonies. By 1860, New England alone was operating "over half of the manufacturing operations, and consumed [or used] two-thirds of all the cotton used in U.S. mills."[35]

In 1734, Georgia became the first colony to produce and sell cotton commercially, and Mississippi is noted as the New World's largest cotton-producing colony. Economists calculate that nearly 90 percent of the cotton sown and picked for over 160 years in the South was exported through trade alliances in the North (primarily New York) to Britain's textual industry. When Eli Whitney's cotton gin emerged on the Southern scene in 1793, the production and distribution of cotton soared, outperforming the production of tobacco and sugar. Cotton was in such high demand that the American North and South as well as countries outside of Europe made millions from its distribution. Without a doubt, "slave-produced cotton connected the country's regions, provided the export surplus the young nation desperately needed to gain its financial 'sea legs,' brought commercial ascendancy to New York City, was the driving force for territorial expansion in the Old Southwest, and fostered trade between Europe and the United States."[36]

By the 1830s, "cotton was king" in the US and the foundation of the antebellum Southern economy. But the American financial and shipping industries were also dependent on slave-produced cotton. So was the British textile industry. According to the Schomburg Center for Research in Black Culture, Cotton was not shipped directly to Europe from the South. Cotton was shipped to New York and then transshipped to England and other cotton manufacturing centers in the United States and Europe. As the cotton plantation economy expanded in the South, banks and financial houses in New York supplied the loan capital or investment capital to purchase land and slaves.[37]

Although the production, sale, and trade of cotton were economic gold mines for American colonists and Europeans, it was a brutal enterprise for enslaved women, men, and children. The "whip-driven regime of cotton" was unrelenting and exacting.[38] By the nineteenth century, "systematic violence had become an economic necessity on America's cotton frontier."[39] The sounds of drivers' whips echoed through the fields, and public floggings ensured continuous work. Women were also subjected to rape and other forms of sexual assault and taunting while working in the fields. As with tobacco and rice production, cotton cultivation was a long, tedious, and repetitive process that depended heavily on free labor for mass production. Cotton was the one cash crop that integrated a high volume of women and children as young as seven years old in the workforce because of their ability to pick cotton sometimes at a faster rate than men.

As with other crops, so with cotton: under the lash of the whip and the heat of the day, enslaved laborers worked from sunup to sundown and beyond to clear fields and till soil for planting cottonseeds. Harvesting began once the cotton flowered and the head (boll) ripened and burst, revealing a white fiber, which covers the seeds of the plant. Then came the picking, which required "sharp eyes, speedy hands, and good coordination."[40] In the heat of the day, enslaved women, men, and children walked up and down the fields with large sacks, picking bolls and placing them in their sacks in preparation for weighing. Prior to the arrival of Whitney's cotton gin, laborers cleaned and dried the harvested cotton by hand, separating the seeds and debris from the cotton fibers.

On average, enslaved workers were expected to handpick 200 to 350 pounds of cotton per day depending on the region and the slave-owning property. Ninety-three-year-old Sarah Ashley, a former enslaved woman, vividly remembered her experiences tolling on a cotton field in Cold Springs, Texas. The length of her testimony quoted below is intentional to capture the full breadth of her life as a cotton picker. Ashley told her interviewer,

> I was born in Miss'ippi and Massa Henry Thomas buy us and bring us here. . . . Us family was sep'rated. My two sisters and my papa was sold to a man in Georgia. Den day put me on a block and bid me off. Dat in New Orleans and I scairt and cry, but dey put me up dere anyway. . . . After 'while Massa Mose Davis come from Cold Spring, in Texas, and buys us. He was buyin' up little chillen. . . . I used to have to pick cotton and sometime I pick 300 pound and tote it a mile to de cotton house. Some pick 300 to 800 pound cotton and have to tote de bag de whole

mile to de gin. Iffen dey didn't do dey work dey git whip till dey have blister on 'em. Den iffen dey didn't do it, de man on a hose goes down de rows and whip with a paddle make with holes in it and bus' de blisters. I never git whip, 'cause I allus git my 300 pound. Us have to go early to do dat, when de horn goes early, befo' daylight. . . .

When de boss man told us freedom was come he didn't like it, but he give all us de bale of cotton and some corn. He ask us to stay and he'p with de crop but we'uns so glad to git 'way dat nobody stays. I got 'bout fifty dollars for de cotton. . . . I got no place to go, so I cooks for a white man name' Dick Cole. He sposen give me $5.00 de month but he never paid me no money. He'd give me hats and clothes, 'cause he has de little store. Now, I's all alone and thinks of dem old times what was so bad, and I's ready for de Lawd to call me.[41]

Ashley, along with other enslaved laborers throughout the mainland North American colonies, lived according to the will of their masters—as human chattel, commodities more valuable than the cash crops they produced. They were not human in the eyes of many of their owners. They were, as one former enslaved woman put it, simply "cattle," livestock and assets being used and awaiting slaughter to further colonists' endeavors. This became more evident as the demand for cotton and its dividends increased throughout the new American frontier.

Unlike rice production that diminished after the Civil War, colonists producing cotton turned to their now free laborers and offered them "deals" to stay on the slave-owning properties as sharecroppers or tenant farmers and receive pay for their services. Unfortunately, as Ashley points out, in reality, most laborers received little or no pay from their former masters. While Ashley and other enslaved and later freed laborers struggled to define their place on American soil, colonists were solidifying their presence and economic prominence in the New World, from small half-acre farms to lavish estates. Ashley's world was a stark contrast to that of her white female counterparts. For example, Mistress Adelicia Hayes Franklin Acklen, one of the wealthiest women in antebellum America, inherited one million dollars from her deceased husband, Isaac Franklin, a wealthy cotton planter and slave trader.

The million included seven Louisiana cotton plantations; one 2,000-acre plantation in Gallatin, Tennessee; more than 50,000 acres of undeveloped land in Texas; stocks and bonds; and 750 slaves. She later married Joseph Acklen, a war hero and slave owner. The two set out to build an elaborate 20,000-square-foot summer villa called the Belmont Mansion in the mountains of Tennessee on land inherited from her deceased father and away from the day-to-day grind of her cotton plantations. The thirty-six-room villa with 10,000 square feet of living space and 8,400 square feet of service area in the basement was filled with fine furniture, paintings, and marble statues. Several buildings along with a two-hundred-foot-long greenhouse and conservatory, zoo, aviary, bear house, bowling alley, lake, and large water tower outlined the perimeter of the mansion.[42]

Each year, Adelicia gave a grand ball, hosting US presidents like Andrew Jackson along with senators, businessmen, clergy, representatives, and dignitaries. In the foreground of this haunting reality are women and men like Sarah Ashley, who after years in labor was seeking a mere $5 a month from her former master for whom she cooked but now found herself sharecropping in the fields after the American Civil War.

On the heels of the Civil War and to the turn of the twentieth century, Black-bodied laborers—enslaved, sharecropping, and tenant—had picked nearly ninety million bales of cotton (which is equivalent to over forty-five billion pairs of socks—this means that roughly everyone in the world in 2018 would receive a pair of socks over a six-year period). To some degree, "cotton's financial and political influence in the 19th century can be compared to that of the oil industry in the early 21st century."[43] From 1803 to 1937, cotton was "America's highest yielding export."[44] The cotton industry birthed in the American colonies and Europe by the hands of enslaved laborers, sharecroppers, and tenant farmers aided an economy that provided colonists and Europeans a lucrative textile industry for generations to come.

## Queen Sugar

Sugar was a rare expensive commodity in Europe reserved primarily for the wealthy. Cotton was king, and sugar was queen, a cash crop often referred to as white gold. When the production of the commodity began in the New World, sugar was already producing high profits for the West Indies, South America, and regions throughout Europe. By the fifteenth century, these countries had devised elaborate plans for cultivating sugarcane on large plantation estates and for processing and packaging the commodity in the West Indies and Brazil for sale and trade throughout Europe.

By the mid-eighteenth century, in addition to the sale of enslaved Black women, men, and children, sugar surpassed grain in sales. Sugar became the most valuable commodity in the transatlantic slave trade, "making up a fifth of all European imports and four-fifths of the sugar came from the West Indies."[45] As sugar production increased, sugar became accessible to the broader populations of Europe, both the wealthy and the nonwealthy. The growing affinity for the sweet taste of sugar was also used for more deceptive purposes, such as enticing little girls in Africa to trust European strangers and luring them to board slave vessels on the African coast. Recalling her childhood, a former enslaved woman said,

> I was playing by the sea-coast, when a white man offered me sugar-plums, and told me to go with him. I went with him, first into a boat, and then to a ship. Every thing seemed strange to me, and I asked him to let me go back, but he would not hear me; and when I went to look for the place where he found me, I could see nothing of land, and I began to cry. There I was for a long time, with a great many more of my own colour, 'til the ship came to.[46]

Sugar production first arrived on mainland North American shores in the Carolinas by way of Barbados. In 1663, eight European men were given land grants for their diligent and noble service during the English Civil War (1642–51). These eight men were known as the Lords Proprietors, an esteemed title given by the king to reward people with land grants as a means of expanding Europe's reach in the New World. The eight men combined their land shares to establish a profit-seeking settlement in an area between English Virginia and Spanish Florida now known as Carolina. In an effort to make Carolina as lucrative as Barbados, the men sent surveyors to study the probability of successfully planting sugarcane in the area. They also made use of enslaved laborers in Barbados versed in sugar planting to work the sugar fields in Carolina.

Drawing on the West Indies' slavery model, the Lords Proprietors drafted the Fundamental Constitution of Carolina granting colonists rights to establish plantations and "absolute Power and Authority over his Negro slaves."[47] The Lords Proprietors granted the colonists "twenty acres of land during the first year of settlement for every Black male they owned, and ten acres for every Black female."[48] This provided colonists with small and large slave-owning properties in Barbados the opportunity to migrate to Carolina with their human chattel and set up dual enslaved labor systems—in West Indies and on mainland North American shores. As early as the seventeenth century, enslaved women, men, and children from the West Indies, specifically Barbados and Haiti, became "Carolina's chief source of labor."[49]

Though the sweet white gold was lucrative for white colonists, it was deadly for enslaved women, men, and children. As with tobacco, rice, and cotton, sugar production was a grueling twelve- to eighteen-month process from cane planting to sugar exportation. On most occasions, enslaved laborers began their workdays before dawn and continued well into the night, with short breaks for breakfast and lunch. They were required to clear the woods and till the fields for planting. Months later, when the cane was ready for harvesting, in the heat of the day, laborers set sections of the sugarcane ablaze to remove the outer leaves around the stalk and kill toxins. Then the leaves were dried, and the cane was cut and harvested and loaded onto carts or railroad cars or carried by laborers and taken to the mill for the time-consuming and dangerous milling process that all too often cost a laborer their life or limb. Upon arrival, laborers removed the debris from the cane and cleaned the cane in warm water. After cleaning, the cane went through a juice-extraction process and was then purified and crystalized. Finally, they packaged the dried sugar crystals in preparation for exportation and trade with Europe and other regions across the globe. An enslaved labor force also became essential for keeping up with the global demand for sugar and for keeping the sugar industry afloat.

Although Carolina had a successful West Indies model on which to base their enterprise and a large labor pool for producing sugar, the sugar industry in that region eventually failed due to poor soil and climate. Colonists soon discovered that coastal regions like Mississippi,

Georgia, Alabama, Florida, Texas, Missouri, Tennessee, and Louisiana were better regions for sugar production.

Within time, Louisiana became queen sugar in the New World, producing the highest yield of sugar on northern American soil. During the antebellum period, 95 percent of the sugar produced in the Southern colonies came from Louisiana. In its early stage, this sugar colony was colonized by Spain and then France, until English colonists gained control of the region in 1803, twenty-seven years after the signing of the Declaration of Independence and twenty years after the American Revolution.

After Thomas Jefferson, the framer of the declaration, became president of the United States in 1801, he commissioned a group of US Army men known as the Corps of Discovery Expedition to survey the Louisiana Territory for its potential for producing agriculture economically viable for the United States. Soon after, Jefferson finalized the Louisiana Purchase (Vente de la Louisiane, or "Sale of Louisiana"), acquiring the land from the French for $15 million, equivalent to roughly $335 million in 2018. This acquisition served Jefferson's purpose of expanding the economic and geographic reach of the Union.

Jefferson was so committed to the United States' economic viability and to the smooth transition of power in the region that he later commissioned House Representative William Charles Cole Claiborne and US Army general James Wilkinson, who served in the Continental Army, to travel to Louisiana and take possession of the region. Claiborne was appointed governor, and Wilkinson was advised to receive the territory from the French officially. Wilkinson began establishing and increasing US Armed Forces in the area while Claiborne provided reports to the House of Representatives and the president about the financial solvency of the region. In his March 1806 letter to the legislature of the Territory of Orleans, Claiborne writes, "Fellow Citizens . . . I cannot deny myself the pleasure of congratulating you on the prosperous situation of the Territory. . . . I surely do not mistake when I observe that our Citizens have great cause to be content with their destiny. . . . This territory enjoys so great a share of felicity . . . a genial climate and a fertile Soil that would yield an abundant harvest . . . an extensive and free Commerce that secures a liberal increase of fortune."[50] In his July 1806 correspondence to President

Jefferson, Claiborne writes, "The facility with which the sugar Planters amass wealth is almost incredible. . . . Planters are now generally free of Debt, and many have added considerably to their fortunes. It is not uncommon with 20 working hands to make from 10 to 14 thousand Dollars, and there are several Planters whose field negroes do not exceed forty who make more than 20,000 Dollars each year. The sugar Plantations . . . have increased in value . . . since the Province was Ceded to the United States; and it is not probable that they have yet reached their true value."[51]

In that same letter to Jefferson, Claiborne speaks admiringly of the wealth obtained by sugar plantation owners and notes that among them are politicians, military officers, merchants, clergymen, and everyday families. He references military officer "Col Macarty's" large sugar estate and considerable wealth and businessman "Mr. Destrehan," whom he describes as the "wealthiest" and "best Sugar Planter in the Territory," who amassed "nearly $30,000 a year" from sugar production.[52] Plantation mistress Rachel O'Conner's letters reveal "planters cultivated sugar cane along the rivers and streams for quick profits."[53]

Some planters invested in sugar because sugar production was important to the "prosperity and independence of the United States and that culture was confined exclusively to south Louisiana."[54] Most Louisiana sugar was exported by sea to Atlantic ports and upriver to western states. In 1802, the Louisiana region harvested 5,000 hogsheads (a large barrel containing approximately one thousand pounds of sugar) and, in 1853, 449,000 hogsheads (equivalent to four billion American apple pies, equipping every grandmother in the US enough sugar to make apple pies for the next two and a half years). In 1853 alone, the total value of Louisiana's sugar crop was $25 million, equivalent to nearly $820 million in 2018. Through slave labor, the sugar industry in the West Indies and the mainland North American colonies enriched the colonial economy and provided colonists and Europeans with an addictive supplement for their coffee, teas, candies, desserts, pastries, and so on for generations to come.

# Conclusion

Tobacco, rice, cotton, and sugar, along with other commodities cultivated by enslaved hands, were the lifeblood of the birth of a new nation and elevated the nation's status in the global economy. Not only the American South but the entire existence and prosperity of the United States depended on slave labor, as did European immigrants and companies that were heavily involved in the slaveholding business as slavers, merchants, investors, entrepreneurs, land owners, real estate industrialists, politicians, lawyers, priests, and clergyman. All were connected to the transatlantic slavocracy through slave ownership, banks, commerce, railroads, and steel, lumber, insurance, tobacco, rice, cotton, and sugar companies.

The North kept the American slave industry afloat through various means. Among them were horses and cattle for powering the sugar mills; lumber for building farms, plantations, seats of government, shipping crates, and summer villas; and wooden staves for constructing hogsheads and crates to store sugar and rum. Both the American South and North benefited economically and politically from the sale and trade of human beings and the commodities produced by them in the United States. In addition to the names of individuals offered throughout this chapter, chart 1.1 provides a mere snapshot of present-day American companies and universities whose origins or parent companies are rooted in the selling and trading of human beings and the commodities produced by them. Many of these companies came into existence as a direct result of the institution of slavery and the slave trade.

## Chart 1.1. A snapshot of companies/institutions that benefited from American slavery and enslaved labor

| Name | Type of company/ institution | Purpose |
|------|------------------------------|---------|
| US government | Government | Used enslaved laborers to build and renovate the White House, the US Capitol, and other federal and nonfederal buildings, roads, canals, and fortifications |
| Aetna | Insurance | Insured the lives of enslaved Black people |

## Chart 1.1. A snapshot of companies/institutions that benefited from American slavery and enslaved labor (*continued*)

| Name | Type of company/institution | Purpose |
|------|------|------|
| Alex Brown & Sons (acquired by Deutsche Bank in 1999) | Merchant and investment banking | Bought and sold cotton and tobacco from plantations with enslaved labor |
| American International Group (AIG) | Insurance | Insured the lives of enslaved Black people |
| *The Appeal* (newspaper of Memphis; became the *Commercial Appeal*, part of the *USA Today* Network) | Newspaper | Sold ads advertising sale of enslaved laborers |
| Baltimore & Ohio Railroad (became a part of CSX) | Railway | Started with money from George Brown's family business that bought/sold products from slave plantations |
| Bank of America (originally Boatman Saving Institution & Southern Bank of St. Louis) | Banking | Accepted enslaved Black people as collateral |
| Bank of Charleston (became part of Wells Fargo Bank) | Banking/finance | Accepted enslaved Black people as collateral |
| Bank of Metropolis (connections with Bank of America) | Banking/finance | Accepted enslaved Black people as collateral |
| Black Heath Company | Coal mining | Enslaved laborers—miners/blacksmiths |
| Brooks Brothers | Apparel | Sold clothes to slave owners for enslaved laborers |
| Brown Brothers Harriman | Banking/finance | Wall Street bank—owned hundreds of enslaved laborers and lent millions to Southern planters, merchants, and cotton traders |
| Brown Shipley and Company | Investment/banking | Started with money from the Brown family and hid money for plantation owners |
| Brown University | University | Made use of enslaved laborers |
| Central of Georgia | Railways | Rented enslaved laborers to work on railroads |
| *The Charleston Courier* (became the *Post and Courier*, owned by Evening Post Industries) | Newspaper | Sold ads advertising sale of enslaved laborers |
| Charter Oak Life Insurance Company | Insurance | Insured the lives of enslaved Black people |

## Chart 1.1. A snapshot of companies/institutions that benefited from American slavery and enslaved labor (*continued*)

| Name | Type of company/ institution | Purpose |
| --- | --- | --- |
| Chesterfield Coal and Iron Mining Company | Coal mining | Enslaved laborers—miners/ blacksmiths |
| *Christian Index* | Newspaper | Sold ads advertising sale of enslaved Black people |
| The Citadel | Military academy | Made use of enslaved laborers |
| Citizens Bank & Canal Bank in Louisiana (became part of JP Morgan Chase) | Banking/finance | Accepted 13,000 enslaved people as collateral and took 1,250 from owners who defaulted on their loans |
| Clemson University | University | Made use of enslaved laborers and convicts |
| College of Charleston | University | Made use of enslaved laborers |
| Columbia University | University | Made use of enslaved laborers / slave traders |
| *The Connecticut Courant* (became the *Hartford Courant*) | Newspaper | Sold ads about enslaved laborers and products made from enslaved labor |
| CSX Corporation | Railway | Rented enslaved laborers to build rail lines |
| Dartmouth College | University | Made use of enslaved laborers |
| Emory University | University | Made use of enslaved laborers / slave owners |
| Freshfields Bruckhaus Deringer | Law firm | Clients—slave owners; lawyers acted as trustees of owners' estates |
| George Mason University | University | Strong ties to slavery; namesake prominent slaver |
| Georgetown University | University | Funded by sale and labor of enslaved Black people |
| Georgia Railroad & Banking Company | Banking/finance | Accepted enslaved Black people as collateral |
| Harvard University | University | Slave owners provided funding |
| Jack Daniels | Whiskey production | Learned distilling from enslaved man, Nathan Green |
| Jean Étienne de Boré (first mayor of New Orleans—willed to Charity Hospital of New Orleans, later owned by Louisiana State University System; closed after Hurricane Katrina in 2005) | Sugar plantation | Enslaved laborers |

## Chart 1.1. A snapshot of companies/institutions that benefited from American slavery and enslaved labor (*continued*)

| Name | Type of company/ institution | Purpose |
|---|---|---|
| The Jesuits | Religious institution | Owned and sold enslaved Black people |
| Knight Ridder | Newspaper | Benefited and profited from slave labor |
| Lehman Brothers Holdings Inc. | Banking/finance (prior to 2008, fourth largest investment bank in US) | Cotton traders; helped finance Alabama's reconstruction after Civil War and helped found the New York Cotton Exchange |
| Midlothian Mining Company | Coal mining | Enslaved laborers—miners/ blacksmiths |
| *The Mobile Register* (became the *Mobile's Press-Register* and owned by the Alabama Media Group) | Newspaper | Sold ads advertising sale of enslaved Black people |
| Mount Gay Distillery (Barbados) | Sugar plantation and rum producer | Enslaved laborers |
| Mount St. Mary's University (Maryland) | University | Made use of enslaved laborers |
| New York Life | Insurance | Of its first 1,000 insurance policies, 339 were policies on enslaved laborers |
| N M Rothschild & Sons Bank in London | Investment bank/insurance | Accepted enslaved laborers as collateral on mortgaged property or loans |
| Norfolk Southern Railroad | Railways | Rented enslaved laborers to work on railroad |
| Pepperell Manufacturing | Cotton textiles | Bought cotton from the South produced by enslaved laborers and also made enslaved laborers' clothing |
| *The Picayune* (became the *Times-Picayune*, owned by NOLA Media Group—part of Advance Publications with Condé Nast and American City Business Journals) | Newspaper | Sold ads advertising the sale of enslaved laborers |
| Presbyterian Church | Religious institution | Owned and sold enslaved laborers |
| Princeton University | University | Made use of enslaved laborers / slave owners |
| Providence Bank (Fleet Boston) | Banking/finance | Owned ships used in the slave trade |
| Rutgers University | University | Made use of enslaved laborers |

## Chart 1.1. A snapshot of companies/institutions that benefited from American slavery and enslaved labor (*continued*)

| Name | Type of company/ institution | Purpose |
|---|---|---|
| South Carolina College (became the University of South Carolina) | University | Leased enslaved laborers to cook, clean, and make repairs |
| Tennessee Coal, Iron, and Railroad System | Coal mining | Enslaved laborers—miners/ blacksmiths |
| Tiffany & Co | Jewelers | Originally financed with profits from a cotton mills picked by enslaved laborers |
| Tribune | Newspaper | Benefited and profited from enslaved labor |
| Union Pacific | Railways | Bought and used enslaved laborers |
| University of Alabama | University | Made use of enslaved laborers |
| University of Buffalo (New York) | University | Made use of enslaved laborers |
| University of Delaware | University | Made use of enslaved laborers |
| University of Georgia | University | Made use of enslaved laborers |
| University of Maryland | University | Made use of enslaved laborers |
| University of Mississippi | University | Made use of enslaved laborers |
| University of North Carolina (Chapel Hill) | University | Made use of enslaved laborers |
| University of Pennsylvania | University | Made use of enslaved laborers |
| University of Richmond | University | Built over the site of a plantation and slave cemetery |
| University of Virginia | University | Made use of enslaved laborers |
| *USA Today* (parent company is Gannett) | Newspaper | Links to slavery |
| US Life Insurance Company (owned by American General Financial and presently known as AIG) | Insurance | Insured the lives of enslaved Black people |
| Virginia Commonwealth University | University | Enslaved bodies illegally exhumed, used for medical experiments and then discarded |
| Virginia Theological Seminary | Seminary | Made use of enslaved laborers |
| W. & F. C. Havemeyer Company (American Sugar Refining Inc., became part of Domino Sugar) | Sugar production | Processed sugar produced by enslaved laborers |

**Chart 1.1. A snapshot of companies/institutions that benefited from American slavery and enslaved labor (*continued*)**

| Name | Type of company/institution | Purpose |
|---|---|---|
| Wachovia | Banking | Accepted enslaved Black people as collateral |
| William and Mary | College | Made use of enslaved laborers / slave owners |
| Yale University | University | Made use of enslaved laborers |

The growth and sustenance of the mainland North American colonies hinged on European settlement in the colonies and also the production of commodities by Black people and the distribution of those commodities within the colonies and their export to Europe and beyond.[55] Early on, because of the American slave trade, England rose as one of the prominent players as exporters and importers of human cargo and other cash crops and material commodities. Equally beneficial to European prominence were the stolen artifacts and precious minerals taken from Africa and later housed in European museums and science labs. Explorations to the New World followed by the slave trade created the conditions by which mainland North American colonies and Great Britain were intrinsically linked. But how long could it continue?

Within this exploitative and economically lucrative slave-dependent American institutional network, the colonists who gathered at the Continental Congress were faced with a desire to sever ties with the country of their forebears and turn their backs on its oppressive taxation and parental stability. The colonists were now resolute in their decision "to be free and independent" and "absolved from all allegiance to the British Crown" that they once relied upon to start their pursuits.[56]

When the Declaration of Independence framers—Jefferson, Adams, Livingston, Sherman, and Franklin—met to craft their written response to the tyrannies of the king, they did not have in mind the millions of enslaved women, men, and children toiling away in the colonies, the West Indies, and Europe. They did not consider the deep yearnings for freedom so evident among the people on whose backs they were becoming wealthy. America's Founding Fathers contemplated their own freedom while choosing not to free the bondswomen, men, and children in their care. Instead, after signing the declaration, they went home to these involuntary workers laboring in their fields; growing their tobacco; planting their rice; picking their cotton; draining their sugarcane; building their plantations, mills, and seats of governance; and serving in their homes. These enslavers sought their freedom from Great Britain with the sole objective of building a new democratic society and buttressing their personal strivings in the New World.

After crafting the declaration, Thomas Jefferson, the primary author, returned home to his elaborate five-thousand-acre Monticello plantation resolute in his belief that the six-hundred-plus enslaved Black people in his possession were "racially inferior" and as "incapable as children."[57] Jefferson's enslaved laborers and those rented out by his colonist friends built the University of Virginia and his elaborate Monticello ("little mountain") estate. For the University of Virginia alone, Jefferson and his estate after he died made use of nearly five thousand enslaved laborers to help build and sustain the University of Virginia from its inception to 1865. Black people, purchased and rented, brought his dreams to fruition and created a legacy for his claimed children for generations to come.

Among his enslaved laborers was a young Black girl named Sally Hemings, who began laboring in his homes in Monticello and Paris as a servant and seamstress. During her time serving in the Jefferson household, Sally bore six of Jefferson's children. Modern history portrays Sally as Jefferson's mistress, implying that she possessed some degree of willingness and agency. Yet Sally was a sixteen-year-old enslaved teen with no rights or powers to reject Jefferson's advances or exploitative sexual abuses. We do not know how she felt each time the forty-six-year-old Founding Father approached her. We do not know of Sally's yearnings for freedom from Jefferson's tyranny because the world in which she lived memorializes, to this day, only her master and his Declaration of Independence. Thomas Jefferson and his band of colonist friends received their independence from Britain by declaration and war.

The Declaration of Independence and the American Revolution became the new nation's freedom papers. But neither declaration nor war afforded Sally Hemings her freedom papers. Master Jefferson worked her like a mule, impregnated her, and never freed her. She was permitted to leave the Monticello grounds only after his death. But where could she go with his children and no Jefferson heir to claim them?

On the Monticello grounds, Jefferson's tombstone reads, "Here Was Buried THOMAS JEFFERSON Author of the Declaration of American Independence of the Statute of Virginia for Religious Freedom and the Father of the University of Virginia." Nothing in this inscription acknowledges the six-hundred-plus human beings he owned in his lifetime or the sixteen-year-old enslaved girl who gave birth to his children. On the Monticello grounds lies his pristine gated cemetery with his family crest and markers of his descendants and the headstones of his Black children conspicuously nonexistent. On the same grounds, at a distance, lies the enslaved cemetery, unkempt and barren, no headstones honoring their presence or labors.

Forty-one of the fifty-six signers of the Declaration of Independence were slave owners and slave traders who profited from the buying and selling of human beings and their labor—labor that included the production and export of cash crops, the nurturing of European immigrant families, the upkeep of their household, and the building of a new nation's infrastructure. These women, men, and children laborers died unnoticed and insignificant to the framers of the Declaration of Independence and other European immigrant colonists. Many of these enslaved persons fought in the white man's war for freedom while they themselves remained in bondage.

There was no member of the Continental Congress who benefited more from the lucrative generational cycle of immigrant migrations, land acquisition, slave ownership, cash crop production, export profit, and economic and sociopolitical standing in the New World than the commander in chief of the Continental Army, George Washington. Following the signing of the Declaration of Independence, Washington received official word from John Hancock, president of the Continental Congress, in a letter dated July 6, 1776, saying, "The Congress have judged it necessary to dissolve the Connection between Great Britain and the American Colonies, and to declare them free & independent States; as you will perceive by the enclosed declaration, which I am directed to transmit to you, and to request you will have it proclaimed at the Head of the Army in the Way, you shall think most proper. . . . It is with great Pleasure I inform you, that the Militia . . . will be every Day in Motion . . . ready to receive such Orders as you shall please to give them."[58] Such pursuits, Hancock writes, is "a Duty we owe ourselves and Posterity."[59] George Washington, in service and duty, upon receipt of the Declaration of Independence, had it read to the troops along with his general orders. The orders served as an inspiration to these Christian men as they united with righteous indignation to protect *their* country. Portions of the order stated,

> The blessing and protection of Heaven are at all times necessary but especially so in times of public distress and danger—The General hopes and trusts, that every officer, and man, will endeavour so to live, and act, as becomes a Christian Soldier defending the dearest Rights and Liberties of his country. The General hopes this important Event will serve as a fresh incentive to every officer, and soldier, to act with Fidelity and Courage, as knowing that now the peace and safety of his Country depends (under God) solely on the success of our arms: And that he is now in the service of a State, possessed of sufficient power to reward his merit, and advance him to the highest Honors of a free Country.[60]

Emboldened by the Declaration of Independence, these soldiers, many of them self-avowed Christians, forged to the battlefield with muskets and flints in hand while Black bodies, held against their will, were toiling away throughout the colonies.

General Washington, after fighting an extensive war against his British brethren, returned home with a sense of victory while the hands of his enslaved workforce were building and expanding the seat of his forebears' home, Mount Vernon, and the seat of the American empire, Federal City. It is the misuse of these hands and the hands of other enslaved Black-bodied people and a microcosmic scope of the European immigrant's pursuit of the American dream on stolen lands to which we turn our attention in the next two chapters.

# CHAPTER TWO

## Black Hands
### *Native Lands, and the Making of Mount Vernon*

*Death is better than slavery.*

    —HARRIET ANN JACOBS, *Incidents in the Life of a Slave Girl*

*I Augustine Washington of the County of King George . . . give unto my Son Lawrence Washington and his heirs forever all that plantation and tract of Land at Hunting Creek [Mount Vernon] in the County of Prince William containing by estimate, two thousand and five hundred acres and all the Slaves, Cattle and Stocks of all Kinds whatsoever.*

    —AUGUSTINE WASHINGTON, LAST WILL AND TESTAMENT

*There is not a man beneath the canopy of heaven that does not know that slavery is wrong for him.*

    —FREDERICK DOUGLASS, "THE MEANING
    OF THE 4TH OF JULY FOR THE NEGRO"

American history memorializes General George Washington as a man of valor who abhorred slavery. Yet George Washington, the descendent of a wealthy Virginia tobacco planter, profited hugely from the very system he abhorred and did so from a very early age. Slavocracy was George Washington's birthright. By age eleven, young George had inherited ten Black people and parcels of land throughout Virginia. Before he understood what it meant to be a man, George Washington was the owner of conquered lands and Black people. His legacy, beginning with his great-grandfather John Washington, afforded him the privilege and power to envision the contours of a new nation that was coming into being. This vision included a plantation estate named Mount Vernon and a metropolis named Federal City to house the nation's seat of government and legalize its existence. Though elite and influential whites, like the Washingtons, made up a small percentage of the mainland North American colonies, the vast majority of white people had access and opportunities not afforded to Black and Indigenous peoples. As noted in chapter 1, before and after Jefferson and others crafted a document to declare the new nation's independence from Great Britain, Black and Indigenous peoples were fighting for their lives against European immigrants hell-bent on living out their vision of what the colonialist later termed the American dream, a dream that encompassed economic solvency, opportunity, access, social and political power, and European expansion, all at the expense of others. The dream was built upon their sense of entitlement and divine providence and achieved through the violent overtaking of Indigenous peoples' territories and the commodification of enslaved Black-bodied people.

The history and legacy of America's first family, the Washingtons, and their forebears, and the erection of Mount Vernon exemplify the immigrants' pursuit of the American dream. Land acquisition and slave labor were critical to the Washingtons' and other European immigrant families' livelihoods in early American history.

## George Washington's Legacy and the Native Peoples' Territory Called Epsewasson

George Washington inherited the colonialist dream when his paternal great-grandfather, John Washington (1631–77), left England and headed to the New World. Already in the late fourteenth century, Europeans from various parts of Europe began relocating in large numbers to territories occupied by the Indigenous peoples of the United States, with over fifty thousand English immigrants arriving in the two decades between 1620 and 1640 alone.[1] Although Portugal and Spain were among the first colonizing European regions to make their way to the New World, neither they nor any other colonizing country (the Netherlands, Denmark,

France) made a more indelible mark on the thirteen American colonies than Great Britain. It is estimated that between 1750 and 1780, about 70 percent of the British government's total income came from taxes on goods from its colonies.[2] European nations made vast amounts of money from the transatlantic slave trade, capital that allowed them to garner tremendous influence in the world. In Britain, those who acquired much wealth from the trade not only built elaborate mansions but also "established banks such as the Bank of England and funded new industries."[3]

Prior to Europeans' arrival, there was no legalized concept of citizenship or land ownership in the New World. For the most part, the Indigenous peoples of the United States did not hold such classifications and believed land could not be owned but rather shared and revered. The first European settlers and subsequent generations did not become citizens of the New World (namely, the United Colonies) until they legislated themselves as such under the Naturalization Act of 1790. The act was one of the first steps in establishing some form of citizenry in the American colonies and a uniform rule of naturalization.

The Naturalization Act also extended Europeans' self-declared rights to occupy inhabited lands by creating a pathway to citizenship for new arrivals. The law they instituted in a world to which they were strangers restricted citizenship "to any alien, being a free white person who shall have resided within the limits and under the jurisdiction of the United States for the term of two years."[4] The broad parameters of this act made citizenry accessible to many white Europeans regardless of their social location, unlike enslaved Black laborers, European convicts, refugees, and working-class and poor European indentured servants who remained in the colonies for a specified period of time before being granted citizenry status. The act also made provisions for these early settlers' children born in Europe and the New World, granting them dual citizenship and classifying them as "natural-born citizens" of the United Colonies if they were under the age of twenty-one. This provision protected the citizenry rights of European immigrants before and after the Naturalization Act and a series of stronger adopted measures.

Though they were settlers in already occupied lands, these early European arrivals did not see or classify themselves as illegal aliens. Rather, they viewed themselves as pilgrims and pioneers charting a new course in search of new opportunities. The colonialist dream had different meanings. For many it meant a new beginning, a life of employment, hard work, hope, financial security, protection, and land and home ownership. For others it meant freedom from prison life or religious and political prosecution. For some it was an opportunity to gain cultural capital and enrich themselves and build a lasting legacy. At the heart of its meaning, the dream gave Europeans a license to displace and destroy all who stood in their way. As immigrants in a New World that was not their own, they forged ahead with little regard for the Indigenous peoples—their tribes, families, customs, rituals, dreams, and ways of life.

Without hesitation, those arriving in the New World encouraged other Europeans to migrate to help bolster a growing economy. European explorers, settlers, planters, convicts, refugees, working class and poor, businessmen, slave traders, and the elites were all a part of the wave of European arrivals. Between 1718 and 1775, 10 percent of the European immigrants who traveled to the American colonies were convicts sent by the British government.[5] They were not political prisoners but rather British criminals, women and men who had committed a range of felony crimes and misdemeanor offenses.[6] In other cases, many European religious dissenters fled Europe seeking asylum and religious freedom in the United Colonies. The conditions in Europe for many of these religious refugees were grim. Some were unsuccessful in fleeing and were imprisoned, drowned, and burned alive. Working-class and poor Europeans also traveled to the New World to work as indentured servants for European settlers, wealthy European businessmen, and aristocrats with business ties to the colonies. European servants were given provisions for a year or more, work tools, and parcels of land in exchange for their labor. Some European immigrants, like John Washington, George Washington's great-grandfather, arrived not as convicts, refugees, and indentured servants but persons seeking to expand their financial network. Nearly 135 years before the Naturalization Act, John Washington migrated in anticipation of venturing into the transatlantic trade business.

John's life in England was bittersweet and sketchy at best. His father, the Reverend Lawrence Washington (1602–52), an Anglican priest, was expelled from his position as rector of Purleigh in Essex, England (approximately forty-five miles northwest of London), for allegations of being "a common frequenter of ale-houses, not only himself sitting daily, tippling there, but also incouraging [sic] others" to do so.[7] Reverend Washington's supporters argued that he was wrongfully accused due to his loyalty to King Charles I, who was unseated during the English Civil War. As a result, the family was barred from their ancestral home, the Sulgrave Manor in Northamptonshire, England, and John was no longer permitted to attend a prestigious school in the area. Amid these allegations, the priest found solace pastoring a small, impoverished congregation in a nearby town named Little Braxted, England. He later died a pauper.

After the Reverend Lawrence Washington's death, John's mother, Amphillis Twigden, and her six children (including John) moved to the home of a relative, Margaret Washington Sandys. Margaret's husband, Sir Edwin Sandys, was archbishop of York and an influential tobacco investor and treasurer of the Virginia Company of London, a joint-stock company instrumental in establishing colonies in the New World. Sir Edwin introduced John to influential businessmen vested in the transatlantic slave trade and American colonization. By 1657, after his mother's death, with little opportunity remaining in England, and with a small inheritance in hand, John boarded a ship headed to the New World, becoming the first immigrant of George Washington's paternal line to settle for an extended period in the mainland North American colonies.

Upon arrival in Virginia (a colony named after England's "virgin" queen, Queen Elizabeth), John worked as a bookkeeper for a wealthy merchant. He began familiarizing himself with the import and export of commodities between Europe, the West Indies, and the mainland North American colonies. John's interest in the lucrative benefits of the tobacco industry led him to use his inheritance to purchase a small merchant ship called the *Sea Horse* to export tobacco from the New World to England. A raging storm later damaged the ship, leaving it docked in Virginia, and John decided to remain in the colony and build a new life there. Nathaniel Pope, a wealthy tobacco planter and landholder, took John under his wing, advancing him "£80 in gold" and "700 acres of riverfront land" upon marrying Pope's daughter, Anne Pope, in 1658.[8] Within a year, they had their first child, Lawrence Washington, who would become George Washington's grandfather.

John then joined the local militia to assist European immigrants in Maryland and Virginia gain control of lands occupied by the Indigenous peoples. In one battle, leading up to Bacon's Rebellion of 1676, John and his troops assisted Maryland colonists in killing five native chiefs from the Susquehanna and the Piscataway tribes. The chiefs and their peoples were living in territories across the Potomac River. During the battle, the five chiefs began waving a truce flag in hopes of negotiating with the colonists. John and his men ignored their request for negotiations, murdering the five chiefs with impunity. An outcry was heard throughout the Susquehanna and Piscataway villages. As a result of these blatant murders, tensions between Indigenous peoples and European immigrants intensified, resulting in more battles and increasing numbers of casualties.

As the battles raged, John Washington became known among the natives throughout the region as "Conotocarious," a Native American name from the Iroquois peoples meaning "town destroyer," "burner of towns," or "devourer of villages." For good reason, the Indigenous peoples did not see John Washington as his European counterparts saw him. The honorable immigrant and defender of the colonies was a "town taker," and generations later, the same name, Conotocarious, was bestowed upon his great-grandson, General George Washington.[9]

John, through a series of land grants, began acquiring substantial Indigenous peoples' territories in the Virginia colony. During the seventeenth century, the "English government promoted settlement of Virginia by granting unclaimed land of fifty acres to any person who paid his or her own transportation costs or the costs of other people."[10] A land grant was also a gift of real estate bestowed by a government or other authority as an incentive for land development, farming, or enabling work or as a reward for military service. One such area was Epsewasson, a five-thousand-acre lot situated on the banks of the Potomac River near the battlefield where his militia killed the Native American chiefs.[11] John acquired Epsewasson with his friend Colonel Nicholas Spencer, the cousin of Thomas Culpeper, second baron of Thoresway and governor of Virginia, who controlled lands in the Northern Neck of Virginia (often referred to as the "Athens of the New World"). The long-established Indigenous name faded into obscurity once John moved indentured and enslaved laborers onto the land to build his one-and-a-half-story home. He renamed his section of the land Little Hunting Creek after a nearby stream that flowed into the Potomac River.

Through his marriage to Anne Pope, John acquired a mill, tavern, and courthouse with a jail, which he, in turn, rented to Virginia's government.[12] He seized this opportunity to engage in insider trading by making a "secret pact with the secretary of the colony."[13] When speculators along the Potomac failed to quickly settle their ties to grants of royal lands, Washington and the secretary "had the land surveyed just before its original grant expired and then quickly patented [deeded] it for themselves."[14] Within twenty years of boarding a ship bound for the New World in hopes of a new life, John Washington's assets had grown from a small inheritance to a profitable legacy on which to build. The £80 in gold and seven hundred acres that he received from Nathaniel Pope by the time of John's death had grown to over five thousand acres along with indentured servants and enslaved laborers.

During this time period, John also received "paid emoluments from the royal Governor while serving as a trustee of estates, guardian of children, county judge and coroner of Westmoreland, and lieutenant colonel in the Virginia militia."[15] John, like many prominent English immigrants, served as the enforcer of law and order in Westmoreland County and throughout the Virginia colony. This power and privilege to enforce the laws that ordered and governed their existence were also passed down from generation to generation to preserve their rights and to protect and keep their families and colonies safe from any outside threat of violence against their personhood, property, or colony. John and each of his male descendants, George Washington included, held these and other related offices, including the county sheriff, throughout their lifetimes, clearly a way of protecting his family's rapidly increasing assets.

In the final days of his life, John sat down to craft his last will and testament in hopes of being absolved of any wrongdoing in the New World. John ascribes his wealth to God's favor rather than to his intentional oppression of others. He writes,

Being hartily sorry from the bottome of my hart for my sins past, [and] most humbly desireing forgiueness of the same from the Almighty god (my sauiour) & redeimer, in whome & by the meritts of Jesus Christ, I trust & beliene assuredly to be saued, .S: to haue full remission & forgiueness of all my sins. . . . My body at the generall dav of ressurrection shall arise againe [with] joy: through the merits of Christ death &

passion posses & inherit the Kingdom of heauen, prepared for his ellect
& Chossen & my body to be buried in ye plantation wheire I now liue.[16]

In the final lines of his will, John, the English immigrant, went on to say,
"It has pleased God to give me far above my deserts."[17] He then proceeded
to divide his land estates, human chattel, livestock, and other commodities among family in the American colonies and Europe, leaving one
thousand pounds each to his sister and brother-in-law in England along
with four thousand pounds of tobacco. Yet John chose not to free any of
his enslaved laborers upon his death. Instead, he willed them to his wife
and children, granting his eldest son, Lawrence Washington, the Little
Hunting Creek tract (Epsewasson) in addition. The rector of his church
received four thousand pounds of tobacco with orders that a tablet akin
to that of the Ten Commandments serve as John's memorial stone.

Years later, when John Washington's friend Nicholas Spencer died,
Lawrence divided the Epsewasson land between himself and Spencer's
heirs. Spencer's descendants occupied the portion of the territory bordering Dogue Creek and paid Lawrence 2,500 pounds of tobacco for
the 2,500 acres. Although Lawrence followed in his father's footsteps
by serving in the military and as sheriff of Westmoreland County, his
primary interests were in law and politics, and thus he often traveled
between the New World and England, where he studied law.

When Lawrence died in 1698, his daughter Mildred inherited Little
Hunting Creek and a portion of his enslaved laborers. Lawrence's second-
born son, Augustine (George Washington's father), also received a portion
of his father's enslaved laborers and one thousand acres of land on Bridges
Creek. Augustine soon expanded his forebears' colonialist dream by
acquiring more enslaved laborers and property, including purchasing the
land known as Little Huntington Creek from his sister Mildred for £180.

Augustine's land purchases along the Northern Neck of Virginia
placed him in the elite class of English slave owners and tobacco planters.
These owners collectively acquired nearly five million acres of Native
American peoples' territories on the northernmost part of three peninsu-
las (traditionally called "necks") on the western shore of the Chesapeake
Bay in the Commonwealth of Virginia. Augustine became a prominent
tobacco planter while, like his forebears, serving in the military and as
justice of the peace and county sheriff of Westmoreland.

In 1743, Augustine became fatally ill while surveying his land on horseback in cold weather. At the time of his death, Augustine increased his one-thousand-acre inheritance to over ten thousand acres, leaving his descendants beneficiaries of the American dream:

I Augustine Washington of the County of King George . . .

give unto my Son Lawrence Washington and his heirs forever all that plantation and tract of Land at Hunting Creek in the County of Prince William containing by estimate, two thousand and five hundred acres and all the Slaves, Cattle and Stocks of all Kinds whatsoever. . . .

I give unto my son Augustine Washington and his heirs forever all my lands in the County of Westmoreland [a.k.a. Popes Creek plantation] . . . with twenty five head of neat Cattle forty hogs and twenty sheep and a negro man named Frank. . . . I also give unto my said son Augustine three young working Slaves to be purchased for him out of the first profits of the Iron Works.

I give unto my son Samuel Washington and his heirs my land at Chotank in the County of Stafford containing about six hundred acres and also the other moity [half] of my land lying on Deeps Run.

I give unto my son John Washington and his heirs my land at the head of Maddox in the County of Westmoreland containing about seven hundred acres.

I give unto my son Charles Washington and his heirs the land I purchased [and] adjoining my said son Lawrence's land. I also give son Charles and his heirs the land I purchased of Gabriel Adams in the County of Prince William containing about seven hundred acres.

I give and bequeath unto my said wife and four sons George, Samuel, John and Charles, all the rest of my Personal Estate to be equally divided between them . . .

I constitute and appoint my son Lawrence Washington and my good friends Daniel McLarity and Nathaniel Chapman—Gentlemen Executors of this my last will and Testament. In witness whereof I have hereunto set my hand and Seal the Eleventh day of April 1743. AUGUSTINE WASHINGTON (L.S.)[18]

Augustine, with the stroke of his pen, sealed his legacy and the fate of his wife and children. Regardless of the ebb and flow and losses and gains of their wealth, the Washingtons were rooted in a system of access and resources that was afforded neither to the Indigenous peoples whose lands they were occupying nor to the involuntary laborers and indentured servants that sustained the Washingtons' livelihood.

The Washingtons, like many European colonists, were steeped in a system of appreciating assets, conquest, and entitlements since the day John Washington boarded the ship in England and headed to the New World. Augustine was both an inheritor and a sustainer of this legacy, and portions of that legacy he willed to his young son George: "I give to my son George Washington and his heirs the land I now live on [Ferry Farm]. And one moiety [half] of my land lying on Deeps Run and ten negro Slaves . . . and it is my will and desire that my said four sons Estates may be kept in my wife's hands until they respectively attain the age of twenty one years."[19] Although George was too young to fully comprehend the lasting legacy bequeathed to him as a Washington, he quickly acclimated to the lifestyle that afforded European immigrants and their descendants a life free of human bondage from birth to the grave. For the upper echelon of Europeans, such life was also free of indentured servanthood, and in most cases, such life came with social, economic, political, and diplomatic privileges. These privileges enculturated George into a world in which land and human ownership were not only permissible but also a notable means for securing and sustaining one's standing and respectability in the New World.

As young George grew, so did his appetite to own Epsewasson and the Little Hunting Creek Plantation, which was now in the hands of his elder brother, Lawrence. Although George had inherited Ferry Farm and a portion of land on Deeps Run, he envisioned owning the plantation situated on the banks of the Potomac River near the battlefield where his great-grandfather's militia killed the Native American chiefs. George became intimately connected to the estate while spending the bulk of his teenage years there involved in its day-to-day operations with Lawrence, the brother whom he admired.

Lawrence admired Admiral Edward Vernon, a British commanding officer in the Royal Navy. Vernon's military career was fraught, but one successful battle earned him more military medals than any British figure in the eighteenth century. His fleet of six ships took Porto Bello, Panama (Portobelo, Colón), another indigenous region colonized by Spain. Vernon's victory was one of many signifiers that Great Britain was winning the battle in taking over other previously colonized regions and placing Britain's mark in the world as a supreme power. Lawrence, enamored by his commanding officer's heroism, returned home to Virginia and renamed Little Hunting Creek, Mount Vernon, a name in honor of his triumphant leader, Edward Vernon. When Lawrence Washington died in 1752, his widow, Ann, inherited his estate, and his enslaved laborers were divided between herself and their daughter Sarah. In 1754, George leased Mount Vernon from Ann and her new husband, George Lee. In 1761, following Sarah's and Ann's deaths, George finally gained sole possession of the land and its one-and-a-half-story white house that was built with the help of enslaved hands. George Washington was twenty-nine years old.

## Mount Vernon

In 1754, the Indigenous peoples' territory called Epsewasson, once in the possession of John Washington, the "town taker," was in the hands of his great-grandson, George Washington. Mount Vernon stood as a symbol of the Washingtons' material wealth passed down from generation to generation. On a larger scale, Mount Vernon was a signifier of American colonization, a direct representation of how some European immigrants such as the Washingtons got their start and sustained their existence in the New World through land seizures, forced labor, and cash crop production. Though their degree of access and wealth differed for each European immigrant family, the Washingtons were a part of a tribal class of European immigrants who secured a better life for themselves in the New World at the expense of others.

The transatlantic slave trade, the enterprise by which African women, men, and children were captured and commodified, benefited English-speaking European Christians with assets. Eventually, these tribal classes lost or abandoned their immigrant identity and assumed the collective identity of being "white." This new white identity afforded them the privilege of citizenship in the United States and, with it, inalienable rights. As a citizen of the New World, John Washington could pass down to his white male heirs a way of life by which his great-grandson, George Washington, could now expand his vision. George Washington had inherited the colonialist dream upon which he could now build.

## Washington's Expansion of Mount Vernon

Washington was committed to creating a grand estate that would sustain his livelihood and social standing in the world. We know this estate today as Mount Vernon.

Washington's expansion of Mount Vernon began with surveying the surrounding territories and notating the land tracts that aligned to his new vision for Mount Vernon. This was a natural endeavor for George given his work as one of the youngest surveyors in Virginia in the period between 1747 and 1752. Washington had a sense of what he wanted to achieve with the estate and knew that in order to do so, he needed to own the lands bordering the property from the east, west, north, and south.[20]

After leasing Mount Vernon from his sister-in-law, Washington began familiarizing himself with the local owners and their businesses and political interests in hopes of leveraging that information to gain possession of their land tracts. In 1757, Washington purchased land bordering the northern portion of Mount Vernon for £350, which included three hundred acres on Little Hunting Creek and two hundred acres on Dogue Run, all owned by Sampson Darrell.[21] The price that Washington paid for Darrell's land tract is equivalent to $70,000 in the 2018 US market—clearly vastly under its real value.

In 1761, he procured 135 acres from John Ashford for £150 (roughly $32,000 in the 2018 US market) and, a year later, 135 acres from Ashford's brother, George.[22] Around 1764, he purchased a 178 acre land tract near Dogue Run from Simon Pearson and 200 acres from William and Diane Whiting to construct a mill race and pond for his grist mill.[23] Five years later, Washington bought approximately 100 acres from George Mason, which bordered the land he purchased from Darrell. In that same year, he purchased 200 acres of land facing the Potomac from Captain John Posey, his neighbor.[24] In 1770, he obtained land from John West and an additional 193 acres next to his mill, owned by Valinda Wade and John Barry.[25]

The acquisition of some tracts proved more challenging than others. In 1760, for example, Washington sought possession of 500 acres west of Mount Vernon owned by Thomas Hanson Marshall and an additional 500–650 acres south of Marshall's tract, owned by Penelope Manley French, the widow of Daniel French.[26] However, he did not procure these traits until later years. Washington remained resolute in convincing colonists to sell their plots of land. In some instances, he offered them English pounds. When he was unable to pay in pounds, he offered cash crops, whiskey from his distillery, produce from his garden, or any other means necessary. In a letter written to colonist Lund Washington dated August 15, 1788, Washington writes,

> I have premised these things to shew my inability, not my unwillingness, to purchase the Lands in my own Neck at (almost) any price & this I am yet very desirous of doing if it could be accomplished by any means in my power, in the way of Barter for other Land—for Negroes (of whom I every day long more & more to get clear of)—or in short for any thing else (except Breeding Mares and Stock of other kinds) which I have in my possession—but for money I cannot, I want the means. Marshalls Land alone, at the rate he talks of, would amount to (if my memory of the quantity he holds is right) upwards of £3000, a sum I have little chance, if I had much inclination, to pay; & therefore would not engage for it, as I am resolved not to incumber myself with Debt.[27]

In those cases in which he desired to rid himself of problematic enslaved laborers (runaways, resistors, or those he deemed "lazy" and "lame"), he offered to sell or trade them for land deeds. In the same letter to Lund Washington, Washington, referring to three particular land tracts owned by Marshall, French, and Barry, goes on to say, "If Negroes could be given in Exchange for this Land of Marshalls, or sold at a proportionable price, I should prefer it to the sale of Morriss Land as I still have some latent hope that Frenchs Lands may be had of D——for it. but either I wd part with. . . . Having so fully expressed my Sentiments concerning this matter, I shall only add a word or two respecting Barry's Land . . .—For this Land also I had rather give Negroes—if Negroes would do. For to be plain I wish to get quit of Negroes."[28]

Washington's relentless pursuit of some properties eventually paid off. In 1779, nineteen years after seeking possession of Marshall's tract,

Washington succeeded. Shortly thereafter, he obtained French's (in 1785) and Barry's (in 1783) tracts. In addition to the aforementioned tracts, Washington continued "acquiring additional plots of land on the (northern) neck between Dogue and Little Hunting creeks until in 1786 with the acquisition of the French parcels he owned the entire neck and several contiguous tracts as well."[29]

While acquiring land, Washington simultaneously commenced reconstructing Mount Vernon, personally supervising the renovations to the main house—design, construction, and decoration—which occurred in stages from 1758 to 1778.[30] Even while in the trenches fighting against the British for freedom, Washington, general of the Continental Army, sent and received several correspondences to and from his property managers outlining the repairs, extensions, and improvements to the Mount Vernon estate. Washington, "conscious that the world was watching, selected architectural features that expressed his growing status as a Virginia gentleman planter and ultimately as the leader of a fledgling democratic nation."[31] His preoccupation with preserving Mount Vernon during the Revolutionary War is evident in a letter he sent to his property manager at the time, Lund Washington, urging him to protect his estate at all costs. He writes, "I will not conclude it without expressing my wish that something should be done this Winter to prevent Armed Vessels from running up the River, in order to destroy the property. . . . I have no doubt of your using every endeavour to prevent the destruction of My Houses, if any attempts should be made thereon by the Men of War & their Cutters, but I would have you run no hazards about it, unless an oppertunity presents of doing some damage to the Enemy. The Height of the Hill—& the distance from the Channel gives it many advantages."[32]

Washington began converting the main house from its original one-and-a-half-story Virginia farmhouse structure to a two-and-a-half-story English-style white plantation home, which he and his property managers, overseers, and enslaved workers referred to as the Great House. Central to the remodeling was the expansion of the estate to twenty-one rooms, which included eight bedrooms with vaulted ceilings—four bedrooms on each floor. Repairs and additions were made to the flooring, windows, closets, basement, cellar, and roof. Washington also retained some of the house's original features, such as the corner fireplaces, and, where possible, preserved its original wooden siding and rusticated the entire house to give it the appearance of sandstone blocks.[33] Several other features were added, such as an elegant staircase with slender banisters that led from the back to the front of the house and to the second-floor bedrooms. Later came a library (study) and banquet room (called the New Room) on the ground floor and ninety-foot first- and second-floor porches with eight wooden columns to the rear of the home for shade and breathtaking views of the landscape, river, and workers. He also added a new roof with a copper cupola, an oval ox-eye window just above the second floor and centered with the front door, and two semienclosed passageways that connected the outbuildings—the kitchen, storage rooms, and artisan shops—to the main house. Washington chose the cupola (a symbol normally affixed to public buildings during this time period) as a distinct insignia representing his estate.

Upon completion, the 3,500-square-foot Virginia farmhouse had been expanded into an 11,000-square-foot plantation mansion, approximately ten times the size of an average home in colonial Virginia.[34] His expansive idea of Mount Vernon extended well beyond the main house to the surrounding gardens, fields, outbuildings, and marshlands. This all-inclusive area became known as the Mansion Farm.

With the acquisition of additional lands, George Washington's Mount Vernon estate now encompassed a grand Great House with five adjoining farms—the Mansion House Farm, Dogue Run Farm, Muddy Hole Farm, River Farm, and Union Farm. In addition to the five farms, the estate encompassed a bowling green, stables, blacksmith and shoemaker shops, gardens (including botanical) and a garden shop, a spinning house, a wash house, a coach house, a storehouse, a salt house, an icehouse, a smokehouse, clerks' quarters, overseers' quarters, and a greenhouse (slave quarters), plus a renovated gristmill and distillery. Some argue that Washington deliberately oriented his mansion not to the water, as most other planters would do, but inland—a political statement of turning away from Britain to the New World's interior.[35]

Within ten years, like his immigrant forebear John Washington, Washington had become a wealthy statesman and planter in Virginia.[36] His preoccupation with the expansion of Mount Vernon and renovations to the main house was on par with his fixation on the production and profitability of his cash crops. All were at the heart of his life at Mount Vernon. He desired to stand on the front porch of his Great House and see with delight the spread of crops growing in his fields. In a letter written to William Pearce, his farm manager at the time, he expressed, "I shall begrudge no reasonable expence that will contribute to the improvement & neatness of my Farms for nothing pleases me better than to see them in good order, and every thing trim, handsome, & thriving about them; nor nothing hurts me more than to find them otherwise."[37] From the time he leased the property until his death, Washington wrote more correspondences about the growth of Mount Vernon and his cash crop production than any other subject. He was interested in not only showcasing a grand estate with the Washington crest but also turning Mount Vernon into a "paying plantation."[38] His interests in planting for profit also extended beyond Mount Vernon to his other slave-owning properties along the York River and to his dower properties obtained in marriage to Martha Dandridge Custis.[39] When Martha's former husband, Daniel Parke Custis, died, he left Martha approximately 17,500 acres of land, 300 enslaved laborers, and a large sum of investments and unspecified cash. At the time of his death, Daniel, through inheritances and investments, was one of the wealthiest Virginia tobacco planters and slave owners. Martha brought a portion of her enslaved laborers to Mount Vernon. A large number continued laboring on the Custis estate, also known as the White House.

Washington's intention to make Mount Vernon and other plantation properties a profitable enterprise, like the Custis estate and other Virginian estates, is clear from several correspondences, including one addressed to his distributor and insurer, Robert Cary & Company, a London-based mercantile firm. In 1767, Washington wrote, "I am possessed of several Plantations on this River (Potok) and the fine Lands on Shannondoah, and should be glad if you would ingeniously tell me what prices I might expect from you for Tobaccos made thereon of the same Seed of that of the Estate & managd in every respect in the same manner. . . . I ask this question purely for my own private information & my Shipping of these Crops will be governed in a great measure by the answer You may give."[40] When away from the battlefield or convening with the Continental Congress, Washington spent his days on horseback riding about his estate and inspecting his workers, livestock, gardens, and fields. He also devoted much time to surveying his soil and determining which crops worked best in a particular soil and climate. He experimented with over sixty field crops. Among them were alfalfa or lucerne, barley, cabbage, clover, corn, cotton, flax, hemp (for rope and sails for ships), oats, orchard grass, peas, potatoes, pumpkin, rye, silk, spelt, tobacco, turnips, and timothy grass.

## Washington's Tobacco

Of all these crops, tobacco and wheat were his most profitable. And indeed, the early American economies during the seventeenth and eighteenth centuries were primarily tobacco based. The growth of cities, towns, neighborhoods, businesses, plantations, warehouses, and shipping ports is attributable to the production, distribution, sale, and export of tobacco.[41] By late 1620, tobacco was central to the Commonwealth of Virginia's economy. In 1624, the commonwealth in one year alone produced 60,000 pounds of tobacco. In 1627, they increased their shipment of tobacco to England to 500,000 pounds and tripled that shipment to 1,500,000 pounds within two years.[42] Virginians planted *Nicotania tabacum* strain seeds, which the immigrant John Rolfe introduced to the colony upon his arrival from England. The tobacco yield was enormously profitable to individual landowners and to the American colonies. Virginia and Maryland, for example, paid their taxes, tithes, and insurance and purchased indentured servants, slaves, livestock, land, and household goods with tobacco leaves. Both regions also assessed penalties by the courts in pounds of tobacco.[43]

The use and flow of tobacco as currency among government officials and clergy showed the interconnectedness of church and state in the New World. On most occasions, "colonial government expenses were paid in tobacco. The Government-established Anglican Church clergy were, by law, paid 16,000 pounds of tobacco annually. The vestry, a local governing body responsible for overseeing the established church, estimated how many pounds of tobacco was necessary for their parish needs, and then required families in the church's neighborhood, whether Anglican or not, to pay a certain amount of tobacco for every member of each household."[44]

Tobacco's currency and value provided Washington with an agricultural means for paying his Virginia taxes and church tithes with tobacco. Washington likewise used tobacco to purchase farming tools, livestock, and enslaved women, men, and children to help him build his agricultural economy. His sights were set on producing the highest-quality tobacco in Virginia, boasting often to local colonists and London merchants that his sweet-scented tobacco, which his laborers produced at Mount Vernon, was "the best" in Virginia. He also complained often to Robert Cary & Company that his tobacco, which "commands great prices" and "sells more quickly and for a better price than other tobacco," was priced "pitifully low," with tobacco sales seldom covering his expenses.[45] Despite these realities, Washington continued to produce as much tobacco as he could for sale and trade between his fellow colonists and the European markets.[46]

By 1750, tobacco's trading popularity was waning in the Commonwealth of Virginia, but not before Washington had the opportunity to gain from the enterprise. The expansion of Washington's Mount Vernon estate was due in large part to his production, sale, and export of tobacco. Tobacco was the cash crop that early on helped establish and seal his socioeconomic standing in the Commonwealth of Virginia, placing him, like his forebears, among the prominent "planters who dominated the economic and political life of Virginia."[47]

His sale of tobacco is evidence of this prominence. Within a three- to five-year period, Washington had over 100,000 pounds of tobacco packaged in hogsheads and loaded onto merchant ships—the *Swift*, *Nugent Only*, *Vessel*, *Arnold*, *Lawrence*, *Jane*, *Bland*, *Sarah*, and *Argo*— ready for sale in European markets.[48] Washington's estate alone, in a two-year period, had harvested and exported more tobacco than the entire colony of Virginia exported in 1624. Washington's 120,000 pounds from 1757 to 1758 was double the 60,000 pounds the Commonwealth produced and sold. Humphrey Knight, his overseer at the time, wrote to Washington,

> I hope all things will be taken cair of that your Honr was pleasd to Interest me with, as to our crop I beleive we have as good as any in the County our corn is Exceeding good . . . and I Dont See a better crop

of Tobco any where. . . . We have about 50 thousand that will soon be In the house the others a smaller Size but I hope will be good. . . . Our negros has bin very Sickley but lost none 2 or 3 is Sick now but I hope soon will got out. . . . As to the oats I think we shall make 300 bushels and I hope more I believe theyr the best sort. . . . The Crptrs has repaird some old Tobco houses at muddy hole. . . . As to the wheat our people has thrasht it out and Safe headed in hhd [hogshead] their is 45 bushels of old wheat the Rest went in Colo. Carlyle's Sloop which was 168 bushels. . . . I have 70 thousand Tobco hills which we tended Last year at muddy hole.[49]

A large quantity of Washington's tobacco was shipped overseas to help cover debits, to defray shipping costs and freight insurance, and to purchase household goods and personal items that were better quality or unavailable in the mainland North American colonies. Among the common items shipped for himself, Martha, and her two children, "Patsy" Parke Custis and John "Jacky" Parke Custis, "were clothing, shoes, spirits (alcohol), wine, toys, chocolates and other sweet indulgences. Other items included quality textiles (silk and cotton), crystal glasses and plates, chinaware, furniture including draperies, porcelain figurines, artifacts, books, metal, and whips."[50] The surplus of tobacco produced at Mount Vernon over the years and other properties owned by Washington provided the Washington family a luxurious lifestyle. The family later expanded to include John's children, Eleanor "Nelly" and George Washington "Wash" Parke Custis.

Washington desired to live a lifestyle akin to the Fairfaxes, Carters, and Robinsons of Virginia, and this desire resulted in Washington oftentimes living beyond his means. Washington spent lavishly; included on his lavish wish list, some of which he later owned, were a chariot of the finest quality with his crest engraved, a seven-and-a-half-foot tester bed with blue-and-white curtains to match the wallpaper, and busts of prominent European figures such as Alexander the Great, Julius Caesar, and the king of Prussia for his mantelpiece.[51]

From the early seventeenth century to Washington's era, tobacco had proven to be a promising pathway to prosperity for European immigrants, English merchants, and the British Crown. However, as more and more hogsheads entered British ports from the mainland North American colonies and the West Indies, the British Crown recognized this and began capitalizing on tobacco imports by imposing higher tariffs. The tobacco market eventually slowed due to those tariffs, leading to lower prices and less profit for Washington and those like him. Anxious about this outcome, Washington wrote in a letter to Robert Cary & Company on September 20, 1765,

> It cannot reasonably be imagined that I felt any pleasing Sensations upon the receipt of your Letter of the 13th of February covering accts of Sales for 153 Hhds . . . the Sales are pitifully low. . . . I cannot readily conceive that our Tobacco's are so much depreciated in quality as not only to sell much below other Marks of good repute, but actually for less, as I before observd. . . . It appears pretty evident to me from the prices I have generally got for my Tobacco in London, & from some other concomitant Circumstances, that it only suits the Interest of a few particular Gentlemen. . . . The Stamp Act, imposed on the Colonies by the Parliament of Great Britain engrosses the conversation of the speculative part of the Colonists, who look upon this unconstitutional method of Taxation as a direful attack upon their Liberties, & loudly exclaim against the violation . . .—What may be the result of this . . . who is to suffer most in this event—the Merchant, or the Planter.[52]

In addition to higher tariffs and depreciating profits, Washington found it difficult to sustain the production of tobacco because as more and more tobacco was planted in the same ground over the years, the soil was being depleted of its nutrients, causing lower yields and the ground to harden. As a result, Washington and other colonists faced with the same dilemma decided to pursue other viable cash crops or streams of revenue to sustain their livelihood and prominent status in the New World.[53] Now in debt, Washington became fixated on growing wheat and becoming versed in learning innovative farming techniques. Drawing on English farming techniques, Washington switched from single-crop production and invested in both manure and a seven-year crop rotation, a method that helped him revitalize his soil and plant a variety of crops to replenish the soil's nutrients.

Washington did not abandon growing tobacco altogether. In the mid-1760s, he stopped producing tobacco for consignment to Robert Cary & Company on his Bullskin quarters in Frederick County and at Mount Vernon. But continued producing "tobacco for shipment on his York River dower plantations and on John Parke Custis's plantations."[54] While keeping his eye on his remaining tobacco production, Washington began focusing on wheat as his main cash crop. From the 1760s until his death, he produced an abundance of wheat at Mount Vernon, and this became the gateway to other lucrative investments.

## Washington's Wheat

Wheat, unlike tobacco, did not deplete the soil and was less labor intensive, allowing Washington to remove some of his enslaved labor force from the fields to work in various locations around the estate. The many uses of wheat also freed him from the strongholds of Europe and its tobacco-taxing industry and from the London markets. Washington had the advantage of selling his grain locally because he could mill his crop.[55] He experimented with various wheats such as summer, red-straw, lammas, double-headed, yellow-bearded, early, Russian, and white and eventually settled on producing white wheat. He devoted three thousand acres to cultivating wheat at Mount Vernon. Shortly after planting wheat, Washington harvested nearly 250 bushels in 1764. By 1769, the number increased to six thousand bushels.[56]

As a result of the growing public demand for wheat and its by-products, Washington, in his later years, constructed a multifaceted site on the Dogue Run Farm for treading wheat. The site included a well-constructed, sixteen-sided, two-story barn along with two stables for raising horses, mules, and oxen; livestock pens; and corn houses. The barn was built so horses could walk in circles to grind/winnow the grain.[57]

In addition to constructing this sixteen-sided barn, Washington also redesigned his father's decaying gristmill. He transformed it into an elaborate two-story stone mill, which contained a wooden, sixteen-foot pitch-back waterwheel with forty buckets that weighed 160 pounds each when filled with water. The new commercial gristmill, located a half mile from the old mill, was later upgraded to an automated system for processing great volumes of commodities such as flour and corn-meal. Wheat and flour were often exported to foreign markets (England, Portugal, and Jamaica) and sold to local colonists and markets in the Alexandria and Fredericksburg areas. Large quantities of cornmeal were rationed to enslaved laborers and livestock for their daily meals. Washington also opened his gristmill to neighboring plantation owners, who processed their grain at Mount Vernon for a fee. With a new gristmill, Washington increased his productivity to approximately five thousand pounds of wheat and three thousand pounds of cornmeal per day. In 1791 alone, "the gristmill produced, 117 pounds of profit—the third highest of any activity at Mount Vernon."[58] In that year, the mill ground "more than, 275,000 pounds of wheat and 178,000 pounds" of corn.[59]

Washington's interest in wheat led him to grow flax for linen cloth. Over time, he started manufacturing his own textiles, becoming less reliant on imports from England. He tasked his laborers with working around the clock, but even then, it took them approximately three weeks to produce twelve yards of linen. Yet in 1768 alone, over 1,300 yards of linen was fabricated in the spinning house, a small space just north of the Great House and dedicated solely to spinning.[60]

Washington also took up commercial fishing, casting twelve-foot-long and over one-hundred-foot-wide seine nets from small vessels he owned into the Potomac to capture fish for sale in Alexandria as well as Jamaican and Portuguese markets. The river contained an abundance of fish each year and provided Washington an income stream that "consistently surpassed earning from the cultivation of wheat and other food crops."[61] Washington often appraised the Potomac as a river with an abundance of fish, noting excitedly in his diary entry dated April 11, 1769, "The white fish ran plentifully at my sein landing having catchd abt. 300 at one Hawl [in one day]."[62]

Open to such innovative streams of income, Washington also decided to venture into the whiskey business upon heeding the advice of James Anderson, his plantation manager at the time and a former distiller from Scotland. Anderson thought of the idea while providing oversight of Mount Vernon's rye and cornfields. The ground corn was not only fed to Washington's enslaved laborers and livestock but also a vital asset for producing whiskey.[63] There was a market for whiskey and rum, two popular spirits in the American colonies, especially among landowners, merchants, politicians, and soldiers. Mount Vernon was a prime location for distilling fine whiskey because the three essential compositions were in surplus at the estate—crops (rye, corn, and barely), a large gristmill, and access to an abundant water supply from the Potomac River, which ran adjacent to the property. Though reluctant at first to invest his time in the enterprise, Washington soon yielded and in time became known as the Whiskey Baron of Mount Vernon. His whiskey, sold in round barrels, not bottled, became known as George Washington's Straight Rye Whiskey. As the demand for Mount Vernon whiskey grew, so did the need for a distillery. He also began constructing, next to the gristmill, a distillery made of sandstone and river rocks and large enough to fit five big copper pot stills.[64]

By 1810, Virginia had more than 3,600 operating distilleries.[65] Washington's distillery was one of the largest in not only Virginia but also the American colonies. His distillery was 2,250 square feet, while other distilleries averaged approximately eight hundred square feet. Washington's distillery, which operated year-round, produced more spirits per year than any other distillery in the Virginia colony. In 1799, for example, the distillery produced nearly 11,000 gallons of whiskey, valued at $7,500 (approximately $145,000 in 2018), while 650 gallons of whiskey, valued at $460 (approximately $8,460 in 2018), were produced by other Virginia colonists.[66] From the 1790s to the present day, Washington's whiskey continues to be distilled and sold at Mount Vernon.

Though George Washington's financial success ebbed and flowed during his tenure at Mount Vernon and his debt often mounted, one variable remained constant. Washington's multifaceted agricultural enterprise yielded him substantial socioeconomic revenue. But what about the enslaved and free laborers who helped him build his enterprise? Washington's profit and social standing depended entirely on the laborers who tilled, seeded, and nurtured the soil. His innovative ventures, for which he was lauded as an esteemed planter and entrepreneur, were impossible without those who packaged the tobacco, harvested the wheat, spun the cotton, distilled the whiskey, and cast nets into the river. The same is true of Washington's vision to build upon his forebears' legacy by expanding the Mount Vernon estate and its four outlying farms. The manifestation of Washington's vision rested on the laborers who cleared the lands, quarried the stones, chopped the wood, carried the pillars, and laid the planks. Most of these women, men, and children received no wages or access to education; they received only deficient health care, dismal housing, unhealthy food, shabby clothing, and worn shoes and were afforded no public recognition for their contributions, time, and sacrifice.

Much is written about Washington's legacy and Mount Vernon. But little is written or said about the hands that built the Mount Vernon estate and sustained the Washington legacy for generations to come. In the next section, we recognize some of the enslaved women, men, and children who made it possible for the first Washington immigrant, John Washington, and his descendants to dream of a better life after leaving Great Britain's shores. By bringing to light some of their names, we create a fractional representation of these enslaved Black people to stand alongside voluminous writings and memorials about George Washington, his forebears, and their Mount Vernon estate. We bring these laborers from the shadows of history because it is inconceivable and disingenuous to think of the Washingtons' migration, progress, and legacy in the New World without taking into consideration the lives sacrificed to make the Washingtons' colonialist dream a reality.

Chapter 1 reminds us that there would be no new nation for which to wage a revolution or seek independence without the enslaved laborers. They helped fashion that nation before and after the American Revolution. The same can be said about Mount Vernon. Mount Vernon, the memorialized public site revered to this day as a symbol of the American dream, came into being in large part thanks to those who labored against their will and without the benefit of rest or access to the dream that their enslavers enjoyed. For most enslaved Black people, the dream of freedom without punishment was plausible only upon their deaths or upon the death of their masters, as dictated in their master's will. For a more complete account of history, in this book, I seek to remember them, those women, men, and children whose names are unknown and omitted from historical accounts of the Washington family, Mount Vernon, and the birth of a new nation.

## Hidden in Plain Sight: Washington's Enslaved Laborers

On January 17, 2016, Scholastic Books terminated the sale of a popular children's book, *A Birthday Cake for George Washington*. The book tells a story about Mount Vernon's cook Hercules and his daughter, Delia, preparing a birthday cake for George Washington's birthday. The illustrations depict them as contented and happy slaves who smile ecstatically while preparing the cake for their master, a misleading representation of Hercules's and Delia's real lives and the lives of other enslaved people at Mount Vernon. The public found the book's story line and illustrations problematic, earning the book criticism, writes an NPR columnist, for "whitewashing the history of slavery."[67] Real life for Hercules, Delia, and others enslaved at Mount Vernon was far from happy and content.

The real-life Hercules was born into slavery around 1754, the same year that George Washington acquired Mount Vernon from his sister-in-law. At a young age, he was given the name Hercules. Europeans likened his strong, muscular frame to the Hercules in Greek and Roman mythologies. The enslaved community, however, referred to him as Uncle Hekles or Harkles, pronounced as "heke" in Sierra Leone, a Mende noun meaning "a strong man" or "a large wild animal."

Young Hercules worked as a ferryman for his owner, John Posey, Washington's neighbor. At the age of thirteen, Posey sold Hercules to George Washington, who three years later in 1770 listed Hercules among his taxable income. Washington knew that Hercules's strength and stature would add value to the enslaved workforce tasked with renovating the Mount Vernon estate. Hercules also served as the estate's ferryman and in time began assisting Old Doll, an elderly enslaved woman serving as the chief cook in the main house. During his time at Mount Vernon, Hercules married Alice, another servant in the Washington household. We have no record of the date of their marriage.

By 1786, Hercules had advanced to the position of chief cook of Mount Vernon and became widely known throughout the estate and surrounding regions as a chef with a knack for extraordinary cuisines. He was one of the few enslaved workers on the Mount Vernon estate allowed to travel without an escort, attend community events, and secure profit from selling to the public meals made from leftover scraps. One year after becoming chief cook, Hercules's wife, Alice, died. Martha Washington expressed her condolences by giving Hercules "three bottles of rum," which she offered in benevolence for him having to "bury his wife."[68] Hercules and Alice had three children, Richmond,

Evey, and Delia. Richmond (not Delia) often accompanied him when traveling to Philadelphia to prepare meals for dignitaries.

It would appear Hercules was a contented slave given his special privileges, notable recognition for his skills, and sometimes favor with the Washingtons. However, beneath the surface of it all, Hercules often contemplated absconding. Washington, having discovered his plan, decided temporarily to strip Hercules of his privileges and move him from the mansion kitchen to the fields to labor under harsh conditions. Journalist Adrian Mille describes Hercules now as being "relegated to hard labor alongside others, digging clay for 100,000 bricks, spreading dung, grubbing bushes, and smashing stones into sand to coat the houses on the property."[69]

On Washington's sixty-fifth birthday, Hercules was neither working in the fields nor joyously baking a cake for his master. Hercules was gone. He had managed to escape undetected and make his way north to freedom. Infuriated, Washington solicited friends for months to help him find Hercules. In the opening lines of a letter addressed to his nephew George Lewis, Washington writes in great distress, "The running off of my Cook, has been a most inconvenient thing to this family; and what renders it more disagreeable, is, that I had resolved never to become the master of another Slave by *purchase*; but this resolution I fear I must break. . . . Mr Brooke (late Governor) informs me that he had a very excellent Cook, with no other fault than a fondness for liquor . . . who is now in Fredericksburg, and is to be sold. I shall write to the Gentleman who has him, not to sell him till he hears from you."[70] Uncle Hekles never returned to George Washington's kitchen or fields. He remained a free man until his death but had one regret—of leaving behind his sons and his beloved daughter, Delia. His children, like most enslaved laborers, continued working on the Mount Vernon estate and other Washington properties until they died or were traded or bequeathed to another family member. These and other key historical truths about Hercules, his family, and his slave life at Mount Vernon were missing from *A Birthday Cake for George Washington*.

Unlike most of Washington's enslaved workers, Hercules had been afforded a modicum of freedom to move about the community and earn wages for himself. But even special privileges were not enough to keep Hercules from absconding to gain freedom. He and all enslaved laborers in the New World were keenly aware that escape could lead to severe punishment, relentless bounty hunters, starvation, imprisonment, death, or being sold as a slave to the West Indies. In 1766, Tom, a foreman at the River Farm and one of the first of several enslaved overseers that Washington appointed, ran away and was captured and punished before being sold to the West Indies.

Regardless of the privileges an enslaved person possessed, in the end, their owners saw them as commodities whose survival depended on their usefulness. Karl Marx's 1867 discussion on the commodity in his seminal work *Capital* is helpful here in assessing antebellum slave owners' mindset concerning their enslaved labor force. Washington, for example, did not purchase, rent, or make use of the enslaved without considering their utility and value in building his personal capital. For the most part, he regarded each enslaved laborer as a commodity that performed a particular function. As a commodity, an enslaved laborer, unlike an indentured worker, was considered an object that through its usefulness to the owner satisfies a human need of one kind or another.[71] An enslaved laborer was assessed based on their "use value"—their usefulness in relation to skill level, skill set(s), age, fitness, competency, adaptability, versatility, quantity produced, and performance quality.

Washington makes these points clear in his notations regarding the usefulness of particular workers. He describes Lucy in his notation as "lame, or pretends to be so occasioned by rheumatic pains, but is a good knitter, & so employed."[72] Moses, he writes, is a good "plowman and carter," who at "26 is in his prime."[73] As the people who labored on his various properties aged, Washington became more descriptive in articulating their usefulness and ability to perform mentally and physically. Hannah, who served the Washingtons for multiple generations, was sixty years old when Washington wrote next to her name, "Partly an ideot." Hannah later died on Washington's Dogue Run Farm with no notation from Washington as to the cause of her death. "Nearly done" is how Washington described Ben, another long-standing Washington family servant who at age seventy worked his final days on the River Farm. Washington included no notation about how Ben contributed to the labor force or to the Washington family over the years, noting only that after years of service, Ben was close to death.

When workers did not perform well or defied the farm managers and overseers, Washington permitted his overseers to flog them. In 1793, Charlotte, an enslaved house servant, was "whipped for being very impudent." Washington threatened to sell another fifteen-year-old servant named Ben to the West Indies if he did not cease his "rogueries, & other villainies." In some instances, Washington appears offended by some of his overseers' treatment of the enslaved. In a letter to William Pearce, his farm manager at the time, Washington expressed his discontent, saying, "McKoy, or indeed from most of his class . . . they seem to consider a negro much in the same light as they do the brute beasts, on the farms; and oftentimes treat them as inhumanly."[74] Washington, however, did not remove these abusive overseers from their authoritative roles.

These and similar notations from Washington and others reveal how steep the idea that Black people were nothing more than commodities was ingrained in the colonial worldview. Not only were enslaved people treated harshly under the conditions of slavery, but slaveholders listed them as transferrable property, willed and passed them on to family members. For example, in his will, Augustine Washington's enslaved persons were counted among the inventory of his estate and divided among his wife, children, and relatives, especially his son, George Washington. Each laborer was listed by name, value, and numeric worth at the time of Augustine's death.

George Washington's inherited laborers continued working on the Ferry Farm plantation, Washington's birthplace home, until he turned eighteen. Once Washington assumed legal ownership of them in 1750, they were more than likely sent to labor on the Bullskin plantation, the first land that Washington purchased in Frederick County, Virginia, then to Mount Vernon, where some, like Jenny and Frank, remained until their deaths. Upon ownership, Washington inventoried and accounted for them in the same manner as his cattle, livestock, cash crops, and so on. He listed them in his ledgers as taxable and tithable income.

Chart 2.1 displays the valuation of Washington's inherited Black people as noted in Augustine's will and recorded in Washington's ledger. At some point the number increased from ten to eleven. Each laborer is listed by name, accompanied by a numeric assessment of their worth. Their total worth was estimated at £202.10, equivalent to a cash value of $45,600.25 in 2018.[75]

## Chart 2.1. George Washington's inherited enslaved persons

| Name | Value in 1750 (£) | US dollar ($) value in 2018 |
|------|---|---|
| Fortune | 30.00 | 6,768.96 |
| George | 20.00 | 4,512.64 |
| Long Joe | 30.00 | 6,768.96 |
| Winna | 30.00 | 6,768.96 |
| Bellindar | 25.00 | 5,640.80 |
| Jenny | 12.10 | 2,730.15 |
| Adam | 10.00 | 2,256.32 |
| Natt | 10.00 | 2,256.32 |
| London | 20.00 | 4,512.64 |
| Milly | 10.00 | 2,256.32 |
| Frank | 5.00 | 1,128.16 |

From the time Augustine Washington purchased Fortune, George, Long Joe, Winna, Bellindar, Jenny, Adam, Natt, London, Milly, and Frank to the moment George Washington assumed legal rights of their Black bodies, we learn nothing of their thoughts, interests, or passions, merely these scant notations regarding their worth and the usefulness of their Black hands and bodies. The same can be said of Hercules, Tom, Lucy, Moses, Hannah, elderly Ben, Charlotte, young Ben, and all of Washington's enslaved laborers. Little is known of them and what they yearned for beyond the gates of Mount Vernon. Washington's notations and the notations of other like-minded slaveholders make evident their disregard for enslaved individuals' well-being beyond their usefulness as laborers to support the economic and social pursuits of their enslavers. In most instances, enslaved persons were also unable to reveal candidly in written form their sentiments about life under the conditions of slavery. Yet Hercules, Tom, and other enslaved individuals who contemplated and succeeded in running away provide us a glimpse into what enslaved individuals thought and felt: they desired freedom, the ability to escape slavery and the harsh conditions that came with being held in bondage and to make a life for themselves on their own terms. Though Washington was often characterized as a "difficult and demanding taskmaster" and the enslaved at Mount Vernon often "felt the sting of his anger,"

his enslaved laborers, as many throughout the nation, possessed "a resolute determination to use their labor for their ends as well as his."[76] The
enslaved at Mount Vernon were a kind, creative, and hospitable people
who built the house of their master, tended his lands, and cared for his
family, "but they also had lives and dreams of their own to fulfill."[77]

Though there are scant detailed accounts of each of these enslaved
women, men, and children at Mount Vernon, one can only imagine how
they felt being held against their will by George Washington and his family. Did Washington and his loved ones ever think to ask them of their
dreams? Imagine how the enslaved at Mount Vernon helped the Washington legacy grow while they and their forebears died on the estate without proper burials. Imagine them involuntarily cultivating lands that
they could never call their own. Picture them watching and internalizing
someone else's immigrant dreams come to fruition generation after generation while their own legacies typically died on the vine.

Those of us who experience freedom today can only imagine what
it must have felt like to be reduced to a commodity, a tool, a thing, and
pushed like a workhorse and treated like a mule. We can only imagine
what it must have felt like to be herded like cattle every morning onto
fields and other places throughout the estate while their own dreams
remained deferred. Imagine working year-round, eight hours a day
during the winter and up to fourteen hours per day in the summer.
Imagine working year-round from sunup to sundown with only Sundays, Christmas, Easter, and Pentecost as your days off. Imagine as your
daily meals nothing short of pig slop and hoecakes made of cornmeal
to keep you sturdy for work and, when night falls, retiring to a one-
or two-room slave quarter shack not worthy to call home. Their lives
consisted of all work. As Sarah Gudgers, a formerly North Carolinian
enslaved woman, described, "I sho' has had a ha'd life. Jes wok, an' wok,
an' wok. I nebbish know nothin' but wok."[78]

When George Washington assumed ownership of Mount Vernon in
1754, the population of Fairfax County in which he lived was approximately 6,500 people, with 28 percent or approximately 1,800 of them of
African descent. By the end of the American Revolution, the number
of enslaved Africans in the county had risen to over 40 percent of the
overall population, with no rights to citizenship and little or no monetary compensation for their time.[79]

The eleven enslaved Black bodies that George Washington inherited in 1743 increased to more than 315 during his lifetime. The women, men, and children who worked on the Mount Vernon estate and the five outlying farms included people George Washington owned outright through inheritance (e.g., from his father, mother, brothers, and sister-in-law) or purchase. Others Washington had received, as previously stated, as part of Martha's dowry. Washington also rented skilled enslaved bricklayers, carpenters, spinners, and painters from Mrs. Penelope French and other neighboring slave owners and acquaintances.

Historical accounts of the Washington family do not include the voices of those who turned the Washington family legacy into an asset. The absence of these voices is particularly startling given that there are incredibly detailed accounts of the building materials necessary to construct Washington's properties—the number of bricks and other materials needed for building the Mount Vernon estate, the intricate details that went into renovating the Mount Vernon estate and the five outlying farms, and the construction of the sixteen-sided barn, which required nearly 140,000 bricks.

Absurdly, there are few details about the persons who worked to make Washington's dream a reality: the enslaved laborers who had to dig soft mud (clay) from the ground to turn those 140,000 small mud blocks into bricks or who had to transport those blocks to a kiln on the estate to bake them and make them durable for the construction of the barn or the enslaved women and men who cut trees, sawed wood into planks, and built the barn structure from yellow pine, white oak, and cypress trees. There is little account of those who maintained the fields and cultivated and helped export various vegetables, plants, and cash crops, those tasked with clearing the land, tilling the soil, and sowing and reaping seeds, over "61 percent" of whom were "women who hoed, ploughed, harvest, and built fences around the estate."[80]

Even the task of fishing from the Potomac required enslaved laborers, who maintained three areas of commercial fishing on the estate—one fishery near Union Farm, another by the wharf, and the third in the River Farm area. Nearly one million fish were caught using large seine nets. These women, men, and children sorted, gutted, cleaned, salted, and then stored the fish in large barrels in the salt house. These workers also disposed of the by-products left after gutting and cleaning the fish. For their labor, the enslaved received a pint of rum each day.

Spinning and weaving likewise generated revenue for Washington. Through the work of enslaved spinners, predominately girls and young women, "fluffs of raw fiber were twisted and counter-twisted with a hand-held spindle or spinning wheel into strong, smooth lengths of thread for weaving."[81] The enslaved weavers, typically males, wove cotton, wool, linen, and silk patterns and types of fabric into "cotton and wool plaids; a pattern called Ms and Os; cotton striped with silk; linsey-woolsey, a mix of linen and wool; fustian, a rough cloth of cotton and linen; shalloon, a woollen material used for linings; and jean, sometimes spelled 'jane,' a thick, twilled cotton that only later was associated with the blue jeans we wear today. The name of another fabric the weavers produced, diaper, also had yet to take on its modern meaning. They also turned out fishnets, harness, carpets, counterpanes and coverlets, and bed ticking."[82]

All enslaved persons on the Mount Vernon estate were put to work. Sick, injured, or physically disabled and, on occasion, young and elderly enslaved laborers were tasked with nondemanding work assignments such as "making clothing or shoes, or picking the seeds of wild onions out of the oat seeds" and tending personally to the Washingtons, their children, and the main house.[83] It was this labor and sacrifice, this blood and sweat equity of enslaved Black laborers along with indentured European immigrants that built Mount Vernon and brought it such success. The enslaved women and men who built the estate, maintained the five outlying farms, tilled the fields, and cared for Washington; his wife, Martha; and their children were considered commodities. And as commodities, they were not valued for their day-to-day sacrifices.

In 1782, Virginia passed legislation allowing slave owners to free their enslaved workers of their own accord and without a special act of the Virginia General Assembly. Despite this legislation, Washington retained nearly all the enslaved laborers on the Mount Vernon plantation well into the early nineteenth century. In 1786, Washington took an inventory of the enslaved laborers that remained at Mount Vernon, listing them in his diary for posterity. A total of 216 women, men, and children composed Washington's inherited and purchased human beings and those from his wife's dowry, not including those he rented from his associates and neighbors.[84] The list included ninety children under the age of eleven. By 1799, the total number of human beings owned by George Washington, in some capacity or another, was more than 315 persons, as illustrated in chart 2.2.

Washington regarded his enslaved workforce as commodities, but they were more than possessions itemized on his cash account ledgers. They were women, men, and children with origins, names, families, skills, and dreams. In the following charts, I list the names of these women, men, and children. I include their names here rather than in appendixes because enslaved Black people have been appendixes in American history for far too long. The names of all these women, men, and children and their contributions to the first family and Washington's immigrant forebears have also been scant or nonexistent in public discourse and publications about George Washington and the emergence of Mount Vernon. I therefore name them intentionally in an effort to memorialize them, honor their stories, acknowledge their presence and sacrifice, and underscore the work of their hands. I do this aware that the recognition that white indentured servants and Native American peoples whose lands were stolen are due is also lacking. I celebrate the writings, websites, documentaries, and social media platforms that have given attention to these workers and anticipate related publications that will detail their realities and forced sacrifices in the building of the New World.

As noted earlier, enslaved women and men possessed a wide range of skills who worked in and around the Mansion House (a.k.a. the Great House) and the estate's five outlying farms—Mansion House, Muddy Hole, River Farm, Dogue Run Farm, and Union Farm. Twenty-eight percent of Washington's enslaved laborers were skilled laborers. Among them were barrel makers, blacksmiths, bricklayers, carpenters, carters, cooks, coopers, dairy maids, distillers, ditch diggers, gardeners, house servants, knitters, midwives, millers, postilions (carriage drivers), seamstresses, shoemakers, spinners, waggoners, weavers, and personal servants to the Washingtons.[85] Most of these artisans (about ninety persons) labored at the Mansion House and the immediate surrounding work areas and shops. Some of their names (and age, skill level, and spouse, where applicable) are noted in chart 2.3. Blank spaces in the trade column more than likely indicate the enslaved laborer was a house servant or assisted in other areas germane to the mansion house.

## Chart 2.2. George Washington's enslaved laborers

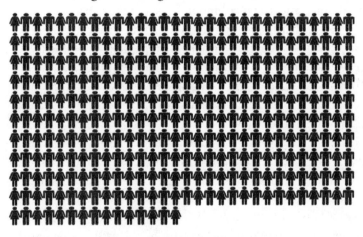

George Washington's enslaved laborers

## Chart 2.3. Mansion (the Great House) farm:
## Enslaved women and men

| Name | Age | Trade | Spouse |
| --- | --- | --- | --- |
| Alce | | Spinner | Charles (freeman) |
| Alla | | Knitter | James |
| Anna | | | name unk. |
| Ben | | Ditcher | Penny |
| Ben | | Miller | Sinah |
| Betty Davis | | Spinner | Dick |
| Boatswain | | Ditcher | Myrtilla |
| Caroline | | Housemaid | Peter Hardman |
| Charles | | Ditcher | Fanny |
| Charlotte | | Sempstress | None |
| Chriss | | House serv. | name unk. |
| Cyrus | | Postilion | Lucy |
| Daniel | | Distiller | None |
| Davy | | Carpenter | Edy |
| Delia | 14 | | None |
| Delphy | | | None |
| Dolshy | | | Joe |
| Dundee | | Ditcher | name unk. |
| Eve | 17 | | None |
| Forrester | | Miller | None |
| Frank | | House serv. | Lucy |
| George | | Blacksmith | Lydia |
| George | | Gardener | Sall |
| Godfrey | | Carter | Mima |
| Grace | | | Juba |
| Hanson | | Distiller | None |
| Harry | | Gardener | None |
| Isaac | | Carpenter | Kitty |

## Chart 2.3. Mansion (the Great House) farm: Enslaved women and men (*continued*)

| Name | Age | Trade | Spouse |
|---|---|---|---|
| Jacob | | Cooper | None |
| James | 40 | Carpenter | Darcus |
| James | | Carter | Alla |
| Joe | | Carpenter | Dolshy |
| Joe | | Postilion | Sall |
| Juba | | Carter | None |
| Judy | 21 | | None |
| Kitty | | Milkmaid | Isaac |
| Letty | | | None |
| Lucy | | Cook | Frank |
| Lucy | | | None |
| Marcus | | House serv. | None |
| Matilda | | Spinner | Boson |
| Mike | | | None |
| Mima | | | Godfrey |
| Molly | | | None |
| Moses | | Cooper | None |
| Nancy | | | None |
| Nat | | Blacksmith | Lucy |
| Nat | | Distiller | None |
| Nathan | | Cook | Peg |
| Peter | | Distiller | None |
| Peter | | Knitter | None |
| Rachel | 12 | | Daughter to Caroline |
| Sall | | Housemaid | None |
| Sambo | | Carpenter | Agnes |
| Simms | | Carpenter | Daphne |
| Sinah | | | Ben |

## Chart 2.3. Mansion (the Great House) farm:
## Enslaved women and men (*continued*)

| Name | Age | Trade | Spouse |
|------|-----|-------|--------|
| Slamin Joe | | Ditcher | Sylla |
| Timothy | | Distiller | None |
| Tom | | Cooper | Nanny |
| Tom Davis | | Brick layer | name unk. |
| Viner | | | None |
| W. Muclus | | Brick layer | name unk. |
| Will | | | Aggy |
| Will | | Shoemaker | None |
| Wilson | 15 | Postilion | None |

As is evident in chart 2.3, a large percentage of the Mount Vernon enslaved laborers were married. The chart reveals that more than half of those enslaved persons working at the Mansion House Farm were married (thirty-eight persons out of sixty-one). An owner allowing their enslaved persons to marry was not a common practice in antebellum America. Washington permitted the practice. However, Washington, like many slave owners, separated enslaved families, especially if an enslaved spouse was rented out to a merchant or another slave owner. In this case, the rented enslaved person worked at another plantation or business, and the enslaved person's owner received the payment for their labor. If the laborer was paid, the amount was minimal. In other cases, enslaved laborers met and married enslaved workers at adjoining plantations. As noted in chart 2.3, W. Muclus, one of Washington's enslaved bricklayers, worked from sunup to sundown at Mount Vernon, while his wife (name unknown) lived and worked across the Potomac from Mount Vernon in Charles County, Maryland, on Captain Thomas Hanson Marshall's property.

Although most of Washington's enslaved married couples resided on the estate, some did not live in the same quarters. At Mount Vernon, it was also common for one spouse to reside on the farm where they worked while the other spouse resided and worked at another farm on the estate. James, a carpenter assigned to Mansion House renovations, for example, worked and lived in the slave quarters near the mansion, while his wife,

Darcus, worked and lived on the Muddy Hole Farm. The same is true of Tom, a cooper assigned to the Mansion House, and his wife, Nanny, who worked on the Muddy Hole Farm. Although enslaved couples sought to raise families, continuous labor left little time for family life. Throughout the antebellum world, enslaved couples were often given specific days and times to see each other. Some were granted more privileges than others. Normally, the family visitation times were evenings, Sundays, and holidays (Easter Monday, the Monday after Pentecost, Christmas, and other official days established by Washington or the colony).

Some parents were separated from their children on the Mount Vernon estate, and when a child's parents died, others in the slave community either willingly or as required assisted in raising the child. Such is the case of Isbel (Muddy Hole Farm), whose mother, Sarah (Dogue Run Farm), died when she was young, and Hannah (River Farm), whose mother, Daphne, also died. Darcus's, Nanny's, and Isbel's names are listed, along with other Muddy Hole Farm laborers, in chart 2.4. Blank spaces in the trade column in chart 2.4 and the remaining preceding charts more than likely indicate the individual worked in the field or some specified rudimentary task.

## Chart 2.4. Muddy Hole Farm: Enslaved women and men

| Name | Age | Trade | Spouse |
|------|-----|-------|--------|
| Alce | 38 | | Sam |
| Amie | 30 | | None |
| Darcus | 36 | | James |
| Davy | 56 | Overseer | Molly (age 76) |
| Gabriel | 30 | | Judy |
| Isbel | 16 | | Daughter to Sarah (deceased) |
| Kate | (old) | | Will |
| Kate long | 18 | | Daughter to Kate |
| Kate sht. | 18 | | Daughter to Alce |
| Letty | 19 | | None |
| Lucy | 11 | | Daughter to Peg |
| Mary | 11 | | Daughter to Betty |
| Molly | 26 | | None |

## Chart 2.4. Muddy Hole Farm: Enslaved women and men (*continued*)

| Name | Age | Trade | Spouse |
|------|-----|-------|--------|
| Moses | 19 | | Son to Darcus |
| Nancy | 28 | | Abram |
| Nanny | (old) | | Tom |
| Oliver | 11 | | Son to Nancy |
| Patience | 14 | | Daughter to Dolly |
| Peg | 34 | | Nathan |
| Sacky | 40 | | None |
| Townshend | 14 | | Son to Darcus |
| Uriah | 24 | | |
| Virgin | 24 | | Gabl |
| Will | 60 | Mink | Kate |

The fear of separation often haunted slave communities, especially when the owner died and the enslaved persons were inherited by other family members or sold to other enslavers. Records of enslaved laborers on the River Farm are similarly revealing. By 1799, there were approximately fifty-seven enslaved laborers living on the River Farm, and most had families. These laborers either belonged to Washington, were a part of Martha's dowry, or were rented by Washington from his neighbor, Mrs. French. Those who belonged outright to Washington had worked and lived at River Farm for a minimum of thirteen years with and without their families. Their names are listed in chart 2.5.

## Chart 2.5. River Farm: Enslaved women and men

| Name | Age | Trade | Spouse |
|------|-----|-------|--------|
| Agnes | 36 | | Sambo |
| Alce | 26 | | John |
| Anderson | 11 | | Son to Agnes |
| Ben | 22 | Carter | |
| Betty | 20 | | Reuben |
| Cecelia | 14 | | Daughter to Agnes |
| Cloe | 55 | | None |

## Chart 2.5. River Farm: Enslaved women and men (*continued*)

| Name | Age | Trade | Spouse |
| --- | --- | --- | --- |
| Daniel | 15 | | Son of Suckey |
| Doll | 58 | | Natt |
| Doll | 16 | | Daughter to Doll |
| Esther | 40 | | Johny |
| Fanny | 30 | | Alexander |
| Hannah | old | Cook | Ned |
| Hannah | 12 | | Daughter to Daphne (deceased) |
| Henry | 11 | | Son to Sall |
| Heuky | 17 | | Son to Agnes |
| Jack | 12 | | Daughter to Doll |
| Joe | 22 | | |
| Johny | 39 | | Esther |
| Judy | 55 | | Gunna |
| Lucy | 18 | | Cyrus |
| Lydia | 11 | | Daughter to Lydia |
| Lydia | 50 | | Smith Geo |
| Nancy | 11 | | Daughter to Bay Suke |
| Natt | 55 | | Doll |
| Ned | 56 | | Hanh |
| Ned | 20 | | |
| Peg | 56 | | Old Ben |
| Penny | 20 | | Ben |
| Richmond | 20 | | None |
| Rose | 28 | | None |
| Sall | 30 | | Joe |
| Suckey | 50 | | None |
| Suckey Bay | 46 | | Name unk. |
| Suckey Bay | 46 | | Name unk. |

On the Dogue Run Farm, some couples did manage to survive without feeling the brunt of separation from their families. As identified in chart 2.6, Ben and Peg, Long Jack and Molly, Dick and Charity, and

Carter Jack, and Grace, along with their children, were among those families that were not separated due to labor assignments. However, Judy's fate was different. She was not fortunate enough to have her husband, Gabriel, by her side to help her as she managed the difficult terrain of slave life while blind. Gabriel worked on the Muddy Hole Farm, while Judy, along with a few others, are listed as living on Dogue Run Farm.

## Chart 2.6. Dogue Run Farm: Enslaved women and men

| Name | Age | Trade | Spouse |
| --- | --- | --- | --- |
| Agnes | 25 | | Will |
| Barbary | 11 | | Daughter to Sall T. |
| Ben | 57 | | Peg |
| Betty | 16 | | None |
| Carter Jack | 40 | | Grace |
| Charity | 42 | | Dick |
| Dick | 46 | | Charity |
| Fomison | 11 | | Daughter to Charity |
| Grace | 35 | | Carter Jack |
| Judy | 50 | "Blind" | Gabriel |
| Kate | 18 | | name unk. |
| Lawrence | 14 | | Son to Matilda |
| Linney | 27 | | None |
| Long Jack | 60 | | Molly |
| Lucy | 50 | | Nat |
| Molly | 45 | Cook | Long Jack |
| Ned | 14 | | Son to Lucy |
| Peg | 30 | | Ben |
| Penny | 11 | | Daughter to Siller |
| Priscilla | 36 | | Slamin Joe |
| Sall Twine | 38 | | George |
| Sarah | 20 | | None |
| Simon | 20 | | None |
| Sophia | 14 | | Daughter to Siller |

Union Farm had two smaller farms known as Ferry and French and had a seven-field crop system and eventually became the location where the new barn was built. Approximately seventy enslaved persons lived and worked at Union. The majority of these workers were single women who worked the fields, which is evident by the omission of a trade in chart 2.7.

## Chart 2.7. Union Farm: Enslaved women and men

| Name | Age | Trade | Spouse |
| --- | --- | --- | --- |
| Betty | 62 | Cook | None |
| Caesar | 50 | | None |
| Edy | 26 | | Davy |
| Ephraim | 11 | | Son to Rachel |
| Fanny | 36 | | Charles |
| Gideon | 13 | | Son to Betty |
| Jamie | 11 | | Son to Fanny |
| Jenny | 34 | | George |
| Joe | 24 | | |
| John | 16 | | Son to Betty |
| London | 64 | | None |
| Lucretia | 20 | | None |
| Lucy | 50 | | None |
| Milly | 22 | | None |
| Paul | 36 | | None |
| Rachell | 34 | | None |
| Sam Kitt | 78 | | Name unk. |
| Sucky | 11 | | Daughter to Doll |

Throughout his time at Mount Vernon, Washington also rented enslaved workers from neighboring plantations and associates to help meet the demands of estate renovations and cash crop production. Listed in chart 2.8 are those enslaved laborers rented from one associate, Mrs. French. Washington also provides a graphic assessment of some individuals' physique, mental capacity, and performance.

## Chart 2.8. Rented from Mrs. French: Enslaved women and men

| Name | Age | Trade | Spouse | Washington's remarks |
|------|-----|-------|--------|---------------------|
| Abram | | | Nancy | "In his prime" |
| Betty | 13 | | | Daughter of Delia |
| Briney | 12 | | | Daughter of Lucy |
| Daniel | 16 | | | Son of Delia |
| Daphne | 40 | Plower | Simms | "Ploughs very Well and is a good hand at any work." |
| Delia | 35 | Spinner | None | "Equally good at the Spinning Wheel or Hoe, but has been kept chiefly at the former." |
| Grace | 12 | | | Daughter of Rose |
| Grace | 28 | Plower | Davy | "A very good Plougher—and equally so at all sorts of Work." |
| Hannah | 14 | | | "Nearly at her full growth and a woman in appear[anc]e." |
| Isaac | 29 | | None | "In his prime" |
| Isaac | 14 | | | Son of Rose (deceased) |
| James | 24 | Works at distillery | | |
| Julius | 23 | Carter | | "A very good Carter, and can do any other work, although defective in Shape from his Infancy." |
| Lucy | 55 | Knitter | George | "Lame, or pretends to be so occassioned by rheumatic pains, but is a good knitter, & so employed." |
| Matilda | 13 | | | Daughter of Daphne |
| Milly | 18 | | None | "A full grown Woman, and [*illegible*]ly; has been used to Common Work only." |
| Moses | 26 | Plowman and carter | | "In his prime" |
| Nancy | 16 | | None | "The same—in all respect.s"— (i.e., "A full grown Woman and [*illegible*]ly; has been used to Common Work only.") |
| Paschall | | | Cornelia ("lately lost") | "In his prime" |
| Sabine | 60 | | Name unk. | "A good working woman, notwithstanding her age." |

## Chart 2.8. Rented from Mrs. French:
## Enslaved women and men (*continued*)

| Name | Age | Trade | Spouse | Washington's remarks |
|------|-----|-------|--------|----------------------|
| Siss | 25 | Plower | Jack | "Ploughs Well—and can Milk & Churn" |
| Spencer | 20 | Carter and mower | | "A very good Carter and Mower and able at any business." |
| Tom | 28 | | None | "In his prime," "getting blind" |
| Will | | "Looks after Stock" | | "Old but hearty" |

Children made up a large percentage of Africans transplanted on slave ships to the New World for mass involuntary labor. Children were important to the institution of slavery and Mount Vernon, and "even the unborn children of expectant mothers were marked with a monetary value."[86] A young girl was considered an adult at eleven or older, an age that typically marked the beginning of menstruation and her ability to conceive children. Her ability to conceive and also endure strenuous labor meant to slave owners that she had transitioned from a girl to a woman, from a teen to an adult. As many enslavers remarked of young girls on the auction blocks, "She is good for breeding." Perhaps this is one reason Washington describes fourteen-year-old Hannah, in chart 2.8, as "nearly at her full growth and a woman in appear[anc]e." Moreover, young girls and boys eleven or older were also considered able to work the fields and complete other skilled tasks. In his ledger, Washington often describes these individuals as being "a full-grown woman" or "in his prime." Such notations imply that these individuals were a good source of reproduction and labor and therefore were particularly valuable to him.

Enslaved children of any age seldom experienced what it meant to be and feel like a child. Older children also worked from sunup to sundown, and while younger children were often joyfully at play with their young masters. Most were fully aware of the day-to-day realities of their enslavement, which came with its share of violence, sexual assault, suffering, public flogging, and famine. Enslaved children also had to deal with abandonment and separation issues when their parent(s) died or when they or their parent(s) were inherited, sold, and sent to work on other plantations. Enslavement, involuntary labor, punishments, and loss or separation from a parent or both parents were always realities on the horizon. As chart 2.9 notes, three siblings lost their mother, Cornelia, when she died of unspecified causes. Alce was two, Davy six, and Lewis four.

## Chart 2.9. Enslaved children

| Name | Age | Parent |
| --- | --- | --- |
| Abbay | 10 | Daughter to Sall T. |
| Adam | 7 | Son to Alce |
| Alce | 8 | Daughter to Darcus |
| Alce | 2 | Daughter to Cornelia (deceased) |
| Alexander | 3 | Son to Peg |
| Ambrose | 1 | Son of Delia |
| Anna | 4 | Daughter to Anna |
| Augusta | 1 | Daughter of Grace |
| Barbara | 10 | Daughter to Kitty |
| Bartley | 6 | Daughter to Linney |
| Beck | 4 | Daughter to Rachel |
| Billy | 2 | Son to Letty |
| Billy | 6 | Son to Peg |
| Bob | 10 | Son of Grace |
| Burwell | | Son to Lucy |
| Cecelia | 2 | Daughter to Alce |
| Charity | 2 | Daughter to Sall |
| Charles | | Daughter to Alce |
| Charles | 1 | Son to Sall |
| Charles | 1 | Son to Fanny |
| Christopher | 1 | Son to Siller |
| Daniel | 6 | Son to Anna |
| Daphne | 5 | Daughter to Fanny |
| Darcus | 1 | Daughter to Peg |
| Davy | 6 | Son to Cornelia (deceased) |
| Davy | 8 | Son to Rachel |
| Dennis | 2 mo. | Son to Dolshy |
| Dennis | 5 | Son to Sall |
| Diana | 8 | Daughter to Peg |
| Diana | 1 | Daughter to Milly |
| Dick | 3 | Daughter to Charity |
| Elias | 2 mo. | Son to Doll |

## Chart 2.9. Enslaved children (*continued*)

| Name | Age | Parent |
|------|-----|--------|
| Elijah | 7 | Son to Sall |
| Eliza | | Daughter to Charolette |
| Elizabeth | 9 | Daughter to Doll |
| Elvey | | Daughter to Charlotte |
| Emery | | Daughter to Alce |
| Eneas | 1 | Son to Rachel |
| Felicia | 7 | Daughter to Jenny |
| Fendal | 2 | Son to Peg |
| George | 8 | Son to Alce |
| George | 1 | Son to Sall T. |
| Guss | 3 | Son to Rachel |
| Gutridge | 3 | Son to Sall |
| Guy | 2 | Son to Agnes |
| Hagar | 6 | Daughter to Rose |
| Hannah | 4 | Daughter to Sall T. |
| Hellam | 1 | Son to Jenny |
| Henriette | | Daughter to Alce |
| Henry | 1 | Son to Letty |
| Israel | 10 | Son to Siller |
| Isrias | 3 | Son to Siller |
| Jack | 7 | Son of Delia |
| James | 7 | Son to Molly |
| Jemima | 9 | Daughter to Caroline |
| Jenny | | Daughter to Charlotte |
| Jenny | 3 | Daughter to Grace |
| Jesse | 6 | Son to Patt |
| Joe | 1 | Son to Rose |
| John | | Son to Mima |
| Jonathan | 3 | Son to Jenny |
| Jude | 1 | Daughter to Alce |
| Judy | 4 | Daughter of Grace |
| Julia | 4 | Daughter of Delia |

## Chart 2.9. Enslaved children (*continued*)

| Name | Age | Parent |
|------|-----|--------|
| Leanthe | 8 | Daughter to Caroline |
| Levina | 6 | Daughter to Kitty |
| Lewis | 4 | Son to Cornelia (deceased) |
| Lucinda | 2 | Daughter to Betty Davis |
| Lucy | 2 | Daughter to Sarah |
| Maria | 2 | Daughter of Daphne |
| Martin | 1 | Son to Nancy |
| Matilda | 1 | Daughter to Linney |
| Milley | 1 | Daughter to Betty |
| Molly | 6 | Daughter to Grace |
| Morgan | 2 | Son of Lucy |
| Nancy | 9 | Daughter to Betty Davis |
| Nancy | | Daughter to Sinah |
| Nancy | 2 | Daughter to Darcus |
| Nancy | 4 | Daughter to Bay Suke |
| Nancy | 1 | Daughter to Edy |
| Nancy | 10 | Daughter of Sabine |
| Nelly | 2 | Daughter of Delia |
| Oney | 6 | Daughter to Betty Davis |
| Patty | | Daughter to Lucy |
| Peg | 8 mo. | Daughter to Peg |
| Peter | 9 | Son to Doll |
| Peter—B. | 4 | Daughter to Caroline |
| Phil | | Son to Lucy |
| Phoenix | 1 | Son of Lucy |
| Polly | 6 | Daughter to Caroline |
| Polly | 1 | Daughter to Sall |
| Polly | 9 | Daughter of Daphne |
| Rainey | 8 | Daughter to Annie |
| Raison | 3 | Daughter of Lucy |
| Ralph | 9 | Son to Sall |
| Randolph | | Son to Mima |
| Renney | 6 | Daughter of Lucy |

## Chart 2.9. Enslaved children (*continued*)

| Name | Age | Parent |
| --- | --- | --- |
| Roger | 10 | Son to Grace |
| Sall | 8 | Daughter of Grace |
| Sandy | 1½ | Son to Anna |
| Sarah | 6 | Daughter to Edy |
| Simon | 4 | Son to Rose |
| Siss | 8 | Daughter to Nancy |
| Stately | 10 | Son of Lucy |
| Suckey | 4 | Daughter to Alce |
| Sucky | 5 | Daughter to Dolshy |
| Sylvia | 10 | Daughter to Molly |
| Teney | 10 | Daughter to Lucy |
| Tom | | Daughter to Alce |
| Tom | 2 | Son to Rose |
| Urinah | 2 | Daughter to Annie |

Chart 2.9 identifies those enslaved under the age of eleven (aged two months to ten years between 1779 and 1799) who were children of the aforementioned enslaved laborers. The children's duties included fanning flies, scaring crows from fields, fetching water, being playmates to their young masters, and fanning owners and their guests during humid weather. Most did not receive an education and were forbidden to read.

Unlike their enslavers, the women, men, and children in this and the previous charts are people whose dreams were often thwarted at the borders of Mount Vernon or indeed long before. Because Washington's immigrant forebears sailed in pursuit of boundless discoveries, anticipating new beginnings as far as their eyes could see, and because George Washington consequently lived the life he dreamed, he had access to a world that his laborers would never acquire. While each Washington heir passed away with honorable ceremonial burials, their enslaved laborers died with neither recognition nor proper burial. They worked. They died and did not live to see freedom or even know, as one formerly enslaved man put it, "what it was like to own your own body."[87]

By 1799, Washington listed eighteen deceased enslaved persons at Mount Vernon. No markers were left on their graves to indicate their names or acts of service. As noted in chart 2.10, they labored from their youth well into their seventies and eighties, never fully knowing what it meant to own their own body and live out the American dream on their own terms.

## Chart 2.10. Dying or deceased enslaved women and men

| Name | Age | Trade | Location of service | Spouse | Washington's remarks |
|------|-----|-------|---------------------|--------|----------------------|
| Ben | 70 | | River Farm | Peg | "Nearly done" |
| Breechy | 60 | | | Ruth | "Not better" |
| Cornelia | | | Muddy Hole | Mother of Alce, Davy, and Lewis | "Deceased" |
| Daphne | 70 | | Union Farm | Mother to Hannah | "Deceased" |
| Doll | | | Mansion House | None | "Deceased" |
| Doll | 52 | | Union Farm | | "Deceased," "lame & pretds to be so" |
| Flora | 64 | | Union Farm | None | "Deceased" |
| Frank | 80 | | Mansion House | None | "Deceased" |
| Gunner | 90 | | Mansion House | Judy | "Deceased" |
| Hannah | 60 | | Dogue Run | | "Deceased," "partly an ideot" |
| Jenny | | | Mansion House | None | "Deceased" |
| Patt | | | | Mother to Jesse | "Deceased" |
| Robin | 80 | | River Farm | | "Nearly passed laborer" |
| Rose | | | Rented from Mrs. French | Mother of Isaac and Grace | "Deceased" |
| Ruth | 70 | | River Farm | Breechy | "Deceased" |
| Sam | 40 | Cook | Mansion House | Alce | "Deceased" |
| Sarah | | | Dogue Run | Mother to Isbel | "Deceased" |
| Sue | 70 | | Dogue Run | None | "Deceased" |

By the turn of the century, Mount Vernon's enslaved burial ground included an estimated 150 graves, with no record of the deceased persons' identities—who they were and how they contributed to the building of Mount Vernon. Instead, in 1929, a stone marker was laid as a fixed reminder of those who labored and died there. The marker reads,

**In Memory of the**
**Many Faithful Colored Servants**
**of the**
**Washington Family**
**Buried at**
**Mount Vernon**
**from**
**1760 to 1860**
**Their**
**Unidentified Graves**
**Surround This Spot**
**1929**

Within time, the stone marker was soon lost in the underbrush and weeds at Mount Vernon. While tombs and monuments honoring Washington and the first family are affixed throughout Mount Vernon and the nation's capital, there are no notable monuments or tombstones of the enslaved laborers whose hands and sacrifice sustained Mount Vernon. Within these realities remains the ongoing saga of whether George Washington; his adopted son, John "Jacky" Parke Custis; and his grandson, George Washington Parke Custis ever fathered enslaved children.

George Washington expanded Mount Vernon as a plantation estate in an effort to secure and legitimize his socioeconomic and political standing. This expansion provided him the latitude to dream new possibilities for the newly emerging nation and for himself, which included envisioning a city from whence to govern and legitimate the nation. The acquisition of Mount Vernon, the native land upon which it sits, and the enslaved women, men, and children who built and sustained it for the benefit of European immigrants would foreshadow the building of

Federal City, which later became Washington's District of Columbia. The steps that George Washington took to expand his Mount Vernon estate became the same process he used to bring Federal City to fruition. Both required a plan and the acquisition of land and enslaved women, men, and children.

# CHAPTER THREE

# Black Minds
## *Blueprints, and the Enslaved and Free Black Artisans of Federal City*

*We the People of the United States, in Order to form a more per-fect Union, establish Justice, insure domestic Tranquility, provide for the common defence, promote the general Welfare, and secure the Blessings of Liberty to ourselves and our Posterity, do ordain and establish this Constitution for the United States of America.*

—US CONSTITUTION

*Sir, I have long been convinced, that if your love for your Selves, and for those inesteemable laws which preserve to you the rights of human nature, was founded on Sincerity, you could not but be Solicitous, that every Individual of whatsoever rank or distinction, might with you equally enjoy the blessings thereof, neither could you rest Satisfyed, short of the most active diffusion of your exertions, in order to their promotion from any State of degradation, to which the unjustifyable cruelty and barbarism of men may have reduced them.*

—BENJAMIN BANNEKER, LETTER TO THOMAS JEFFERSON

The "We the People" clause in the Preamble to the US Constitution was not written to include the domestic tranquility and freedoms of the women, men, and children whom George Washington, Thomas Jefferson, and other colonists held in bondage and used to advance their new nation's agenda. The evidence of this could not be more striking than the image of ten of Mount Vernon's servants toiling in the Presidential Mansion in Philadelphia shortly after Washington assumed office in 1789. Washington the planter was now Washington the first slave-owning president of the new nation. The ten forced to serve on the grounds and in the house of the president's Executive Mansion were Austin, Christopher Sheels, Giles, Hercules, Joe Richardson ("Postilion Joe"), Molly ("Moll"), Paris, Richmond, William "Billy" Lee, and Ona "Oney" Maria Judge, who became Martha Washington's maid-in-waiting.

Ona was born into slavery on the Mount Vernon estate around 1773 and became one among hundreds of laborers, domestic servants, and artisans who made it possible for the Washingtons to fulfill their aspirations. Ona, her siblings, and their mother, Betty, were a part of Martha Washington's dowry. Upon the death of Betty's husband, Daniel Parke Custis, Martha had gained possession of Ona's family and nearly one hundred other enslaved women, men, and children. Because Martha had no legal right to sell or free them, these enslaved laborers became a part of Martha's dowry and subsequently a part of George Washington's estate.

While laboring at Mount Vernon, Ona's mother, Betty, had met Andrew Judge, a white indentured servant and tailor from Leeds, England. As part of his six-year contract from 1772 to 1780, Andrew became the estate tailor and was tasked with teaching his skills to some of Washington's enslaved laborers. He was responsible for custom making Washington's military attire, the buff and blue-colored uniforms that Washington wore throughout his time in Philadelphia. Upon fulfilling his contract, Andrew left the estate and purchased a small plot of farmland in nearby Alexandria, Virginia. During his time at Mount Vernon, Betty had four children fathered by Andrew: Nancy, Philadelphia ("Delphy"), Lucinda, and Ona.

Ona learned the art of domestic servanthood and sewing from her mother, who was beloved by the slave community. Betty, a significant contributor to Martha Washington's sewing circles, was an expert in making clothes, weaving fabric, spinning thread, and tailoring. She made clothes both for the Washingtons and for the slave community. Betty also spent her days in the main house preparing food, churning butter, making soap, dipping candles, and doing laundry.

Ona became useful to the Washington family at the age of ten, when she was sent to the main house to work. In time, like her mother, she began spending long days sewing, churning, spinning, threading, weaving, dipping, prepping, and washing. Ona's expertise in sewing and her contributions to the Washington household were so evident that George Washington described her as "a perfect Mistress" and especially "a perfect Mistress of her needle." Ona was fifteen years old, just crossing the threshold between adolescence and young adulthood, when Washington became US president. Yet unlike most young adults today, Ona was separated from her mother to serve in the president's mansion in Philadelphia as Martha Washington's maid-in-waiting. Ona spent her days helping Martha prepare official receptions and traveling with her on various outings and daily errands. Several times a week, she accompanied the First Lady on her visits to the wives of other legislators and political leaders. Ona remained with the family through the eight years of Washington's presidency and his pursuit of a permanent seat of government, and as Ona's world grew, so did her desire for freedom.

Ona Judge's journey is among thousands of known and unknown stories of artisans, people of European descent, free Blacks, and enslaved laborers who contributed to the sustenance and building of the nation's capital cities—New York, Philadelphia, and later the city of Washington in the District of Columbia. Many of them worked, resisted, and died without memorialization on American soil. Of particular note are those late eighteenth- and early nineteenth-century artisans, such as French immigrant Pierre Charles L'Enfant, Quaker adherent Andrew Ellicott, and a free Black man named Benjamin Banneker. Often under duress, these men, along with hundreds of enslaved and free Black artisans, helped construct the permanent seat of government that became known as Federal City and later the city of Washington in the Territory of Columbia. Each played an innovative role in the city's design, survey, and construction.

Their collective stories reveal a tapestry of people who offered their gifts despite misrepresentation, adversity, disregard, and subjugation. Each of these artisans, the first contributors and first builders of the nation's capital, possessed an instinctive and strategic inclination to preserve their dignity while working to bring the young nation into being. Though Washington, Jefferson, and other colonizers plowed ahead, failing to consider their contributions, these artisans' stories are worth consideration, for they illumine the stark contrast between the lived commitments of the men who conceived of, sponsored, and supervised the construction of the nation's capital and those artisans whose dreams they deferred. Weaving all these lived realities together not only invites us to reappraise the nation's first leaders but also casts them and the contributions of L'Enfant, Ellicott, and Banneker in a new light. Most importantly, it highlights the contributions of the many unacknowledged enslaved and free Black-bodied workers who made conceiving and completing this national project possible.

## Setting the Context for the Building of the Nation's Capital

With the American colonies separation from Britain firmly secured through the 1776 Declaration of Independence and the subsequent Revolutionary War victory in 1783, the new nation was now poised to establish itself as a free and unified republic. After much deliberation, in May 1787, Congress met in Philadelphia in hopes of ratifying a written constitution to establish a national government representing northern and Southern colonies' interests. Under this constitution, the colonies, which later became independent states, would become one federal republic known as the United States of America. Congress believed that a centralized government would bring stability to the young nation and create a more perfect and stronger union, especially among states divided by ideologies of governance, slavery, and individual rights. A written constitution would solidify new, comprehensive provisions for governance.

On September 17, 1787, Northern and Southern delegates to the Constitutional Convention in Philadelphia signed the United States Constitution and established a national government.[1] Different from reigning monarchies in France, Britain, and other European regions of the time, this established authority would be democratic, with delineated power shared between the federal government and the states. It placed power in the hands of the people and safeguarded its citizens' freedoms of speech, press, religion, and peaceful assembly/protest and their right to petition the government without fear of punishment. The Constitution served as the universal law of the new nation. Shortly after establishing the Constitution, the delegates also deliberated ad nauseam over a permanent location for the national seat of governance.

The selection of the permanent location for the nation's capital did not come without multiple deadlocks and controversy because politicians representing the North and South understandably desired the nation's capital to be in their respective regions.[2] Congress continued its debate for years.[3] The matter was resolved by what become known as the Compromise of 1790. On June 20, 1790, Jefferson hosted a dinner and invited his fellow Virginian and protégé, James Madison, and Alexander Hamilton, secretary of the treasury. During the dinner, Jefferson and Madison convinced Hamilton on their position to place the nation's permanent capital in the South within Maryland and Virginia's borders near George Town (later named Georgetown), a matter Jefferson and Washington had discussed privately.[4] Hamilton convinced Jefferson and Madison that the national government should assume and pay all debts incurred by the states from the Revolutionary War. Hamilton's plan benefited Northerners because Northern states had accumulated an enormous war debt, whereas the Southern states had already resolved their financial obligations. Hamilton reasoned that the Department of the Treasury could raise money to pay off the debts by selling bonds to wealthy colonists. In return, these investors would profit from the venture. By the end of the dinner, the three men reached a compromise. Congress later accepted Jefferson, Madison, and Hamilton's plan, which made way for two bills, the Residence Act of 1790, which placed the nation's capital in the South, and the Funding Act of 1790, which authorized the federal government to absolve the states' war debts.[5] The Residence Act authorized President Washington to locate "a district of territory, not exceeding ten miles square, to be located as hereafter directed on the river Potomack [Potomac], at some place between the mouths of the Eastern-Branch and Connogocheague [Conococheaque Creek]" for the purpose of constructing "the permanent seat of government of the United States." Philadelphia would serve as the second and temporary seat of government while the new district was under construction. Washington was granted a ten-year period to select the site and build the nation's capital and transfer power from Philadelphia to the new national capital city.

In August and September 1790, Washington, Jefferson, and Madison met in New York and at Mount Vernon to discuss possible locations. In October, Washington toured areas along the Potomac and near Georgetown. He envisioned a central waterway that "connected the Atlantic Ocean to the Mississippi River with navigable rivers, canals, and a land portage through what is now West Virginia."[6] He feared that if trade routes to eastern markets were not established, France and Spain would take control of western territories. By late January 1791, Washington had selected the location, outlined in a written proclamation to Congress dated January 24, 1791, which read,

> *Gentlemen of the Senate and*
> *House of Representatives.*
>
> *United States January 24th, 1791.*
>
> *In execution of the powers with which Congress were pleased to invest me by their Act intitled "An Act of establishing the temporary and permanent seat of the Government of the United States" and on mature consideration of the advantages and disadvantages of the several positions, within the limits prescribed by the said Act, I have, by Proclamation, bearing date this day, a copy of which is herewith transmitted, directed Commissioners, appointed in pursuance of the Act, to survey and limit a part of the territory often miles square, on both sides the river Potomack, so as to comprehend George Town in Maryland, and to extend to the Eastern branch. I have not by this first Act given to the said territory the whole extent of which it is susceptible in the direction of the River; because I thought it important that Congress should have an opportunity of considering whether by an amendatory law, they would authorize the location of the residue at the lower end of the present, so as to comprehend the Eastern branch itself, and some of the Country on its lower side in the State of Maryland, and the town of Alexandria in Virginia. If, however, they are of opinion that the federal territory should be bounded by the water edge of the Eastern-branch, the location of the residue will be to be made at the upper end of what is now directed. I have thought best to await a survey of the territory before it is decided on what particular spot on the North Eastern side of the River the public buildings shall be erected.*
>
> *Go: Washington*[7]

The selection of lands along this area would transform the new capital city into a formidable commercial and political metropolis, he reasoned.[8] Yet such selection required its share of tactical maneuvering to acquire the land needed to build his city.

## The Acquisition of Land

Although Virginia and Maryland gifted the US government portions of land, other areas within Washington's ten-mile radius stood in the way of his vision. The lands, encompassing small farms and large plantations, were owned by eighteen landowners—Robert Peter, David Burnes (sometimes spelled Burns), James M. Lingan, Uriah Forrest, Benjamin Stoddert, Notley Young, Daniel Carroll of Duddington, Overton Carr, Thomas Beall, Charles Beatty, Anthony Holmead, James Peerce (Pierce), Abraham Young, Edward Peerce, John Waring, William Prout, William King, and Eliphas Douglass (Eliphaz Douglas). A breakdown of their plots is shown in figure 3.1.[9]

Washington concluded that purchasing land from these proprietors at a reasonable rate to build a federal city might prove challenging for his administration. Given this, he solicited two associates who owned

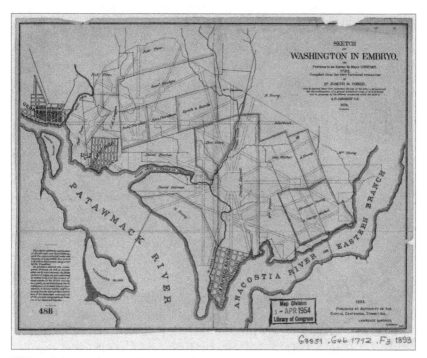

**Figure 3.1.** *Sketch of Early Washington with Names of Proprietors.* Library of Congress.

land in Georgetown and knew the proprietors well. In a letter addressed to William Deakins Jr. and Benjamin Stoddert dated February 3, 1791, Washington writes, "There are lands which stand yet in the way . . . if they could be obtained, for the purposes of the town, would remove a considerable obstacle to it."[10] Washington asked the men to serve "in secrecy" as "his confidential agents" and "purchase these grounds of the owners for the public . . . but as if for yourselves, and to conduct your propositions so as to excite no suspicion that they are on the behalf of the public."[11] The men agreed but were ultimately unable to acquire the lands.

When that approach failed, Washington sent Jefferson and other officials to meet with the owners to discuss the terms and advantages of the land deal. Following a series of meetings, Jefferson organized a dinner between the owners and President Washington. From March 28 to March 30, 1791, Washington met with twelve owners at Suter's Tavern in Georgetown to finalize the deal. On March 30, Washington left the meeting with a signed agreement from twelve owners—Peter, Burnes, Lingan, Forrest, Stoddert, Young, Carroll of Duddington, Carr, Beall of George, Beatty, Holmead, and J. Peerce (Pierce).[12] After the meeting, six more signatures were added—E. Young, Peerce, Waring, Prout, King, and Douglass (Douglas). Washington noted in his March 30 diary entry that upon obtaining "the signatures of eighteen proprietors of land within the federal district, constituting most of the landowners within the proposed federal city" that his business at the tavern was "happily finished."[13] Three landowners—Joseph Coombs Jr. and Enoch and Thomas Jenkins—were not present at either signing. The finalized agreement read as follows:

*Agreement of the Proprietors of the Federal District*

*[Georgetown, Md., 30 March 1791]*

*We the subscribers, in consideration of the great benefits we expect to derive from having the Federal City laid off upon our Lands, do hereby agree and bind ourselves, heirs, executors & administrators, to convey in Trust, to the President of the United States, or Commissioners, or such person or persons as he shall appoint, by good and sufficient deeds in fee simple, the whole of our respective Lands, which he may think proper to include within the lines of the federal City for the purposes and on the Conditions following—*

*The President shall have the sole power of directing the Federal City to be laid off in what manner he pleases. He may retain any number of squares he may think proper for public Improvements, or other public uses, and the Lots only which shall be laid off shall be a joint property between the Trustees on behalf of the Public and each present Proprietor, and the same shall be fairly and equally divided between the Public and the Individuals, as soon as may be, after the City shall be laid off.*

*For the streets, the Proprietors shall receive no compensation, but for the squares, or Lands in any form which shall be taken for Public buildings or any kind of Public Improvements, or uses, the Proprietors, whose Lands shall be so taken shall receive at the rate of twenty-five pounds ℙ Acre, to be paid by the Public.*

*The whole wood on the Lands shall be the Property of the Proprietors: But should any be desired by the President to be reserved or left standing, the same shall be paid for by the Public at a just and reasonable valuation, exclusive of the Twenty-five pounds ℙ Acre, to be paid for the Land, on which the same shall remain.*

*Each Proprietor shall retain the full possession and use of his Land, untill the same shall be sold and occupied by the purchasers of the Lotts lain out thereupon, and in all cases where the public arrangements, as the streets, lotts &c. will admit of it, each Proprietor shall possess his buildings and other Improvements and grave yards, paying to the public only one half the present estimated value of the Lands, on which the same shall be, or twelve pounds ten shillings ℙ Acre—But in cases where the Arrangements of the Streets, lotts, Squares &c. will not admit of this, and it shall become necessary to remove such buildings Improvements &c. the Proprietors of the same shall be paid the reasonable value thereof, by the Public.*

*Nothing herein contained, shall affect the Lotts which any of the Parties to this Agreement many hold in the Towns of Carrollsburgh or Hamburgh.*

*In Witness whereof we have hereunto set our hands and Seals, this thirtieth day of March 1791.*[14]

Though Washington had a signed agreement, he had not secured bonds of conveyance for the land. As a result, some landowners who had promised to give the government their land later modified their agreement. These landowners only gave a portion of their land to the government and kept the remaining part. This caused confusion once the planning and construction commenced, as some owners refused to move or demanded higher prices for their lots. An example is the Carroll estate, Duddington Manor, the largest estate among the proprietors that covered most of what became the National Mall area and all of Capitol Hill. Upon learning that the US Capitol would be placed adjacent to his estate, Carroll "immediately demanded exorbitant prices for building-lots."[15]

David Burnes's land covered most of the northwestern quadrant of DC, presently the land north of Constitution Avenue and the White House. Burnes operated a large plantation and owned a small cottage near the river adjacent to where the Washington Monument rests today. The Burnes family delayed the sale of their land surrounding the cottage even after the monument was erected in 1848. Others, like Uriah Forrest, bought land and sold it at a higher price to other investors, who, in turn, sold the same property at a still higher rate to the federal government.

All the owners stood to gain enormous wealth from the land deals. Like Washington and Jefferson, the majority of the proprietors had inherited their wealth and increased their revenue through slave and indentured labor and through the manufacturing of tobacco and other commodities. They also acquired land through treaties and war against the Indigenous peoples. The Nacotchtank (Anacostank) peoples, part of the Piscataway chiefdom, along with several related tribes (Pamunkey, Mattapanient, Nangemeick, and Tauxehent), were the central occupants of the new territory outlined for the nation's capital. The Nacotchtank (or Anacostank, from which the name Anacostia derived) was the largest Native American village in the area and operated a major trading center. Their removal from the land was a result of battles, wars, treaties, and diseases contracted from Europeans. The eighteen proprietors were able to sell their lands to the government under the protection of such treaties, laws, and land grants set in place by Europeans upon their conquest of the Indigenous peoples' territories. These men and other colonizers were also emboldened by a sense of nation building as set forth in documents such as the Declaration of Independence, the Immigration Act of 1790, the US Constitution, and the Residence Act of 1790. These and other enforceable documents provided them and their descendants' entitlements and security for centuries to come.

Guided by the US Constitution and the Residence Act, George Washington acquired the land he needed to build the nation's capital. But land alone was not sufficient to make his vision a reality. Central to Washington's building project was assembling a team consisting of commissioners, designers, and surveyors. The three commissioners selected to supervise the project were General Thomas Johnson of Fredericktown of Maryland, Dr. David Stuart of Hope Park in Fairfax County and Washington's family physician, and the Honorable Daniel Carroll, son of the aforementioned landowner Charles Carroll of Duddington.

Washington's vision would also require the ingenuity of the artisans. Washington also appointed French-born engineer and artistic designer L'Enfant to design Federal City and Ellicott, a Quaker, to survey the ten-mile square. A four-person team assisted Ellicott—his brother Benjamin Ellicott, Isaac Briggs, George Fenwick, and Benjamin Banneker, a self-educated free Black man. Though Ellicott and L'Enfant saw the emerging metropolis from different vantage points, their work came together through "surveying the grounds of the city and forming them into lots."[16] Both men shared a mutual commitment to play a role in the erection of Washington's dream city.[17] But their pursuits were fraught with conflict, deceit, and misrepresentation. How these artisans negotiated the difficult terrain of imposing commissioners and politicians is important to America's national story. It brings to light and provides a fuller perspective of L'Enfant and Ellicott's accomplishments amid bickering, defamation, and adversity and shades the often told narrative of patriotic white men working together to build this great nation. The nuancing of their stories and the inclusion of Benjamin Banneker's and countless other enslaved and free Black artisans' contributions are patriotic acts that rightly honor those often devalued and forgotten in building the nation's capital.

## Major Pierre Charles L'Enfant (1754–1825)

Pierre Charles L'Enfant was born in Paris, France, on August 2, 1754. From 1771 to 1776, L'Enfant studied at the Royal Academy of Painting and Sculpture and served in the French Colonial Troops. In 1776, at the age of twenty-two, he left France to join the American cause for freedom. He served on the Continental Army Corps of Engineers at Valley Forge, Pennsylvania, from 1777 to 1779 under General George Washington. In 1783, L'Enfant was appointed to the rank of major. He became known for his sketches of soldiers and his illustrations in the *Army Blue Book* (*Regulations for the Order and Discipline of the Troops of the United States*). He designed halls, homes, and monuments in Philadelphia and New York.

## L'Enfant's Contribution to the Formation of Federal City

After serving in the military, L'Enfant expressed to Washington in a letter dated September 11, 1789, his "embition and desire of becoming a usefull Citizen" in hopes of being "appointed the Engineer . . . in the establishment of the Capital."[18] In 1791, Washington hired L'Enfant with deadlines and provisions to submit drafts of his plans.

Washington's vision of the city was modest. It included basic squares for the Capitol, the President's House, federal office buildings, residences, open markets, public walks, a prison, and a slave pen. His vision changed after meeting with L'Enfant on March 28, 1791. L'Enfant envisioned a grand capital city and urged Washington to seize the moment to build a center of power unlike any European country.[19] What began to emerge in collaboration with Washington was a replica of European cities being established in the United States. In one draft, L'Enfant incorporated a general layout of the city center and the distances of structures like the Capitol, the President's House, gardens, public walkways, and a park.[20] The design included "wide diagonal avenues superimposed on a grid of narrower streets . . . to promote rapid settlement."[21] L'Enfant added a grand cascade resembling that at Versailles, with a large waterfall running beneath the Capitol. Since the overall plan dated June 22, 1791, was incomplete, L'Enfant advised Washington that he would submit a more comprehensive plan of the city, "giving a perfect Idea of the effect of the whole in the Execution" once the surveyors had completed accurate measurements of the area.[22]

At the end of August, L'Enfant traveled to Philadelphia to hand deliver an updated plan to Washington along with a copy for the engraver. In a letter to Washington dated August 19, 1791, L'Enfant expressed, "[My] heigest embition [was] Gratified in having met with your approbation in the project of the Plan which I have now the Honor of presenting to you altered agreeable to your direction, Steel [still] leaving me some thing to wish for until I see the execution of that plan effected to the full attainement of your object."[23] The updated version included a canal, elaborate ceremonial spaces, monuments, foundations, picturesque landscapes resembling English-style gardens, and tree-lined streets. Integrated into the plan was a diamond-shaped layout of the city's streets, "a system of orthogonal streets with intersecting diagonal avenues radiating from two of the highest points in the city."[24] The grand avenues would be named after the states in the Union (at the time). All of these avenues led to the Capitol, symbolizing both the independence of the states and their efforts toward unification at the foot of the Capitol. L'Enfant also shaded in fifteen thousand squares designated for public use—residential and commercial—for sale to the public. He cautioned Washington, however, not to sell lots to the public without "contemplating cooly."[25] He felt that a buying frenzy would ensue, resulting in avaricious investors purchasing large blocks and causing problems later.

Following their meeting, Washington advised Jefferson to review L'Enfant's plan with Madison.[26] After their meeting, the two met with commissioners Johnson, Stuart, and Carroll on September 8, 1791, to discuss further both the plan and the impending sale of lots.[27] Guided by their advisement, Washington decided to proceed with the sale of lots and scheduled this for October 17–19. In preparation for the sale, the commissioners advised L'Enfant to have copies of his map denoting the lots for sale available for distribution to the public. The commissioners also advised L'Enfant to make several printed copies of his plan available for circulation to Washington and other noted persons and to leave copies in their offices in Georgetown and other locations before the lot sale.[28] L'Enfant was also told to rename his plan *A Map of the City of Washington in the Territory of Columbia* in honor of George Washington and Christopher Columbus.[29]

L'Enfant became annoyed by the commissioners' constant directives, and tensions mounted between them. Though accustomed to taking directives from the president, L'Enfant resented the commissioners telling him what to do. The commissioners, on the other hand, felt that L'Enfant was circumventing their authority by reporting directly to the president, especially since Washington had hired them to supervise the planning and construction of the city, which encompassed L'Enfant and Ellicott's work.[30] The commissioners were also troubled that they were not being included in deliberations between Washington and L'Enfant. On October 17, 1791, as the sale of the lots officially commenced, the bidding was "hampered by the lack of a printed plan of the city for prospective buyers."[31] Prospective buyers were privy to "plats of the divided squares prepared by Ellicott but had to rely on L'Enfant's verbal descriptions to understand how those squares fit into his city plan."[32] Tensions escalated further between L'Enfant, the commissioners, and Washington.

## L'Enfant's Exit

President Washington found himself in the middle of a controversy that he had in some way ignited due to his failure to establish clear boundaries and responsibilities between himself, the commissioners, and L'Enfant. In a letter dated October 29, Commissioner Stuart advised Washington of their dismay that L'Enfant had failed to make maps available as instructed.[33] Washington responded that he shared their grave concerns and advised L'Enfant at their next meeting that he was no longer to report directly to him but rather to the commissioners and to adhere to their instructions.

Tensions reached their boiling point in November when L'Enfant, without the commissioners' approval, began demolishing a house owned by Daniel Carroll. The house extended six feet onto public property, impeding L'Enfant's layout for the US Capitol. On November 21, Carroll appealed to Washington, and seven days later, Washington offered Carroll two alternatives: "pull down the building in its present state, and raise it to the same height next spring," or build the house "at your own cost, and occupy it 6 years from the present date, and then remove it" in time for the Capitol.[34]

Carroll immediately hired a lawyer, who in turn obtained an injunction with a summons for L'Enfant to appear before a judge in December. L'Enfant demolished the house without the consent of Carroll and the commissioners and was quickly admonished by Washington. Washington advised L'Enfant to lay out his plan for the city "but only on condition" he would act "in subordination to the authority of the Commissioners, to the laws of the land, and to the rights of its citizens."[35] L'Enfant defended his actions and continued with his plans for the city, but within time, it would all prove futile. The men continued bickering and haggling over who was in charge and who should report to whom, with Washington appeasing both sides.[36]

To make matters worse, Washington announced to Congress in October that a copy of L'Enfant's plan would be available for perusal at their mid-December meeting. When December came, L'Enfant failed to show, so Washington made an earlier version of the plan available for Congress. Days later, L'Enfant met Washington with an updated plan in hand along with a strong assertion that he would neither be subordinate to nor take orders from the commissioners. Inevitably, more bickering followed among the men, and Washington reprimanded L'Enfant in a letter drafted by Jefferson and Alexander Hamilton.[37] L'Enfant, however, stood his ground.

On February 26, 1792, Washington summoned Jefferson, Madison, and the attorney general, Edmund Randolph, to resolve the matter. On February 27, 1792, Jefferson notified L'Enfant that his "services must be at an end."[38] L'Enfant appealed, but to no avail.[39] His vision to design the city he called "grand" had come to a close. On March 8, 1792, Commissioner Stuart, under Washington's directive, offered L'Enfant "five hundred guineas and a lot in a good part of the City" (equivalent to nearly $19,000 in 2019).[40] L'Enfant refused. The offer did not compensate him for the damage to his reputation or for his design and contribution to the new metropolis.[41] L'Enfant appealed to Congress for appropriate compensation, but Congress denied his claim. Though he went on to design structures in New York and New Jersey, L'Enfant struggled financially and personally most of his adult life.

On June 14, 1825, at the age of seventy-one, Pierre Charles L'Enfant died a pauper and without recognition for his contribution to the city of Washington in the Territory of Columbia. After decades of mounting pressure from Washingtonians and the Columbia Historical Society, the US government signed a resolution (the Sundry Bill of 1908) to exhume L'Enfant's body and give him a proper burial and recognition of his service to the nation.

On April 22, 1909, L'Enfant's body was duly exhumed from its unmarked grave on a friend's farm in Prince George's County, Maryland, and transported to a vault at Mount Olivet Cemetery. On April 28, 1909, the Second Battalion of the Corps of Engineers escorted L'Enfant's casket, draped with the American flag, to the US Capitol rotunda to lie in state for three hours, where the French ambassador, President William Taft, the vice president, and district commissioners offered tributes.

Following an artillery gun salute, the funeral procession made its way to Arlington National Cemetery among crowds holding flags at half-mast. At Arlington, L'Enfant's body was reinterred, this time with full military honors and on a hill overlooking the city he had designed. Chiseled on top of his white marble grave was a circle enclosing his blueprint with an inscription that read,

> **ENGINEER, ARTIST, SOLDIER / UNDER THE DIREC-
> TION OF GEORGE WASHINGTON DESIGNED THE
> PLAN FOR THE FEDERAL CITY / MAJOR US ENGI-
> NEER CORPS 1789 / CHARTER MEMBER OF THE
> SOCIETY OF THE CINCINNATI AND DESIGNED ITS
> CERTIFICATE & INSIGNIA / BORN IN PARIS, FRANCE
> AUGUST 2, 1755 / DIED JUNE 14, 1825 WHILE RESIDING
> AT CHILHAM CASTLE MANOR PRINCE GEORGE'S
> CO MARYLAND AND WAS INTERRED THERE /
> REINTERRED AT ARLINGTON APRIL 28, 1909**

Private citizens did for L'Enfant what the US government chose not to do: they rallied and gave proper respect to one of the artisans of the nation. Because of their actions, "thousands who never heard of the Frenchman's name, thousands who have praised the broad avenues of the Capital City yet knew not whose hand designed them or in whose brain the scheme of the city was born now knew the name of Pierre Charles L'Enfant."[42] Figure 3.2 is L'Enfant's plan of the city.[43]

## Major Andrew Ellicott (1754–1820)

Andrew Ellicott was born in Bucks County, Pennsylvania, on January 24, 1754. Though he and L'Enfant lived worlds apart, the two men found themselves in one location for one cause—to bring to fruition the new seat of government. Andrew was the eldest of nine children born to Judith and Joseph Ellicott. His lineage dates back to seventeenth-century

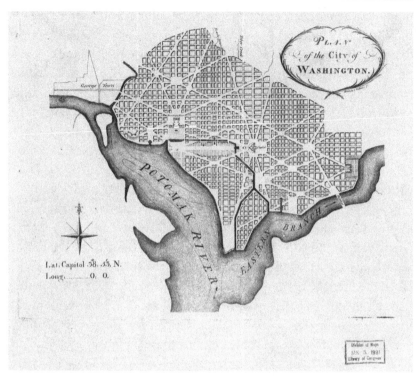

**Figure 3.2.** *Plan of the City of Washington, Pierre Charles L'Enfant.*
Library of Congress.

England; eventually, his forebears fled religious persecution as members of the Devonshire Society of Friends (Quakers). Andrew's father, Joseph, a clockmaker and surveyor, mentored Andrew. At age fifteen, he assisted his father in designing clocks, making a four-sided astronomical and musical clock in 1767 that is presently housed among the Smithsonian collections.

Around 1770, Andrew's family migrated to Maryland, where his father and two uncles, John and Andrew, purchased land and built the Ellicott's (Upper and Lower) Mills, which included gristmills, cotton mills, sawmills, and an iron shop. The family also built a mansion (called Fountainvale), the Friends Meeting House at Elk Ridge Landing, and schoolhouses. In 1775, Andrew married Sarah Brown, a prominent Quaker. He spent a vast amount of time surveying lands throughout the colonies for colonists and local governments until he joined the military, where he was commissioned as a captain and later a major in the Elk Ridge Battalion, Maryland Militia, under General Washington. Andrew was recommended by his father's friend, Benjamin Franklin, to survey lands in the Niagara Falls River area and was noted for completing the Mason-Dixon line, a line surveyed initially by Charles Mason and Jeremiah Dixon to resolve a border dispute between Maryland, Pennsylvania, and Delaware. The line later denoted the demarcation between Southern slave states and free states in the North.

## Ellicott's Contribution to the Formation of Federal City

Ellicott's original four-man surveying team included Isaac Briggs, George Fenwick, Benjamin Ellicott, and Benjamin Banneker.[44] At different points, Ellicott's brother, Joseph Ellicott, and Isaac Roberdeau also joined the team. Ellicott's team began their survey of the lands designated for the nation's capital in early February 1791. Washington selected Ellicott as chief surveyor of the federal district because he felt there was no "better [man] than Mr. Ellicott for all matters, at present."[45] Washington later considered Ellicott as L'Enfant's replacement.

In March 1792, Jefferson, in consultation with Washington, advised the commissioners to "employ Ellicott to finish laying out the Federal city and discuss his past and future wage."[46] Ellicott was now tasked with two assignments: continue surveys of Federal City and complete L'Enfant's Federal City plan in preparation for the engravers. L'Enfant's dream was now in the hands of Ellicott.

Ellicott began to feel the weight of his enormous responsibility and the demands of the commissioners, and all the more so when he received word that the commissioners had accused him of inaccurate measurements and subpar surveys. Ellicott was experiencing a taste of L'Enfant's dismay with the early founders and commissioners. The commissioners obtained their information from James Reed Dermott, whom the commissioners recently hired as an assistant surveyor on March 26, 1792.[47] Dermott, who was originally assigned "as an Overseer to overlook the Negroes in cutting down the trees in the Streets and Avenues," began to take an active role in the surveyors' field office, bragging while drunk that he would one day have Ellicott's job.[48] Ellicott suspected that Dermott was sabotaging his team's efforts by stealing maps, plans, and journals;

tampering with boundary markers; and altering surveys, measurements, layouts, and documents to make Ellicott appear incompetent.[49]

## Ellicott's Exit

As expected, on December 10, 1792, the commissioners expressed to Washington their displeasure with Ellicott.[50] Dismayed, Ellicott lamented to his wife, saying, "I begin to dislike the whole place, and have become too ill-natured to associate with any beings except my four assistants."[51] Ellicott worked vigorously through the holidays and forwarded on January 1, 1793, a signed certificate of his completed work for the commissioners' review along with a deadline for his remaining work.[52] Three days later, he submitted his letter of resignation as chief surveyor of Federal City effective May 1, 1793.[53] The commissioners forwarded his resignation to Washington, asserting, "There is Uncertainty whether we shall much longer have Majr Ellicott's services, he has however shewn such a Temper in our Verbal intercourse, that we have no Apprehension of his purposely leaving the work, in a State to create Embarrasment."[54] Though the commissioners were dissatisfied with Ellicott, they approved his submission, which in turn led to Jefferson's approval. On February 18, 1793, Jefferson sent the following declaration to both houses of Congress: "The Commissioners of the Territory of the United States on the Potomac having, according to law, had the said Territory surveyed and defined by proper metes and bounds, and transmitted their report with a plat of the boundary, I have now the honor to lay them before you. As this work has been executed under the authority of the Legislature."[55]

Shortly after, the commissioners fired Ellicott, overriding his May 1793 resignation.[56] Ellicott was undone by the commissioners and also displeased with Washington for not defending him.[57] After several registered complaints by landowners and officials, Ellicott was reinstated. His suspicions about the commissioners and Dermott eventually proved correct when the commissioners admitted to Washington that Ellicott's office had been pillaged and documents seized.[58]

In December 1793, Ellicott notified the commissioners that the map of the Territory of Columbia had been completed and was now at the engravers. He also submitted another letter of resignation officially ending his term. On February 28, 1794, Washington received two copper plates of *A Map of the Territory of Columbia* and a letter from Ellicott saying,

> I am in hopes the map will be found sufficiently correct, however if it should not, I have only to lament that it has been . . . in consequence of the original, together with my field notes, being more than a year ago privately carried away from the office. Although being one of those with whom the City of Washington . . . originated, I feel no desire of resuming my former station at that place, being convinced from severe experiance that no mans reputation can be safe, when in the power of men, who avail themselves of their right to censure, and remove from office, without allowing the object of their resentment the benefit of a scientific enquiry . . . the injustice which I have experienced, will not only at some future period be manifest; but perhaps sap the foundation, and injure the whole business of the City in its infancy.[59]

Ellicott went on to survey regions throughout the colonies, playing a major advisory role in the Lewis and Clark Expedition in 1803 and establishing the western border between Canada and the US in 1817. He spent most of his days teaching mathematics at West Point. On August 28, 1820, Ellicott, age sixty-six, died from a stroke. He was buried at West Point with full military honors. Among his accomplishments listed on his tombstone, a mere one line refers to his role in the nation's capital: "In 1791, he surveyed for Washington the future city of Washington, DC."[60] Figure 3.3 is his revised city plan. In contrast to L'Enfant's plan, Ellicott provided more details, showing block numbers and proposed government buildings. Washington purchased lots near the White House and along the river.

The waters become murky when applying percentages to the roles L'Enfant and Ellicott played in authoring maps of the region. L'Enfant conceived the design of the nation's capital, and Ellicott (more or less) carried it out. Washington, DC, exists because of the contribution of these two men. But the district also owes its existence to the contributions of a Black man named Benjamin Banneker, whose story follows.

**Figure 3.3.** *Plan of the City of Washington, Andrew Ellicott.* Library of Congress.

## Benjamin Banneker (1731-1806)

Early on, while the men were bickering, Benjamin Banneker, a self-taught Black astronomer and member of Ellicott's team, was lying on his back, looking up at the stars to determine the exact starting point to lay the first boundary marker for the new metropolis. Banneker was born on November 9, 1731, in Baltimore County, Maryland. He was the son of a free woman named Mary Banneky (Bannaky) and an enslaved man from Guinea named Robert, who later purchased his freedom. Banneker, a free Black farmer, astronomer, mathematician, inventor, and surveyor, was twenty-three years older than L'Enfant and Ellicott.

A dominant narrative that weaves through oral accounts and written biographies connects Banneker's lineage to white ancestry. These accounts identify Banneker's maternal grandmother as a "white English dairymaid" named Molly Welsh (or Walsh or Welch) imprisoned in

Europe for stealing.[61] In 1683, she was sent to the mainland North American colonies to serve her seven-year term as an indentured servant on a tobacco farm in Maryland. Upon fulfilling her contract, Molly became a tobacco planter, acquired a small farm, and purchased two enslaved men to maintain it. One of the men, a recent arrival from Africa, "refused to work" because "his royal heritage as the son of a king made it improper for him to be a slave, or to convert to Christianity."[62] By 1696, Molly freed the men and married one of them, named Bannaka.[63] The two remained in Maryland and had four children, among them the girl who would become Benjamin Banneker's mother, Mary. Molly and Mary were the primary influences in young Banneker's education. His grandmother also introduced him to prominent Quakers in Maryland, among them the Ellicotts.

Other accounts present Molly Welsh as a white female slave owner who owned and later freed Banneker.[64] These accounts debunk Molly as grandmother, citing that Banneker himself neither mentions a white grandmother in his writings nor speaks of a Molly Welsh as an enslaver or as someone who played a formative role in his education or in shaping his future. Some of these accounts suggest that a white woman was inserted into Banneker's narrative to make a case for his intellectual aptitude.

Outside of these dominant narratives is a less-known story of Banneker's African lineage by way of his maternal or paternal grandfather, Bannaka.[65] Banneker's grandfather was a royal member of the Wolof kingdom of Walo or Dogon peoples. Bannaka was taken from either the coastal areas along Senegal and Gambia or farther inland in the Mali region. During the transatlantic slave trade, the regions encompassing Senegal, Gambia, and Mali were commonly and collectively referred to as Senegambia. These diverse ethnic groups shared commonalities. Their societies were similar in structure, and most were "stratified into tripartite arrangements consisting of a free population, caste groups, and slaves," with the upper strata "enjoying greater wealth and power."[66] Many of these groups spoke common languages, and their religious traditions were either Islamic or traditional African. A large percentage of the ethnic groups from these regions were enslaved and taken to labor to labor in South Carolina, Georgia, Virginia, and Maryland.

The Dogon were literate people with a writing system that predates European arrival.[67] The Dogon people were "well known for their ancient and highly sophisticated knowledge of astronomy, numerology, and irrigation."[68] They understood that "the Earth orbits around the su[n]" before Europeans accepted the science and "knew about other planets and even worlds beyond the solar system."[69] Their technologies and knowledge in "mining, metal processing, cotton planting and textiles, food storage, architecture, erosion control, and irrigation [were] widely respected."[70] This was the world of Benjamin Banneker, whose knowledge of mathematics, astronomy, and other sciences reflected this Dogon heritage. His love for the sciences was influenced by an African cosmology passed down from his grandfather and cultivated by his father, an African worldview transplanted from Africa to the New World.

On March 10, 1737, Banneker's father, Robert, owned a twenty-five-acre plot in Timber Point, Maryland. He also purchased, for seven thousand pounds of tobacco, one hundred acres of land in Oella, Maryland, from Richard Gist, a prominent Quaker landholder.[71] Banneker, at age six, was added to the deed. Robert developed an irrigation system, which included digging ditches and building dams to control the water flow to produce an abundance of good tobacco. The irrigation system became known in the area as Banneky Springs. Banneker spent most of his life on the farm learning and implementing farming techniques, later making innovative improvements to the system by creating a continuous water flow over a larger land mass. To date, there is no evidence that the Bannekers maintained the farm by use of enslaved or indentured labor.

### Banneker's Education and Skills

Upon his father's death in 1759, Benjamin Banneker took over the family farm. He continued his love for knowledge by reading the Bible and borrowing books in the natural sciences, mathematics, and religion from his neighbor and friend George Ellicott (cousin of chief surveyor Andrew Ellicott). As noted earlier, the Ellicotts were devout European Quakers and antislavery advocates known for their surveys, mills, school, meeting house, and small town along the Patapsco River. Banneker engaged in lively discussions with the Ellicotts, becoming interested in the classics and in the Latin, Greek, German, and French languages. Among the books he read were self-taught German mathematician and astronomer Johann Tobias Mayer's work *Lunar Tables* and Scottish astronomer James Ferguson's *Astronomical Tables*.

In 1753, Banneker, enamored by a watch he had received, made a wooden clock from scratch. His clock was among the first known wooden clocks produced in the United States. Banneker's reading, research, and discussions with others interested in the sciences resulted in him authoring a series of almanacs published in the US from 1791 to 1797. On the editor's page of Banneker's almanac, entitled *Benjamin Banneker's Pennsylvania, Delaware, Maryland, and Virginia Almanack and Ephemeris, for the Year of Our Lord 1792; Being Bissextile, or Leap-Year, and the Sixteenth Year of American Independence which Commenced July 4, 1776*, his publishers wrote,

> The editors of the Pennsylvania, Delaware, Maryland, and Virginia Almanack, feel themselves gratified in the opportunity of presenting to the public, through the medium of their press, what must be considered an extraordinary effort of genius—a complete and accurate Ephemeris for the year 1792, calculated by a fabled defendant of Africa, who, by this specimen of ingenuity, evinces, to demonstration, that mental power and endowments are not the exclusive excellence of white people, but that the rays of science may alike illumine the minds of men every clime, (however they may differ in colour of their skin) particularly those whom tyrant-custom hath too long taught us to depreciate as a race inferior in intellectual capacity.[72]

Scientists in the US and throughout Europe respected Banneker's findings, and it drew the attention of Thomas Jefferson, who, upon receiving Banneker's almanac, forwarded a copy to Marie Jean Antoine Nicolas de Caritat (Marquis de Condorcet). Condorcet, a well-known French philosopher, mathematician, and politician, was active in the French Revolution and also secretary of the French Academy of Sciences.

After studying tides in the region, conducting astronomical observations, and researching how to write an almanac that identified coming solar and lunar eclipses, Banneker also became proficient in surveying lands. His skills, intellect, and networks led him to participate in the early formation of the new seat of government.

## Banneker's Contribution to the Formation of Federal City

When Andrew Ellicott was selected to identify the boundaries of the new city and survey lands in preparation for its construction, he asked his cousin George Ellicott to serve on his team. George declined and instead recommended Banneker, his neighbor and friend, whom Ellicott then hired in March 1791. The *George-Town Weekly Ledger* published an article dated March 12, 1791, highlighting Banneker's appointment—and intellect: "Some time last month arrived in this town Mr. Andrew Ellicot, a gentleman of superior astronomical abilities. He was employed by the President of the United States of America to lay off a tract of land, ten miles square on the Potomack, for the use of Congress;—is now engaged in the business, and hopes soon to accomplish the object of his mission. He is attended by *Benjamin Banniker*, an Ethiopian, whose abilities, as a surveyor, and an astronomer, clearly prove that Mr. Jefferson's concluding that race of men was void of mental endowments, was without foundation."[73] Martha Ellicott Tyson, George Ellicott's daughter, in *A Sketch of the Life of Benjamin Banneker*, also noted Banneker's role: "Banneker was but once absent, at any distance, from his domicile. An appointment having been made after the adoption of the Constitution, in 1789, of commissioners, to run the lines of the District of Columbia—then called the 'Federal Territory,' they wished to avail themselves of his talents, induced him to accompany them in the work and retained him with them until the service was completed."[74] On August 30, 1791, Jefferson wrote to Condorcet regarding his approval of Banneker and employing him on Ellicott's survey team:

> I am happy to be able to inform you that we have now in the United States a negro, the son of a Black man born in Africa, and of a Black woman born in the United States, who is a very respectable Mathematician. I procured him to be employed under one of our chief directors in laying out the new federal city on the Patowmac, and in the intervals of his leisure, while on that work, he made an Almanac for the next year, which he sent me in his own handwriting, and which I inclose to you.[75]

Jefferson likewise noted Banneker's African heritage, saying he was "the son of a Black man born in Africa, and of a Black woman born in the United States."[76] But though Jefferson identified him as a "respectable

Mathematician" who was a "worthy and respectable member of society,"
he thought little of his intellect, and whatever acumen Banneker possessed, it was neither equal to whites nor representative of Black people
in general.[77] Aware of Jefferson's opinion about Black people's inferiority, Banneker not only sent his almanac but also used the opportunity
to school Jefferson. On August 19, 1791, he wrote to Jefferson, saying,

> Sir I am fully sensible of the greatness of that freedom . . . a liberty which
> Seemed to me scarcely allowable . . . we are a race of Beings who have
> long laboured under the abuse and censure of the world, that we have long
> been looked upon with an eye of contempt, and that we have long been
> considered rather as brutish than human, and Scarcely capable of mental
> endowments. . . . One universal Father hath given being to us all, and that
> he hath not only made us all of one flesh, but that he hath also without
> partiality afforded us all the Same Sensations, and endued us all with the
> same faculties, and that however variable we may be in Society or religion,
> however diversifyed in Situation or colour, we are all of the Same Family,
> and Stand in the Same relation to him.
>
> Sir I freely and Chearfully acknowledge, that I am of the African
> race . . . and it is under a Sense of the most profound gratitude to the
> Supreme Ruler of the universe . . . that I am not under that State of tyran-
> nical thraldom, and inhuman captivity, to which too many of my breth-
> ren are doomed. . . . Sir, Suffer me to recall to your mind that time in
> which the Arms and tyranny of the British Crown were exerted with
> every powerful effort in order to reduce you to a State of Servitude, look
> back I intreat you on the variety of dangers to which you were exposed . . .
> a time in which you clearly saw into the injustice of a State of Slavery . . .
>
> . . . Sir how pitiable is . . . that altho you were so fully convinced
> of the benevolence of the Father . . . that you should at the Same time
> counteract his mercies, in detaining by fraud and violence so numer-
> ous a part of my brethren under groaning captivity and cruel oppres-
> sion, that you should at the Same time be found guilty of that most
> criminal act, which you professedly detested in others, with respect to
> yourselves. . . . This calculation [Almanac], Sir, is the production of my
> arduous [Astronomical] Study. . . . And altho I had almost declined to
> make my calculation for the ensuing year, in consequence of that time
> which I had allotted therefore being taking up at the Federal Territory
> by the request of Mr. Andrew Ellicott.[78]

Though Banneker's letter and almanac did little to dissuade Jefferson
of his opinion, Banneker took a bold and unapologetic position in his

letter to Jefferson, a position that suggests that he was likewise not passive in his approach and discourse surrounding the surveying of Federal City. Jefferson acknowledged receipt and did not change his opinion on Black people's inferiority and lack of mental capacities.[79]

Jefferson's position, however, was not aligned with the realities of Black people's contributions to the nation's early formation, nor were Banneker's gifts and intellectual prowess anomalies. Among those who helped build the colonies, economically and structurally, were innovators and inventors like Banneker who, despite their status, early on helped improve the United States' standing in the world. Most contributed knowing that they would not be publicly recognized for their talents, own exclusive rights to their innovations, or be able to patent their inventions.

Indeed, US patent laws of 1793 specifically identified Black people as noncitizens and therefore as having no rights to any of their inventions. Whites were credited with Black people's inventions. Jefferson, aware of these laws and gross injustices, still upheld the Black people's intellectual inferiority, even though in his lifetime alone, between 1743 and 1826, there were a number of Black visionaries like Banneker. One in particular was Onesimus, an enslaved Black man laboring in Massachusetts who provided a treatment for smallpox, drawing from the West African practice of inoculation to cure diseases.[80] Another was James Forten, a free Black man from Philadelphia who worked with a Philadelphia sailmaker and, at the age of twenty, invented an apparatus for managing sails to improve a ship's control, balance, and speed. James Derham, an enslaved man from Philadelphia who later purchased his freedom in 1786, was the first known Black man allowed to practice medicine formally in the US.

In 1794, Jo Anderson, an enslaved Black man, became the coinventor of a mechanical reaper that revolutionized agriculture by facilitating harvesting and thus increasing food production. By 1800, another enslaved Black man from Massachusetts named Ebar created a broom made from broomcorn and in doing so forged a new way of manufacturing brooms. In 1820, six years before Jefferson's death, Lewis Temple, a formerly enslaved Black man from Richmond, Virginia, moved to Boston, Massachusetts, where he invented a harpoon called the Temple's toggle or Temple's blood. The tool helped colonists capture whales for whale oil, a popular commodity throughout the New World and Europe. In 1821, Thomas Jennings, a free Black tailor from New York, created a new method for washing clothes called "dry scouring," known today as dry cleaning. Not without much controversy, in 1821, Jennings became the first Black man to receive a patent. In 1826, as mourners gathered around Jefferson's deathbed, Henry Boyd, an enslaved Black man from Kentucky, was conceiving a corded bed known as the "Boyd Bedstead." Boyd's wooden-railed bed that connected the headboard to the footboard more firmly was the first of its kind in the early nineteenth century and is still commonly used today. Banneker, these men, and the unnamed and unrecognized Black women inventors among them were not anomalies. They were among those Black people who contributed to the building of this nation.[81]

Banneker was keenly aware of Jefferson's short-sightedness and lived in a world in which men who did not look like him governed and fashioned laws that kept Black people and Native Americans in a perpetual state of inferiority and bondage to further their own personal and public causes. In his appeal to Jefferson, Banneker underscored that what Black people lacked in the new nation was not mental capacity but rather the same access, freedoms, and entitlements as people of European descent. Banneker appealed to Jefferson to recognize the injustice, hoping that Jefferson would acknowledge publicly that God had endowed all humans, without partiality, with the same capacities and sensations. Jefferson's refusal and willful neglect did not deter Banneker, the self-taught Black astronomer, from laying the boundary stones of the nation's capital.

## The Laying of Boundary Stones

In the early months of 1791, Banneker left his family farm to begin the process of laying forty stones to mark the boundaries of the new capital city. The forty stones, each weighing about half a ton, were commissioned by President Washington, quarried near Aquia Creek in Virginia, and placed on the ground a mile apart in a diamond configuration to mark the federal territory borders during the late eighteenth century. Larger stones were placed at each corner of the diamond to signify the most southerly, easterly, northerly, and westerly points of the new territory. Four noteworthy inscriptions were chiseled on each of the forty stones. As Ellicott notes, "On the sides facing the Territory [nation's capital] is inscribed, 'Jurisdiction of the United States.' On the opposite sides of those placed in the state of Virginia, is inscribed, 'Virginia.' And of those in the state of Maryland, is inscribed, 'Maryland.' On the fourth side, or face of the stone, is inscribed the Year, and the present position of the magnetic-needle at that place."[82] Figure 3.4 is a blueprint of the stone markers:[83]

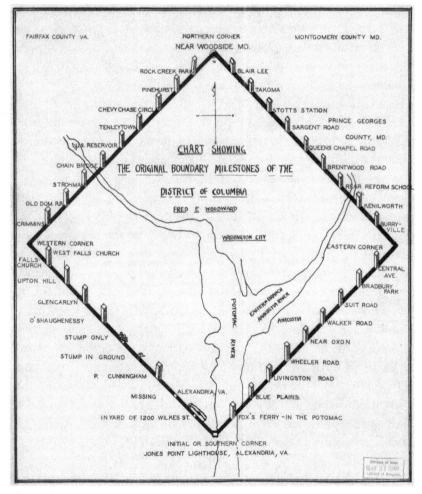

**Figure 3.4.** *Chart of the Original Boundary Milestones of the District of Columbia.* Library of Congress.

Before placing the first stone, Banneker was tasked with making the astronomical observations and calculations needed to establish the most southerly point of the diamond located at Jones Point in Alexandria. Banneker "fixed the position of the first stone by lying on his back to find the exact starting point for the survey . . . and plotting six stars as they crossed his spot at a particular time of night"[84]—the anecdote with which I began this section. Through written proclamation, President Washington declared Jones Point as the starting point of the new nation's capital.

On May 7, 1791, the *Columbian Centinel* newspaper reprinted an article dated April 15, 1791, describing the ceremonial placement of the first cornerstone at Jones Point. The newspaper also made note of the processional that included Ellicott; Commissioners Stuart and Carroll; the Reverend James Muir, a mason and pastor of Presbyterian Church of Alexandria; members of the Alexandria Masonic Order fraternity; and other dignitaries and citizens. When Ellicott and his team identified the precise point from which the first line of the district was to proceed, the master of the lodge and Dr. Stewart (Stuart) placed the stone.[85]

Once the cornerstone was placed, the men performed a Masonic ritual by putting "corn, wine and oil . . . upon it [the stone], then, words delivered by Reverend Muir."[86] The three elements—corn, wine, and oil—were significant to Masonic ritual practices. Drawing from Psalms 104:15, the corn, representing food, reminded masons to be nourished by righteousness; wine, a refreshment, reminded them to be refreshed by God's word; and the oil, symbolizing divine anointing/joy, reminded them to rejoice with joy, unspeakable in the riches of divine grace. In 1794, the original ceremonial cornerstone marking the spot of the initial southernmost boundary point of the new federal district was buried at a nearby church and replaced by a larger one with the words "The beginning of the Territory of Columbia" chiseled into the stone. Ironically, it was Banneker, a free Black man, who marked the spot where slave owners placed the first stone. A remnant of the replacement stone is currently located in the lighthouse seawall at Jones Point. Aboveground near the stone marker is a fixed display honoring Ellicott and Banneker along with one of Banneker's mathematical puzzles from his 1798 astronomical journal. The marker reads in part,

**Major Andrew Ellicott, owner of one of the finest sets of surveying instruments in the country, was put in charge of the DC boundary survey and established the first base camp on Jones Point. On-site measurements and round-the-clock astronomical calculations were conducted by Benjamin Banneker, a free Black, self-taught in math and astronomy.**

After the placing of the first ceremonial stone, Ellicott and his team continued on, clearing lands, marking boundary lines, and placing more stones. They began surveying ten-mile lines first along the southwest line, then, northwest, followed by the northeast and southeast lines, until the diamond shape of the new federal district took shape. A remnant of another stone known as the SW-9 Intermediate Boundary Stone (an Intermediate Stone of the District of Columbia), marked the western tip of the new district. Ellicott and Banneker laid this stone in 1791. At the urging of the Afro-American Bicentennial Corporation, the marker was later renamed and dedicated in honor of Benjamin Banneker for his role in installing the stone markers along the perimeter of the new district. Due to land retroceding to Virginia in an 1846 Act of Congress and other factors, the original DC boundary to which this marker stands shifted. Presently, it marks the boundary between Falls Church, Virginia, and Arlington County, Virginia. The stone, which is approximately one foot square at its top and has fifteen inches visible aboveground with two feet being belowground, is the first Federal City boundary marker recorded on the National Register of Historic Places. Other markers throughout the city highlight Banneker's work with Ellicott's team.

On January 1, 1793, Andrew Ellicott submitted to the commissioners a report with a map attached to it indicating that the boundary survey had been completed and all boundary stone markers had been installed. The map displayed the boundaries, streets, and structural features of the city of Washington in the Territory of Columbia.

## Banneker's Death

Over the course of history, accounts of Banneker's contributions to the building of the nation's capital have been rather mixed. Some have concluded that Banneker was a field laborer who hauled wood and cleared lands, while others attribute the completion of L'Enfant's plan and subsequent city grid to his skill and ingenuity. As discoveries about Banneker's role in the building of the nation's capital continue to be unearthed, some conclusions about Banneker's position have been refuted and others confirmed. By the time Ellicott submitted his final reports to the commissioners, Banneker was no longer working with his team. He returned to his farm in Oella, Maryland, but continued to help maintain the project's astronomical field clock, make astronomical recordings, and determine latitudes. Banneker also continued producing almanacs until 1802 but ceased publishing them when sales declined in 1797.

On October 9, 1806, after a long walk, Benjamin Banneker died in his sleep just one month before his seventy-fifth birthday. Two days later, on October 11, Banneker was buried in the Banneky family graveyard near his farm. As mourners gathered, they became alarmed by smoke rising in the distance. Banneker's home was in flames, and burning with his family's legacy were his writings, inventions, calculations, keepsakes, clothing, books, furniture, and other possessions. The cause was never determined. Family members suspected arson. Though Banneker was a respected man in many circles, he suffered discrimination and jealousy at the hands of whites, and his calculations often came under scrutiny. He received threats from whites who were renting portions of his lands. He had been shot at and his home vandalized. A 1797 journal entry of his recalls one incident in which bullets entered his home: "Standing at my door I heard the discharge of a gun, and in four or five seconds of time, after the discharge, the small shot came rattling about me, one or two of which struck the house; which plainly demonstrates that the velocity of sound is greater than that of a cannon bullet."[87]

Banneker's ability to turn any moment into something of scientific interest later led newspapers in the area to publish a poignant obituary about this free Black man who contributed substantially to the nation and to the building of the nation's capital. On October 28, 1806, three weeks after his burial, the *Federal Gazette* and the *Baltimore Daily Advertiser* published an obituary that read in part, "On Sunday, the 9th instant, departed this life at his residence in Baltimore county, the 73d [sic] year of his age, Mr. BENJAMIN BANNEKER, a Blackman, and immediate descendent of an African father. He was well known in his neighborhood for his quiet and peaceable demeanor, and among scientific men as an astronomer and mathematician. . . . Mr. Banneker is a prominent instance to prove that a descendant of Africa is susceptible of as great mental improvement and deep knowledge into the mysterious of nature as that of any other nations."[88]

In Europe, upon learning of his death in 1806, Banneker "was eulogized before the French Academy by the Marquis de Condorcet, and William Pitt placed his name in the records of the English Parliament."[89] But in the United States, Banneker's obituary was placed in the newspaper next to advertisements offering rewards for runaway enslaved women, men, and children. Over the course of time, shrubbery overtook his grave site until citizens during the late twentieth century urged the Maryland Bicentennial Commission and the State Commission on Afro American History and Culture to honor Banneker with a new memorial. In 1977, a tombstone in the form of an obelisk was erected on Mt. Gilboa AME Church cemetery grounds in Oella, Maryland. The plaque on Banneker's obelisk reads, "Buried in an unmarked grave near here lie the remains of Benjamin Banneker, distinguished son of Maryland, who was born, lived and died in this area. Erected in Memoriam by the Maryland Bicentennial Commission and the State Commission on Afro American History and Culture 1977." Banneker was not the only Black person who contributed to the building of the nation's capital.

## The Enslaved and Free Black Laborers' Roles in the Building of the Nation's Capital

Hundreds of enslaved and free Black laborers contributed significantly to the emerging young nation. One must wonder how many of their stories have been lost because, as a country, we do not value Black people's stories and remain indifferent to their contribution. Our choice not to value, however, does not negate their presence and the work of their hands that carried out the plan.

By the end of the American Revolutionary War, slavery was legalized and practiced in all thirteen colonies, with Black people, enslaved and free, representing 20 percent of the overall US population. In 1790, there were approximately 757,208 Black people residing in the United States. By 1800, the number had increased to 1,002,037 and to 1,377,808 in 1810 (an upsurge of 32.3 percent and 37.5 percent, respectively, within a two-decade period).[90] In 1790, over half of the US Black population lived in Virginia and Maryland alone. Virginia's total Black population was approximately 305,493 persons (292,627 enslaved and 12,866 free), and Maryland's total reached nearly 112,000 persons (103,036 enslaved and 8,043 free).[91] These numbers only increased with time.

Given the high density of enslaved and free Blacks in these two slave states, it is not surprising that they also became the primary source of labor. As Lane points out, "From a geographical standpoint alone, it should come as no surprise that slave laborers were used to build the nation's capital."[92] Washington and Jefferson's grand desire to hire Europeans from Ireland, Scotland, and other parts of Europe seemingly fell short, and the commissioners eventually turned to enslaved labor, a pursuit that neither Washington nor Jefferson overruled or prohibited. The commissioners considered purchasing enslaved women, men, and children rather than rent them to avoid foreseeable conflicts with landowners and slavers, but they did not follow through with their plan. Instead, they hired Captain Elisha Williams to recruit enslaved workers, tasking him, in a resolution dated April 13, 1792, "to hire good laboring negroes by the year, the masters clothing them well and finding each a blanket, the Commissioners finding them provisions and paying twenty pounds a year wages. The payment if desired to be made quarterly or half yearly. If the negroes absent themselves a week or more such time will be deducted."[93] The commissioners advertised for enslaved laborers, offering hefty wages to owners through flyers, news ads, and posters that read, "Seeking a number of Slaves to labor in the Brick Yards, Stone quarries, etc. for which generous wages will be given. Also, Sawyers to Saw by the hundred or on wages by the month or year." Over the course of the new city's construction, many more advertisements for enslaved and free Black workers were posted throughout the region with the caption "Negroes for Hire" or "Negro Men Wanted" printed in bold.

The commissioners rented large numbers of enslaved workers from owners at a lower rate than free whites. They believed any signs of monetary competition and discord among white workers could be curtailed by integrating enslaved workers and low-paid free Black workers within the white working pool. The commissioners established compensation parameters between white, Black, and enslaved workers. They referred often to whites as workmen or skilled workmen, free Blacks as Negroes and skilled workers, and the enslaved as laborers or Negroes. This monetary and title designation is denoted in a correspondence between the commissioners and Jefferson dated January 5, 1973. The commissioners wrote, "The provisioning the workmen draws after it so many expences and so much waste that we have hitherto left them to provide for themselves. We are under the necessity of doing otherwise with the labourers, a part of whom we can easily make up of negroes and find it proper to do so. Those we have employed this summer have proved a very useful check and kept our affairs cool."[94] The monies the government saved by integrating free and low-rate Black-bodied laborers into the workforce allowed them to cover relocation and travel expenses for European immigrant workers. This tactic is outlined in the workmen's "Terms for Mechanics" contract, which was written by the commissioners and had Washington and Jefferson's approval. Dated January 3, 1793, it reads as follows:

> Advance up to 30/sterling to mechanics in Europe for expenses and to pay their passage upon arrival in the Federal District, and to make the same advances for wives in some instances; promising to pay the same wages as mechanics of similar skills in the United States, namely the daily wage of 4/6 to 5/sterling presently earned by stonecutters and good masons; giving assurances from the projected expenditure of $2,000,000 over eight years that there was "no probability of any considerable decline of wages"; and stipulating that half their weekly wages would be retained until the advance and passage were repaid.[95]

In an earlier correspondence dated January 2, the commissioners forwarded the same "Terms for Mechanics" contract to James Traquair, a Philadelphian stonecutter from Scotland, "requesting him to induce fifty plain stonecutters in Great Britain to emigrate to the United States to work in the Federal District . . . and inviting him to visit the Federal District for consultation."[96] Free involuntary labor did not require such maneuvering or accommodations. Enslaved laborers worked unpaid in a controlled environment where noncompliance was punishable by violence, imprisonment, and termination. Throughout the ten-year span of the construction of the new metropolis, it was not uncommon for enslaved laborers and free Blacks to be assigned multiple tasks at a time. Both were involved in all aspects of the construction of federal buildings, private homes, and other public and private structures and green spaces. Among them were skilled and unskilled persons whose work included but was not limited to agriculture (chopping, clearing, farming), carpentry, masonry, mining, carting, sawing, rafting, roofing, hauling, milling, blacksmithing, bricklaying, brick making, nailing, hammering, surveying, plastering, quarrying, glazing, and painting. Enslaved women, men, and children were forced to multitask in hostile working environments and under harsh seasonal climatic conditions. Many served dual roles, working as skilled laborers and field hands while also working at construction sites. Their ability to multitask, however, posed a risk for slavers, who feared the enslaved were prone to escape due to their necessary mobility at construction sites to complete the wide range of tasks. An exploration of some of the tasks previously outlined shows the roles that enslaved laborers and free Blacks played in the formation of the nation's capital.

In the preliminary stages of the city's design, for example, enslaved and free Blacks were instrumental in assisting Ellicott's team by clearing lands and debris, hacking through brushes, wading through creeks, and preparing the ground for plotting and laying the stones of the ten-mile sides of the diamond-shaped federal district. The commissioners also advised L'Enfant and other district architects to rent enslaved workers on a month-to-month and sometimes yearly basis to prepare the foundation of various public and private buildings. On one federal construction site, the commissioners assigned sixty enslaved Black men, and approximately eight hundred enslaved laborers at one time were needed to paint, roof, saw, glaze, and perfect the US Capitol from 1793 to 1826.[97]

As construction progressed, some people worked in the quarry cutting stone to build the foundation of federal buildings, with some stone coming from as far away as Aquia Creek in Stafford County, Virginia. Once quarried, they dragged the large stone pieces excavated with pick-axes, mauls, and wedges to the waterfront and loaded them on small boats bound for Washington. Oftentimes upon arrival in Washington, they did not have enough stone for the masons because "it took six slaves two days to unload one shallop [small boat] load. And then it took eight slaves three days to put that load on the drags [tow]" with no indication of the "time it took the horses to pull the stone" to the work sites. The heaviness of the stone slabs and the amount of manual labor exerted did not matter to the commissioners, who directed the overseer "to keep the yearly hirelings at work, from sunrise to sunset, particularly the negroes," until the task was complete.[98] While several worked with stone from Aquia Creek, others were tasked with excavating rock at Rock Creek, Maryland. Once excavated, some of this rock was transported to mills to be crushed and boiled by enslaved hands to make plaster for the interior walls of public and private buildings.

In addition to quarrying stone and rock, enslaved laborers were charged with hauling building materials such as nails, lumber, saws, and so on to construction sites. Because building materials were scarce in the area, the commissioners obtained materials from as far north as Massachusetts, New England, and New York. Other laborers spent their days digging trenches for the canal or working in sawpits cutting timber for carpenters.

While whites were hired as master brick makers, enslaved and free Blacks did the dirtier work of digging the clay from the Anacostia River and other areas. Once gathered, they mixed the clay with water and sand, then molded it into bricks and fired it, before setting it aside for cooling. This was an ongoing process to produce the number of blocks needed to build federal offices, the US Capitol, the White House, private homes, and so on. Enslaved brick makers were paid fifty cents more than those assigned to other tasks. On most occasions, however, it was actually their owners who received payment for their services.

Brick making was in high demand because in the early stages of construction, President Washington set the "terms and conditions" for buildings erected in the new city, and these included that they be made of brick or stone. In his October 8, 1792, correspondence regarding the "Broadside: Sale of Lots in Federal City," Washington stipulated that "the Materials and Manner of the Buildings and Improvements on the LOTS in the CITY of WASHINGTON" shall be as follows: first, "THAT the outer and party-walls of all houses within the said City shall be built of brick or stone."[99] Throughout his presidential term in office and afterward, Washington's terms and conditions were revised to include wooden structures. By 1800, millions of bricks had been made by enslaved hands to lay the foundation and build many of the structures in the permanent seat of government.

## Conclusion

While the demand for enslaved laborers was on the rise in the nation's capital, slavery was coming to a gradual close in Philadelphia. In March 1780, ten years before Philadelphia was named the temporary seat of government, the Pennsylvania legislature passed An Act for the Gradual Abolition of Slavery. The act put an end to the importation of Black-bodied people into Pennsylvania. And to ensure the end of this practice, the colony required slaveholders to register their enslaved laborers annually. Failure to do so would result in an enslaved person's freedom. The law also declared that those enslaved in Pennsylvania before 1780 remain in bondage but that children born of an enslaved woman after 1780 were born free. However, these children were classified as indentured servants and made to work for their mother's owner until age twenty-eight. Since the Continental Congress met in Philadelphia, Congress members were exempt from the statute. Nonresident slaveholders could hold their enslaved laborers in the colony for up to six months.

Aware that his term in office was longer than six months, Washington faced a dilemma while awaiting the completion of the new President's House in the city of Washington: How could he continue to reap the benefits of his enslaved labor force toiling away in the Philadelphia mansion without running the risk of their manumission? In response, Washington devised a rotation scheme to evade the Pennsylvania law. He instructed Tobias Lear, his secretary, to send his domestic servants back to Mount Vernon before they reached their six-month limit. In a correspondence to Lear dated April 12, 1791, Washington writes,

> The Attorney-General's case and mine I conceive, from a conversation I had with him respecting our Slaves, is some what different. He in order to qualify himself for practice in the Courts of Pennsylvania, was obliged to take the Oaths of Citizenship to that State; whilst my residence is incidental as an Officer of Government . . . in case it shall be found that any of my Slaves . . . shall attempt their freedom at the

expiration of six months, it is my wish and desire that you would send the whole, or such part of them . . . home [Mount Vernon] . . .

. . . the idea of freedom might be too great a temptation for them to resist . . . it might, if they conceived they had a right to it, make them insolent in a State of Slavery . . . it behoves me to prevent the emancipation of them, otherwise I *shall* not only loose the use of them, but may have them to pay for. If upon taking good advise it is found expedient to send them back to Virginia, I wish to have it accomplished under pretext that may deceive both them and the Public. . . . I request that these Sentiments and this advise may be known to none but *yourself* & *Mrs. Washington*.[100]

As proposed by Washington, close to the end of their six-month stint in Philadelphia, Tobias sent his laborers back to Mount Vernon to work. Some were immediately returned to Philadelphia as a means of resetting the clock. Although an amendment in 1788 was passed by the Pennsylvania legislature prohibiting the rotation of enslaved workers, Washington violated the law throughout his term in office. The scheme worked, and all seemed well in Washington's world—a new government in session in Philadelphia with a new US Constitution, a national capital city on the horizon, the turmoil of L'Enfant and Ellicott behind him, and an ongoing rotation of enslaved laborers. But all was not right for Washington's house and grounds servants moving between Mount Vernon and Philadelphia. The ten domestic workers mentioned in the opening of this chapter—Austin, Christopher Sheels, Giles, Hercules, Joe Richardson ("Postilion Joe"), Molly ("Moll"), Paris, Richmond, William "Billy" Lee, and Ona "Oney" Maria Judge—felt the weight of enslavement in a free state.

On May 21, 1796, Ona Judge, whose story began our conversation, decided that she had had enough. She would no longer participate in a forced servitude system that sought to annihilate her. Upon overhearing that the First Lady would be bequeathing her as a wedding gift to her granddaughter, Elizabeth, Ona decided, "I'm done." One Saturday evening while the Washingtons were dining, Ona walked out of the front door of the Presidential Mansion in Philadelphia. She was twenty-two years old. Ona did not turn to the Philadelphia law to support her pursuits. She turned within. She had been planning her escape for months, leaving a few of her belongings at a time with friends each time she visited. When asked in an 1845 interview how she had escaped, she stated, "Whilst they were packing up to go to Virginia, I was packing to go, I didn't know where; for I knew that if I went back to Virginia, I never should get my liberty. I had friends among the colored people of Philadelphia, had my things carried there beforehand, and left while they were eating dinner."[101] With the aid of white and Black abolitionists, Ona then boarded a ship headed to Portsmouth, New Hampshire.

Upon learning of the plot and her escape, the president and First Lady were furious. Washington made use of the Fugitive Slave Act he had signed into law three years prior. Without hesitation, Washington went in dogged pursuit of Ona, posting advertisements in public spaces. The ad was published in the *Pennsylvania Gazette* on May 24, 1796, and read,

---

Advertisement. ABSONCDED from the household of the President of the United States, on Saturday afternoon, ONEY JUDGE, a light Mulatto girl, much freckled, with very Black eyes, and bushy Black hair.—She is of middle stature, but slender and delicately made, about 20 years of age.

She has many changes of very good clothes of all sorts, but they are not sufficiently recollected to describe. As there was no suspicion of her going off, and it happened without the least provocation, it is not easy to conjecture whither she is gone—or fully, what her design is, but she may attempt to escape by water, all masters of vessels and others are cautioned against receiving her on board, altho' she only, and probably will endeavour to pass for a free woman, and it is said has, wherewithal to pay her passage.

Ten dollars will be paid to any person who will bring her home, if taken in the city, or on board any vessel in the harbour; and a further reasonable sum if apprehended and brought home, from a greater distance, and in proportion to the distance.[102]

FREDERICK KITT, Steward. May 23.

On several occasions, Washington solicited friends and family members such as Thomas Lee Jr. and Burwell Bassett to help him reclaim his property. In one instance, upon learning of her whereabouts, Washington sent Bassett to convince Ona to return, but she refused. Bassett advised her that if she returned, Washington would free her, but she retorted, "I am free now and choose to remain so."[103] Furious, Washington wrote to John Whipple, the collector of customs in Portsmouth, bidding him to send authorities to apprehend Ona. The collector did not comply but instead warned Washington of the political consequences of apprehending her.

Washington, determined to have what he deemed to be his, advised Bassett and Lear to use force to return Ona and her infant child, to which she had given birth after her escape. Bassett advised Pennsylvania governor John Langdon over dinner of Washington's plan to use force. The governor immediately sent word to Ona, urging her to leave town until it was safe to return. Washington and his men, however, continued their relentless pursuit of Ona until Washington's death in 1799. Ona told a reporter, "They never troubled me anymore after he was gone."[104] Washington died without capturing Ona and also without seeing his city along the Potomac River come fully to fruition. He died in his bed at Mount Vernon without ever occupying the White House in the city that bore his name.

Though history has recorded George Washington as a noble man who made provisions in his will to free his enslaved laborers, it is important to note that Washington made sure such freedom would only come to be after he and Martha died—when they both had no more use for Black bodies. Upon her death, Martha did not free her dowry slaves, including Ona's mother and siblings. They, like most enslaved persons whose owners died, were separated from their family members and were willed by Martha to her surviving relatives.

Ona felt safer in the world without president and slaveholder George Washington and his First Lady, Martha Washington. She was free, though labeled a fugitive. A woman of faith active in the church and the abolitionist movement, Ona remained in New Hampshire, where she learned to read and spent time painting. In 1797, she fell in love and married a young Black sailor named Jack Staines. The two had three children—Eliza, Nancy, and William. Ona outlived her husband

and children, and as age and illness set in, she was forced to move in with a friend living in Greenland, New Hampshire. The two women struggled to make ends meet. Ona eventually became a pauper, leaning often on the kindness of friends to survive. When asked if she regretted running away from servitude at the President's House, she said that she was motivated by one thing and one thing alone—freedom. "I am free," she said, "and have, I trust been made a child of God by the means."[105]

On February 25, 1848, Ona "Oney" Maria Judge Staines died poor and alone. She was buried in an unmarked grave in Greenland, New Hampshire. She was seventy-five years old. Ona's story is one of many of those artisans, first builders, and first contributors of the nation's capital who died without public recognition for their labors. Ona worked. Ona gave. Ona sacrificed. She yearned for domestic tranquility and freedoms in the colonizers' world that she and others helped build. Her story, too, is not an anomaly.

# CHAPTER FOUR

# Black Builders
## *Slave Pens, and the Construction of the National Seat of Government*

*We have indeed come into a new part of the world, and amongst a new Set of inhabitants; it is a city in name, and that in a wilderness, a beautifull Spot by nature—but it must be commerce; and the introduction of a more hardy and industerrus race than its present inhabitants to build up and raise it to any degree of respectability: The effects of Slavery are visible every where.*

—FIRST LADY ABIGAIL ADAMS, LETTER TO COTTON TUFTS

*Generations of people who felt the lash of bondage, the shame of servitude, the sting of segregation, but who kept on striving and hoping and doing what needed to be done so that today I wake up every morning in a house that was built by slaves. And I watch my daughters, two beautiful, intelligent, Black young women playing with their dogs on the White House lawn.*

—FIRST LADY MICHELLE OBAMA, "DEMOCRATIC NATIONAL CONVENTION ADDRESS"

Every year, millions of people from all over the world and within US borders travel to the United States' capital in anticipation of seeing the majestic city that Washington and L'Enfant envisioned just beyond the Potomac River. In crowds, they make their way along the National Mall, a serene two-mile botanical display of American elm trees and water flowers situated among iconic landmarks and statues. Within its reach, a tidal basin lies surrounded by three thousand cherry blossom trees that visitors travel to see in full bloom at springtime. It is here, on the National Mall and surrounding area, that many citizens and immigrants of the metropolis honor, read about, and show respect to those who sacrificed their lives for the general welfare of the country. Many also have stood, and continue to stand, in protest of policies and injustices that have plagued the nation since its founding. In the center of this two-mile stretch stands the tallest structure in the District of Columbia, a 555-foot stone obelisk overlaid in white marble in honor of America's first president, George Washington. The monument towers over the nation's capital as if Washington himself were peering like a god examining the city he envisioned that would expand his ideals of a new independent republic.

In the opposite direction, approximately one mile west of Washington's monument, sits the grandeur of the Lincoln Memorial, an enormous and ancient thirty-six-columned, four-sided limestone edifice designed to resemble a Greek temple and dedicated to America's sixteenth president, Abraham Lincoln. Once visitors reach the top of this ascending structure, they are overtaken by a nineteen-foot-tall, 175-ton statue of Lincoln seated in a large armchair. Etched into the walls around him are his words taken from his Gettysburg Address, delivered in 1863. The chamber memorializing him is adorned with an inscription behind him, which reads,

**IN THIS TEMPLE**
**AS IN THE HEARTS OF THE PEOPLE**
**FOR WHOM HE SAVED THE UNION**
**THE MEMORY OF ABRAHAM LINCOLN**
**IS ENSHRINED FOREVER**

As Lincoln sits, visitors stand in solemn awe of him and of the reflecting pool, an iridescent body of water that begins just beyond the foot of the monument and stretches into the distance. A closer look into the water allows onlookers to see a reflection of themselves with the memorial behind them, mirroring back the past and the present, the old and new, the then and now.

About one mile east of Washington's monument sits the US Capitol, the permanent seat of the legislative branch of government, which houses two chambers of governance—the Senate and the House of Representatives. In 1793, when construction work began on the US Capitol, Washington laid the first cornerstone, and within weeks the judicial branch of government—the US Supreme Court—made its temporary home in the US Capitol. During the early days of the republic's formation, the Library of Congress and the Protestant Church also resided inside the Capitol. By using the Capitol as the repository of law, knowledge, and Protestant Christianity, the young nation early on enunciated its identity, governance, and sovereignty.

Less than a two-mile walk from the US Capitol toward Pennsylvania Avenue lies a three-story white mansion known as the White House, the working and living residence that has housed forty-four of the forty-five leaders of the free nation, forty-four of whom were white males. The forty-fourth leader, President Barack Obama, was the nation's first African American leader. From the White House, the presidents have presided over the executive branch of government.

Beyond these aforementioned institutions lies the Smithsonian Institution, an intentional cluster of museums commissioned by the US government that signifies America's openness to intellectual, cultural, and scientific query, and the Department of the Treasury, the nation's financial epicenter. Scattered throughout these physical structures on or near the National Mall are other landmarks and memorials.

Millions travel from near and far to take in and feel the dynamism of America's political power center and to connect with the Founding Fathers, who conceived, fought for, and built this great nation. People stand filled with a sense of nostalgia and national pride as they survey the National Mall, the surrounding institutions of sovereignty, and iconic symbols enshrined with the sentiment of brave men and noble eras.

For many people, the National Mall is indeed sacred ground, a place to honor and remember America's triumphs and greatness. But for others, it is a place of grief and profane human deprivation etched into the history of the entire landscape. For many, it is a traumatization of Native Americans violently driven off their lands and later enslaved Black bodies shackled, chained, and paraded over the terrain for sale to prospective buyers. The area was also daunting for those tasked with building the nation's capital, those forced into domestic servitude, or those who fled across the National Mall to pursue a life of freedom beyond city borders. From the perspective of generations of enslaved and free Black-bodied people, the National Mall has been a site of legalized domestic terror upheld and indeed sanctioned by all three branches of government.

The impact of this terror is seen in the lives of two enslaved girls, Mary Edmonson, age fifteen, and her younger sister Emily, age thirteen. Mary and Emily remember the National Mall as a site where Black lives did not matter. On April 15, 1848, Mary, Emily, and seventy-four other enslaved laborers fled to the wharf to board the *Pearl*, a sixty-five-foot vessel anchored in the Potomac River. Among the runaways were servants of the US president, politicians, Supreme Court justices, clergymen, merchants, and dignitaries. Despite knowing what their powerful and influential owners might do to them, these seventy-six Black-bodied persons risked their lives to escape.

Daniel Drayton, a white merchant seaman versed in successful slave escape voyages, aided their efforts. During his voyages carrying sellable goods between DC, New Jersey, and Philadelphia, Drayton offered his colleague Edward Sayres, captain of the *Pearl*, one hundred dollars to transport Mary, Emily, and others from DC to Frenchtown, New Jersey. From there, allies along the Underground Railroad would assist them.[1] Sayres agreed, bringing with him Charles English, his young white cook.

So it was that on the night of Saturday, April 15, 1848, the *Pearl* disembarked carrying seventy-six fugitives beneath its deck. But a lack of wind halted the journey. Sayres anchored the vessel until daybreak Sunday. The *Pearl* made its way through the channel for several hours until a turbulent wind troubled the waters, forcing Sayres to anchor the *Pearl* in Cornfield Harbor near Point Lookout. There, the group anxiously waited for the seas to calm.

In DC, meanwhile, slave owners awoke to discover that their workforce had fled. A Black hackman (cab driver) seeking monetary reward told owners that a vessel carrying fugitive slaves had headed toward free states on Saturday night. Church bells began ringing the alarm throughout the city, notifying the region of the escape. Furious owners and a band of citizens armed themselves with muskets, guns, and pistols and darted aboard a steamboat called the *Salem* in search of the *Pearl*. Once they spotted her, they boarded, weapons in hand. One man unbolted the lower deck latch, looked in, and cried out to the others, "Niggers, by G—d!" The men began cheering and banging the ends of their muskets against the deck. They had found their human property. The enslaved, determined to be free, rose to fight. But Drayton halted them midstream, urging them to concede that they had no chance—their captors held weapons, and they held only a deep yearning for freedom. The men commandeered the *Pearl* and took its enslaved passengers back to captivity. Drayton, Sayres, and English were taken aboard the *Salem*. As the vessels drew closer to the DC wharf, another enraged mob shouted obscenities from the shoreline. The closer they drew to the riverbank, the more the *Pearl's* captured passengers realized their chance at freedom had faded. They were back where they had started, now fugitives in the city where they were forced to labor. The men ordered the passengers off the vessel and paraded them two by two into the DC streets and through the dreaded National Mall. The journey seemed endless. The mob encircled the enslaved and the three white men, loudly ranting, "Lynch them! Lynch them! The damn villains! Lynch them!" One slave owner lunged at Drayton with a knife, cutting his ear. Within seconds, a taxi was called to escort Drayton and the two other white men safely to the jail while Mary, Emily, and the other enslaved laborers continued on foot, heads held high, navigating the treacherous terrain of slave markets, slave pens, and the angry mob. One by one, they filed into the city jail to await their fate as the crowd outside grew larger by the minute. The enslaved were not hopeful. For them, the nation's capital, the center of America's alleged democracy, was the site of national trauma, a place of the loathing of Black lives. The consequences of their escape now rested in the hands of the people who enslaved them—lawmakers, judges, merchants, and the US president.

Stories like Mary, Emily, and the seventy-four other enslaved laborers fleeing for their lives to the *Pearl*, captured, and paraded back like cattle are not a part of the tours of the nation's capital. Historical accounts of the nation's capital often exclude or minimize stories of Washington, DC, as a significant hub in human trafficking. Seldom do we hear about Black-bodied people toiling away on plantations and farms before the city's construction and serving as domestics to government officials, prominent white families, and wealthy landowners and businessmen.

Seldom do we learn about those who contributed to the building and everyday maintenance of the National Mall, the White House, the US Capitol, and the US Supreme Court, primarily between 1790 and 1863. A nuanced history of the nation's capital and the contributions and voices of enslaved Black-bodied people matter.

## The National Mall

The design of the National Mall was inspired by two plans: Pierre Charles L'Enfant's plans of the city submitted to George Washington in the early 1790s and the Senate Park Commission's (known as the McMillan Commission) plan introduced to Congress in December 1900 by Daniel Burnham, Frederick Law Olmsted Jr., Charles McKim, and Augustus Saint-Gaudens. L'Enfant's city plan included a design of a "Grand Avenue," which the McMillan Commission later renamed the National Mall.

L'Enfant envisioned a "Grand Republic" with a picturesque "Grand Avenue," approximately "400 feet in breadth, and about a mile in length, bordered with gardens, [and] ending in a slope from the houses on each side."[2] But between the late seventeenth and mid-nineteenth centuries, as federal buildings, private homes, parks, landmarks, and monuments began to fill the landscape, so too did bustling slave markets and slave pens. The emerging city, mapped out from two slave states, Virginia and Maryland, became a prime location for the nation's capital and for the domestic slave trade. In 1790, enslaved laborers were the largest source of labor in the nation. In 1800, the enslaved Black population in Washington, DC, was 3,244 persons, and the free Black population was 793 persons. Free Blacks, however, were not immune to mistreatment, kidnapping, and enslavement, even when they presented, on demand, their freedom papers to whites. The number of enslaved Blacks doubled in the district by 1820, because Washington, DC, was one of the most active slave depots in the US. Abolitionists nicknamed the city the Great Man Market of the Nation.

Initially, enslaved labor was needed to meet the demands of a growing city. But as construction slowed in the district and slave owners in DC, Maryland, and Virginia were producing fewer cash crops, the region had a surplus of enslaved laborers. DC became a bustling slave market for the Deep South, an area in need of enslaved laborers to produce cotton, sugar, and other cash crops. Domestic servants and "fancy girls" (i.e., prostitutes) were also in high demand for white merchants, investors, and travelers. It was not uncommon to see Black women, men, and children trudging up and down the undeveloped National Mall and surrounding areas in slave coffles. With the rise of this lucrative slave economy, owners seeking to make a profit could sell their laborers to slave dealers in the district, who in turn shipped enslaved laborers to Southern slave markets.

Slave markets prompted the rise of slave pens throughout the nation's capital as well as the Georgetown and Alexandria areas. Slave pens, often called gaols (an eighteenth-century term meaning "jail"), were scattered about the National Mall, the US Capitol, the White House, and the Smithsonian Castle. Behind the walls of the pen, Black bodies were inspected like cattle and detained like prisoners while awaiting sale or transport South. Edward Strutt Abdy, a European traveler writing about race and racism in the US, described his visit to a DC slave pen between 1833 and 1834:

> One day I went to see the "slaves' pen"—a wretched hovel, "right against" the Capitol. . . . The outside alone is accessible to the eye of a visitor; what passes within being reserved for the exclusive observation of its owner, (a man of the name of Robey,) and his unfortunate victims. It is surrounded by a wooden paling fourteen or fifteen feet in height, with the posts outside to prevent escape, and separated from the building by a space too narrow to admit of a free circulation of air. At a small window above, which was unglazed and exposed alike to the heat of summer and the cold of winter, so trying to the constitution, two or three sable faces appeared, looking out wistfully. . . . In this wretched hovel, all colors, except white—the only guilty one—both sexes, and all ages, are confined, exposed indiscriminately to all the contamination which may be expected in such society and under such seclusion.
>
> The inmates of the gaol, of this class I mean, are even worse treated; some of them . . . having been actually frozen to death, during the inclement winters which often prevail in the country. While I was in the city, Robey had got possession of a woman, whose term of slavery was limited to six years. It was expected that she would be sold before the expiration of that period, and sent away to a distance, where the assertion of her claim would subject her to ill-usage. Cases of this kind are very common. There was at the time a man in the gaol, who had

been taken up on suspicion; and, as no one claimed him, he was to be sold to pay his fees. On these occasions, free papers would be of little avail to the accused; as the gaoler has it in his power, and frequently takes an opportunity, to destroy them, unless some person . . . give evidence in his favor.[3]

Abdy's observation of the gaol rings true of Solomon Northup's experience, a free Black farmer and violinist from New York. Two men whose real names were Alexander Merrill and Joseph Russell approached Northup and convinced him to travel with them South for employment. The men were involved in a scheme with DC slave traders designed to deceive free Blacks with papers into traveling with them for work. Shortly after arriving in Washington, Northup was drugged and kidnapped. Upon waking, he found himself in Williams's slave pen at the mercy of James H. Burch, a well-known slave trader in the district whose business partner, Theophilus Freeman, owned a large slave market in New Orleans.

The pen, known as the Yellow House, owned by William H. Williams, was situated approximately eight blocks east of the US Capitol. It was a multistoried yellow house nestled within trees and contained behind a twelve-foot wall. The yard was used for breaking in and selling the enslaved, and the basement of the house is where some were kept, chained to walls. The monies Williams acquired from the bartering of human beings allowed him to purchase two slave ships, the *Tribune* and the *Uncas*, to transport enslaved women, men, and children from the nation's capital to other slaveholding states, principally Louisiana. Northup was not alone in the slave pen; there were others, including a mother and her two young children, Emily and Randall. Children were often confined in the same pen "for a short time to fatten" and then were sold at slave markets in the Deep South.[4] Northup was beaten severely and sold to a Louisiana slave owner to work the cotton field. His owner changed his name to Platt Hamilton.

A simple trip to the nation's capital by a free Black looking for work to support his family turned into twelve years of captivity and hard labor in the Deep South. When Northup was eventually freed, he made known his dismay, bemoaning the fact that this slave pen was "within the very shadow of the Capitol."[5] He was unaware, at the time, that there were over a dozen slave pens, jails, and markets scattered about the emerging metropolis from the late eighteenth to the mid-nineteenth century.

In addition to Williams's pen, other pens along the National Mall and federal buildings included William Robey's pen and Tavern (near Williams's pen), Isaac Beer's pen and Tavern / Mechanics Hall (on Seventh Street near Robey's pen), Lafayette Tavern (F Street between Thirteenth and Fourteenth Streets), Thomas Lloyd's Tavern (Seventh Street and Pennsylvania), Miller's Tavern (F Street Tavern), Montgomery Tavern (1300 block of Wisconsin Avenue), Neal's slave pen (just east of Robey's pen), St. Charles Hotel (Third Street and Pennsylvania Avenue), Gadsby Hotel / National Hotel (Sixth Street and Pennsylvania Avenue), Washington Jail (near Fourth and G Streets), Carroll Row Prison (the annex to the Old Capitol Prison on First and A Streets, presently the site of the Library of Congress), and the Decatur House (opposite the White House on Lafayette Square).[6]

From 1828 to 1836, Isaac Franklin and John Armfield's slave-trading firm called Franklin & Armfield was the largest and most prosperous slave-trading business in the United States. Their pen was located just a few miles from the National Mall in Alexandria, Virginia, at Duke and West Streets.[7] Every month, in 1830 alone, Franklin & Armfield shipped from Alexandria thousands of enslaved people from their pen to Mississippi and Louisiana.[8] In 1846, the partners sold the business to other slave dealers, who continued the practice until 1862. Not far from the Franklin & Armfield slave pen was Joseph Bruin and Henry P. Hill's slave pen (Bruin & Hill), which held Mary and Emily Edmonson and others aboard the *Pearl*.

It was not uncommon to have temporary pens located within taverns and hotels, allowing patrons to "store" women, men, and children in pens while they enjoyed a meal, drink, and good night's sleep in close proximity to their human investment. Taverns and hotels were also perfect locations for cloak-and-dagger activities for illegal operations. In DC, it was unlawful to kidnap and sell people with freedom papers. But at night, traders were known to transport kidnapped free Blacks to the rear of taverns or hotels, away from the watchful eye of others. Thousands of Black bodies were housed in pens within the nation's capital under the gaze of the White House and US Capitol. This helped signify to the nation that Black lives have no intrinsic value.

By the early twentieth century, the grotesque imagery of slave coffles trudging through the National Mall to slave pens and markets was overlaid with a picturesque park terrain, replaced with L'Enfant's image of a tree-line promenade filled with botanical gardens, green spaces, iconic landmarks, and monuments dedicated to the Founding Fathers and patriotic men.

In 1902, a US Senate commission inspired by L'Enfant's plan issued the McMillan Plan, a reimagined Mall as "the centerpiece of a larger, grander federal district." The McMillan Plan extended beyond the boundaries of the "Grand Avenue" outlined by L'Enfant's plan to include memorials to Lincoln and Jefferson as well as other memorials, landmarks, and federal buildings. By 1912, over three thousand cherry blossoms gifted by the mayor of Tokyo, Yukio Ozaki, transformed the area even more by creating a serene atmosphere as a complement to the picturesque terrain. L'Enfant's vision and the McMillan Plan soon beautified the grotesque reality of a bustling slave market, with its cesspool of slave pens scattered about. Gone are the slave markets and pens and shackled Black people on display for perspective buyers. In their place, monuments and buildings were erected to memorialize the men and the city that held them in bondage. Hidden in plain sight in the city, once known as the "Great Man Market of the Nation," is the pain of the captured and their contributions to the nation's capital. The White House, the US Capitol, and the US Supreme Court, housed within the Capitol building, are just a few structures they helped construct.

## The White House

Construction of the White House began in 1792. The building was opened as the official residence and workplace of the US president in 1800. Early in its inception, the White House was referred to as the President's Palace, President's House, Presidential Mansion, and Executive Mansion.[9] Washington did not live to see the completion of the Presidential Mansion he envisioned.

His successor, President John Adams, the second US president, and his wife, Abigail, were the first to occupy the White House beginning in November 1800. Adams and his son, John Quincy Adams, the sixth president, did not own human beings in their lifetime and often spoke out against slavery in the US. Although First Lady Abigail Adams grew up in a prominent slaveholding family, she too publicly expressed her objection to slavery as a national institution. On November 28, 1900, shortly after moving into the Executive Mansion, the First Lady wrote a letter to Cotton Turfs, her husband's cousin, to share her observations of the city: "We have indeed come into a new part of the world. . . . The effects of Slavery are visible every where; and I have amused myself from day to day in looking at the labour of 12 negroes from my window. . . . It is *true Republicanism* that drive the Slaves half fed, and destitute of cloathing, or fit for . . . labour, whilst the owner waches about Idle. . . . Such is the case of many of the inhabitants of this place."[10] The White House was just one site among many where both free and enslaved Black people labored under poor and inequitable working conditions. Free Blacks were paid less than whites and were often degraded at construction sites. The enslaved were forced to work all day without pay. The mistreatment, lack of attention to basic human needs, and disparities in pay intensified enslaved Blacks' yearning for freedom, causing many to flee the nation's capital. The *Pearl* story is one among many accounts that shed light on the enslaved person's desire for freedom.

### They Built: Enslaved Black People and the White House

From the beginning of the construction of the White House to its final renovations in the mid-twentieth century, hundreds of Black people, enslaved and free, participated in its construction and renovations. Hundreds more have also served inside the Executive Mansion and on the grounds. Surviving payroll records and diaries and correspondences of former presidents and First Ladies attest to their presence, an indisputable record of enslaved and free White House workers.

The commissioners, acting on behalf of the US government, relied heavily on an enslaved labor force to build the White House and the US Capitol. They rented laborers from local owners and paid the owners accordingly. Figure 4.1 is a rental voucher that the commissioners gave to James Clagett, a local landowner and descendent of Georgetown's prominent Clagett family, for the rental of one of his laborers named George.[11] According to the voucher, George was rented to work at the White House construction site for five months and three days, from July to December 1794.

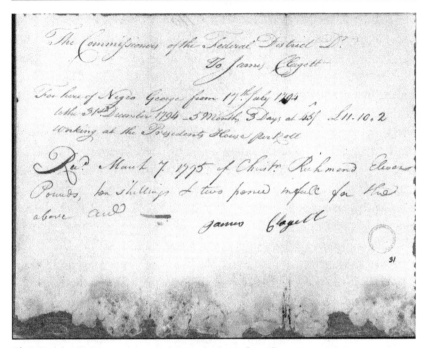

**Figure 4.1.** *US Government Pay Voucher: Paid to Slave Owner James Clagett for Work Completed at the President's House by His Enslaved Laborer, Negro George.* National Archives, Records of the Commissioners of the City of Washington (Record Group 217).

Local landowners and slave dealers like Clagett as well as politicians, merchants, traders, landowners, clergypersons, military personnel, and city designers were among those who hired out their enslaved laborers and profited from doing so.[12] Most often, the Treasury Department paid slave owners the wages earned by enslaved laborers, as enslaved laborers were not permitted to directly receive the wages they earned.

In addition to Clagett, James Hoban, the chief designer of the White House, also received compensation from the government for both his White House design and his enslaved laborers who worked on the Presidential Mansion. Hoban, an Irish Catholic immigrant, born circa 1758, migrated, shortly after the Revolutionary War, from Ireland to Philadelphia, Pennsylvania, to pursue the American dream. In 1787, he relocated to Charleston, South Carolina, later designing the state's Capitol building in Columbia.

In March 1792, Hoban entered the design competition for the White House. Shortly after, the commissioners and George Washington "awarded Hoban first prize in the competition" and hired him the next day "to supervise the execution of his design."[13] Washington, pleased with the selection, wrote Tobias Lear, his secretary, saying, "The Plan of Mr Hoben" has been chosen "for the President's House. . . . He . . . appears a master workman—and has a great many hands [enslaved laborers] of his own."[14] Both Hoban's design and his enslaved laborers were assets to Washington and the nation.[15]

Hoban arrived in the district with two carpenters, Pierce Purcell, his business associate, and Pierce's brother, Redmond Purcell. The men also brought some of their enslaved laborers and rented workers with them. The building project required skilled and unskilled workers, most of whom were enslaved and free Black-bodied people assigned to various tasks. Early on, Redmond was tasked with overseeing the White House carpenters, among whom were a handful of enslaved Black carpenters. Black carpenters and other Black skilled laborers worked as masons, bricklayers, and stonecutters. Other enslaved Black laborers were tasked with hauling building materials from various locations to the construction site, breaking ground, and digging to build the White House foundations. They also were tasked with clearing trees and cutting them for lumber, excavating sandstone to make bricks, and firing bricks for the interior walls. Skilled and unskilled enslaved and free Blacks were involved in virtually all aspects of the initial construction of Hoban's Georgian-style presidential house, which took nearly eight years to build.[16] When the British set fire to the President's Palace following the War of 1812, Black people were also involved in the rebuilding process from 1814 to 1818. Samples of the commissioners' payrolls, from December 1794 to November 1797, give us a window into the government's use of enslaved and free Black laborers to build the White House. The February 1795 payroll (figure 4.2) identifies five enslaved Black male carpenters—Peter, Tom, Ben, Harry, and Daniel—belonging to Hoban and Pierce who worked at the White House alongside Hoban, the Purcell brothers, and other workers.[17]

On payrolls, free whites (and sometimes free Blacks) were listed by first and last names, unlike enslaved laborers, who were normally listed by their first names under the subheading "Negro." The nationality

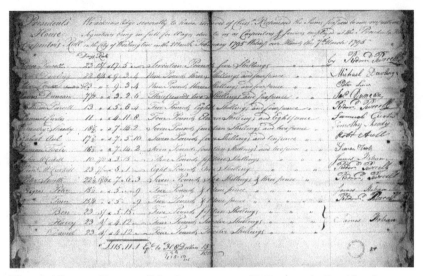

**Figure 4.2.** *Monthly Payroll for Carpenters and Joiners at the President's House, February 1795.* National Archives, Records of the Commissioners of the City of Washington (Record Group 217).

of the free workers listed on the payroll is not as apparent. Yet some researchers have concluded that the workers listed on the February payroll were more than likely white indentured workers whose contracts were held by Hoban, Purcell, and other landowners in the area.

The February payroll and other related wage-earning documents not only provide evidence of enslaved laborers' contribution to the construction of the White House but also highlight the wage disparity between Blacks and whites and the absence thereof regarding wages for enslaved laborers. Such disparity is noted in the February payroll and illustrative of disparities for those working at the White House and other construction sites in the area. Most often skilled white nonindentured workers were at the top of the pay scale and unskilled enslaved Black laborers at the bottom. The February payroll also identifies wage differences among free workers as noted in Hogan's, the Purcell brothers', and the other carpenters' monthly earnings. There also existed a racial pay disparity among skilled whites and skilled enslaved laborers completing the same task. Enslaved carpenters, for example, were known to work longer hours than whites per day or per week and yet received less pay than their white counterparts. On rare occasions, skilled enslaved laborers were paid higher or equal wages as white skilled workers. The February 1795 payroll, for example, shows two enslaved men, Peter and Tom, receiving the same pay rate as Peter Smith. A May 1795 payroll also shows Peter and Tom earning more than John Dickey, a free worker.

Enslaved laborers without skills were at the very bottom of the pay scale. On average, unskilled enslaved laborers earned approximately $4 to $5 a month or $50 to $60 per year in comparison to skilled enslaved laborers who earned approximately $4 to $7 a month or about $50 to $85 per year, equivalent to roughly $1,000 to $1,700 in 2018 terms. Though the owners received their enslaved laborers' earnings, it was at the owners' discretion to pay or not pay their workers for their contribution to the nation's capital. In some cases, enslaved laborers, especially skilled workers, did receive a small incentive pay for their services.

Whites were known to complain when enslaved and free skilled Black laborers—carpenters, stonecutters, and bricklayers—on rare occasions made higher wages. At one point, the commissioners responded to whites' outcry by temporarily banning skilled Black workers from the White House construction site. White laborers often lamented that hiring enslaved laborers would depress wages and discourage whites from migrating to the colonies.[18] But the commissioners and most of the builders and framers of the Federal City were driven by money. They knew all too well how enslaved labor provided a "very useful check" on white workers because "it was difficult to fight for higher wages or better working conditions when employers could hire dirt cheap replacement off nearby plantations."[19] The temporary banning of skilled Black workers in no way minimized their contribution. Despite the ban, surviving records show that "Peter and the others were among the seventeen carpenters that worked at the site and completed a significant amount of interior carpentry work."[20] Though the White House has undergone fires and renovations since Hoban's original design, this 1900s photo from the Library of Congress (figure 4.3) represents the contribution of enslaved Black-bodied people involved in the building, rebuilding, and renovation of the White House from the 1790s leading into the Civil War.[21]

**Figure 4.3.** *The White House, 1918.* Library of Congress.

## *They Served: Enslaved Black People in the White House*

Enslaved laborers, often referred to as domestics, house servants, or the help, also served inside and on the grounds of the White House. They worked as housekeepers, house managers, valets, stewards, carters, horsemen, blacksmiths, butchers, gardeners, and planters. Some were personal servants, body servants, maids-in-waiting, wet nurses, nannies, fanners, and fly swatters. Others were butlers, ushers, doorkeepers, ironers, laundresses, servers, food shoppers, dressmakers, seamstresses, cooks, and so on.

Head cook and assistant cook were two positions enslaved and free Blacks maintained throughout the years at the White House, from George Washington's presidency to modern times. Nearly two hundred Black laborers, enslaved and free, have worked as chief cooks/chefs or assistant cooks or in food preparation in the White House kitchen from the Washington to the Obama administrations. Forty-five of these individuals held positions during American slavery and post-Reconstruction. Hercules and Laura "Dolly" Johnson are notable among them.

In 1790, Hercules, also known as Herculas or Uncle Harkless, Washington's former enslaved cook, likewise traveled with Washington from Mount Vernon to serve as the chief cook in the President's House in Philadelphia. In 1797, Hercules ran away and never looked back. Long after Hercules, Laura "Dolly" Johnson worked as chief cook for the Grover Cleveland administration and continued her position into the Benjamin Harrison administration, the grandson of ninth president William Henry Harrison, in 1889. Johnson was born in Lexington, Kentucky, in 1852.

Prior to her appointment to the White House, Johnson served as the family cook of Colonel John Mason Brown, Union Army commander of the Forty-Fifth Kentucky Volunteer Mounted Infantry Regiment during the Civil War. Local and national newspapers made much to do about the hiring of a local Black woman to serve as the White House chief cook. Johnson began her tenure at the White House at a time when culinary training was not a requirement for free Black cooks to be hired in prominent locations like the White House, the Capitol, or local restaurants. As chief cook, Johnson was responsible for planning menus; buying groceries, meats, and fresh produce; managing the White House kitchen staff; and preparing meals for the president, the first family, and dignitaries and for social gatherings. At the close of President Harrison's term, she continued as chief cook, working for President Grover Cleveland in his second term.

After serving as chief cook at the White House, Johnson returned to Lexington. She continued providing culinary consultation throughout the William McKinley and Theodore Roosevelt administrations. In 1905, she married Ed Dandridge, and the two opened a restaurant. They opened a second restaurant and catering service in 1910 called the White House Café. Local and national newspapers covered the opening of both restaurants, highlighting Johnson's reputation as former White House chief cook. Soon after news of Johnson's restaurant broke, dignitaries, politicians, and local residents began piling into her restaurant. Johnson was later invited to be the chief chef at the Central Hotel in Lexington, where she served a few years. On February 1, 1918, Laura

Dolly Johnson passed away. The *Kentucky Herald-Leader* included a small mention of her death tucked away in the obituary section with no public recognition of her service to Lexington and the nation. The White House similarly failed to acknowledge publicly her service over four presidencies as the White House chief cook. There was no gesture of gratitude from the White House or former presidents for her culinary talents, fame, and commitment to feeding the first families and their guests.

During the early stages of the US presidency, from 1789 to 1850, newly elected presidents were responsible for hiring their household staff and paying them from their own pockets. Because of this, most presidents brought their enslaved laborers to the White House to cut costs. Selected enslaved servants, such as Oney Judge, were forced to accompany their owners. Twelve of the first eighteen US presidents who served prior to the Reconstruction era (1789–1877) owned enslaved individuals, and the majority of them brought their servants with them to the White House. Of the presidents who did not own Black people in their lifetimes, only John Adams and John Quincy Adams were outspoken critics of the institution. Though their views on slavery evolved over time, they publicly and privately addressed the immoral and unjust practice of slavery in the New World.

For some slave-owning presidents, the institution of slavery functioned like a family system. President Jackson's Hermitage plantation, for example, was sustained solely by enslaved labor. He encouraged his enslaved women, men, and children to see themselves as family units for the betterment of Hermitage. Jackson and many slave owners saw themselves as father figures, benevolent masters providing care for Black people who were too ignorant and childlike to care for themselves. As James Fisher, a formerly enslaved man recalling his owner's rationale for enslavement, said, "[Master] sometimes talked to me an hour at a time, to convince me that I was better off than I should be if I were free. He said slaves were better off than their masters, much better off than the free colored people, and vastly better off than they would have been if left in the wilds of Africa; because there they fought, killed, and ate each other. . . . He told me that the reason why they murdered and devoured one another in Africa was because there was no white people there to make them behave themselves."[22]

When proslavery advocates President John Tyler and First Lady Julia Tyler finished their presidential term, they returned to their plantation in Virginia. Julia spent her days writing about slavery at Sherwood Forest, expressing how grateful Black people felt being enslaved at Sherwood, so much so that those who ran away often returned willingly. She reasoned that at Sherwood, her enslaved women, men, and children lived lavishly, engaged in work others would envy, and were blessed with the gifts of Christian baptism and conversion. President Andrew Johnson's benevolence extended to a fourteen-year-old girl named Dolly, whom he purchased in 1842. Dolly, who was for sale at a slave market, asked Johnson to buy her because she "liked his looks." Compelled by her plea, Johnson purchased Dolly. While living with him, she gave birth to three children of unknown paternity—Liz, Florence, and William.

Stories like these provide us a window into the self-indulged and entitled white mind and serve to perpetuate the myth of the benevolent white slave owner. This myth conceals both the reality of slavery as morally reprehensible and the role slavery played in securing slaveholders'—including the nation's presidents'—personal and economic well-being. Their lives as American slaveholders should stand alongside their dominant narratives of American patriotism. A more nuanced version of their lives should inform how we enshrine and memorialize them. Chart 4.1 lists, in chronological order, the nation's first eighteen presidents and their positions on slaveholding, according to four categories: those presidents who owned enslaved people and brought some to serve in the White House, owned enslaved Black persons but did not bring them to serve in the Executive Mansion, never owned enslaved Black persons yet appeared ambiguous in their position on slavery, and never owned enslaved Black persons and consistently opposed the practice.

From the presidencies of George Washington to Ulysses Grant, slavery constituted the soul of the nation. Slavery was the economic engine that drove the US economy, and slaveholding sensibilities were engrained in the new republic's national identity. At the heart of this enterprise was the disregard for Black life. Such was deeply engrained in the ethos of the new republic's way of life. During the eighty-eight years that these presidents served, the majority, through their actions and inactions, signaled from the most powerful office in the United States that Black

## Chart 4.1. The nation's first eighteen presidents and their positions on slavery

| Years in office | US presidents during slavery and the Reconstruction era | Owned enslaved Black persons and brought them to the White House | Owned enslaved Black persons but did not bring them to the White House | Did not own enslaved Black persons but held ambiguous positions on slavery | Never owned enslaved Black persons and publicly opposed slavery |
|---|---|---|---|---|---|
| 1789–97 | 1. George Washington | ✓ | | | |
| 1797–1801 | 2. John Adams | | | | ✓ |
| 1801–9 | 3. Thomas Jefferson | ✓ | | | |
| 1809–17 | 4. James Madison | ✓ | | | |
| 1817–25 | 5. James Monroe | ✓ | | | |
| 1825–29 | 6. John Quincy Adams | | | | ✓ |
| 1829–37 | 7. Andrew Jackson | ✓ | | | |
| 1837–41 | 8. Martin Van Buren | | ✓ | | |
| 1841–41 | 9. William Henry Harrison | | ✓ | | |
| 1841–45 | 10. John Tyler | ✓ | | | |
| 1845–49 | 11. James Polk | ✓ | | | |
| 1849–50 | 12. Zachary Taylor | ✓ | | | |
| 1850–53 | 13. Millard Fillmore | | | ✓ | |
| 1853–57 | 14. Franklin Pierce | | | ✓ | |
| 1857–61 | 15. James Buchanan | | | ✓ | |
| 1861–65 | 16. Abraham Lincoln | | | ✓ | |
| 1865–69 | 17. Andrew Johnson | | ✓ | | |
| 1869–77 | 18. Ulysses S. Grant | | ✓ | | |

lives do not matter. Their actions and inactions had a direct impact on Black people's well-being. The aftermath of their decisions was felt well into the Reconstruction period and beyond. Under their watch, slavery and its reverberations echoed more intensely each year throughout the nation. Adverse vibrations of this syncopation continue to affect Black people and other disenfranchised individuals and groups to this day.

As discussed in chapter 2 and noted in the chart, George Washington, the United States' first president (1789–97), owned over three hundred enslaved women, men, and children in his lifetime. Prior to the relocation of the White House to the nation's capital, Washington brought some enslaved servants, like Oney Judge and Christopher Sheels, to work in the Executive Mansions in New York and Philadelphia. Though it is often noted that Washington toward the end of his life appeared conflicted about the institution, he continued the practice of owning slaves until his death.

John Adams, the second president (1797–1801), did not own Black people. As Adams wrote in a letter to abolitionists George Churchman and Jacob Lindley dated January 24, 1801, "My opinion against it [slavery] has always been known, and my practice has been so conformable to my Sentiment that I have always employd freemen both as Domisticks and Labourers, and never in my Life did I own a Slave." Adams continues in his letter, addressing the other "Evils in our Country" that appear to weigh more heavily on him than slavery—namely, the oppression of poor whites in the South. With this dual focus, Adams supported a gradual nonviolent end to slavery in the New World rather than its immediate abolition.[23]

In contrast, Thomas Jefferson, the third US president (1801–9) owned over six hundred enslaved women, men, and children in his lifetime. He was the first to bring approximately twelve enslaved women and men from his Monticello plantation to work as domestics at the new White House. One in particular was fourteen-year-old Ursula Granger Hughes. Jefferson brought the young pregnant teen specifically to learn the cooking trade in hopes of appeasing his taste for French cuisine. Ursula's husband, Wormley Hughes, was the nephew of Sally Hemings, Jefferson's enslaved concubine and the mother of his enslaved children. When Ursula gave birth, she and her baby made history as the first woman to give birth and the first baby born at the White House.

Though often noted that Martha Jefferson Randolph (Jefferson's daughter) was the first to give birth to a child, James, in the White House, "in actuality Hughes' child was the first baby born in the residence."[24] During his presidency, Jefferson also purchased John Freeman to work at the White House as a footman, one who set the table for each meal and helped serve the Jefferson family and their guests.

Jefferson sold Freeman to James Madison, the fourth president (1809–17), in 1809 to serve as Madison's footman while at the White House. Both Jefferson and Madison knew the sale was improper, as Jefferson had stipulated Freeman would be granted his freedom after a certain period of time in Jefferson's service. In addition to acquiring Freeman, Madison brought Paul Jennings, his personal body servant, to Washington with him. Jennings had served him well at his Montpelier estate in Virginia. After Madison's death, Jennings purchased his freedom and was among those who aided enslaved laborers in the *Pearl* escape. In 1865, he published his story about life as a servant in the White House entitled *A Colored Man's Reminiscences of James Madison*. During his lifetime, Madison owned over one hundred enslaved persons.

James Monroe, the fifth president (1817–25), was Jefferson's mentee. He owned nearly eighty enslaved persons in his lifetime and was a member of the American Colonization Society. The society supported the return of freed enslaved persons to the new country of Liberia for US expansion. Liberia's capital city, Monrovia, was named after Monroe. He brought a number of enslaved laborers with him to the nation's capital from his Highland estate in Virginia. Among the domestics were Datcher, Monroe's body servant; unnamed assistants; a valet; a maid; and a cook. After his presidency, Monroe sold most of his enslaved women, men, and children to Southern plantations—namely, the Casa Bianca estate in Jefferson County, Florida, in 1828.

As noted previously, John Quincy Adams, the sixth president (1825–29), followed his father's footsteps and insisted that slavery be an immoral institution. He advocated for the end of slavery from the White House. Adams later became the principal lawyer defending fifty enslaved Africans in their rebellion and pursuit of freedom aboard the *Amistad* vessel (*United States v. Schooner Amistad*). Adams successfully argued and won the case before the US Supreme Court.

Adams's antislavery stance stood in contrast to Andrew Jackson, the seventh president (1829–37). Jackson owned over three hundred enslaved women, men, and children in his lifetime. He brought a large number of enslaved domestics from his Hermitage estate in Tennessee to serve at the White House. While serving as president, he also purchased in Washington enslaved persons from Marine Corps commander Clement Dorsey Hebb. "Old Nancy" was among those he purchased to serve during his term. Old Nancy had three daughters, Gracey, Louisa, and Rachel, and one son, Peter.

Both Martin Van Buren, the eighth president (1837–41), and William Henry Harrison, the ninth president (1841–41), owned enslaved laborers but did not bring any to serve at the White House. Although Van Buren's father was a noted slaveholder, Van Buren owned only one enslaved man, named Tom. In 1814, decades before Van Buren assumed office, Tom ran away, and upon his capture, Van Buren sold him for fifty dollars on condition he would not be harmed by his owner in any way. When Van Buren headed to the White House, he no longer owned Black people.

Although Harrison did not bring his enslaved servants to the White House, when he assumed the presidency, he hired George DeBaptiste, a free Black man, to serve as his steward and valet. DeBaptiste's time at the White House was cut short because Harrison died one month after his inauguration on March 4, 1841. DeBaptiste left Washington and continued his work with the Underground Railroad, which operated out of his barbershop in Ohio.

It is important to note, before serving one month as president, Harrison did take seven of his inherited enslaved laborers with him when he became governor of Indiana. Since Indiana was a free territory at the time, new enslaved persons were not permitted. Harrison, in an attempt to get around this law, changed the status of his enslaved laborers to indentured servants. In 1805, Harrison also adopted a law that allowed slave owners to convert the status of their enslaved laborers to indentured servants for a ninety-year term. In 1810, the law was repealed, freeing all indentured servants after twelve years of service. Harrison, who often described himself as "the ardent friend of Human Liberty," later as a presidential candidate maintained, "Congress had no power to eliminate slavery in the states or the District of Columbia."

Presidents John Tyler (the tenth, 1841–45), James Polk (the eleventh, 1845–49), and Zachary Taylor (the twelfth, 1849–50) followed the other presidents who benefited from owning human beings and making use of them at the White House. Tyler, a fervent proslavery advocate and defender of states' rights, owned over seventy enslaved laborers during his lifetime. He brought a number of them from his Sherwood Forest Plantation in Virginia to Washington. Tyler sold Ann Eliza, the most beloved mother figure among the enslaved community, to help pay for his travels to Washington to assume his Senate seat before becoming president. He was a strong advocate for the expansion of slavery throughout the US, arguing that such pursuits would improve the condition of enslaved persons. He also maintained that free Blacks should not be considered US citizens.

Polk owned about twenty-five enslaved persons. His White House servants included enslaved and free laborers taken from his Polk Place mansion in Tennessee and purchased and hired in Washington. Polk was known for using violence to discipline his enslaved laborers and for separating and selling Black families for a profit. In one rare instance, Polk purchased an enslaved couple, Henry and Mariah Carter, to prevent them from being separated and sold to different buyers. But when Henry and Mariah gave birth to their son, Henry Jr., Polk behaved as expected, separating Henry Jr. from his parents when he was around ten years old and bringing him to Washington to serve as his personal house servant at the White House.

Taylor, a wealthy slaver and army general war hero, owned a home in Baton Rouge, Louisiana, and a plantation called the Cypress Grove (later Buena Vista) along the Mississippi River in Jefferson County, Mississippi. Taylor was a proslavery advocate who maintained that slavery was a constitutional right. During his lifetime, he owned nearly two hundred enslaved persons, some of whom picked cotton and other cash crops and built levees on the Mississippi River. Taylor brought fifteen enslaved workers, some of them children, with him to the White House. Among them, Charles Porter, his body servant who traveled with him during the US's war with Mexico, later died in the White House. Because public opposition to enslaved labor in the White House heightened, Taylor kept his enslaved laborers out of sight to avoid public rebuke. Taylor died in the White House with his servants by his side.

After Taylor, several people who did not own slaves during their lifetimes assumed the office of president, including Millard Fillmore (the thirteenth, 1850–53), Franklin Pierce (the fourteenth, 1853–57), James Buchanan (the fifteenth, 1857–61), and Abraham Lincoln (the sixteenth, 1861–65). However, like some of their predecessors, these presidents more often than not appeared ambiguous in their position on slavery. Their verbal and written opposition to slavery often conflicted with their political practices, resulting in legislative support or the perpetuation of the institution.

Fillmore, for example, signed into federal law on September 18 the 1850 Fugitive Slave Law Act, which enforced stricter penalties than the previous fugitive law. The act prohibited persons from assisting runaways. Those who violated the law faced strict fines and imprisonment. Fugitive slaves were ordered to return to their owners, were denied a jury trial, and were not allowed to testify on their own behalf. Pierce supported the 1854 Kansas-Nebraska Act, which repealed the ban on slavery in Kansas. The 1820 Missouri Compromise set the ban in place. As a result, Pierce and other colonizers upheld that citizens, not Congress, could determine whether a territory or state would permit slavery. This meant the citizens of a given state could decide, by popular vote, whether to continue or allow the practice of slavery within their borders. The move emboldened Southern states and opened doors of possibility for new states joining the Union.

When James Buchanan took office, he remained steadfast in maintaining that the US Constitution supported slavery. During his term in office, the Confederacy was established on February 4, 1861. The Confederacy (or South) was made up of those lower and upper Southern states that seceded from the United States (Union)—South Carolina, Mississippi, Florida, Alabama, Georgia, Louisiana, Texas, and later Virginia, Arkansas, Tennessee, and North Carolina. These proslavery states, especially those in the Lower South, had the highest density of enslaved laborers and plantation agriculture and were unwilling to lose or compromise their economic and sociopolitical leverage. A month after Buchanan's departure from office, the Civil War began.

Soon after Abraham Lincoln took office in 1861, he signed the Emancipation Proclamation (1863) with the intention of freeing not all enslaved persons but only those residing within the "rebellious states" or those "states that had seceded from the United States, leaving slavery untouched in the loyal border-states."[25] Lincoln saw the Emancipation Proclamation as a political war measure intended to take down the Confederacy and not as a full-throated negation of slavery. Yet in truth, Lincoln was more motivated to punish the "rebellious states" than free enslaved persons.

Andrew Johnson, the seventeenth president (1865–69), and Ulysses S. Grant, the eighteenth (1869–77), served their terms after the signing of the Emancipation Proclamation. Johnson and Grant were the last two presidents who owned Black people. Prior to the Emancipation Proclamation's signing, Johnson, a Tennessee slave owner and strong supporter of states' rights, lobbied Lincoln to exclude Tennessee from the Emancipation Proclamation. When Johnson assumed the presidency after Lincoln's death, he remained a staunch supporter of slavery and upheld the notion that freed Blacks had no right to vote or rights to equality under the law. Grant, the successful leader of the Union Army, owned an enslaved man named William Jones. On March 29, 1859, shortly before the start of the Civil War, Grant entered a St. Louis, Missouri, courthouse and handwrote a manumission paper legally freeing Jones from slavery.

These eighteen former presidents' stance on slavery is relevant to the stories of enslaved laborers within Washington, DC, and its surrounding areas. Because of their unwillingness to adjudicate and permanently abolish slavery, its ill effects further perpetuated the exploitation and dehumanization of Black people during slavery and for generations to come. Their firm stance in support of the institution or their ambiguous duplicitous inaction contributed to the nation's overall attitude about the worth of Black people. It also helped foster an ethos of disrespect regarding Black people's potential, then and now, as citizens of the United States.

## The US Capitol

As with the White House, when construction began on the US Capitol in 1793, the area consisted of unpaved roads, rustic landscapes, and emerging slave pens. L'Enfant envisioned placing the Capitol on the east end of his Grand Avenue on the crest of a hill known as Jenkins Heights or Jenkins Hill. He saw the hill as "a pedestal waiting for a monument."[26] The monument became the US Capitol, the legislative branch of the US government, and the permanent seat of Congress. In 1793, President Washington laid the first ceremonial cornerstone of the Capitol, dubbing the area during the Masonic ceremony as Capitol Hill, a moniker inspired by the Temple of Jupiter Optimus Maximus in ancient Rome, one of most sacred temples on the Capitoline.

After L'Enfant's termination, the commissioners, in consultation with Washington and Jefferson, held a design competition to find his successor. The commissioners accepted the design submitted by Dr. William Thornton (1759–1828), a Scottish physician and self-trained architect from the British West Indies. At a young age, Thornton lived with Quaker relatives in Europe, where he studied medicine in London, Paris, and later Scotland. In 1787, he relocated to Pennsylvania. His lack of formal training did not prevent him from submitting his design, which proved to be more akin to Washington and Jefferson's idea of the Capitol. The plan included a building with three sections: a center section topped with a large dome and two adjoining rectangular sections on each side to house the Senate and the House of Representatives.

On April 2, 1793, Washington, in agreement with Jefferson, wrote to the commissioners applauding the design's "Grandeur, Simplicity, and Beauty," saying, "I approve of the Plan of Doctr Thornton for a Capitol to be erected in the City of Washington."[27] Thornton moved to the nation's capital and was appointed by Washington to serve as one of the commissioners from 1794 to 1802. When Jefferson assumed the presidency, he appointed Thornton to head the US Patent and Trademark Office, a position he held until his death in 1828.

In 1793, the commissioners, having rejected Étienne Sulpice Hallet's (Stephen Hallet) submission, hired the French designer to study Thornton's plan and make revisions where needed and also to supervise and estimate the cost of the Capitol construction.[28] But conflicts soon ensued, resulting in Hallet's termination in 1794. A succession of other persons replaced Hallet. These men and the years they assumed supervision of construction or served as chief architect are as follows: George Hadfield (1795), James Hoban (1798), Benjamin Henry Latrobe (1803 and 1815, second chief architect), Charles Bulfinch (1818, third chief architect), and Thomas Ustick Walter (1851, fourth chief architect). Each of these men played an instrumental role in constructing a specific aspect of the building.

During Hoban's term, the unfinished Capitol opened its doors in 1800. Latrobe saw the building through to completion but was called upon later to serve as the second chief architect when the Capitol nearly burned to the ground during the War of 1812. Latrobe designed and completed the Supreme Court Chamber housed in the Capitol building and Bulfinch, the Library of Congress section. In 1829, the US Capitol building was complete, nearly thirty-six years after its construction began.[29] But the need for more space resulted in hiring Thomas Ustick Walter, who expanded both wings of the Capitol. By the end of the Civil War, the Capitol's expansion was complete. None of these men's efforts could have come into fruition without the help of skilled and unskilled enslaved and free Black workers.

## They Built: Enslaved Black People and the US Capitol

Throughout the various construction phases, enslaved Black people were essential workers in building the seat of governance to which many politicians refer to as the "Temple of Liberty." They also contributed to the expansion project from 1850 until the enforcement of the DC Compensated Emancipation Act in 1862. Between 1790 and 1863, enslaved laborers made up more than 50 percent of the US Capitol construction workforce. At a given time throughout the Capitol construction, an estimated eight hundred or more enslaved Black people helped build or perfect between 1790 and 1826 alone. The federal government turned to enslaved laborers early on. As in the case of the White House, the commissioners rented laborers from nearby slave owners. These essential workers labored from morning to night, serving as axmen and women, blacksmiths, brick makers, bricklayers, carpenters, carters, craftspeople, casters, diggers, glazers, haulers, land clearers, masons, miners, rafters, painters, plasters, quarrymen and women, roofers, sawyers, stonecutters, and other positions.

One of their first essential tasks in preparation for building the Capitol was clearing the lands, a trade many enslaved laborers acquired from West Africa and others from their American-born forbears. Enslaved women, men, and children removed debris, trees, branches, and stumps to allow the formation of new streets. They also cut tress on the hill where the Capitol was slated to stand and dug trenches for the Capitol's foundation. Once the groundwork for the Capitol was clearly defined and ready for construction, skill and unskilled enslaved laborers were incorporated into various phases of the construction and design.

A large number of the enslaved laborers throughout the region served as carpenters, sawyers, stonecutters, brick makers and bricklayers. These laborers were in high demand. Enslaved sawyers did most of the sawing of lumber and the cutting of stone for the Capitol building project. Once cut, enslaved laborers hauled the stone and lumber to the construction site for building the interior walls and floors. Because sawing and cutting was such arduous work, as an incentive, the commissioners suggested that enslaved sawyers and those who worked at sawmills should earn their freedom after serving five to six years. This remained only an idea.

There was also a high demand for brick makers and bricklayers. Enslaved women and children made bricks by molding clay into blocks and stacking them in kilns. Once ready, the bricks were placed in a brick hod (a three-sided box on a long stick) and carried on mostly enslaved men's and boys' shoulders to the bricklayers. The number of bricks in each hod was based on the amount of weight an individual enslaved person (hod/hoddie carrier) could carry. Skilled enslaved and free Black and white bricklayers then laid the bricks for the foundation and walls of the Capitol.

President Washington, an admirer of stone architecture, decided that the White House and the Capitol's exteriors should be faced entirely with sandstone. This proved to be a difficult task for the commissioners because brick was easier to manage and less time consuming to work with and access to clay was closer to the construction site than quarries for stone. One of the closest locations to excavate sandstone was a quarry in Stafford County, Virginia, nearly forty-five miles away. The government later purchased the quarry for $6,000, turning it into a "public" quarry with a supervisor and enslaved laborers. Large numbers of enslaved stoneworkers labored at the Stafford quarry and at the Capitol building site.

In Stafford, enslaved laborers endured the challenging task of excavating the stone from mosquito- and snake-infested Aquia Creek. From morning to night, they continuously chiseled, cut, and pulled until large stone pieces broke from their massive boulders. At the quarry, enslaved laborers continued the process of chiseling the stone with pickaxes until it formed into the desired sandstone for the Capitol's foundation, exterior, and interior walls and columns. One can only imagine how time consuming and difficult it was to refine a large piece of stone into the desired shape to create a habitable structure. Once work ended in the quarry, enslaved laborers helped deliver the stone to the Capitol construction site. One formerly enslaved man, George Pointer, was among those boat owners and captains who carried stone back and forth from the quarry to the district. Once the stone arrived at the Capitol, enslaved laborers assisted skilled masons in setting the stone.

Enslaved laborers, in significant numbers, also painted, glazed, and roofed the Capitol building. Many carved and polished the present-day three-story-high marble columns in Statuary Hall, a large two-story semicircular room devoted to sculptures of well-known Americans. Black people performed various other known and unknown tasks in the heat of the day and the cold of winter. They did so without modern-day equipment, mostly using their hands, garden tools, pickaxes, and saws to help construct the Capitol without pay.

Before 1797, the US government paid slave owners up to $60 per year for each laborer they hired out. In 1797, the amount rose to $70 a year. Enslaved women, men, and children earned on average $5 a month for twelve-hour days, six days a week. Slave owner James Hollingshead Blake received a one-month pay voucher from the US government for his enslaved laborers, Abram and Charles. Abram and Charles worked at the Capitol for ten months. The voucher reads, "The Commissioners of the Federal District' paid James Hollingshead . . . for the hire of Negroes Abram and Charles from 1st Sept. 1 to 1st October 1795–10 Months at 5 Dollars each p mo. . . . . . . . . . . . . . . . . . . Drs. 10.00."

On occasion, the more "generous" owners paid their enslaved laborers a small portion of their earnings. Enslaved women, men, and children who worked on Sundays received minimal pay for working on the Sabbath. Also, some enslaved laborers were allowed to live apart from their owners and hire out their services.

Chart 4.2 is a listing of one hundred slave owners living in and around the nation's capital who hired out their laborers. The list is not exhaustive but rather represents a mere snapshot of those paid by the US government for the "rental" of Black people over a six-year period, from 1795 to 1801.[30] Though the list does not identify the name of the enslaved

## Chart 4.2. Partial list of DC-area slave owners compensated by the US government for renting out their enslaved laborers for the construction of the US Capitol (1795–1801)

| | | | |
|---|---|---|---|
| Adderson, J. | Burns, James | Hollinshead, James B. | Reintzell, Valentine |
| Barber, Ann | Carr, Overton | Hunt, Gladen | Scott, Alexander |
| Barber, Barnard W. | Carroll, Daniel of Dudd | Ireland, Joseph | Scott, Gustavus |
| Barber, Barnett | Cartwright, William | Jackson, Jasper M. | Sewell, Clemont |
| Barber, Luke | Causeen, Gerrard | Jackson, John | Short, Peter |
| Beck, Joseph | Chew, Margaret | Jackson, Joseph | Simmes, Edward |
| Beck, Richard | Dant, Joseph | Johnson, Susannah | Simmes, Joseph |
| Belt, Middleton | Dare, Nathaniel | Kearney, John | Simmes, Mary |
| Belt, Mitchell | Deakins, William | Kent, Richard | Simpson, James |
| Bond, Sarah | Dermott, James R. | Key, James | Slye, J. S. |
| Bond, Thomas | Digges, Ann | Latimer, James | Smallwood, Samuel |
| Boone, Edward | Digges, William | Law, Thomas | Somerville, William |
| Brent, Elizabeth | Dixon, Thomas | Love, Charles | Stone, James |
| Brent, James | Dobson, John | Lynch, John | Sunderland, Benjamin |
| Brent, Jane | Douglass, Robert | Magruder, William B. | Syle, John L. |
| Brent, Mary | Duncanson, William M. | Matthews, Luke F. | Tarlton, Charles |
| Brent, Miss | Fenwick, Bennett | Millard, E. J. | Thomas, Elizabeth |
| Brent, Teresa | Fenwick, George | Mills, Susanna | Thornton, William |
| Briscoe, Samuel | Forrest, Joseph | Mills, William | Turner, Joseph |
| Brooks, Hammett | Graves, Catherine | O'Neill, Bernard | Varnal, Caleb |
| Broome, James | Hammersly, Francis | Parren, Thomas | Walker, Nathan |
| Brown, Catherine | Heard, James B. | Plowden, Edmund | Wolfe, Francis |
| Bryan, William | Heighe, James | Prather, Zephaniah | Wolfe, Thomas |
| Bryon, Richard | Hith, James | Queen, Joseph | Wood, Leonard |
| Burch, Henry | Hoban, James | Reiley, Michael | Young, Robert |

woman, man, or child who contributed to the building of the US Capitol, it is evident by the listing of the owners' names that Black people were working against their will to build the temple of freedom. Washington area elites as well as everyday individuals and families benefited from Black people's free labors.

As enslaved laborers continued working on the capital, Thomas Ustick Walter, the building's fourth architect, replaced the Capitol's wooden dome, designed by Bulfinch, with a 287-foot cast-iron dome.

Walter drew inspiration for his design from Michelangelo's St. Peter's Basilica's dome in Rome. Walter also advocated for his sketch of a sixteen-foot statue inspired by the Roman goddess Libertas (Liberty) to stand at the Capitol dome's apex. In 1855, the federal government commissioned Thomas Gibson Crawford (1814–57), and shortly after, Crawford submitted two statue models, entitled *Freedom Triumphant—in Peace and War* and later *Armed Liberty.* Jefferson Davis, a prominent slave owner and the US secretary of war in charge of the Capitol's construction between 1853 and 1857, rejected Crawford's submissions. Davis was offended by its symbolism of freed enslaved laborers and did not want any representation of American slavery enshrined at the Capitol.[31] To meet Jefferson's needs, Crawford, in 1856, submitted his third design of a statue symbolizing American patriotism and conquest atop a globe encircled with the words "E Pluribus Unum" (out of many, one).[32] Davis approved Crawford's third model, entitled *Triumphant in War and Peace,* later renamed the *Statue of Freedom.* Crawford died after finishing the full-size plaster model, which arrived in the US in six crates and was reassembled in the Capitol in 1859.

The federal government appointed Clark Mills (1810–83), a self-taught sculptor and slaveholder, to cast Crawford's *Statue of Freedom* at his iron foundry in Washington.[33] Mills and his workers struggled with how to disassemble Crawford's 19.5-foot plaster model and transport it from the Capitol to Mills's foundry. The statue remained at the Capitol until one of Mills's enslaved workers, Philip Reid (ca. 1820–92), also a master craftsman, "skillfully devised a method of separating and then casting the individual sections."[34] Reid "figured out that using a pulley and tackle to pull up on the lifting ring at the top of the model would reveal the joints between the sections," thereby allowing the statue to be separated at the joints.[35] As a result, "the statue was successfully separated into its five sections for easier transport to Mills' Foundry." At Mills's foundry, under hazardous, humid, and dirty working conditions, Reid helped cast the bronze statue. Once meant to pay homage to enslaved workers and their freedom, the sculpture owed a part of its successful completion to the skill and ingenuity of an enslaved Black man.[36]

## The Master Caster: Philip Reid and the Capitol Dome

Reid was born into slavery in Charleston, South Carolina. Reid learned how to work with clay and wood from an enslaved elder. Reid was purchased by Mills at a young age for $1,200 at a Charleston, South Carolina, slave market. Mills chose Reid because he displayed craftsmanship and talent for the foundry business. Reid was nearly forty years old when he began working on the *Statue of Freedom*. Reid was joined by other enslaved workers. Despite their significant roles in the building of the Capitol, Reid and others were also victims of pay disparity.

Reid played a pivotal role in not only the disassemblage, transport, and casting of the statue from plaster to bronze but also installing the statue on top of the US Capitol dome. At the time of the installation, Reid had already gained his freedom due to the passage of the DC Compensated Emancipation Act in April 1862.

On December 2, 1863, at noon, the *Statue of Freedom* was raised above the Capitol and affixed to the cast-iron dome. A reporter from the *New York Tribune* described the moment between Reid and the statue, writing in 1863, "The Black master-builder [referring to Reid]

**Figure 4.4.** *The US Capitol and the Installation of the Statue of Freedom, 1863.* Library of Congress.

lifted the ponderous uncouth masses, and bolted them together, joint by joint, piece by piece, till they blended into the majestic 'Freedom' who to-day lifts her head in the blue clouds above Washington, invoking a benediction upon the imperiled Republic! Was there a prophecy in that moment? The slave became the artist and, with rare poetic justice, reconstructed the beautiful symbol of freedom for America."[37] The installation was followed by a thirty-five-gun salute as the Civil War raged on in the background. The firing of thirty-five guns represented the thirty-five states, including Confederate states. In response to the salute, cannons were fired from twelve surrounding military forts. Thereafter, the "flag of the nation" was raised above the center of the dome indicating a successful installation. As the symbol of freedom stood affixed defiantly above the US Capitol dome, weary enslaved and free Black bodies throughout the nation were still under the threat of domestic terrorism.

Although Reid became known as the enslaved man who saved the fifteen-thousand-pound *Statue of Freedom*, he was not sufficiently compensated for his service to the nation. Reid worked six days a week at $1.25 a day—but he himself received no pay except for when he worked on Sundays, a day most enslaved people were not required to work. Reid's owner received his wages and paid Reid for working thirty-three Sundays between July 1, 1860, and May 16, 1861. In short, Reid earned a paltry $41.25 for nearly three years of work on the Capitol and no public recognition of his contribution to the nation.

Upon freedom, Reid changed the spelling of his last name to Reed as a statement of his freedom from Mills and the institution of slavery in the US. He remained in Washington with his wife and son and worked as a self-employed plasterer. On February 6, 1892, the master craftsman Philip Reed died. He was born enslaved and died a free man in the city that exploited his ingenuity and labor. One must wonder what Reed contemplated as he passed the statue atop the Capitol on his way to plastering jobs throughout the city, what it felt like for him to watch onlookers admire the work of his hands with no knowledge that he, a formerly enslaved Black man, played a role in its magnificent creation for which he received meager pay and no public recognition.

Though the *Statue of Freedom* now stood at the apex of the Capitol, its symbolism did not represent those hired out by their owners and forced to build the seat of America's legislative branch under dire conditions without recognition and pay. For these disenfranchised builders and subsequent generations of Black people, the Capitol and the White House were not the only harmful institutions delegitimizing Black existence. The judiciary branch proved to be yet another system of inequality to traverse. One must wonder as Black people were building the Capitol whether these disenfranchised builders knew that they were constructing a space to temporarily house the US Supreme Court and that the decisions made from that windowless chamber would impact their lives and their descendants for generations to come.

Though the US Capitol has undergone renovations since Thornton's original design, figure 4.5, which is an 1860s-era photo from the Library of Congress, represents the contribution of enslaved Black-bodied people involved in the building, rebuilding, and renovation of the Capitol from the 1790s leading into the Civil War.

**Figure 4.5.** *The United States Capitol, c. 1865.* Library of Congress.

## US Supreme Court

In 1800, when the seat of government transferred to its permanent location in Washington, DC, the Supreme Court, the judicial branch of government, did not have a permanent home in the new capital city. Congress agreed to house the court in the US Capitol. At the time, the north wing was the only section of the Capitol near completion. But in 1803, when Latrobe arrived, faulty construction led to an interior redesign. Both the Supreme Court Chamber on the ground floor and the Senate Chamber on the north wing's upper floor needed repairs. In 1810, the court moved into its room and remained there for nearly fifty years. In 1860, the court relocated to the upper chamber, initially occupied by the US Senate, and remained in the Capitol for another seventy-five years. In 1935, the Supreme Court moved to its present location, across the street from the Capitol.

Enslaved laborers were involved in the court's building and restoration process throughout all of its construction phases. Parts of the original stonewall, columns, and room borders where the court met in both the lower and upper chambers were installed with enslaved laborers' help. Given this, it is safe to conclude that laborers already working on the Capitol building project were equally involved in the court's redesign and renovation before and after the War of 1812. These laborers were instrumental in bringing Latrobe's neoclassical vision—a semicircular-shaped courtroom with striking columns—into fruition. Enslaved laborers were used to make, transport, and lay bricks for the vaulted sphere-shaped fireproof ceiling, domes, and columns. Latrobe made use of new materials in his design by integrating marble from the Potomac. During the Capitol's construction, since enslaved laborers were used to excavate, cut, process, transport, and set stone taken from Aquia Creek at Stanford, the same holds for marble taken from the nearby Potomac River. After Latrobe departed, enslaved laborers continued working under Bulfinch's leadership. In 1819, the Supreme Court Chamber was ready for occupancy. In 1860, when the court relocated to the upper chamber, the lower room was converted into a law library.

One must wonder what was going through enslaved laborers' minds while constructing and cleaning the chamber where the justices deliberated and legislated their oppression; what was going through their minds the first day the justices met in their newly renovated room, with Chief Justice John Marshall, a slaveholder, presiding; what it must have felt like for them to build, clean, and polish the highest Court in the land, knowing their fate rested in the hands of people who cared little about their humanity. The majority of the initial justices were slaveholders, proslavery advocates, lukewarm on abolition, or outspoken about Black people's inferiority. How could justice bend toward Black people's emancipation when Chief Justice Marshall believed slavery was evil and "contrary to the law of nature" but owned more than two hundred Black people, which he inherited and purchased, and freed none?

One must wonder what it must have felt like for enslaved Black people to walk throughout the Capitol, among sculpted tobacco leaves and corncobs signifying America's wealth and bounty with no financial assets of their own to show for their labors, only their dignity and a deep yearning for freedom. One must wonder how many times they cried. How many times did they moan when there was nothing left to say? How many mourners' bench prayers did they pray? How many times did they plead with God to smite the men and women who held them in bondage or remained complicit and silent?

One must wonder how many times they held their breath waiting for that moment of vindication, that sign of relief that never came as Marshall read opinion after opinion denying Black people's petition for freedom and justice. *Scott v. London*, 7 US 324 (1806); *Scott v. Negro Ben*, 10 US 3 (1810); *Wood v. Davis*, 11 US 271 (1812); *Mima Queen v. Hepburn*, 11 US 290 (1813); and *Henry v. Ball*, 14 US 1 (1816); and many more, all denied. How could any suit on behalf of freedom have a chance? What chance at freedom did Dred Scott have when Charlotte Dupuy's petition seventeen years earlier before the DC Circuit Court against her owner, Secretary of State Henry Clay, was denied?

In 1836, one year after Chief Justice Marshall's death, Roger Brooke Taney became the chief justice. In 1857, when Scott's case (*Dred Scott v. Sandford*) reached the Supreme Court, the justices ruled 7–2 against him. Taney wrote about the court's majority opinion, finding that neither Scott nor any person of African descent, enslaved or free, were US citizens. Black people, he ruled, were a "subordinate and inferior class of beings . . . and had no rights or privileges but such as those" granted by white people. Taney also concluded Scott's petition for freedom was unconstitutional because the Fifth Amendment protected his owner's property rights, and enslaved laborers were property. Dred Scott died in 1858, merely one year after the Supreme Court decision.

## Conclusion

For centuries, Black lives, from the time of American slavery to the present, have been litigated in the White House, the US Capitol, and the Supreme Court. Although there were key turning points in American history at which the three branches of government tried to right their wrongs against Black people, the trajectory of their decisions and inactions have harmed Black lives. Behind the veil of democracy and freedom, which the nation's capital seeks to project, is the reality of a cruel and calculated antebellum world that held Black people in bondage and used their bodies and minds to build a national metropolis. Black people found little solace from America's three branches of government institutions, which, for the most part, protected the rights of their owners. A grassroots civil rights movement was inevitable. The *Pearl* story with which this chapter opened signals one of those seminal moments when Black people simply had enough and risked their lives to flee crimes against their humanity.

The escape of seventy-six persons aboard the *Pearl* was attempted not because these three branches of government were operating as though Black lives matter. Mary and Emily Edmonson and the others found no recourse in America's justice system. The Declaration of Independence and the US Constitution were not written to grant them the same access, protections, and equalities as their white counterparts. They escaped aboard the *Pearl* with the support of their white allies, Drayton and Sayres, to rid themselves of human bondage in the nation's capital.

Now after an unsuccessful attempt, Mary, Emily, and the others found themselves sitting in a local slave pen awaiting their fate while a crowd of whites stood outside furious, shouting their demise. It did not matter to the white crowd that Mary, Emily, and the others and their forebears spent decades cleaning their homes, serving their meals, and building and polishing the White House, US Capitol, and Supreme Court. What mattered was their source of income fled and the lifestyle to which they felt entitled was in jeopardy. How dare the help rise up and flee. In outrage, the whites rioted in the streets, breaking windows, destroying property, and threatening Black people and their white allies.

Drayton and Sayres were charged with seventy-six counts of theft and seventy-six counts of illegal transportation of slaves. Bail was set at $76,000 ($1,000 for each enslaved person). At trial, both were found guilty and imprisoned for illegal transportation. Drayton was ordered to pay $10,060 in fines.

Fearing another escape attempt and subsequent profit loss, frantic owners of the captured enslaved laborers began selling them to DC slave dealers. Joseph Bruin of Alexandria and his partner, Henry Hill, two known dealers in the area, purchased Mary, Emily, their four brothers, and some of the others.

Mary and Emily's distraught parents, Paul, a free Black man, and Amelia, an enslaved woman, were heart stricken and worried that Bruin and Hill were about to sell their daughters at one of the largest slave markets in New Orleans to endure a cruel life of prostitution. In desperation, Paul raised $1,000 to purchase their freedom, but Bruin refused, foreseeing a higher return on his investment down South. Months later, Mary and Emily were transported to New Orleans and paraded in fancy dresses on auction blocks for sale as prostitutes. Their sale, however, was impeded by the rise of the yellow fever epidemic in the area. Bruin and Hill returned the sisters to their depot in mid-October 1848 until the epidemic waned.

After public outcry from both Blacks and whites and media visibility, Bruin succumbed to mounting pressure and sold Mary and Emily to their father for $2,250. Paul immediately traveled to the Anti-slavery Society in New York to solicit financial assistance. Society members urged him to see renowned abolitionist Reverend Henry Ward Beecher, pastor of Plymouth Church in Brooklyn. Beecher, moved by Paul's plea, appealed to his congregation to fund the sisters' release and later their education.

On November 4, 1848, Mary and Emily Edmonson were freed. The two attended New York Central College in Cortland with the financial support of the congregation and by working as domestics to support themselves. After attending the Slave Law Convention in Cazenovia, New York, in protest of the Fugitive Slave Act of 1850, Mary and Emily became actively involved in the abolitionist movement, sharing public platforms with Frederick Douglass. Within time their paths crossed with Drayton, who after serving four years and four months in prison received a pardon, along with Sayres, from President Fillmore. The two were released in 1852.

Sayres relocated and was never heard from again. Drayton began speaking publicly against slavery. In summer 1857, Drayton checked himself into a room at the Mansion House in New Bedford, Boston, and committed suicide. Imprisonment had left him physically weak, emotionally distraught, and financially ruined. His courageous actions in the face of unjust and cruel adversity bore witness to the arduous and lonesome journey to freedom taken not only by the enslaved but also by their white allies. It was clear from Drayton's ingenuity and courage that the road to freedom for those who are oppressed necessitates the joint efforts of Blacks and whites working together to challenge the nation's government and systems of oppression.

In 1853, Mary Edmonson died. She was twenty years old. Emily, heartbroken, returned to Maryland. She eventually attended the Normal School for Colored Girls in DC and continued speaking publicly against slavery. In 1860, she married Larkin Johnson and purchased a home in Anacostia near Frederick Douglass. On September 15, 1895, forty-seven years after the *Pearl* incident, Emily Edmonson died.

Mary, Emily, and the others who fled viewed the nation's capital through the lens of generations of Black people and their allies, who longed for basic human decency, equality, and freedom. These Black people believed their bodies mattered. They held no nostalgic memories of the nation's capital and its inhabitants who humiliated, tortured, and used their bodies as tools of labor for economic gains. Their recollection of the National Mall was merely one of captivity, exploitation, and betrayal.

Generation after generation, they longed for the day when they could claim their rights to own their bodies. Although their escape attempts were not always successful, they did not shy away from repeatedly risking their lives to secure their freedom. Their stories and countless others reveal how enslaved people labored and resisted in an emerging democratic nation since the day they arrived on Indigenous peoples' soil and quarried the first stones to lay the foundations of the capital city of the new republic.

# CHAPTER FIVE

# Black Laborers
## *Prophetic Abolitionists, and Iconic Institutions in the Nation's Capital*

We pray for his excellency, the governor of this state, for the members of the assembly,
for all judges, magistrates, and other officers who are appointed to
guard our political welfare, that they may be enabled, by Thy
powerful protection,
to discharge the duties of their respective stations with honesty
and ability.

—ARCHBISHOP JOHN CARROLL

It is said that the Negro is ignorant. But why is he ignorant? It comes
with ill grace from a man who has put out my eyes to make a parade
of my blindness,—to reproach me for my poverty when he has
wronged me of my money. . . . If he is poor, what has become of the
money he has been earning for the last two hundred and fifty years?
The Negro helped build up that great cotton power in the South,
and in the North his sigh was in the whir of its machinery, and his
blood and tears upon the warp and woof of its manufactures.

—FRANCES ELLEN WATKINS HARPER

On May 9, 1848, Frederick Douglass stood before a large crowd gathered for the fourteenth annual meeting of the American Anti-slavery
Society at Broadway Tabernacle Church in New York City. By the time

Douglass rose to give his speech, entitled "Triumphs and Challenges of the Abolitionist Crusade," the crowd had dwindled. After standing for several hours, most had grown weary listening to a succession of long-winded speakers, including Douglass. Douglass, annoyed by those exiting during his address, immediately voiced his frustration.

Douglass began retelling the perils of the *Pearl* incident, which had occurred just two weeks earlier. Most were aware of the story and were anxiously awaiting news about the fate of seventy-six fugitive enslaved laborers following their capture and painstaking trek to the slave jail and slave pens. The crowd was also awaiting the fate of the fugitives' white allies, who had courageously aided them on the journey. Douglass, advocating for the runaways, reminded the crowd that "a MAN IS A MAN; that every man belongs to himself and to no one else."[1]

Douglass referred to the *Pearl* incident to emphasize the solidarity among Black and white people who collectively opposed Black people's marginalized status in the US, those who courageously stood against institutionalized racism and involuntary labor and worked to counter disparaging stereotypes and claims about Black people's humanity. Douglass maintained that the new republic's unwillingness to accept Black people's right to freedom and legitimate quest for human decency and justice delegitimized the principles of democracy upon which the young nation was founded. It also exposed the true nature of the US to the world. The crowd, still silent, was now captivated by Douglass's words. To illustrate his point, Douglass held up a large drawing, Richard Doyle's *The Land of Liberty* (figure 5.1), taken from England's *Punch Magazine* (1847).[2] The sketch was a satirical depiction of the duplicitous nature of the United States. Douglass, having captured the crowd's attention, proceeded to interpret the caricature, saying,

> I want to show you how you look abroad in the delectable business of kidnapping and slavedriving . . . a long, lean, gaunt, shrivelled looking creature, stretched out on two chairs, and his legs resting on the prostrate bust of Washington; projecting from behind was a cat-o'-nine tails knotted at the ends; around his person he wore a belt, in which were stuck those truly American implements, a bowie-knife, dirk, and revolving pistol; behind him was a whipping-post, with a naked woman tied to it, and a strong-armed American citizen in the act of scourging her livid flesh with a cowskin. At his feet was another

**Figure 5.1.** *The Land of Liberty: Recommended to the Consideration of Brother Jonathan.* Richard Doyle, *Punch Magazine*, December 13, 1847.

group:—a sale going on of human cattle, and around the auctioneer's table were gathered the *respectability*—the religion represented in the person of the clergy—of America, buying them for export to the goodly city of New Orleans. Little further on, there was a scene of branding—a small group of slaves tied hand and foot, while their patriotic and phil-anthropic masters were burning their name into their quivering flesh. Further on, there was a drove of slaves, driven before the lash to a ship moored out in the stream, bound for New Orleans.

Above these and several other scenes illustrative of the character of our institutions, waved the star-spangled banner. Still further back in the distance was the picture of our gallant army in Mexico, shooting, stabbing, hanging, destroying property, and massacring the innocent with the innocent, not with the guilty, and over all this was a picture of the devil himself, looking down with satanic satisfaction on pass-ing events. Here I conceive to be a true picture of America, and I hesi-tate not to say that this description falls short off the real facts, and of the aspect we bear to the world around us. . . . I have been frequently denounced because I have dared to speak against the American nation, against the church, the northern churches especially, charging them with being the slaveholders of the country.[3]

For Douglass and many other abolitionists, the illustration was a true depiction of the US, a depiction that expressed the experiences of many enslaved and free Black people, including those who boarded the *Pearl* and later headed to slave markets in New Orleans. It also expressed the experiences of their forebears, many of whom had contributed, along with others, to the building and daily maintenance of the National Mall, the White House, the US Capitol, and the US Supreme Court. These women and men also made significant contributions to the Department of the Treasury, the Smithsonian Castle, Georgetown University, and the Library of Congress and Protestant Church housed within the US Capitol build-ing. This is quite important—as is, by extension, the leading (but often unacknowledged) role of Black people in the armed forces and their con-tribution to the building of military installations to preserve American slavery and to protect Americans from enemies, foreign and domestic.

These institutions reflect the young nation's foundational commit-ments and sense of identity. Evinced from its inception and extending to the present day, the nation prioritized and established the Depart-ment of the Treasury for the preservation of the nation's currency, wealth, and capital and the Smithsonian Castle for the preservation of science and artifacts. The nation likewise prioritized and established Georgetown University and other like-minded colleges and universities to preserve historically nuanced and critically informed Western thought. The Library of Congress served as a repository of knowledge, and the fact that church services took place inside congressional chambers signified the prominence of the Protestant Church in the US.

The presence of these five spheres of influence reflects rather ironically the state of Black life in the US. Black people not only played a role in their erection and maintenance; their lives were also determined by the ideologies and practices espoused by what these landmark institutions represented. Black people helped build the Department of the Treasury and the economic infrastructure of the US yet were not granted fair wages and credit for their labors. The Smithsonian Castle stood as a beacon of the preservation and advancement of scientific discovery and research, while Black-bodied people were often the unwilling subjects of their dissection, research, and scientific query or were omitted altogether from their archival preservation. Black people helped build Georgetown University, one of the leading academic institutions in the nation's capital, yet they were denied entrance and equal access to education in the young nation's early inception. Black people helped build and prepare the room where the Library of Congress was housed, yet they were forbidden to read, and writings from their perspective were underrepresented on its shelves. Black people helped build and prepare space inside the Capitol for Protestant worship services, while throughout the nation, churches were complicit in their subjugation and vilified African traditional and Islamic religious traditions. These five institutions, situated on or within a three-mile radius of the National Mall, are a mere microcosm of a larger institutional network that adversely affected Black lives. Each of these institutions brings to light how the loathing of Black people in the US leads to the institutional denigration of Black people and the co-optation of their contributions.

## The Department of the Treasury

Following the meeting of the First Congress in New York on March 4, 1789, the new government established a permanent institution for managing government finances.[4] Washington appointed Alexander

Hamilton as the secretary of treasury because of Hamilton's financial and managerial astuteness.[5] Though it remains questionable whether Hamilton owned enslaved individuals, the nation's first secretary of treasury played a central role in bartering, purchasing, and selling Black people on behalf of family members and friends. But Hamilton is not memorialized in front of the present-day Treasury Department Building in our nation's capital for his slave deals. He is lauded for his development of America's financial system.[6] When the seat of government transferred from Philadelphia to the nation's capital in 1800, the Treasury Building was the only federal structure completed and ready for occupancy. Hamilton died before seeing America's financial epicenter completed in the nation's capital.

Between 1795 and 1869, seven architects were called upon to build, rebuild, and expand the building. Over the course of its seventy-four-year history, the building underwent a series of additions and renovations. George Hadfield was the first chief architect of the Treasury Building. James Hoban, the White House designer and US Capitol building construction supervisor, also oversaw the Treasury Building's construction during the initial production phase. Construction began in 1795, and by 1800, the two-story building measuring one hundred and forty-seven feet in length and made of sandstone quarried from Aquia Creek by enslaved hands was complete. The first floor had sixteen rooms, and the second floor had fifteen. The fifty-seven-foot-wide building, which stood at the southeast end of the White House, became the financial headquarters for the US government.

A year later, the Treasury Building was engulfed in flames and partially destroyed. In 1806, Benjamin Henry Latrobe, second chief architect of the US Capitol, who also renovated and fireproofed parts of the Capitol building, renovated and fireproofed the Treasury Building, including the vault. The fireproofing proved fruitful when the Treasury Building was again struck by fires during the War of 1812 and when a former clerk set the building ablaze to destroy incriminating pension records in 1833. Between 1836 and 1842, the designs of Latrobe's protégé, Robert Mills, for the east and center wings were implemented and completed. Thirteen years later, Ammi B. Young and Alexander H. Bowman were selected to extend and enlarge the south wing. That project was completed in 1861. In 1864, Isaiah Rogers's construction of the west wing was finalized, and

Alfred B. Mullet's modifications to the west and south wings ended in 1869. Mullet was also instrumental in designing and completing the north wing, which included a grand Italian palazzo–style bank called the Cash Room. The Cash Room quickly became a national symbol of the new nation's banking system.

By 1870, the Treasury Building was firmly established in the nation's capital. Its presence is due in large part to Hamilton, its designers, and those enslaved and free Black laborers who participated in its construction. Although later employment records from 1836 to 1869 highlight enslaved and free Black laborers' role in various aspects of the building process, it is reasonable to conclude they were also involved in the construction process from the very start in 1795. It is likewise reasonable to conclude that since the commissioners, Hoban, Latrobe, and other supervisors and designers used enslaved laborers to build the White House, US Capitol, and other federal buildings, these men continued similarly with the construction of the Treasury Building.

Presumably enslaved laborers cleared lands at ground zero, set the building's foundation, built its infrastructure, and carried and installed iron columns and beams used to reinforce the building's brick vaults. It is reasonable to conclude that since enslaved and free laborers loaded stone onto ships and unloaded and carried it to the White House construction site, such laborers were used to do the same for the nearby Treasury Building. And equally reasonable is the possibility that they hauled away the ashes and rubbish after the Treasury Building was engulfed in flames in 1801, 1814, 1833, and 1851. They also were instrumental in firing and laying the bricks and carrying the thirty-six-foot-tall columns that grace the breadth of the building.

Black men, enslaved and free, worked with white immigrant workers on the Treasury Building between 1795 and 1869. Figures 5.2 and 5.3 bring to life a fraction of those enslaved and free Black men who toiled on the ground of the young nation's financial epicenter to help build the physical structure that housed the currency and mission of American commerce. These photographs, taken after 1836, are a part of the American Antiquarian Society collection at the Library of Congress and the National Archives. They are a visual representation of Black people's presence and a workforce delineated by race, pay, and social standing.

**Figure 5.2.** *An Integrated Workforce at the Treasury Department Including Enslaved Black Laborers.* American Antiquarian Society, Library of Congress and National Archives.

## Freedman's Savings and Trust Company

The depiction of Black men laboring at ground zero of the Department of the Treasury is an inescapable reminder of Black people's sacrifice and toil throughout the nation. Buried beneath the rubbish is also a reminder of how this nation treated them. When the Department of the Treasury opened its doors in 1869, enslaved laborers had already been officially freed by the ratification of the Thirteenth Amendment, which occurred in 1865. The emancipation of nearly four million Black people laid bare the daunting disparities in economic status and access to capital between Black people, enslaved and free, and those in power and landholders with assets.

With limited options, millions of formerly enslaved Black people began working as sharecroppers or tenant farmers throughout the district and nation, many of them on the farms of their former masters. As such, they signed an annual labor contract binding them to work

**Figure 5.3.** *Black Men Working on the Front Steps of the Treasury Building.*
Library of Congress.

long hours for minimal pay. However, most never lived to see and enjoy
the monetary fruits of their labors due to the costs of living and housing, which far exceeded their income. Those who broke their contract
were often arrested and imprisoned. Once entrapped in the prison system, they were made to work for state and federal governments clearing
lands, building roads and railroads, and laboring on construction sites.
The imprisoned workforce became known as chain gangs, a new form
of slave labor, what some call "slavery by another name," where persons
were forced to work chained together building federal, state, and local
cities' infrastructures. Many worked year-round, during both humid
summers and brutally cold winters.

Outside of sharecropping and chain gangs, some former enslaved
laborers were hired to work for low wages at construction sites throughout the district. Others worked as domestics, porters, cooks, janitors,
seamstresses, carpenters, nurses, carters, drivers, nannies, butlers, and
other skilled and unskilled positions. Those who fought in the Civil
War and returned home could rely on their war pensions as a source

of income. As formerly enslaved Black people began acquiring revenue from various forms of work, the need for a financial institution for their holdings became more urgent, especially since they were not allowed to open accounts at white banks.

Aware of the inequities, a group of white abolitionists, philanthropists, and business leaders urged Congress to respond to the plight of the disenfranchised. On March 3, 1865, Congress passed and President Lincoln signed into law the Freedmen's Bureau Bill, which provided basic human needs, education, and legal assistance for formerly enslaved Black people. On that same day, as part of the Freedmen's Bureau, Congress and the president also chartered the Freedman's Saving and Trust Company (Freedman's Savings Bank) to provide Black people a safe place to deposit their earnings, build their assets, and work toward a stronger and sustainable economic future.[7]

On April 4, 1865, nearly a month after the bill was passed, Freedman's Savings Bank opened its first banking institution in New York City. The highly publicized opening and subsequent success attracted nearly twenty-three thousand depositors and led to branches being established throughout the nation in cities with large Black populations. By 1867, the bank had moved its headquarters from New York to the nation's capital on the southeast corner of Lafayette Square directly across from the White House and the Department of the Treasury. From this vantage point, Black customers were sure to get a memorable glimpse of the White House and the Department of the Treasury.

Over time, the bank grew to thirty-seven branch offices in seventeen states and over seventy thousand account holders. The depositors were primarily Black low-wage earners and civil war veterans. They opened accounts with amounts ranging from $5 to $60 in hopes of a new beginning and better opportunities in the postslavery era. Prominent Black people, like Douglass, also opened accounts, as did Black businesses, schools, colleges, churches, and other religious institutions. Chart 5.1, taken from Walter L. Fleming's 1906 study on Freedman's Saving Bank, identifies the yearly deposits by Black account holders from 1866 to 1870. In March 1874 alone, Black people's collective deposits and saving power totaled $57,000,000.[8]

A brighter future for Black people in the US seemed to be dawning. They were now free and on a path of financial solvency and security, which translated into self-ownership and business ventures.

## Chart 5.1. Total business of the Freedman's Savings Bank

The following table, compiled from the various reports of the bank and of the government, shows the entire business of the bank to 1874:

TOTAL BUSINESS OF THE FREEDMEN'S BANK.

| Years ending with March. | Total Deposits. | Deposits each year. | Balance due Depositors. | Gain each year. |
|---|---|---|---|---|
| 1866 | $   305,167.00 | $    305,167.00 | $   199,283.42 | $   199,283.42 |
| 1867 | 1,624,853.33 | 1,319,686.33 | 366,338.33 | 167,054.91 |
| 1868 | 3,582,378.36 | 1,957,535.03 | 638,299.00 | 271,960.67 |
| 1869 | 7,257,798.63 | 3,675,420.27 | 1,073,465.31 | 435,166.31 |
| 1870 | 12,605,781.95 | 5,347,983.32 | 1,657,006.75 | 583,541.44 |
| 1871 | 19,592,947.36 | 7,347,165.41 | 2,455,836.11 | 798,829.36 |
| 1872 | 31,260,499.97 | 11,281,313.06 | 3,684,739.97 | 1,227,927.67 |
| 1873 | ............ | ............ | 4,200,000.00 | ............ |
| 1874 | 57,000,000.00 | ............ | 3,299,201.00 | ............ |

The interest paid on deposits amounted to the sums given in the following table:

INTEREST PAID BY FREEDMEN'S BANK :

| | |
|---|---|
| To January 1, 1867,......................... | $ 1,985.47 |
| For 1867 .................................. | 9,521.60 |
| For 1868, to November 1,.................. | 24,544.08 |
| November 1, 1868 to November 1, 1869 ...... | 43,896.98 |
| "      1, 1869 "      "      1, 1870 ...... | 59,376.20 |
| "      1, 1870 "   March    1, 1871 ...... | 20,840.32 |
| March 1, 1871 to Jan. 1, 1873............... | 122,215.17 |
| Total ................................ | $262,379.82 |

## Two Steps Forward, Several Steps Backward: They Built, They Saved, and They Still Got Swindled

Yet after the bank moved its national headquarters to the nation's capital, Congress made changes to the board of trustees of the Freedmen's Bureau, appointing all white men with connections to politicians and businesses. To sustain trust in the community, the board gradually hired local Black leaders—politicians, ministers, and business leaders—to work as bank cashiers and to serve on the advisory board, the latter in name only, however. The bank took Black people's capital seriously by offering Black communities hands-on training, basic financial literacy, and banking skills. Black people felt not only a sense of security depositing their monies in the bank but also a sense of pride when the bank began employing them in large numbers to work in branch offices nationwide.

Some of the all-white male board members convinced Congress to expand the bank's power by modifying the bank's charter. The original charter did not permit the bank to approve loans of any kind, including personal, business, or real estate.[9] The bank served only as a savings institution. Congress accepted the members' recommendations. At first hopeful that they could acquire loans for various purposes, Black people's hopes were crushed when the board denied their loan applications. What had happened? After receiving permission from Congress to distribute loans to clients, the board had instituted stringent rules and requirements—with the purpose of deterring Black people from acquiring loans. White applicants, on the other hand, were readily approved by the board.

The board also sought more control of the bank's holdings and sought to remove bank oversight from the Office of the Comptroller of the Currency (OCC). They wanted the board and Congress to assume oversight of bank operations. Meanwhile, Black people thought that their holdings at Freedman's Savings Bank were secure because they were backed by the US government. Unbeknownst to the bank's account holders, however, the board slowly assumed control and oversight of the bank's operations. The change in the bank's charter soon led to risky investments. Some board members used the bank's funds to obtain unsecured loans for themselves and their families and friends. They also invested half of the bank's deposits in speculative stocks, bonds, and real estate.[10] Inevitably, the lack of oversight by Congress resulted in fraud, mismanagement, abuse—and loss. Henry Cooke, chairman of the bank's finance board, was among those members who used Black people's life savings to advance his own economic interests. Along with other board members and associates, he invested the bank's holdings in railroad companies and DC real estate.[11] In 1866, Cooke and other Georgetown proprietors purchased the Seneca Quarry and renamed it the Seneca Sandstone Company. Cooke was hoping to buy influence in Washington and profit from the post–Civil War economic housing boom in the nation's capital. To fund the quarry's operations, Cooke took out several unsecured loans from the bank.

Cooke and the other quarry owners also sold stock in their quarry company at half price to Republican congressmen, their colleagues, and Ulysses Grant one year before his presidency. Given Cooke's shady dealings, people were shocked when Grant appointed Cooke as the first governor of Washington, DC, in 1871, two years into his presidency. In addition to Seneca Sandstone Company, Cooke also became entangled in an investment with his brother, Jay. Jay, an associate of Grant and other politicians, was the owner of Jay Cooke and Company, a bank that opened in 1861 to support Union war efforts. Cooke approved a large, unsecured loan from Freedman's Savings Bank to help keep his brother's bank afloat and for the two to invest in the Northern Pacific Railway.

The men nearly depleted the bank's assets, and Congress seemed to turn a blind eye to their malfeasance, until public outcry in 1873 forced them to launch a congressional investigation with the aid of the OCC. Meanwhile, several months after the theft was discovered, some of the trustees asked Frederick Douglass to serve as the bank's president and "quietly" oversee the bank's operations. Douglass accepted without knowing the severity of the corruption. He quickly realized that the bank had become what he called "the Black man's cow and the white man's milk," a place where Black people's savings funded privileged men's ambitions. Douglass concluded that the trustees had hired him as a means of reassuring the public and to help save the trustees from a crisis of their own making. Douglass publicly expressed that the trustees had knowingly "married [him] to a corpse."

After six weeks, Douglass ended his service, concluding that Freedman's Savings Bank was "no longer a safe custodian of the hard earnings" of his people. Douglass had invested $10,000 of his personal money to help save the institution, but to no avail—the bank was "insolvent and irrecoverable." Douglass immediately advised Hon. John Sherman, chairman of the Senate Committee on Finance, of the "rampant corruption" and "risky investments across industries being made with depositors' savings."[12] But the trustees turned a deaf ear to Douglass and continued urging Blacks to open accounts. After much debate, the Senate Committee on Finance sided with Douglass, and on June 29, 1874, Freedman's Savings and Trust closed its doors forever.

A few trustees tried to use Douglass as a scapegoat and blamed him for the bank's downfall, but their attempts failed. And though the congressional inquiry led to a recommendation that Cooke and his coconspirators be indicted, the men received no jail time or penalty for their crimes. Cooke resigned as governor and remained in the area. To add insult to injury, in 1875 he received a substantial sum of money as the sole executor of the will of Salmon P. Chase, the twenty-fifth secretary of the treasury.[13] Continuing the pattern, clearly both Cooke and Chase had benefited financially from the hard work of Black people, especially those formerly enslaved and military veterans.

In 1876, Freedman's Savings Bank, along with Seneca Sandstone Company, officially went bankrupt. The bank, which once had an A1 rating (strong financial solvency), closed its doors. The most solvent branches were located in Augusta, Baltimore, Charleston, Louisville, Memphis, Mobile, Nashville, New York, Norfolk, Richmond, Savannah, Vicksburg, and Wilmington[14]—all cities with large Black populations. The bank's closing "did more than shatter the dreams of Douglass and others with high hopes in its future. It left 61,144 Black depositors with losses of nearly $3 million."[15] In compensation, the government promised to reimburse depositors up to "62% of their savings," but many depositors received no compensation. In 1899, the Freedman's Savings Bank headquarters was torn down and replaced by the Department of the Treasury Annex. Forgotten in the debris is the remarkable story of the rise and fall of Black capital generated by Black people between 1865 and 1875. Also forgotten were the enslaved and free Black people who helped build the US Department of the Treasury of the new republic.

On January 7, 2016, the seventy-sixth secretary of the treasury, Jacob J. Lew, in an effort to honor what has been forgotten, commemorated the 150th anniversary of the Freedman's Savings Bank by renaming the Department of the Treasury Annex the Freedman's Bank Building. At the dedication ceremony, Lew noted that Freedman's Savings Bank's legacy serves as a reminder to "continue striving for greater financial inclusion for all Americans—particularly those in underserved communities—so that they can share in the benefits of our growing economy."[16]

## Smithsonian Institution (the Smithsonian Castle)

The bustling nefarious slave pen called the Yellow House once stood near today's red sandstone Smithsonian building known as the Smithsonian Castle.[17] The pen's owner, William H. Williams, publicly engaged in slave trading until the practice was abolished in the district in 1850. Though the slave trade had ended, it was still legal to own human beings in the nation's capital until 1862. When construction began on the Smithsonian in 1847, hundreds of slave coffles were still making their way daily through the National Mall until they reached the Yellow House and other slave pens. As with other federal buildings that filled the DC landscape that slave coffles and enslaved builders traversed, the Smithsonian was another institution Black people helped build. And like other such buildings, the US government sanctioned its construction.

James Smithson, a British scientist, bequeathed his estate to the US for the erection of a research-oriented institution bearing his name.[18] Smithson devoted his life to scientific inquiry, specifically of chemistry, mineralogy, and geology. He had never visited the US but long admired its promise as a budding new nation. On June 27, 1829, Smithson died, leaving his estate to his nephew, Henry James Hungerford, who was directed to give the estate to the US if he died without heirs: "I then bequeath the whole of my property . . . to the United States of America, to found at Washington, under the name of the Smithsonian Institution, an Establishment for the increase & diffusion of knowledge among men."[19]

On July 1, 1836, Congress approved Smithson's gift. Two years later, eleven boxes of 104,960 gold coins, along with Smithson's mineral collection, library, scientific notes, jewelry, and personal belongings, arrived in Washington in August 1838. The coins were melted down and minted into US currency at the US Department of the Treasury. The coins' estimated monetary value was $510,000 (roughly $14 million in 2018). On August 10, 1846, Congress signed into law the establishment of the Smithsonian Institution. On May 1, 1847, accompanied by Masonic ceremony and ritual, the first cornerstone of the Smithsonian Institution, designed by James Renwick, was laid. A metal plate bearing the names of President James Polk and other politicians and wealthy persons was installed beneath the stone. Within time, many more red stones arrived from a quarry in Seneca, Montgomery County, Maryland, to build the Smithsonian. The sandstone's striking redness is what set the Smithsonian apart from the White House, the US Capitol, the Treasury Building, and other buildings erected during the early nineteenth century.

The Peter family of Georgetown owned the Seneca Quarry from 1781 to 1866. In the late 1820s, John Parke Custis Peter, Martha Washington's great-grandson, turned the quarry into a lucrative commercial business, building a stonecutting mill and winning bids to supply stone for the Smithsonian and building projects throughout the city.

Enslaved laborers belonging to the Peters were instrumental in excavating the red sandstone from the quarry for various projects. A few of the workers were either a part of Martha Washington's dowry or passed down through subsequent generations, eventually reaching Martha's great-grandson. Anthropologist Mark Auslander matches names of dowry slaves listed as children or infants on George Washington's inventory of enslaved laborers in 1799 with names listed on John Parke Custis Peter's inventory upon his death in 1848. Among the names common to both lists were Sandy, George, Davy, John, Celia (Cecilia), and Eliza (Elizabeth) and her three children.[20] Some of these workers, along with others, were directly involved in quarrying stone from Seneca. Such is also supported by oral accounts from present-day descendants and community members who live near the quarry and recall stories of Black workers.

When John Parke Custis Peter died in 1848, the family retained ownership of the quarry until 1866, under the management of Gilbert Cameron and James Dixon, supervisor of the Smithsonian construction project. In 1866, the Cooke brothers purchased the quarry for $70,000 using money from the Freedman's Savings Bank scandal. The quarry went bankrupt shortly afterward. Enslaved laborers likely continued working at the quarry after Peter's death until slavery ended, and free Black workers continued working until the quarry temporarily closed.

For many laborers, work at the quarry was long and arduous. Laborers quarried blocks for the Smithsonian from the Seneca rock face and milled them. After milling, the blocks were transported (by barge) down the canal to Georgetown, then onward down the Potomac River to the nation's capital, towards the National Mall, then, finally the Smithsonian construction site.[21]

It is unknown how many enslaved and free laborers excavated stone during the Smithsonian's construction from 1847 to 1855. What is somewhat measurable is the amount of stone used at different points of the building process. Even before the Chesapeake and Ohio (C&O) Canal was completed, Cameron had enslaved laborers preparing sandstone blocks in anticipation of transport.[22] Once the canal opened, workers were tasked with shipping "as much rock as possible."[23] Cameron had, on one occasion, "almost 15,000 feet of stone ready to send" to Washington.[24] The first boat from Seneca, referred to as Scow No. 1, carrying thirty-five perches of rough stone for the Smithsonian Castle, passed through Georgetown on June 12, 1847.[25] Thirty-five perches are equivalent to nearly 9,600 square feet, the size of nearly two professional US basketball courts.[26] Given the amount of stone used to build the Smithsonian, it is likely that large numbers of enslaved and free workers were involved in the excavation process. This includes some of John Parke Custis Peter's laborers as well as those hired out by their owners and free Blacks.

The shipping of stone from the quarry to the nation's capital was only possible thanks to the C&O Canal. The C&O was a 184-mile waterway known as the Grand Old Ditch. It operated along the Potomac from Washington to Cumberland, Maryland, from 1831 to 1924. In addition to excavating stone, John Parke Custis Peter's workers likely helped construct a portion of the C&O near his quarry by removing "twenty thousand cubic yards of soil" at Peter's quarry base, making it convenient for shipping the red sandstone.[27] The men were also involved in constructing the Seneca Aqueduct (Aqueduct No. 1), the only red-sandstone, three-arched bridge crossing Seneca Creek, which also operated near Peter's property. The aqueduct had a canal lock (Lock No. 24) to raise and lower boats, ships, and other water vessels. More than likely, Peter's enslaved laborers and other Black men in the area played a role in building the canal as well as the aqueduct and lock.

Given this, it is also conceivable that enslaved and free Black workers assisted in digging the holes needed to construct the entire 184-mile canal and also in other aspects of the canal construction, including its ten other aqueducts and seventy-three canal locks. Logically, Peter and other slaveholders along the 184-stretch of the canal and the US government would have hired out or used their free labor force rather than rely solely on paid white workers. Throughout the canal's operating history, Black workers were used to make canal repairs, operate the locks, boats, and bridges, and care for the horses and mules.

As this red sandstone began arriving at the nation's capital, the construction of James Renwick Jr.'s design of the Smithsonian got underway.

It is not known whether enslaved and free people were involved in the actual building of the Smithsonian. Although there are records of white workers, scant documentation has been uncovered on enslaved and free laborers' direct contribution. Yet given that enslaved and free persons helped build other sites in the nation's capital, it is likely they did so on the Smithsonian too, though one must wonder why any mention of their contribution is absent from the records. Were some of the same men who labored in quarrying, shaping, and transporting the stone also involved in the building of the Smithsonian? In 1855, eight years after the red sandstone was quarried by Black hands, the Smithsonian Castle (figure 5.4) was complete.[28]

**Figure 5.4.** *The Smithsonian Institution.* Library of Congress.

## Inside the Walls of the Smithsonian: Solomon Galleon Brown

Once the Smithsonian was built, laborers were needed to work inside the building. Little information exists on the Smithsonian's Black workers, with the exception of Solomon Galleon Brown, the first Black person to work at the institution from 1852 to 1906. Brown, a noted scientific technician, poet, and lecturer, was a self-taught free man. He was born on February 14, 1829, in Washington, DC, to former enslaved parents, Isaac and Rachel Brown. In 1833, his father died, which inevitably led to his family becoming homeless. At age fifteen, Brown worked for the Trees, a prominent white family. While serving in the household, Brown asked Lambert Tree, the assistant postmaster of the DC post office, to help him gain employment. Brown was hired, and while working, he met three men, Joseph Henry, the first secretary to the Smithsonian; Samuel F. B. Morse, an inventor and painter; and Alfred Vail, a machinist and inventor. Brown assisted the men in the development of the first magnetic telegraph that ran from the nation's capital to Baltimore, Maryland.

In 1852, Henry, impressed with Brown's work, hired him as a general laborer at the Smithsonian. Brown built exhibit cases, tended to furniture maintenance, and completed other tasks, proving to be an asset to Henry and Spencer Fullerton Baird, the Smithsonian's assistant secretary. By 1866, Brown was supervising Black messengers, drivers, watchmen, and janitors, who were designated as "common laborers" at the Smithsonian. After much prodding from leaders in the Black community and with Baird's support, Henry promoted Brown to registrar in charge of transportation, registry, and storage in 1869. Brown was charged with collecting and storing animal specimens and artifacts for the institution's research.

From the first day he entered the Smithsonian, Brown read more and more books in literature and natural history and became well versed as a naturalist, scientist, illustrator, lecturer, philosopher, and poet. Baird and others relied on him to draw maps and diagrams and illustrate specimens for their scientific lectures at the Smithsonian and other locations. On January 10, 1855, Brown presented his first lecture on entomology at the Young People's Literary Society and Lyceum and thereafter continued lecturing throughout the region on entomology, geology, and the telegraph. His scientific knowledge and poems brought him recognition and respect in the Black community.[29]

Brown was keenly aware of the lack of recognition and acceptance of his achievements, intellect, fortitude, and contributions to the Smithsonian. He alludes to such in an essay published in *Men of Mark: Eminent, Progressive, and Rising*, noting how he received no monetary compensation and recognition for helping create the first magnetic telegraph. Brown sheds light on the historical injustice and privileges given to white men like Samuel F. B. Morse, Alfred Vail, and others who draw on Black people's talents and intellect to advance their agendas and who receive "accolades, fame, and wealth," while the contributions of the American "negro [*sic*] who materially assisted" are largely omitted. Brown knew his promotion within the Smithsonian neither solved the race problem nor changed the hearts of men associated with the Smithsonian that viewed Black people as intellectually inferior. He articulates such in the poem "He Is a Negro Still: The Uncompromising Prejudice towards the Negro American." An excerpt reads,

> "Why don't the Negro keep his place," / Not force himself upon our race? / It matters not what men may say, / They are inferior in every way. . . .
> He's well enough among his race, / And this alone is his true place; / We'll not regard his fame or skill, / But hold him as a Negro still.
> Suppose he has inventive art, / The world acknowledge he is smart, / Intelligent and fills the bill? / He's nothing but a Negro still.

## Brown's Departure: A Tree in My Name

Following Henry's departure from the Smithsonian in 1878, Baird became the second secretary of the Smithsonian and served in that capacity until 1887. When Baird died, the third Smithsonian secretary, Samuel Pierpont Langley (1887–1906), put Brown in his place by significantly decreasing his pay and demoting him to the status of "common laborer." Brown's world spiraled as he lost his privileges and status at the Smithsonian. Debts mounted, and the threat of returning to his desolate origins was becoming a pressing reality. Because of the demotion and decrease in pay, Brown could not retire as planned and worked several years beyond his eligible retirement to make ends meet.[30] On February 14, 1906, Brown retired after fifty-four years of service to the Smithsonian, and on June 24, 1906, he died in his home in Anacostia. No plaques, stones, or memorials were raised for his service. Nearly one hundred years later, in 2004, the Smithsonian National Museum of Natural History planted trees in his honor on the museum grounds. Twelve years later, the National Museum of African American History and Culture, which opened in 2016, recognized Brown for his service by designating a room in his honor inside the halls of the Smithsonian.

Today, the Smithsonian Castle, whose existence is due in part to enslaved and free Black people's contribution, is the first and "most iconic of all the Smithsonian's 769 facilities, including nineteen museums, nine research centers, a National Zoo, and other establishments."[31] Eleven of the nineteen Smithsonian buildings stand in areas within the National Mall once occupied by slave pens, slave markets, and slave-owning plantations and farms.

## Georgetown University

On October 25, 1791, President George Washington stood before the US Senate and House of Representatives in Philadelphia to deliver his first address to members of the Second Congress. In referencing US treaties for the acquisition of Indigenous peoples' lands and the dissenting mood among Indigenous peoples, Washington offered the following recommendation. He stated, in addition to "efficacious provision . . . for inflicting adequate penalties upon all those who . . . shall infringe the treaties, and endanger the peace of the Union," the US government should implement "a System corresponding with the mild principles of religion and philanthropy towards an unenlightened race of men, whose happiness materially depends on the conduct of the United States, would be as honorable to the national character as conformable to the dictates of sound policy."[32] Five months later, on March 20, 1792, John Carroll (1735–1815) responded to Washington's presidential address before Congress. Carroll, who delivered the prayer at Washington's inauguration, was the son of a wealthy Catholic slave owner and one of the original land proprietors who helped Washington secure land to build the nation's capital. In a letter of March 20, 1792, Carroll suggested to his friend Washington a strategy for "handling" the Indigenous peoples:

> The subscriber has the honour of stating, that the President in opening the present session of Congress, was pleased to express a sentiment,

suggesting the propriety of introducing a system of conduct towards the Indians within, and contiguous to the United States, *corresponding with the mild principles of religion and philanthropy*, that experience has shewn, how much this would contribute to put a period to those cruelties and devastations, which have distressed so often the frontier inhabitants of these States; that a few of those Indian tribes having received formerly some instruction in the principles and duties of Christianity, their manners became more gentle, their warfare less savage, and a strong attachment was formed in their minds towards the nation, to whose provident care they were indebted, for enabling the ministers of religion to subsist amongst them; that at present, some worthy and respectable clergymen are willing and desirous of devoting themselves to the charitable employment of reviving and continuing amongst those Indians the lessons of religion and morality, which were deliver'd to them formerly; that a proposal so benevolent in its object, and promising so much advantage to the United States, was warmly encouraged by the subscriber, who flattered himself, that these charitable men would find some provision for their subsistance, during their dangerous and painful employment, in the produce of a body of land.[33]

At the time Carroll penned these words, he was serving as the first Roman Catholic bishop of Baltimore. During his tenure, Carroll worked tirelessly to establish seminaries for native-born white men, mostly of Irish and Italian descent, seeking the Catholic priesthood within the Jesuit order. In 1808, Carroll became the first archbishop in the United States. Under his leadership, the Roman Catholic Church became firmly rooted in the US, with the highest percentage of Catholics residing in Maryland and Pennsylvania.

Though Carroll was a proponent of religious freedom, he tolerated the manipulative treatment of Indigenous peoples and enslaved people in the mainland North American colonies and encouraged their Christianization only because he saw it as an instrument of civility and docility. He also advocated for religious instruction for enslaved communities by European and American missionaries and ministers. Most religious leaders sought to convince reluctant owners that religious instruction would advance the owners' cause by rendering the enslaved persons submissive and less prone to revolt.

In 1789, the same year in which Carroll was consecrated bishop of Baltimore, he also acquired sixty acres of hillside land overlooking a village and the Potomac River. The area was once worked by enslaved laborers for the production and exportation of tobacco. Today, the area is known as Georgetown. The area's namesake was King George II, and its port was the biggest tobacco exporting port in the country.

Carroll was not interested in producing crops on his newly acquired land. The young nation's independence from Britain had ushered in the rise of academic institutions of higher learning that were founded by Protestant Church bodies or clergymen, European monarchs, and American politicians. The majority of these institutions throughout the US were built or maintained by enslaved labor or funded with assets acquired from the institution of slavery. Education was essential to the successful governance of the young nation and advancing its prominence in the world. Carroll envisioned the Catholic Church making its mark by building a Catholic liberal arts college. In 1789, he founded Georgetown College. Carroll also advised his constituents that building his institution during the formation of the nation's capital and within earshot of the permanent seat of government would give "weight to [its] establishment" and be the key to establishing a stable, well-integrated Catholic community within the new republic.[34]

In 1792, the Georgetown College held its first classes, admitting predominately white Christian (both Catholic and Protestant) men, taught primarily by male Jesuits from Europe and the Americas. The college welcomed a small contingent of Jewish male students in the 1830s. Together, the college and the nation's capital grew in size and renown. In 1797, Carroll's small college on the hill soon expanded into Georgetown University, the first Catholic and Jesuit institution of higher learning in the US.

The university was built and maintained by enslaved workers who had been an integral part of Georgetown's history since 1789. Its buildings were erected upon land once used to cultivate tobacco. Enslaved persons worked throughout campus until slavery was abolished in the district in 1862. The majority of the workers were owned by the Jesuits, an apostolic religious community known as the Society of Jesus and founded in the sixteenth century by St. Ignatius of Loyola. The religious community sought to emulate the life of Jesus and offered themselves to the Catholic Church in lifetime service to God and the church. In the early sixteenth century, upon their arrival in Maryland, Jesuits received from Maryland officials over twelve thousand acres of land stretching between the Potomac and Chesapeake Rivers. The area became known as the Jesuit plantations. The plantations produced several tobacco fields, tended first by indentured servants, poor white immigrants, and criminals. But the rise of the cash-crop tobacco industry in the Americas and West Indies precipitated demand for a larger and more cost-effective labor force. Enslaved workers, both those owned by the Jesuits and those hired out by area owners, began populating plantations in the area. Many of these workers and their descendants helped build the university and worked throughout the campus as carpenters, valets, blacksmiths, maids, laundresses, cooks, and other skilled and unskilled positions. Most lived at Georgetown University and on one of the Jesuits' plantations in Maryland. They received little to no pay for their labors and were provided meager housing, clothing, and meals.

Enslaved workers also became a primary source of revenue for the university. Six of these workers, Sukey, Becky, Mary, Nat, James, and Charles, are a mere sampling of the many who contributed to the growth and development of Georgetown University. The university rented Sukey and Becky from William Diggs for $10 a year.[35] Sukey worked at Georgetown from 1792 to 1796 and returned during Becky's term from 1801 to 1803.[36] The Jesuits purchased Mary and her two young children, Hannah and Isaac, from Samuel and John Fulton for £35 in 1792.[37] A year later, the Jesuit priests, after capitalizing from their labor, sold Mary and her children for £40 to nearby landowners, making a £5 profit from the sale.

Nat's labors helped pay for his owner's son's tuition. Such practice of hiring out enslaved laborers to "offset the cost of educating" slave owners' children was a known practice at Georgetown. From 1792 to 1795, Nat earned fifteen pounds a year for his owner, Ignatius Smith, and Ignatius's family.[38] Between 1792 and 1793, prominent slaveholder and planter Clem Hill sold James to a nearby owner and Charles to the university to also cover the college expenses of his sons, Clem Jr. and William.[39] In 1814 alone, 12 out of the 102 persons on the Georgetown campus were women, men, and children "owned by the Jesuits or hired out by local owners whose children attended Georgetown."

Perhaps the biggest single instance of the Jesuits' exploitation of enslaved laborers was their sale of over three hundred enslaved women,

men, and children in an effort to save the university. Georgetown was mired in debt and on the verge of bankruptcy. The sale signified that Black lives possessed no intrinsic value as humans. They were merely a commodity to be bought or sold to rectify the fiscal mismanagement of a Christian institution of higher learning. The price Black-bodied women, men, and children would pay for the Jesuits' mishap was a one-way trip down South to a harsh life of labor and violent assault. Others were sold to local owners, where they continued laboring involuntarily throughout the DC, Maryland, Virginia (DMV) area.

The selling of Black people to save Georgetown was organized by Georgetown University president Thomas F. Mulledy. Mulledy executed the sale with the assistance of former university president William McSherry. The sale was approved by the church in Rome under strict conditions: the enslaved could only be sold to established landowners; the enslaved would continue receiving religious instruction—namely, Catholicism—with the assistance of a priest; enslaved families were to remain intact; special consideration should be given to the elderly and sick; and proceeds from the sale could not pay the university's debt or operating expenses.[40]

Yet the Jesuits and their Louisiana buyers, Henry Johnson and Jesse Batey (Beatty), ignored a majority of the terms. The most egregious was not just the selling of Black people to save an institution but the separation of Black families to do so. Even more egregious was the treatment of the elderly and sick. Seventeen of those who survived the treacherous and humid journey from Georgetown to Louisiana were sixty and older. Isaac Hawkins, for example, was born enslaved and lived most of his life on the Jesuits' White Marsh plantation near Bowie, Maryland. He was sold to a plantation in Louisiana at sixty-five years old. Daniel, another enslaved man, was eighty years old when he was sold.

In the end, the Jesuits, after negotiations with the Louisiana buyers Johnson and Batey, secured $115,000 for the sale of 272 enslaved women, men, and children aged between eighteen months and eighty years. The vast majority of those sold were sent to Johnson's and Batey's estates and other sugar and cotton plantations in Louisiana. In short, "No one was spared: not the 2-month-old baby and her mother, not the field hands, not the shoemaker and not Cornelius Hawkins, who was about 13 years old when he was forced onboard."[41] Their cries for mercy went unheard as they disembarked for another site of domestic terror in the US.

In 1993, a study chronicled the university's role in enslavement, exploitation, and sale of Black people since the opening of its doors and well into the civil rights movement. In 2014, Matthew Quallen, a Georgetown undergraduate history major at the time, also began writing a series of articles about Georgetown's involvement in slavery. One year later, university president John J. DeGioia formed the Working Group on Slavery, Memory, and Reconciliation to investigate the university's role and offer best practices for the university's response.

That same year, Georgetown students galvanized in protest to remove Mulledy's and McSherry's names from campus buildings. A series of sit-ins with the hashtag #GU272 ensued, bringing awareness to the sale, separation, and transport of hundreds of Black people by the Jesuits. Inspired by the students, alumnus Richard Cellini formed the Georgetown Memory Project to help identify the names of those enslaved women, men, and children sold to Louisiana plantations and locate their descendants. In spring 2016, *New York Times* correspondent Rachel L. Swarns's article helped place a national spotlight on the sale. Two-thirds of Georgetown students voted for each student to pay a specified fee per semester to create a monetary fund to honor the enslaved and to serve as a form of reparations to their descendants.

The Working Group on Slavery, Memory, and Reconciliation was composed of faculty, students, alumni, and support staff developed an extensive archival online database, the Georgetown Slavery. The group detailed the role Georgetown University and the Jesuits played in the commodification of Black bodies and held a series of ongoing events, public discussions, and outreach programs related to their findings. Mulledy's and McSherry's names were removed from two campus buildings and replaced by two former enslaved workers' names, Isaac Hawkins and Anne Marie Becraft. These two names honor and represent all the enslaved individuals who served Georgetown, the Jesuits, and the nation.

Georgetown University, along with the Department of the Treasury and the Smithsonian Castle, not only exploited Black bodies but did so recklessly without consideration of Black people's well-being and humanity. Yet Georgetown has taken appropriate and lasting steps to recognize and respond to the institutions' rootedness in slavery. Georgetown serves as a model for other institutions in American society. As of the date of

**Figure 5.5.** *Georgetown University, 1904.* Library of Congress.

this writing, other universities involved in the Universities Studying Slavery project are seeking to explore and address areas of racial inequality in higher education and legacies of slavery. Figure 5.5, taken in 1904, represents the trajectory of service enslaved Black-bodied people provided Georgetown University by constructing, expanding, and maintaining its premises from the 1790s leading into the Civil War.[42]

## Library of Congress

The establishment of a reference library for Congress's use was included in the bill President Adams signed on April 24, 1800, to transfer the seat of government from Philadelphia to the new nation's capital. Adams approved the appropriation of $5,000 to purchase books for Congress's use to be housed in "a suitable apartment," which later became known as the Library of Congress. Initially, between 1800 and 1818, the suitable apartment became different temporary locations throughout the city and US

Capitol. After the War of 1812, workers constructed a more permanent site in the Capitol's north wing and later the main terrace. The Library of Congress remained in these two locations inside the Capitol from 1818 to 1897. Charles Bulfinch, architect of the Capitol, mentioned earlier, moved the library from the north wing to the center of the west facade of the Capitol. Bulfinch created an open-squared, three-level room. The library opened in 1825. The following year, another fire caused by a burning candle resulted in little damage but evoked much alarm. The fire appeared to be a precursor to a Christmas Eve fire twenty-six years later due to a faulty chimney. Nearly thirty-five thousand of the library's fifty-five thousand books burned. In eighteen months, Thomas Walter, the architect of the Capitol who proceeded Bulfinch, decided to build a fireproof room, described as an "eye-popping, incombustible cast-iron library, and an amazing feat of technological innovation."[43] The room became known as the iron library. Figures 5.6 and 5.7 from the Historical Society of Washington, DC, and

**Figure 5.6.** *Black Men Working in the Library of Congress Room Located Inside the US Capitol.* Historical Society of Washington, DC.

MAIN HALL OF THE LIBRARY OF CONGRESS,
U. S. Capitol.

**Figure 5.7.** *Main Hall of the Library of Congress Room Inside the US Capitol.* Library of Congress.

the Library of Congress represent the trajectory of service enslaved Black-bodied people provided the university by constructing, expanding, maintaining, or preserving the Library of Congress and the Jefferson Collection from the 1800s leading into the Civil War.

Congress and the president, vice president, and Supreme Court justices were the only persons granted access to the Library of Congress volumes. Within one year, 740 books and three maps arrived at the US Capitol from noted London distributors Cadell & Davies. But the most significant addition to the library, at the time, was the arrival of the Thomas Jefferson collection.

## Enslaved Laborers and the Jefferson Collection

On January 26, 1802, newly elected president Thomas Jefferson signed legislation outlining the purpose and function of the Library of Congress and noting the selection of a librarian appointed by the US president. That same year, the library holdings increased to 964 books and nine maps. Jefferson also appointed John James Beckley, his fellow comrade in arms, to serve as librarian. Beckley, an English immigrant of meager means, arrived in Virginia around 1768. He worked as an indentured servant and upon completion of his contract acquired land and enslaved laborers. He rose to prominence, studying law and serving twice as mayor of Richmond, Virginia (1783 and 1788). He served as the first librarian of Congress until his death in 1807. The library collection, which increased to nearly three thousand volumes, was almost destroyed during the War of 1812. The British created a bonfire with the books in an attempt to destroy the library and Capitol.

On September 21, 1814, Jefferson wrote to his friend Samuel Harrison Smith, federal commissioner of the revenue and former publisher of the *National Intelligencer*, about the fire: "I learn from the Newspapers that the Vandalism of our enemy has triumphed at Washington."[44] Jefferson then offered his personal library collection of approximately nine to ten thousand books for sale to Congress. Jefferson asked Smith to present his collection, which he acquired during his travels to Amsterdam, Frankfort, Madrid, Paris, and London, to Congress's Library Committee.[45] Smith agreed.[46]

By mid-October, Joseph Milligan, a Georgetown bookseller, traveled to Monticello to appraise the collection.[47] On November 28, 1814, the committee presented a draft of a library bill inclusive of terms, conditions, and purchase price of Jefferson's collection. The result was 6,487 books for $23,950 (equivalent to $345,000 in 2019). Congress approved the bill with noted vocal opposition. On January 30, 1815, President James Madison signed An Act to Authorize the Purchase of the Library of Thomas Jefferson, Late President of the United States. Two months later, Congress passed An Act to Provide a Library Room, and for

Transporting the Library Lately Purchased. George Watterson, the second librarian of Congress, selected the Blodgett Hotel.

Jefferson also requested the committee to hire someone to assist him in revising and updating his handwritten catalog and supervise the packaging and transportation of books to Washington.[48] In April 1815, the committee appointed Milligan to help with revisions and updates and oversee the labeling, wrapping, binding, and packaging of books. Joseph Dougherty, Jefferson's former Irish-born coachman, was hired to oversee the transportation from Monticello to Washington.[49] Jefferson sold 6,707 books and requested his payment in treasury notes payable to his debtors.

By the end of April, "ten wagons filled with Jefferson's nailed up book presses [cases] left Monticello . . . with the last one departing on 8 May 1815."[50] Dougherty, the waggoneers, and crewmen headed toward the city of Washington. Each wagon, weighing approximately 2,458 pounds, made its way along the 125-mile stretch, which took seven to eight days to reach the nation's capital. Upon arrival in Washington, the wagons were unloaded and set up on the third floor of the Blodget Hotel, the library's temporary location on the corner of Seventh and E Streets, present-day Penn Quarter.

Jefferson's collection revitalized the Library of Congress. To this day, the collection is hailed as "the nucleus around which the present collections of the Library of Congress are assembled." Moreover, "for nearly a century the subject arrangement that Jefferson developed from Sir Francis Bacon's division of knowledge was used to organize the Library of Congress book collection."[51] The Jeffersonian collection made it possible for the Library of Congress to reestablish itself, after the War of 1812, as a leading reference center. Over the years, parts of the collection were lost or destroyed, including in a subsequent fire in 1851. The few remaining volumes from that original Jeffersonian collection are presently housed in the Rare Books and Special Collections Section of the library.

No doubt Jefferson's collection was made possible by the work of Jefferson and also Smith, Congress's Library Committee, Milligan, Dougherty, Beckley, and so on. These men's roles in the early stages of the Library of Congress along with the later acquisition of the Jeffersonian collection helped make the institution a national resource center. Equally important to note are the enslaved workers who packaged, carried, and loaded the books on wagons at Monticello and later unloaded and set up the books throughout the library's history in the US Capitol. The omission of these laborers from historical accounts infers that Jefferson, Milligan, Dougherty, and the librarians of Congress acted alone. One need only consider the hundreds of skilled and unskilled enslaved workers at Monticello at Jefferson's disposal who participated in this historic move.

It is irresponsible to overlook or conclude that Milligan, along with seventy-two-year-old Jefferson, who suffered from rheumatism, completed the work alone. It is much more likely that enslaved laborers, especially those working at Monticello's joinery workshop, aided Jefferson and Milligan in emptying each of the heavy nine-foot bookcases filled with books in Jefferson's home and packing the books securely in travel cases. It is disingenuous to intimate in historical accounts that "Jefferson and Milligan" within a two- to three-week period "stuffed [the waste paper] into spaces to secure the volumes," nailed large boards "across the front to prepare them for the journey," and loaded over six thousand volumes into ten wagons for Dougherty and unnamed waggoneers to transport 125 miles to Washington. Enslaved laborers were involved in the lifting, stuffing, securing, nailing, loading, transporting, and delivering of the Jeffersonian collection.

## Master Crafters: John Hemmings, Burwell Colbert, and Joseph Fossett

One particular contributor to preparing the collection was John Hemmings, Jefferson's enslaved carpenter. John, a highly skilled carpenter, joiner, and cabinetmaker, was among those enslaved craft persons who worked in Monticello's joiner workshop. He was born into slavery at Monticello in 1776. His mother, Elizabeth (Betty) Hemings, arrived at Monticello as part of Jefferson's wife's dowry. When John came of age, for some unknown reason, he dropped the second "m" from his last name. His half-sister was Sally Hemings.[52]

John's talents became evident while working as an apprentice to James Dinsmore, an Irish joiner and master builder who worked on the exterior and interior of the main house from 1798 to 1809. Both John and James were instrumental in creating all the architectural features and woodwork throughout the Monticello mansion. John's hands created the Elliptical Arch, wooden shutters, and some furnishings in the Monticello library and home. When James left Monticello in 1809, John became the master crafter and manager of the joiner's workshop until Jefferson's death in 1826. John's young nephews, Madison and Eston Hemings, Sally and Jefferson's sons worked as his apprentices in the joinery shop. John continued making furniture for Jefferson—cabinets, chairs, tables, cupboards, shelves, and so on. Most of the furniture Hemmings crafted was made between 1809 and 1820.[53]

Hemmings also handcrafted bookcases with presses similar to those in the Jeffersonian collection. A revolving "lazy susan-style" walnut bookstand was also handmade in Monticello's joiner's shop. John was also instrumental in constructing the slave quarters at Monticello on Mulberry Row; all the interior joinery at Jefferson's octagonal Poplar Forest summer home in Bedford County, Virginia; and by 1814, a four-person landau carriage, designed by Jefferson. Burwell Colbert and Joseph Fossett, John's enslaved relatives, also worked at the joiner's shop. Colbert, Jefferson's butler, painted the carriage, and Fossett, manager of Monticello's blacksmith shop, fashioned the carriage's ironwork.

John and Colbert were among the enslaved workers who prepared the Jeffersonian collection for sale and transport. John crafted the pine bookcases for Jefferson's books and built the portable book boxes needed to transport the collection to Washington. Edmund Bacon, Jefferson's overseer, had John make additional portable book boxes, while Burwell, other enslaved laborers, and Bacon and James Dinsmore packed the books. Jefferson's granddaughters, Ellen, Cornelia, and Virginia Randolph (then ages eighteen, fifteen, and thirteen), helped sort them.[54]

Once the book boxes were stuffed with paper to keep the books protected and from shifting and being damaged in transit and Hemmings and Colbert had completed their work, enslaved laborers were called upon to load the heavy book boxes onto ten to eleven wagons. Once loaded, each wagon weighed approximately 2,458 pounds. It took seven days for the about 27,038 pounds of books to reach Washington and six days for the wagons and crew to return to Monticello.[55] Upon arrival in Washington, enslaved workers also helped with unloading the collection.

On occasion, Jefferson paid John, Colbert, and Fossett up to $20 a year for their craft and extra labors. The three, as stipulated in Jefferson's will, were freed upon Jefferson's death. John, Colbert, and Fossett spent most of their lives building, crafting, and working on Jefferson's Monticello and Poplar Forest estates without fully tasting the joy of freedom from work. John died in 1831, Colbert in 1862, and Fossett in 1858. All men labored without recognition for their craft and their contributions to Jefferson and the nation. Jefferson's books, however, gained prominence at the Library of Congress. Jefferson's volumes became a major aspect of the library's collection. When some books were lost or destroyed by the second fire in 1851, the library set out to reconstruct Jefferson's library by seeking out identical editions.[56]

In 1864, Ainsworth Rand Spofford, the sixth librarian of Congress, ushered the institution into the national spotlight by transitioning the library "from a congressional reading room into a national institution"— what he termed "the book palace of the American people."[57] By 1872, Spofford increased the holdings, instituted a copyright system, and championed a stand-alone grand structure called the Thomas Jefferson Building.[58] In 1886, Congress authorized the construction of a new facility designed by John L. Smithmeyer and Paul J. Pelz and supervised by Edward Pearce Casey in 1892. It is reasonable to conclude that freed Black people played a role in building and later transporting 787,715 volumes and 218,340 pamphlets to the newly erected library.

On November 1, 1897, the Thomas Jefferson Building on First Street, between Independence Avenue and East Capitol Street, opened its doors to the public. Today, the Jeffersonian collection is the crown jewel of the Library of Congress and frames the foundation of its growing holdings and historical legacy. The imprint of Jefferson, his white comrades and collection, and those visionaries of the Library of Congress are well documented beneath the dome of the nation's library. Forgotten, however, are the stories of those Black-bodied people who carried and packed Jefferson's books and built the furniture and structures that house the collection.

## The US Church

Within a month of officially moving into the partially finished US Capitol in Washington, Congress approved the use of the Capitol as an edifice for Christian worship. Both the House under the leadership of Speaker Theodore Sedgwick and the Senate under its president,

Thomas Jefferson, approved holding Christian services inside the US Capitol. At the time, Jefferson was vice president of the United States and a proponent of both religious freedom and the need for what he termed "a wall of ~~eternal~~ separation between Church and State." In the original text, Jefferson, during his editing, made a strikethrough of the word *eternal* but did not blot it out. Clearly, at the nation's birth, the founders did not conceive a wall of separation between church and state. Most were slaveholders who believed their dominion over lands and people was providential, a divine entitlement that many still cling to today. The wall of separation between church and state in Jefferson's mind and the world he inhabited was tissue-paper thin.

Enslaved laborers were instrumental in building the US Capitol and its congressional and Supreme Court chambers and the Library of Congress room. They were also responsible for cleaning and transforming congressional chambers into an edifice for Christian worship. Each Sunday morning, the podium in the House and Senate Chambers symbolically became the preacher's pulpit. Christian chaplains appointed by Congress and compensated by the Department of the Treasury organized weekly services. Congregants sang from hymnals purchased by Congress, and most services included a Mass choir accompanied at times by the United States Marine Band. Services were often standing room only, with over two thousand attendees by the mid-nineteenth century. Members of Congress from both chambers voluntarily attended 11:00 a.m. services with their families and friends. The US president and vice president and other mainly white slaveholders, merchants, proprietors, and their families also attended church services. Shortly after his inauguration, President Thomas Jefferson was the first president-elect to place his right hand on the Bible and take the oath of office within the Senate Chamber. On Sunday morning, President Jefferson, still a slave owner, could be seen riding on horseback from the White House to the US Capitol to attend morning services. Jefferson's successor, President James Madison, another prominent Virginia slave owner, continued the tradition of arriving at the Capitol each Sunday in a carriage drawn by four white horses.

Although the young nation did not outright identify itself as a Christian nation, its framers were undoubtedly influenced, shaped, and molded by Christian values interpreted and advanced by European religious institutions and well-established American slaveholding churchmen and politicians. The men who wrote the nation's founding documents and who inscribed on America's currency "In God, We Trust" were also slaveholding ministers and politicians guided by religious values driven by economic prosperity and political power. By placing a church inside the Capitol, Jefferson and other founders set a tone and precedence that Christianity was the new republic's religious identity. As long as slavery was alive and well in the American Union, the church and state would remain intertwined. The church and state promoted slavery, the disenfranchisement of Black and Brown people, and the advancement of whiteness. Given this, using enslaved laborers to build the new seat of government and to advance the economic welfare of white colonists and the nation was an act of the church and state.

Formerly enslaved man Henry Highland Garnet (1815–82) understood this all too well. Nearly ninety years after Congress held the first church service in the Capitol building, Garnet became the first African American to preach in the House Chamber. Congress invited him to commemorate the Thirteenth Amendment passage, which abolished slavery on January 31, 1865. Nearly two weeks after the passage, Garnet graced the Capitol pulpit. Garnet's journey to the US Capitol was not an easy one. Garnet, the grandson of a Mandingo chief, was born in slavery. His family was "stolen" from Africa and later owned by William Spencer, a Kent County, Maryland, farmer and War of 1812 veteran. At age nine, his family fled to New York, where they lived as fugitives. In 1843, at age twenty-eight, Garnet delivered a rousing speech at the National Negro Convention in Buffalo, New York, bringing him widespread recognition. The call for retributive justice in the address, known as the "Call to Rebellion," shocked convention-goers. "Brethren, arise, arise!" Garnet said. "Strike the blow. . . . Strike for your lives and liberties. Remember that you are FOUR MILLION!"[59] Frederick Douglass immediately rose to censure Garnet's speech, but Garnet rebuffed him and continued speaking for an additional hour and a half.

By the time Congress invited Garnet to preach at the US Capitol, he had become a renowned abolitionist and pastor of the Fifteenth Street Presbyterian Church in Washington, DC. Now he stood before a packed room of politicians, slaveholders, ministers, and their families who had gathered in the Capitol chamber to hear a Black man applaud them for the passage of the Thirteenth Amendment. But Garnet, aware of the hypocrisy and the labor of millions of Black people who built this country and prepared the room to which he stood, opened his sermon with a title: "Let the Monster Perish."[60] Garnet then proceeded to address the hypocrisy of separation between church and state. For Garnet, the irony was apparent: there was no wall because the Bible, the law, the churchman, the missionary, and the politician were all complicit in the institution of slavery.

Garnet began his sermon by reading aloud from Matthew 23:4. Crowds of Black people stood along the walls anxiously awaiting to hear Garnet's words. "For they bind heavy burdens and grievous to be borne and lay them on men's shoulders, but they themselves will not move them with one of their fingers," Garnet professed.[61] He proceeded by indicting the American church and government as coconspirators in the establishment and perpetuation of slavery. It was time for slavery, America's monster, to die, he said, and the two entities that possessed the power to kill it were the ones most responsible for its rise and perpetuation—the church and state. Drawing parallels between the church and biblical scribes and Pharisees, Garnet noted how Jesus admonished his disciples, "Beware of the religion of the Scribes and Pharisees," whose "great professions" were often "inconsistent" with their practices "and wrong."[62] Garnet scoffed at the politicians, churchmen, and colonists' piety and pomp and circumstance, celebrating a moment that could never overshadow their active and complicit involvement in nearly 250 years of slavery in the American Union.

The passage of the Thirteenth Amendment and his invitation to commemorate the event, though commendable and noteworthy, neither repudiated nor alleviated the American slaveholder, the American church, and the state's involvement in the transatlantic slave trade. It did not redeem the role those gathered played in violently subjugating, colonizing, and traumatizing Black people. It did not render them faultless in an exploitation that began, as Garnet described, with their "heroic . . . Pilgrim" forebears who braved the "treacherous sea" and "joyfully went forth to illuminate" this darkened American landscaped once scattered with "savages."[63] And once they rid themselves of the savages, it did not leave them blameless in forcing Black people to build the nation's capital without pay and in total disregard of their humanity.

Garnet drew from his story of bondage to provide a counternarrative to the often told whites-save-the-world pilgrim narrative. His voice pierced through Congress's celebratory moment. "I was born," he said, "among the cherished institutions of slavery."[64] Silence filled the room as he described his monstrous experience of slavery against the backdrop of a pilgrim story: "My earliest recollections of parents, friends, and the home of my childhood are clouded with its wrongs. The first sight that met my eyes was a Christian mother enslaved by professed Christians. . . . The first sounds that startled my ear and sent a shudder through my soul were the cracking of the whip and the clanking of chains. These sad memories mar the beauties of my native shores and darken all the slaveland, which, but for the reign of despotism, had been a paradise."[65] Though a pastor and free man, Garnet was still entangled in the chains of American carnage and inequality. Experience had taught him that the Thirteenth Amendment's physical removal of chains would do little to change Black people's livelihood in the US. Garnet continued by painting a broader picture of the monster, saying,

> Let us view this demon, which the people have worshipped as a God. Come forth, thou grim monster, that thou mayest be critically examined! There he stands. Behold him, one and all. . . . Slavery preys upon man, and man only. A brute cannot be made a slave. Why? Because a brute has not reason, faith, nor an undying spirit, nor conscience. It does not look forward to the future with joy or fear, nor reflect upon the past with satisfaction or regret. But who in this vast assembly, who in all this broad land, will say that the poorest and most unhappy brother in chains and servitude has not every one of these high endowments? Who denies it? Is there one? If so, let him speak. There is not one; no, not one.
>
> But slavery attempts to make a man a brute. It treats him as a beast. Its terrible work is not finished until the ruined victim of its lusts and pride and avarice and hatred is reduced so low that with tearful eyes and feeble voice he faintly cries, "I am happy and contented. I love this condition."[66]

Garnet proceeded with a declarative statement to Congress followed by an admonishment: "Our poor and forlorn brother whom thou hast labeled 'slave,' is also a man. . . . God made him such, and his brother cannot unmake him. Woe, woe to him who attempts to commit the accursed crime."[67] He cast those guilty of slavery, its sins and benefits, as "Christian," lying in wait, "ruthless traders in the souls and bodies of men."[68]

Garnet then offered a charge: "With all the moral attributes of God on our side . . . let the verdict of death which has been brought in against slavery by the Thirty-Eighth Congress be affirmed and executed by the people. Let the gigantic monster perish. Yes, perish now and perish forever!"[69] Following his pronouncement of death, Garnet reminded Congress that Black people wanted nothing short of justice, nothing short of mattering in America:

> We ask no special favors, but we plead for justice . . . in the name of God, the universal Father, we demand the right to live and labor and enjoy the fruits of our toil. The good work which God has assigned for the ages to come will be finished when our national literature shall be so purified as to reflect a faithful and a just light upon the character and social habits of our race. . . . When caste and prejudice in Christian churches shall be utterly destroyed and shall be regarded as totally unworthy of Christians, and at variance with the principles of the Gospel . . . then, and not till then, shall the effectual labors of God's people and God's instruments cease.[70]

He reminded them that though the passage of the Thirteenth Amendment was a noble endeavor, those who held Black people in bondage and benefited from slavery needed to atone for their "national sins." He asked them to stop instituting laws and religious dogmas that slow slavery's demise and trafficking in Black people's social, material, political, cultural, mental, and spiritual disenfranchisement:

> Great sacrifices have been made by the people; yet, greater still are demanded ere atonement can be made for our national sins. Eternal justice holds heavy mortgages against us and will require the payment of the last farthing. We have involved ourselves in the sin of unrighteous gain, stimulated by luxury and pride and the love of power and oppression; and prosperity and peace can be purchased only by blood and with tears of repentance. We have paid some of the fearful installments, but there are other heavy obligations to be met. Let slavery die. . . . Do not commute its sentence. Give it no respite, but let it be ignominiously executed. . . .

> Emancipate, enfranchise, educate. . . . Thus shall we give to the world the form of a model Republic, founded on the principles of justice and humanity and Christianity, in which the burdens of war and the blessings of peace are equally borne and enjoyed by all.[71]

On February 13, 1882, seventeen years after his sermon in the US Capitol, Henry Highland Garnet died. At the time of his death, many of the freedoms and advantages Black people had received after the passage of the Thirteenth Amendment had been stripped from them by Congress, the White House, the US Supreme Court, and federal and state legislatures. American citizens also played a role in limiting Black people's access and freedoms, often through violent means.

For Black people, the church inside the Capitol had two milestone moments—the Sunday mornings on which enslaved laborers prepared the House and Senate Chambers for Christian worship and the day Henry Highland Garnet gave his rousing sermon. Outside of those two moments, the intermingling of church and state remained in constant conflict with the idea of democracy espoused by the politicians of Garnet's day. Church services continued in the US Capitol building until 1870, even during the rise of church buildings throughout the district.

## Conclusion

In December 1861, Ohio lawyer and politician Thomas Marshall Key, with the aid and sponsorship of Massachusetts senator Henry Wilson, drafted a bill entitled An Act for the Release of Certain Persons Held to Service or Labor Within the District of Columbia. On April 3, 1862, the bill passed the Senate and, eight days later, the House of Representatives. On April 16, 1862, President Abraham Lincoln signed into law the release of all Black women, men, and children forced into labor in the nation's capital. The over seventy-year history of slavery in the District of Columbia had come to an end.

However, the bill freed Black people but did not compensate or acknowledge their contribution to the city and the nation. The act made no allowances for their basic human needs—food, clothing, and shelter—and provided them no land rights. The law did allocate $100,000 toward payment for those willing to leave the US and turn their backs on the country they built and the loved ones they knew. Those choosing to immigrate received $100 from the US government plus transportation across the waters to Haiti and Liberia.

The enslaved who gave years of service to the nation received no realistic compensation from the American government. Instead, the government offered assistance to slave owners for their loss of property and income. The act allocated $1,000,000 to compensate slave owners who were loyal to the Union, paying them up to $300 per enslaved person residing and working within DC and the surrounding area. Within nine months of the act's passage, slave owners had filed nearly one thousand petitions. If owners provided two documents with their petitions—proof of ownership and a statement of their loyalty to the Union—the petitions were approved without delay by the board of commissioners, known as the Emancipation Commission. The compensation to owners became known as the District of Columbia Compensated Emancipation Act.

On April 16, 1862, the US government freed 3,185 enslaved Black people in the District of Columbia. The date became an official city holiday in Washington, DC, in 2005. No doubt, April 16 held a special meaning for Black people seeking to own their bodies in the nation's capital. But beneath the pomp and circumstance of each year's celebration is the handout the US government provided former white slave owners and the meager provisions that same government provided generations of Black people who helped build the new republic and its permanent seat of government. As slavery came to a close in the District of Columbia, millions of Black people were still toiling away their lives in states throughout the new republic. How would their owners be compensated when freedom came?

# Part II

## Blessing the Wings

---

*A Call for a National Memorial*

# CHAPTER SIX

# Black Lives
## Co-opted Memorials, and the Paradox of Not Mattering

*I, too, sing America.*

*I am the darker brother.*
*They send me to eat in the kitchen*
*When company comes,*
*But I laugh,*
*And eat well,*
*And grow strong.*

*Tomorrow,*
*I'll sit at the table*
*When company comes.*
*Nobody'll dare*
*Say to me,*
*"Eat in the kitchen,"*
*Then.*

*Besides,*
*They'll see how beautiful I am*
*And be ashamed,—*

*I, too, am America.*

—LANGSTON HUGHES

The enslaved arrived as early as the 1500s in the mainland North American colonies. However, the year 1619 marks a significant turning point in the history of slavery in the US. In late August 1619, Virginia tobacco planter and Englishman John Rolfe, son of the archbishop of York, wrote to Sir Edwin Sandys, one of Virginia's founders, announcing the arrival of "20 . . . odd Negroes" abroad the Dutch ship *White Lion*. The twenty had begun their journey aboard the *S João Batista* (*São João Bautista*), a vessel bearing Portugal's flag, which had left Lisbon months earlier, headed to West-Central Africa. In 1619, the *Batista* left Luanda (São Paulo de Loanda), a West African city and the capital of Portuguese Angola, and sailed toward Vera Cruz, Mexico (New Spain), carrying approximately 366 African captives. During that period, between 1615 and 1622, the *Batista* was one among other Portuguese slave ships that traveled from Luanda carrying human cargo for sale and labor in Vera Cruz and Cartagena per an agreement with the Spanish Crown.

On this particular voyage, the *Batista*, under the leadership of Captain Manoel Mendes da Cunha, disembarked in Veracruz and Jamaica. En route to Mexico, crewmen aboard two ships, the *White Lion*, bearing a Dutch flag, and the *Treasurer*, an English vessel, attacked and robbed the *Batista* of its human cargo off Campeche Bay in the Gulf of Mexico. Among those stolen and taken aboard the *White Lion* were the "20 . . . odd Negroes" who later disembarked along the James River at Point Comfort near Hampton, Virginia. The *Treasurer* arrived in the area approximately three to four days later. Those captured were purchased and traded among the Virginia colonists and forced to work as indentured or enslaved persons throughout the Virginia colony. The Virginia government also bartered and exchanged the Africans with other colonists to obtain supplies for the province.

While some accounts identify these initial African captives as indentured servants, no account disputes their origins, capture, and subsequent voyage across the waters aboard the *S João Batista*, followed by their arrival in the Virginia colony in August 1619. The year marked a seminal moment in the United States' involvement in the transatlantic slave trade. From this date forward, the number of enslaved Africans arriving in the mainland North American colonies increased steadily. By 1790, an estimated 694,280 enslaved Black laborers were toiling away throughout the American colonies, almost one-fourth of the total US population. The numbers of those enslaved climbed steadily and remained unhampered by Congress's 1807 ban on importing slaves. By 1860, the United States' Black population rose to 4.4 million, of whom 3.9 million were enslaved.

Without question, enslaved Black women, men, and children were the primary workforce involved in building the young nation. From the first arrivals to well into the Reconstruction era, enslaved people contributed to the American colonies' formation and later to the US and its infrastructure. They cleared the forests, sowed the seeds, harvested the cash crops, and prepared them for export. They loaded the ships, excavated the stones, and carried the lumber. They surveyed the ground, set the markers, and laid the foundations. Their hands built American towns, cities, railroads, seaports, and streets. Their hands constructed elaborate plantation mansions, mills, cabins, cottages, farms, stores, and churches.

Their hands fabricated the slave quarters at Monticello, Mount Vernon, and other slave-owning properties throughout the American colonies. Their hands nurtured their masters' families and helped enrich the financial solvency of their enslavers. Their hands constructed slave markets, pens, whipping posts, and depots from which they and succeeding generations were incarcerated, auctioned off, and beaten. Their hands helped build the nation's capital and its seat of government, federal buildings, and landmarks. They helped usher in the Industrial Revolution with their cultivation of raw materials and noteworthy inventions rarely patented under their names. Without any land rights and little protection under the law, they refined an American landscape once occupied by and later stolen from the Indigenous peoples of the Americas. They helped transform that landscape into a metropolis.

Yet after shaping this new nation, after sustaining it structurally and economically, there remains no stand-alone monument in the nation's capital dedicated solely to their labor and sacrifice. No noteworthy tributes or declarations have been inscribed acknowledging the work of these Black people's hands. From the antebellum period to the present day, there exist no notable slave memorials in the nation's capital commissioned by the US government and devoted solely to acknowledging the United States' terrible role in the transatlantic slave trade and the violent institutional subjugation of Black people for free labor.

Monuments are fixed symbols that commemorate a person or past event. They convey what and whom a nation values, and they point to the stories central to that nation's identity. Because monuments signify what society thinks about and how it sees itself and its past, present, and projected future, what does the absence of monuments commemorating enslaved Black laborers say about the value, presence, and place of Black people in American history? What does the selective erasure of their contributions to the formation of a nation that generally honors those who make such contributions say about American patriotism? What does such erasure of their contributions say about American's valuation of essential labor and essential laborers?

Even more, what does it say about America that it tells its history primarily from the perspective of those in power, a history that omits the intrusive and unfair practices indelibly woven into the nation's story? If American patriotism is respect for one's country and caring for those who sacrifice and serve this great nation, and if monuments symbolize such gestures, where are the monuments on the National Mall honoring the patriotic enslaved persons who built this country? How is it possible to honor one's country without honoring the men and women whose backbreaking toil under legalized duress constructed its infrastructure? Where are the monuments commissioned or endorsed by the US government from which today's American citizens can gain fuller insight and moral clarity about the enslaved laborers who built the infrastructure of this nation?

At the close of the Civil War and toward the end of Reconstruction, only one monument stood in the nation's capital near the National Mall as a dedicatory symbol of freedom from American slavery. Yet the US government did not commission that memorial. Formerly enslaved laborers from across the country donated the little monies they earned to erect a monument honoring Lincoln's role in abolishing slavery. Their gesture was an act and model of patriotism. It exemplified their respect for the nation and their enthusiastic support of an American patriot who worked to further the United States' cause of democracy and freedom. But the well-intentioned monument conceived in unselfishness, patriotism, and grace, entitled Freedmen's Memorial (also referred to as Emancipation Memorial, Freedmen's Memorial Monument, Freedmen's National Memorial, Freedman's Memorial, and the Lincoln Emancipation Statue in Lincoln Park), had its shortcomings. Erected in the postslavery era in the nation's capital and in the line of sight of the

US Capitol, the Freedmen's Memorial, the first and only stand-alone memorial and a tacit reminder of American slavery and freedom, reinforces a revisionist history of the master–slave relationship.

## Conceiving Freedmen's Memorial: Charlotte Scott's Offering

By 1865, over four million enslaved women, men, and children serving in the United States were freed. Shortly after emancipation, one former enslaved woman named Charlotte Scott, in gratitude for her freedom, gave the first of her meager earnings to her former owners, Dr. William and Margaret (Meg) Rucker, as seed money for a monument in honor of Abraham Lincoln.

Her story and the story of her gift go like this: Charlotte was born into slavery circa 1803 on a 1,150-acre Virginia plantation owned by Meg's grandparents, Capt. William Scott and Ann Jones Scott of Spotsylvania, Virginia. In 1784, William, an American Revolutionary War veteran, purchased land "lying on both sides of the James River in Bedford, Campbell, and Amherst counties" from James Gatewood for £2,000 (equivalent to over $300,000 in 2019).[1] William was also the beneficiary of land and servants that he inherited from his father, Thomas Scott, a prominent Scottish slave owner in the area.[2]

Kept safe in Thomas's *Oxford Bible* was a list of all his servants, along with his last will and testament. Upon his death, Thomas bequeathed his servants, lands, homes, furniture, material goods, and artifacts to his children and wife. Regarding his sixth son, William, Thomas wrote, "I give William Scott six negro slaves hereafter mentioned . . . one boy named Lewis, one negro girl named Selah, one woman named Ester, one negro boy named Martin, one negro woman named Judah, and one named Charlotte and their future increase to him and his heirs or assignees forever."[3] When William died in 1817, Charlotte and his other servants were divided among his children. Thomas Hazelwood, age fourteen, assumed ownership of Charlotte. Nine years later, when Thomas married Margaret Parks née Burke, Charlotte moved into their household, where she served in a domestic capacity and later as a nursemaid to the couple's newborn daughter, Margaret Ann (Meg). Some reports indicate that when Thomas died in 1861, he willed Charlotte and other laborers to Meg. Other accounts suggest Charlotte was a wedding gift to Meg from her parents upon Meg's 1852 marriage to Dr. William P. Rucker, a prominent Virginia physician. Charlotte worked in the Rucker household well into her fifties. By 1861, at the age of fifty-eight, Charlotte had spent the majority of her life as a bondswoman, serving for four generations in the household of her masters.

Dr. Rucker was an interesting person—a slave owner and Union sympathizer who resided in a Confederate state and was a vocal critic of the Confederacy and secession. His refusal to denounce the Union and pledge his allegiance to the Confederacy resulted in numerous conflicts and death threats by slave-owning loyalists. Under much pressure, at the dawn of the Civil War, Rucker left Virginia and joined the Thirty-Sixth Ohio Infantry under the command of Colonel George Crook. Fearing for his family's safety, Rucker moved Meg, their children, and their servants (including Charlotte) to Marietta, Ohio. During this time, Rucker led a notable attack against Confederate soldiers. Under his direction, seventy-five Union soldiers burned down a central bridge in Virginia to immobilize Confederate soldiers and cut off their access to supplies. Rucker was later captured by Confederates in a surprise attack in West Virginia.

While imprisoned, he and Meg sold some servants to cover living expenses and freed others in anticipation of the passage of the Emancipation Proclamation. The proclamation, authored by Lincoln, did not outright free enslaved people from slavery, but it served as a catalyst. Though slavery did not legally end in the US until the Thirteenth Amendment was ratified on January 31, 1865, Rucker decided to free the now almost sixty-year-old Charlotte before its ratification. Charlotte chose to continue working in the Rucker household as a paid cook and laundress. One year after his capture, Rucker escaped from jail. Upon reaching Union lines, he continued serving to defeat the Confederacy and, at the close of the war, returned home to Marietta.

Shortly after his arrival, word reached the Rucker household that President Lincoln had been assassinated on April 14, 1865. Moved by his death, Charlotte gave $5 of her meager earnings to the Ruckers, saying, "The colored people have lost their best friend on earth; Mr. Lincoln was our best friend, and I will give five dollars of my wages towards erecting a monument to his memory."[4] It was a significant offering.

## Funding the Memorial: Black Soldiers and Other Contributors

Charlotte asked Mr. Rucker, "Who would be the best person to raise money [for the monument]?"[5] Rucker called upon Reverend Cornelius Durant Battelle, an influential Methodist pastor in the area with ties to the community and the press. With Charlotte's contribution in hand, Reverend Battelle announced in the local paper his willingness to accept donations and "cheerfully do what he could to promote so noble an object."[6]

Word spread, and monies from other former enslaved women and men poured in. In consultation with Mr. Rucker and General Thomas Church Haskell Smith, US Department of the Treasury official, Reverend Battelle forwarded the donations to James E. Yeatman, president of the St. Louis Western Sanitary Commission, a volunteer war relief organization composed of influential white philanthropists and spearheaded by William Greenleaf Eliot, a Unitarian minister and founder of Washington University.[7] Knowing his work with the Western Sanitary Commission, the men solicited Yeatman's help in hopes that he would sponsor the project and publicize it to freed persons, specifically Black soldiers. In summer 1865, Reverend Battelle wrote to Yeatman, saying, "I herewith forward you [Charlotte Scott's] contribution, and I hope to hear from you upon its receipt, that I may show to Charlotte and others that the money has gone in the right direction. After hearing from you, I hope to be able to stir up the other colored folks on the subject."[8] Dr. Rucker also wrote to Yeatman, saying, "As a slaveholder by inheritance . . . and as an ardent admirer of our lamented President . . . I feel an enthusiastic interest in the success of the Freedmen's Memorial. I hope it may stand unequalled and unrivalled in grandeur and magnificence. . . . Every dollar should come from the former slaves . . . and the monument should be erected at the capital of the nation."[9] Rucker also vouched for Charlotte, saying, "Her reputation for industry, intelligence, and moral integrity has always been appreciated by her friends and acquaintances, both white and colored."[10]

Battelle's and Rucker's words led Yeatman and the commission to "seize on Scott's offering as a model gesture of Black gratitude" that was "made doubly sentimental by its transmission through the bond of master and slave."[11] The commission immediately "reported that an old negro woman gave the money to build a monument to good Massa Lincoln."[12] Yeatman wrote to the editors of the *Daily Missouri Democrat*, urging them to advertise the fundraising efforts: "Gentlemen: I enclose you a note, received this evening from a gentleman now sojourning in this city, which contains a suggestion worthy of the consideration of those who have been made free by the action of our lamented President. It would be a fitting tribute from the race to the noble and good man who has done so much for them . . . a fund would soon be raised sufficient to rear a noble structure to commemorate their gratitude and love to the man through whose instrumentality enslaved millions of their race have been made free."[13] The newspaper announcement generated much enthusiasm.[14] By late spring 1865, Black troops of the Sixth US Colored Heavy Artillery at Fort McPherson in Natchez, Mississippi, under Lt. Col. John P. Coleman's command, were among the first to contribute to the monument fund. Their company headquarters received from the troops $4,242 (equivalent to $67,000 in 2019). The breakdown is in table 6.1.

### Table 6.1. Freedmen's Memorial in Lincoln Park, Washington DC.

| | |
|---|---|
| Alpha Company | $515 |
| Bravo Company | $594 |
| Charlie Company | $514 |
| Delta Company | $464 |
| Echo Company | $199 |
| Foxtrot Company | $409 |
| Golf Company | $284 |
| Hotel Company | $202 |
| Indian Company | $423 |
| Kilo Company | $231 |
| Lima Company | $142 |
| Mike Company | $354 |

At the same time, 683 Black soldiers of the Seventieth US Colored Infantry in Rodney, Mississippi, under Col. W. C. Earles's command, contributed $2,949.50 (equivalent to $47,000 in 2019). Troops from the

Sixth US Heavy Artillery under Colonel Bernard Gaines Farrar Jr's command also donated $4,700 (equivalent to $74,000 in 2019). Shortly after that, the Alpha, Charlie, and Echo units of the Sixty-Third US Colored Infantry under Lt. Col. Albion L. Mitchell's command raised $263 (equivalent to $4,000 in 2019). The Freedmen of Natchez also contributed $312.38 (equivalent to $5,000 in 2019). Days later, Coleman's men, along with troops from the Fifty-Seventh US Colored Infantry, approximately 1,700 Black soldiers, agreed to additionally give "one dollar per man" at "the next payday," bringing these men's total donations to $10,000 (equivalent to $158,000 in 2019).[15] More and more Black soldiers, upon hearing about the cause, began donating "over half their pay, and in some instances, the whole of it."[16]

The commissioners noted Charlotte's and the soldiers' contributions in their *Western Sanitary Commission's Final Report* (May 9, 1864–December 31, 1865):

> There are those, perhaps, who may think that some other form of testimonial, such as the endowment of some great charity, would be better; but the colored people of the United States, and especially the liberated bondmen, wish something tangible and visible to the eye of present and future generations, that will testify of their love and gratitude to their great deliverer . . . it is peculiarly fitting that from this race alone, a monument should ascend, at the capital of the nation, showing forth, to the whole world of mankind, the appreciation of an emancipated race for their greatest earthly benefactor.[17]

By May 1866, the monument fund rose to over $17,000 (equivalent to $274,000 in 2019), secured by Carlos S. Greeley, treasurer of the commission. Elated by the outcome, the commission began advocating for a striking monument, "nothing less than a great work of art . . . so that the magnificence of the memorial may correspond to the distinguished excellence of the man."[18] The commission increased its fundraising efforts, setting a new goal of $50,000, imploring freed people throughout the US to donate "one week's free work or its equivalent."[19] They also asked John Mercer Langston, a prominent Black abolitionist and lawyer from Ohio, to assist in their fundraising efforts. Langston, the first dean of Howard University School of Law, was highly respected in the Black community. Langston saw the undertaking as an opportunity to mobilize Black communities around a common cause. Ironically, other groups solicited Black people to fund memorials elsewhere dedicated to Lincoln during this same period. In particular, two were the iconic Lincoln Memorial on the western end of the National Mall and the Lincoln Memorial at Lincoln's burial site in Springfield, Illinois.[20] Though Black people made contributions to these memorials, Freedmen's Memorial was the only monument funded solely by Black people.

Yet despite their ingenuity and generous contribution to Freemen's Memorial, Black people were not permitted to participate in the design process. Once funds were obtained, Yeatman, Eliot, and the all-white male commission assumed control of the project. With a particular focus in mind, they set about to create a pomp and circumstance portrayal of Lincoln as a benevolent hero who saved a nation and an entire race of people.

## Erecting the Memorial: The Design Process

The design process spanned over ten years before its public unveiling in the nation's capital. Two proposals were considered: one was from Harriet Hosmer (1830–1908), a renowned Watertown, Massachusetts–born sculptor, and the other from Thomas Ball (1819–1911), a celebrated Charlestown, Massachusetts–born sculptor, painter, and musician. Hosmer was the most prominent American female sculptor of her time. But gender discrimination, marginalization, and lack of recognition for her work caused her to leave the states and head to Italy. In Rome, Hosmer studied with distinguished European sculptors—namely, John Gibson—and produced some of her most notable and lucrative works. She was joined by other noted American female sculptors who fled the US for similar reasons. American-British author Henry James disparagingly described the women's network as an "odd phenomenon," a "strange sisterhood of American lady sculptors" who had "settled upon the seven hills [of Rome] in a white marmorean flock" between 1850 and 1876.[21] James's assessment, though typical, is a misleading representation of these influential and diverse women artists who sought independence and recognition for their work on their own terms.

In 1867, the Western Sanitary Commission rejected Hosmer's inclusive and egalitarian design, citing it as too costly and elaborate.

Her project cast Lincoln on top of a pillar center mass and surrounded by several other pillars. Around Lincoln, Hosmer situated an array of formerly enslaved and free Black women, men, and children and Black abolitionists and soldiers on top of the other pillars as a representation of the diversity of Black life in the United States. The commissioners did not think of inviting a Black sculptor to design the monument. At their disposal was the internationally renowned sculptor Mary Edmonia Lewis (ca. 1844–1907), the daughter of a free Black man and a free Chippewa woman. Her parents died at a young age, and Edmonia, whose Native American nickname is Wildfire, left her birth home in Upstate New York to live with her Chippewa people. While attending Oberlin College in 1859, Lewis's white female roommates accused her of poisoning them. At trial, Lewis was acquitted but severely beaten by whites who accused her of stealing art supplies. In 1863, after expulsion from Oberlin, Lewis moved to Boston to study sculpting with the renowned Edward Brackett. Lewis became known for her sculptures of known abolitionists and soldiers. Determined to perfect her craft, Lewis traveled to work with sculptors London, Paris, and Florence, and finally settled in Rome in 1865. Lewis knew and was well acquainted with Hosmer's work. At the time the commission was seeking a designer, Lewis was working on a sculpture entitled *Forever Free*.

Unlike Hosmer's and Lewis's works, Ball's proposal struck a different tone. Upon hearing of Lincoln's death, Ball drew inspiration from a widely used and well-known abolitionist emblem. The emblem portrayed a kneeling, half-naked Black man, his chained fists gripped tightly together, his solemn brow looking upward to an unknown entity. The emblem also contained a banner flowing beneath the chained man's feet that read, "Am I Not a Man and a Brother?" Inspired by the emblem and Lincoln's death, Ball began sculpting a small design of Lincoln standing over a kneeling Black man, pleading for freedom.

Upon seeing Ball's design during one of his travels, Commissioner Eliot immediately summoned the commission, who in turn authorized Ball to create a larger bronze sculpture with a few minor changes. They desired Lincoln to appear statelier, approximately ten feet tall, and the enslaved man replaced with a known living freedman. Eliot forwarded Ball a photo of Archer Alexander, whom Eliot knew personally.[22] Upon completion, Ball shipped the sculpture from his Florence, Italy, studio to the royal foundry of Herr von Müller in Munich, Germany, for casting. In 1875, the finished bronze sculpture made its way from Europe to the nation's capital. Ball received $17,000 for his work (equivalent to $274,000 in 2019), and Congress accepted the statue as a gift from the "colored citizens of the United States."[23] Congress had also previously approved $3,000 for the construction of a pedestal to hold Ball's bronze sculpture and affix it on public grounds in the city under the direction of General Orville E. Babcock, superintendent of public buildings and grounds. L'Enfant's earlier proposal to "place a park in direct line of the Capitol at East Capitol between 11th and 13th streets" to "hold a monumental column" played a critical role in the sculpture's permanent home.[24]

Before its placement, the monument's site served as a dumping ground and then a hospital, Lincoln Hospital, for soldiers during the Civil War. In 1867, Congress authorized the development of a park on the site bearing the official name of Lincoln Square, the "first site [in the city] to bear his name."[25] Shortly after its arrival, the crew placed the monument in the park, in direct line of the US Capitol.

## Unveiling the Memorial: The Dedication Ceremony

On April 14, 1876, the eleventh anniversary of Lincoln's assassination, the Freedmen's Memorial sculpture, paid for by formerly enslaved Black people, stood veiled in the center of the park. The commissioners hired Langston to organize a dedication ceremony. Among the festive crowd of nearly twenty-five thousand onlookers were dignitaries, soldiers, governmental officials, foreign dignitaries, soldiers, businessmen, domestic workers, field hands, community leaders, ministers, abolitionists, educators, and freed women, men, and children, including Charlotte Scott, now seventy-three years old. All gathered to see Black people's gift to the nation. A reporter from the *Washington Republican* newspaper described the exhilaration in the air, masses of people standing by "to witness the spectacle of a grateful race doing homage to a cherished name."[26]

Undoubtedly, it was the largest gathering of Black and white people to commemorate an American statesman in the nation's capital before the end of Reconstruction. Thousands lined the streets and sidewalks, with many others packed shoulder-to-shoulder, peering through windows, hoping to catch a glimpse of the parade and the unveiling. US flags affixed to the White House, the US Congress, the Supreme Court, and other federal and public buildings were lowered to half-mast.

Several Black organizations, along with mounted police, poured onto Seventh and K Streets, waiting to parade toward Lincoln Square at noon. Leading the march was Chief Marshal Charles Henry Marshall, a prominent businessman in the city with deep ties to transatlantic steamship companies. Behind Marshall, cadres of Black soldiers marched in lockstep, with noted uniformed societies, organizations, and clubs and benevolent associations following behind them. Among these groups joining the parade route were the Knights Templar, Rising Sun Commandery, Knight Templar of Baltimore, Knights of St. Augustine (Nos. 1 and 2), Sons of Purity, Sons of Levi, Young Men's (Island), Good Samaritans, Sons of Zion, Sons of St. John, Labor League, and Pioneer Corps of Alexandria. City bands such as the Philharmonic Band of Georgetown, Monumental Band, Excelsior Cornet Band of Baltimore, Beethoven Band, National Band, and the South Washington Band. Spectators looked in anticipation to catch a glimpse of the guests inside the white horse-drawn carriage that entered the parade behind the bands. Seated inside was Langston, the organizer and master of ceremony; Frederick Douglass, the keynote speaker; and other noted guests. The parade continued along K Street to Seventeenth Street, then onward to Pennsylvania Avenue, across the grounds of the White House. From the White House, they continued until they reached Lincoln Square.

Parade participants were greeted by loud cheers as they entered the park. The day had delivered more than Langston and the others imagined. All had gathered for the dedication of the draped memorial encircled with flags in the center of the park. US president Ulysses Grant, his cabinet members, and the justices of the Supreme Court were seated on the dais directly in front of the monument. US senators Thomas Ferry (Michigan), Oliver Hazard Perry Throck Morton (Indiana), George Boutwell (Massachusetts), George Eliphaz Spencer (Alabama), John Sherman (Ohio), and Blanche Kelso Bruce (Mississippi), the first Black senator to complete a full term, were all seated on the dais. Behind them were other government officials and foreign ministers. Within minutes, members of the Metropolitan Methodist Episcopal Church began to perform a succession of songs accompanied by chimes and bells. Immediately thereafter, the US Marine Band seated to the right of the dais opened the ceremony with "Hail, Columbia," the unofficial national anthem of the US until 1931.

The horse-drawn carriage carrying Langston, Douglass, and others arrived, and the men made their way to the dais. Bishop John M. Brown of the African Methodist Episcopal Church opened with a prayer. Honorable J. Henri Burch, House representative from Louisiana, read aloud the Emancipation Proclamation. There followed a rendition of "La Marseillaise," the revolutionary song of the New French Republic. Yeatman and Eliot stood at the podium to provide a brief historical overview of the Western Sanitary Commission and its involvement with the monument, acknowledging Charlotte's initial $5 contribution as a "grain of mustard seed . . . in gratitude to her deliverer Mr. Lincoln." Yeatman reminded the crowd that it was "this five dollars that was the foundation of this beautiful and appropriate memorial which we now see before us."[27] Yeatman ended his remarks by saying, "Whatever of honor, whatever of glory belongs to this work, should be given to Charlotte Scott, the poor slave woman. Her offering of gratitude and love, like that of the widow's mite, will be remembered in heaven when the gifts of those rich in this world's good shall have passed away and been forgotten."[28] Several reports indicated Charlotte was standing among the crowd as Yeatman and others spoke of her from the dais, but she was not publicly acknowledged or invited to speak. After Yeatman and Eliot, Langston rose to receive the statue from the commission and to unveil it. He said,

> In behalf of our entire nation, in behalf especially of the donors of the fund with whose investment you and your associates of the "Western Sanitary Commission" have been charged, I tender to you, sir, and through you to the commission, our sincere thanks for the prompt and wise performance of the trust and duty committed to your care. The finished and appropriate work of art presented by you we accept and dedicate through the ages in memory and honor of him who is to be forever known in the records of the world's history as the emancipator of the enslaved of our country. We unveil it to the gaze, the admiration of mankind.
>
> Fellow-citizens, according to the arrangement of the order of exercises of this occasion it had fallen to my lot to unveil this statue

which we dedicate to-day; be we have with us the President of the United States, and it strikes me that it is altogether fit and proper to now ask him to take part in the exercises as far as to unveil this monument.[29]

In honor of President Grant's presence, Langston asked him to unveil the monument. Silence filled the square as Grant made his way to the monument. All eyes were fixed on the cord that held together the drapery around the monument. Everything had led to this moment. As Grant pulled the cord, the crowd "burst into spontaneous applause and exclamations of admiration" of Ball's massive bronze sculpture, which towered nearly fifteen feet high.[30] Black peoples' tribute and Ball's creation (figure 6.1) now stood fully viewable in the light of day, affixed forever in Lincoln Square in direct line of the US Capitol.[31] Sounds of

**Figure 6.1.** *Freedmen's Memorial in Lincoln Park, Washington, DC.* Library of Congress.

cannons filled the air, reverberating throughout the park as the band began playing "Hail to the Chief."

Langston returned to the podium to read aloud the words inscribed on the monument, which read,

**Freedom's Memorial**
**In Grateful Memory of**
**Abraham Lincoln**
**This Monument Was Erected**
**By the Western Sanitary Commission**
**Of Saint Louis MO:**
**With Funds Contributed Solely by**
**Emancipated Citizens of the United States**
**Declared Free by His Proclamation**
**January 1st A.D. 1863**
**The First Contribution of $5.00 Was Made by**
**Charlotte Scott, a Freed Woman of Virginia**
**Being Her First Earnings in Freedom**
**And Consecrated**
**By Her Suggestion and Request**
**On the Day She Heard of President Lincoln's Death**
**To Build a Monument to His Memory**

Following the reading, William E. Matthews, a well-respected Black lawyer and activist, read a poem entitled "Lincoln," written by Henrietta Cordelia Ray, a Black woman from New York and graduate of the University of the City of New York (1891). An excerpt of the first stanza speaks of the heroic heartfelt sentiment many shared about Lincoln: "To-day, O martyred chief, beneath the sun / We would unveil thy form; to thee who won / The applause of nations for thy soul sincere, / A loving tribute we would offer here. . . . / And so they come, the freed, with grateful gift, / From whose sad path the shadows thou didst lift."

After the reading, Langston returned to the podium to introduce Douglass, who was met by boisterous admiration from the crowd. He opened his speech by saying,

Friends and Fellow-citizens:

I warmly congratulate you upon the highly interesting object which has caused you to assemble in such numbers and spirit as you have today. This occasion is in some respects remarkable. Wise and thoughtful men of our race, who shall come after us, and study the lesson of our history in the United States; who shall survey the long and dreary spaces over which we have traveled; who shall count the links in the great chain of events by which we have reached our present position, will make a note of this occasion; they will think of it and speak of it with a sense of manly pride and complacency.

I congratulate you, also, upon the very favorable circumstances in which we meet today. They are high, inspiring, and uncommon. They lend grace, glory, and significance to the object for which we have met. Nowhere else in this great country, with its uncounted towns and cities, unlimited wealth, and immeasurable territory extending from sea to sea, could conditions be found more favorable to the success of this occasion than here.

We stand today at the national center to perform something like a national act—an act which is to go into history; and we are here where every pulsation of the national heart can be heard, felt, and reciprocated. A thousand wires, fed with thought and winged with lightning, put us in instantaneous communication with the loyal and true men all over the country.[32]

Black people's gift to the nation moved Douglass. Yet his repeated reference to the monument as an object suggests Douglass was troubled by its appearance. And no wonder: the memorial was a strange juxtaposition between a towering Lincoln portrayed as the Great Emancipator and a kneeling, half-naked Black man appearing docile and beholden. Why is Lincoln standing and the Black man kneeling?

Douglass also seemed to struggle with the characterization of Lincoln as the Great Emancipator. Midway through his speech, he offered a more nuanced perspective of Lincoln and also transitioned from calling the memorial an "object" to a monument. Douglass welcomed the crowd to see both Lincoln and Freedmen's Memorial in a newer and fuller light. He stated,

Truth is proper and beautiful at all times and in all places, and it is never more proper and beautiful in any case than when speaking of a great public man whose example is likely to be commended for honor and imitation long after his departure . . . truth compels me to admit, even here in the presence of the monument we have erected to his memory, Abraham Lincoln was not, in the fullest sense of the word, either our [Black people's] man or our model. In his interests, in his associations, in his habits of thought, and in his prejudices, he was a white man.

He was preeminently the white man's President, entirely devoted to the welfare of white men. He was ready and willing at any time during the first years of his administration to deny, postpone, and sacrifice the rights of humanity in the colored people to promote the welfare of the white people of this country. In all his education and feeling he was an American of the Americans. He came into the Presidential chair upon one principle alone, namely, opposition to the extension of slavery. His arguments in furtherance of this policy had their motive and mainspring in his patriotic devotion to the interests of his own race. To protect, defend, and perpetuate slavery in the states where it existed Abraham Lincoln was not less ready than any other President to draw the sword of the nation. He was ready to execute all the supposed guarantees of the United States Constitution in favor of the slave system anywhere inside the slave states. . . . The race to which we belong were not the special objects of his consideration. Knowing this, I concede to you, my white fellow-citizens, a pre-eminence in this worship at once full and supreme. First, midst, and last, you and yours were the objects of his deepest affection and his most earnest solicitude. You are the children of Abraham Lincoln. We are at best only his step-children; children by adoption, children by forces of circumstances and necessity. To you it especially belongs to sound his praises, to preserve and perpetuate his memory, to multiply his statues . . . for while Abraham Lincoln saved for you a country, he delivered us from a bondage. . . .

The name of Abraham Lincoln was near and dear to our hearts in the darkest and most perilous hours of the Republic. We were no more ashamed of him when shrouded in clouds of darkness, of doubt, and defeat than when we saw him crowned with victory, honor, and glory. Our faith in him was often taxed and strained to the uttermost, but it never failed.

Though he loved Caesar less than Rome, though the Union was more to him than our freedom or our future, under his wise and beneficent rule we saw ourselves gradually lifted from the depths of slavery to the heights of liberty and manhood; under his wise and beneficent rule, and by measures approved and vigorously pressed by him, we saw that the handwriting of ages, in the form of prejudice and proscription, was rapidly fading away from the face of our whole country; . . . we saw two hundred thousand of our dark and dusky people responding to the call of Abraham Lincoln, and with muskets on their shoulders, and eagles on their buttons, timing their high footsteps to liberty and union under the national flag; . . . under his rule, and in the fullness of time, we saw Abraham Lincoln . . . penning the immortal paper . . . making slavery forever impossible in the United States.[33]

Douglass's dedicatory speech moved beyond the typical singular heroic portrayal of Lincoln, as represented visually in the Freedmen's Memorial. Douglass presented a more complex characterization of a man caught in the inevitable tide of self-preservation, power, racism, nation building, and the advancement of whiteness. Though Lincoln's actions, in the end, were courageous, Douglass reminded the crowd that they must be viewed within the context of his commitment to the welfare of white men and his desire to preserve the Union. Black people's well-being and freedom were by-products of those endeavors.

In his final words, Douglass also reminded twenty-five thousand people assembled that their gathering for Lincoln must not overshadow the generous and patriotic acts done by those whom America willfully held in bondage. He closed by pointing to the monument as a symbolic representation of Black people's hospitality, fortitude, and patriotism. Their act alone provided Americans with a new way of seeing what it means to remain hopeful, charitable, loyal, and impartial to a people and a nation while repeatedly being devalued and despised. He stated,

> Fellow-citizens, I end, as I began, with congratulations. We have done a good work for our race today. In doing honor to the memory of our friend and liberator, we have been doing highest honors to ourselves and those who come after us; we have been fastening ourselves to a name and fame imperishable and immortal; we have also been defending ourselves from a blighting scandal. When now it shall be said that the colored man is soulless, that he has no appreciation of benefits or benefactors; when the foul reproach of ingratitude is hurled at us, and it is attempted to scourge us beyond the range of human brotherhood, we may calmly point to the monument we have this day erected to the memory of Abraham Lincoln.[34]

The band softly began playing "Sicilian Vespers" as Douglass took his seat. The Reverend John Philip Newman, pastor of Metropolitan Methodist Episcopal Church and former chaplain to the United States Senate, offered a solemn benediction. Soon after that, the processional reconvened and in lockstep proceeded southeast on Tenth Street to

Pennsylvania Avenue and then B Street and then headed northwest on to First Street to Indiana Avenue until they reached City Hall. The large crowd that had gathered at Lincoln Square slowly dispersed. Charlotte Scott, a Black woman whose name appeared on the monument but not on the program, exited too, quietly among the fanfare.

## Freedmen's Memorial: Beyond the Pomp and Circumstance

Douglass's speech acknowledged the importance of both the moment and a dedicatory marker to remember and honor Lincoln and those formerly enslaved in the US. Yet Douglass and many others had "strong reservations about the appropriateness of this tribute to Lincoln's legacy."[35] Although in his address he did not explicitly critique the monument, many people knew Douglass took issue with its appearance. John W. Cromwell, a prominent Washingtonian who attended the ceremony and stood no more than fifteen feet from Douglass, recalled how Douglass "was very clear and emphatic in saying he did not like the attitude; it showed the Negro on his knees, when a more manly attitude would have been more indicative of freedom."[36]

Thomas Ball also recalled how Wendell Phillips, a white abolitionist who divested himself of social standing to join the antislavery movement, also took issue with the memorial. Phillips opposed the monument erected in Lincoln Square and a second one placed in Park Square in Boston, Massachusetts. Ball writes, "Wendell Phillips, did me the honor to wish I 'would go to heaven soon;' but seeing no prospect of it, and evidently thinking that I had received although too many honors . . . he sent me away with his exceedingly vulgar tirade against me and the Boston statues ringing in my ears,—as if I had made them all! . . . Poor Mr. Phillips! He was generally scolding about something. But he did scold to some purpose for the poor negroes."[37]

Years later, civil rights icon and renowned African American art historian Freeman Henry Morris Murray also offered a scathing critique of the monument. Murray questioned the favorable accolades bestowed upon the statue by prominent Americans, saying the memorial is "far less adequate than it has been popularly regarded. . . . The conception of Lincoln in certain respects is lofty [and] as a whole is an unsatisfactory representation" and appears "to be saying: 'Go, and sin no more: or, Thy sins be forgiven thee.' As for the kneeling—or is it crouching?—figure," he has "little if any conception of the dignity and power of his own personality and manhood. . . . He seems to have a hazy idea that he is, more or less . . . free. . . . If he should speak, he would probably murmur dubiously and querulously, 'O Mr. Lincoln! Am I _____?'"[38]

Douglass's, Phillips's, and Murray's critiques of the monument must be seen within the context of the time. The monument was conceived at the close of slavery in America and erected near the end of Reconstruction, a crucial time in American history when the nation was steeped in racial violence and racial inequality. Though Black people felt inspired by the prospects of equality postemancipation, they were still without due process and access to the privileges afforded their white counterparts. Most of the social, political, and economic advances they achieved during the Reconstruction era were soon curtailed by Black Codes and Jim Crow laws designed to limit their mobility, agency, and civil rights.

White Americans' understanding of Black people as less than human and far less capable and intelligent than themselves or other groups did not diminish or decline after slavery, compounding Black people's postemancipation challenges. Though they built the country and fought to preserve it during the Civil War, Black people received few to none of the entitlements offered to white people in the new republic. Though their legal enslavement ended, the jaundiced worldview and discriminatory practices of their former enslavers often defined the value of their lives.

Though a glorious event, the pomp and circumstance ceremony for the unveiling of Freedmen's Memorial did nothing to alter and advance race relations in the US. After the ceremony and the Reconstruction era's end, race relations became increasingly violent: the period from 1876 to well into the 1920s is often described as "the nadir of American race relations," when racist violence was deemed worse than any other period in US history since slavery.[39] White domestic terrorist groups such as the White Knights, the Knights of the White Camellia, the White League, Kuklos Adelphon (Circle of Brothers founded at the University of North Carolina in 1812), and the Ku Klux Klan (KKK) persistently perpetrated anti-Black violence and propaganda. Black people were harassed, mutilated, murdered, lynched, burned, and jailed at a higher rate than in previous periods.

Segregation, legal racial discrimination, organized domestic terror-ism, mob violence, white power politics, and expressions of white supremacy were normalized in many parts of the US. The Freedmen's Memorial stood in Lincoln Square as a grim reminder of slavery and of the disparity between those in power and those who occupied mar-ginalized places in the world.

Douglass's, Phillips's, and Murray's critiques encapsulate this reality. They saw in the monument a microcosm of the American society they sought to change. Viewed within this context, the erection of Freedmen's Memorial marks a poignant moment in US history—not only because it is the first monument in the nation's capital purported to acknowledge formerly enslaved people's contribution to the country and Lincoln's role in securing their freedom at a tumultuous time in US history but also because it falls short as a national symbol of freedom in a society yet to acknowledge its historical embeddedness in structural racism and discrimination. Beyond the rhetoric and romanticized notions of Black liberation in the US, the monument reinforces a revisionist history of slavery. From the time of American slavery to the present, it purports a rendering of history that mutes the voices of the Black women, men, and children who contributed to the building of this nation and who most severely experienced slavery's horrific impact. After the pomp and circumstance, American officials and prominent figures referred to the statue as a symbol of freedom and racial solidarity. But for a vast major-ity of people living in the US at the time, the memorial was a poor rep-resentation of freedom and racial solidarity. Black people were living in a country where their bent backs became a bridge for the welfare of the people who lorded over them.

Freedmen's Memorial's design and road to completion missed the mark. The memorial as a national symbol falls short in three ways. The monument perpetuates Black people's oppression, whitewashes malevolence, and implies absolution without accountability.

## Perpetuating Black Peoples' Oppression

Freedmen's Memorial ultimately reinforces racial stereotypes. Its depiction of a half-naked Black man kneeling with a forlorn gaze at the foot of a white man perpetuates the white supremacist nature of the master–slave dichotomy in America. The dichotomy between Lincoln and Alexander is striking and yet is undoubtedly indicative of the time. Lincoln, the leader of the free world, stands tall, a stately figure dressed in his signature double-breasted coat representing authority, access, benevolence, and power. Alexander, on the other hand, appears defeated and solicitous of a white male liberator. Douglass, Phillips, and Murray liken Ball's portrayal of formerly enslaved Black people to one of weakness and docility.

The racial stereotypes represented in the memorial played into the larger antebellum world's oversimplified generalizations about various racial groups. These stereotypes held by former enslavers and colonists persist today. Since early American history, some whites still consider slavery as morally justifiable because they believe that Black people are savages, promiscuous, and uncivilized. Europeans and colonists characterize Black people as inherently childish, naturally lazy, resistant to hard work, easily contented, and adaptable to pain. Whites consider Blacks to be simpleminded and unteachable, mentally and biologically inferior, apelike in appearance, violent, and loud. Since Black people are ill equipped to care for themselves, whites believe Black people need an all-wise, all-powerful, and all-knowing white master and other Europeans to guide them. As mentioned previously former enslaved man, James Fisher, recalled how his slave owner told him, "the reason why they murdered and devoured one another in Africa was because there were no white people there to make them behave themselves."[40]

Clearly, these and other stereotypical assumptions do not lend themselves to openness about the value, worth, and agency of Black people and the spectrum of difference between diverse Black communities. These assumptions are deeply held convictions, affixed in early Europeans and American colonists' and present-day white people's minds, and woven into their sense of identity and system of reality. Most early European and American colonists and present-day white people define themselves in contrast to their assumptions about Black people. For example, they often reason that since Black people are savages, they—white people—are civilized. Since Black people are simpleminded and unteachable, white people are highly evolved and intelligent. Since Black people are violent and loud, white people are genteel and self-controlled. Europeans and white Americans are willing to defend this sense of self-identity and system of reality at any cost.

These negative beliefs or prejudices that Europeans and American colonists held about Black people resulted in discriminatory practices that often meant the difference between life and death, thriving and scraping by, and justice and inequality. Discriminatory practices that sought to deny Black people resources, access, and justice because of their racialized identification and social location. Black people's daily lives were steeped in this polarizing and racist worldview. Inevitably, some Black people began to internalize that there was something inherently iniquitous about themselves and inherently pure about white people and at times began inflicting some of the same racist stereotypes, prejudices, and discriminatory practices used against them onto themselves and other Black people. As enslaved preacher Reverend W. B. Allen put it emphatically, "If it wasn't for the influence of the white race in the South, the Negro race would revert to savagery within a year."[41] Another formerly enslaved man, James Reeves, remarked, "We were savages when we came over here. Everything we got and everything we know, good and bad, we got from white folks."[42] Not all Black people shared these views during slavery and postemancipation. Yet regardless of how Black people saw themselves, whites' racially disparaging stereotypes were physically, psychologically, and emotionally harmful to Black people's sense of self and well-being.

Douglass's, Phillips's, and Murray's analyses help us see how Freedmen's Memorial reinforces racist stereotypes and long-held assumptions in American colonists' minds. Rather than serve as a source of inspiration and a symbol of freedom, to this day, the monument memorializes the master–slave dichotomy. Douglass, Phillips, and Murray also suggest that as a racist trope, the monument is an "unsatisfactory representation" of Black people. The kneeling slave does not capture a nuanced portrayal of Black people and their contribution to the nation. It does not adequately represent how Black people collectively saw themselves, nor does it compel us, as a human community, to contemplate the depths of the slave experience in America and Black people's deep yearning for freedom.

Black people were active agents in building this country and securing their freedom. Chapters 1–5 have recounted their ingenuity, sacrifice, intellect, skills, work ethic, creativity, sacrifice, resilience, and wisdom, qualities on which they drew as they labored throughout the US. It is insulting to call Black people lazy during and after emancipation, when 90 percent of the world's cotton alone was produced by Black people laboring in Southern states. Americans in Northern and Southern states depended on Black labor to thrive in the New World. Indeed, Black people were such an essential workforce in the United States that by 1860, their commodified value "outweighed all the money invested in this country's railroads, banking and industry combined."[43] Or as economist David Brion Davis puts it, "In 1860, the value of Southern slaves was about three times the amount invested in manufacturing or railroads nationwide."[44] At the time of the Civil War, enslaved Black people were collectively "the second most valuable capital asset in the United States," the first being land.[45]

Enslaved and free Black people were not a monolithic group of docile, ignorant, and debased persons who waited timidly for Americans with influence to free them. Though their emancipation was not possible without the aid of white American allies, Black people were actively involved in securing their freedom and used a variety of means to emancipate themselves. They absconded, organized and led slave revolts, fought in wars, served as spies, created underground networks and secret societies, led abolitionist movements, established newspapers depicting the horrors of American slavery, and developed strategies and secret codes. The formerly enslaved attacked slave owners' properties as a means of destabilizing them economically, legislated their freedom in courtrooms, and purchased their freedom and their family members' freedom. They also led marches and boycotts and wrote and distributed antislavery pamphlets and autobiographies, which became useful to the abolitionists' cause.

During the Civil War, over ten thousand enslaved persons fled their masters and ran to cross Union lines for protection. The nation's capital became a haven for a majority of enslaved persons fleeing Maryland and Virginia under the threat of violence. These laborers became known as contrabands—and the nation's capital wasted no time in exploiting them. Upon crossing, they helped troops build fortifications to protect federal property and land. Some received forty cents plus rations per day, while others received no wages. These and other pursuits are evidence that formerly enslaved Black people were not simpleminded, docile persons who crawled their way to freedom as the Freedmen's Memorial depicts. Though grateful for freedom, Black people were neither indebted to Lincoln nor helpless in their pursuits.

The monument fell short because it reinforced existing stereotypes. Rucker, Yeatman, Eliot, Ball, and others could have avoided this outcome by including formerly enslaved and free Blacks' design ideas and voices in the production and design process. By silencing their voices, the monument affirmed widely held views about the master–slave relationship. The kneeling position is representative of America's racist assumptions about Black people.

Today, the memorial continues to reinforce harmful tropes about Black and white people. Such representation of Black life within a paternalistic enslaving white culture stifles and robs Americans of the truth about its past and the resourceful agency, dignity, and creative resilience of Black people. All monuments in the US produced with intentional shortsightedness and narrow vision of America's past whitewashes racism in its presentation of white people as heroes, saviors, and men and women of valor and Black people as helpless perpetual victims in need of white benevolence. As an evolving society, we must question how the Freedmen's Memorial came to be, the stories told about it, and the motivations and perceptions surrounding its representation. We must also question the absence of a monument on the National Mall that truthfully depicts the United States' role in American slavery and the contributions of millions of enslaved Black people forced to work, over 250 years, to help build this nation.

## Whitewashing Malevolence

Racialized ideologies were so embedded in the fabric of the US that with time, they normalized American slavery and Americans' valuation of Black people. Though Lincoln apologists often cite him as one who opposed slavery, at the unveiling ceremony, Douglass pointedly reminded those gathered that Lincoln's opposition was not altogether true. Douglass stated, "It must be admitted, truth compels me to admit . . . Abraham Lincoln was . . . entirely devoted to the welfare of white men. He was ready to execute all the supposed guarantees of the United States Constitution in favor of the slave system anywhere inside the slave states. He was willing to pursue, recapture, and send back the fugitive slave to his master, and to suppress a slave rising for liberty."[46] Douglass expressed what many Blacks felt at the time. Lincoln was "an American of the Americans," and Black people "were not the special objects of his consideration." Black people were a by-product of his political ambitions. Lincoln's Emancipation Proclamation did not free Black people, nor did the original Thirteenth Amendment. In fact, the original Thirteenth Amendment proposed by Senator William Seward of New York sought to make American slavery constitutional and permanent. Known as the "Corwin Amendment" or the "Slavery Amendment," Congress passed it in 1861, but it was not ratified. The Corwin Amendment read in part, "No amendment shall be made to the Constitution which will authorize or give to Congress the power to abolish or interfere, within any State, with the domestic institutions thereof, including that of persons held to labor or service by the laws of said State."

In his first inaugural address, Lincoln had insisted that "the Federal Government shall never interfere with the domestic institutions of the States, including that of persons held to service. . . . Holding such a provision to now be implied constitutional law, I have no objection to its being made express and irrevocable."[47] Lincoln's position on slavery was hardly unambiguous, nor were his views on the inferiority and superiority of the races. In 1858, Lincoln and incumbent Democratic senator Stephen Douglas participated in the Illinois senatorial debate. In response to Douglas's charge that Lincoln supported Black people's equality, Lincoln remarked,

> I am not, nor ever have been, in favor of bringing about in any way the social and political equality of the white and Black races. . . . I am not nor ever have been in favor of making voters or jurors of Negroes, nor of qualifying them to hold office, nor to intermarry with white people; and I will say in addition to this that there is a physical difference between the white and Black races which I believe will forever forbid the two races from living together on terms of social and political equality. And inasmuch as they cannot so live, while they do remain together there must be a position of superior and inferior, and I as much as any other man am in favor of having the superior position assigned to the white race.[48]

Lincoln apologists argue that Lincoln's position on slavery and the inferiority of Black people and superiority of whites must be taken in context and do not reflect the full scope of a man whose views evolved overtime, especially concerning race relations. But Lincoln spoke these words. Lincoln was socialized into a world of racial delusion, a world birthed and steeped in racial hatred and inequality. Those who ascribe to such a world often deny that the beliefs they harbor and the actions they do are racist. The views Lincoln expressed at his debate and inauguration are not an aberration. Not only did he express similar convictions on other occasions, but his words reflect the inclinations of those in power in the nation—that is, whites.

Alexander H. Stephens, vice president of the newly formed Confederate States of America, captured this mood of the nation in an extemporaneous speech, delivered on March 21, 1861, at the athenaeum in Savannah, Georgia. Stephens stood before an all-white packed room just weeks before the Civil War began with the Battle of Fort Sumter and said that the "cornerstone" of the Confederate government "rests upon [one] great truth . . . the negro is not equal to the white man; that slavery subordination to the superior race is his natural and normal condition."[49]

Though Lincoln and Stephens were at odds, the two shared views on slavery and on the inferiority and superiority of the races. These views were not limited to the South. Many Northerners held similar views. Though Northern states eventually opposed slavery, one cannot overlook the reality that their existence and their infrastructure are due in large part to enslaved labor, which many colonists exploited and relied upon for two centuries. Nor did the abolition of slavery extinguish Northerners' long-held beliefs about Black people. Black people had a right to freedom but were seen as inferior. Even poor white Americans at the bottom of the sociopolitical and economic ladder considered Black people to be beneath them. As lawyer and civil rights activist Derrick Bell observed in *Faces at the Bottom of the Well*, "Black people are the magical faces at the bottom of society's well. Even the poorest whites, those who must live their lives only a few levels above, gain their self-esteem by gazing down on us. Surely, they must know that their deliverance depends on letting down their ropes. Only by working together is escape possible. Over time, many reach out, but most simply watch, mesmerized into maintaining their unspoken commitment to keeping us where we are, at whatever cost to them or to us."[50]

That the institution of slavery and the inferiority and superiority of the races were intrinsically linked was also expressed by the Christian Church and espoused from the pulpit. Stephen Elliott, the presiding bishop of the Protestant Episcopal Church in the Confederate States of America, referred to the institution of slavery as a "sacred trust from God . . . a divinely guarded system, planted by God, protected by God and arranged for his own wise purposes in the future of him."[51] Such widely held views as expressed by Bishop Elliott fed Americans' notions about the superiority of whiteness and white people's divinely destined presence in the New World. God, they believed, chose them to exercise lordship over other people and lands. Slavery was a divine mandate given to them by God to subdue territories and bring the uncivilized and unsaved darker-skinned people to toil in the New World or garden of Eden as penance for their sins. As Alexander Stephens put it in another speech before the Georgia legislature, "Our first parents, the great progenitors of the human race . . . were led to believe that their condition would be bettered—that their eyes would be opened—and that they would become as gods. . . . I look upon this country, with our institutions, as the Eden of the world, the paradise of the universe."[52] Europeans and American colonists' assumptions about their manifest destiny led some to view themselves as saviors. Claims such as those espoused by Elliott and Stephens support such views: "[White] culture has changed [Black people] from savages into servants, from barbarians into men of Christian feeling and Christian sympathy."[53] White culture and whiteness became associated with purity, beauty, light, sacredness, holiness, privilege, entitlement, supremacy, civility and civilization, sovereignty, faultlessness, propriety, morality, normativity, and benevolence. Blackness, on the other hand, was associated with Black people. By extension, Blackness and Black people represented all that was vile, ugly, dark, profane, burdensome, subordinate, ungodly, inferior, ignorant, shameful, unsuitable, immoral, abnormal, evil, and uncivilized.

So the question becomes, what was it that fueled Yeatman, Eliot, Ball, and the commission's thought processes when they set out to capture the story of Lincoln, emancipation, and the formerly enslaved in the Freedmen's Memorial monument? To judge by the outcome, it is conceivable that these men drew from their personally held views and the larger society's conception of race, slavery, and freedom. Their version contributed to the larger American saga that romanticizes whiteness absent of white people's failures and comports blackness in a perpetual state of depravity void of human worth and agency. In this sense, Black people would find themselves always in need of white people and ideas of whiteness to save them from themselves.

Yeatman, Eliot, Ball, and the others, like their predecessors, gave primacy to whiteness. In their portrayal of Lincoln as the Great Emancipator and savior, Lincoln is rendered well intended, stately, gallant, powerful, paternal, civilized, and benevolent. But Douglass has helped us see that such a message is incomplete and misleading. Lincoln was not altogether a heroic and generous American who cared about the welfare of Black people. By characterizing Lincoln as the Great Emancipator and savior and his actions as benevolent and heroic, we obscure the malevolent layers of his story. We also give Lincoln and others a pass for their role in American slavery and the atrocities inflicted on Black-bodied people. Equally troubling is how influential and privileged white men read and write themselves into American history without acknowledging their failures or any accountability for their actions and role as the primary perpetrators of sins committed against Black-bodied people. The story that the Freedmen's Memorial conveys is one grounded in the values of privileged white men, men who never consulted those Black persons who conceived and funded the monument.

So the questions become, What then are we to do with the Lincoln such white men concealed? Are we to ignore the Lincoln that spent a lifetime asserting Black people's inferiority? Are we to overlook the Lincoln whose ideologies and policies harmed Black people? Are we to downplay the Lincoln who was slow to act when it came to abolishing slavery and only pay attention to his Emancipation Proclamation?

What are we to do, as a nation, with the historical figures we have enshrined on the National Mall and throughout the country that intentionally harm Black-bodied people? How shall we assess our memorialization of them? Should their memorials be taken down, or should a more nuanced version of their lives stand alongside them? How shall we continue in this democratic endeavor with a whitewashed and selective representation of American history? Why are we, as Americans, reluctant to hear the full story of our beginnings, the birth of the nation, and the Founding Fathers and others we revere? Is our reluctance grounded in fear of having to reevaluate long-standing notions of whiteness and blackness, depravity and goodness, and cowardice and heroism? When we portray the Founding Fathers and other slave owners, and those who advocate racist ideologies and enact racialized policies that harm others as benevolent, we cease perceiving them as cruel. When we cease perceiving them as cruel, we fail to hold them accountable.

## Absolution without Accountability

Douglass closes his speech by reminding those gathered (and those reading his words for generations to come) to remember the moment the human community gathered in solidarity to witness the unveiling of the Freedmen's Memorial and to celebrate Abraham Lincoln and acknowledge Black people's contribution. Douglass concludes by saying,

> Fellow–citizens, I end, as I began, with congratulations. We have done a good work for our race today. In doing honor to the memory of our friend and liberator, we have been doing highest honors to ourselves and those who come after us. . . . When now it shall be said that the colored man is soulless, that he has no appreciation of benefits or benefactors; when the foul reproach of ingratitude is hurled at us, and it is attempted to scourge us beyond the range of human brotherhood, we may calmly point to the monument we have this day erected to the memory of Abraham Lincoln.[54]

Douglass's words shed light on Black people's willingness to participate in the American democratic experiment amid relentless ridicule and personal attacks. Douglass points to the memorial as evidence of Black people's appreciation, kindness, and at times forgiving spirit toward those who harm them and show little to no remorse and accountability for that harm. Oftentimes, they double down on their acts of hatred and disdain for Black life, even after Black people forgive them or show some level of graciousness or empathy. Freedmen's Memorial points to the strange juxtaposition of Black people's kindness and forgiving spirit and white people's lack of ownership, accountability, and contrition for harming them. Such has been the case before and during the memorial's unveiling to the present day.

Take for example in 1963, when four Black girls (an eleven-year-old, Denise McNair, and three fourteen-year-olds, Addie Mae Collins, Cynthia Wesley, and Carole Robertson), became a casualty of the civil rights movement following the bombing of the Sixteenth Street Baptist Church in Birmingham, Alabama. A fifth girl, twelve-year-old Sarah Collins Rudolph, who was also in the church's basement, survived the ordeal. The bomb detonated before the little girls ever got a chance to hear the Sunday sermon, titled "The Love That Forgives." Homemade bombs by white terrorist individuals and groups planted in Black people's homes, businesses, and churches were so prevalent in Birmingham that the city became known as "Bombingham." White supremacists saw themselves as defenders and preservers of America, a society wherein Black people's place in the world was on their knees and subservient to white people. The bomb blast was their reminder.

Rallies, protests, and repeated calls for justice to state and national legislators and the justice department went unanswered. Alabama and FBI officers had a strong inclination of the possible suspects involved in the bombing but chose not to bring charges, citing concerns regarding weak convictions. Nearly fourteen years passed before some semblance of justice emerged. In 1977, Alabama native Robert E. Chambliss (a.k.a. Dynamite Bob), a member of the United Klans of America who often bragged to family and friends about the bombing, was convicted. Nearly twenty-five years later, after Chambliss's arrest, two other Klan members, Bobby Frank Cherry, an Alabama native, and Thomas Edwin Blanton Jr., a Washington, DC, native, were also convicted of the bombing. However, the national spotlight faded on the men. Media attention turned to Rudolph, the fifth girl, who had remained relatively quiet and did not publicly speak about the bombing until she was nearly fifty.

In 2016, Rudolph and others in the community attended Blanton's parole hearing, opposing his release. Rudolph, who was still suffering from the effects of the Sunday morning tragedy, told reporters she "found it in her heart to forgive Blanton" and the men.[55] "I had to forgive him," she said.[56] "I didn't want that on me to hate him because

the devil used him. You don't put a bomb in a church and kill innocent children. Hating him and not forgiving him won't bring my sister
back."[57] As Rudolph's words of forgiveness became the focal point of
speaking engagements, the three men convicted of killing four little
girls and injuring over twenty people did not accept any responsibility
for the crime.

In 2020, Rudolph sought restitution from the state of Alabama.
Governor Kay Ivey responded to her letter, saying, "As you noted . . .
'the State Alabama did not place the bomb next to the church.' For this
and other reasons, many would question whether the state can be held
legally responsible for what happened at the Sixteenth Street Baptist
Church so long ago. There is no question," the governor continued,
that many "suffered an egregious injustice that has yielded untold pain
and suffering over the ensuing decades. For that, they most certainly
deserve a sincere, heartfelt apology."[58]

In 2014, nine Black people attending a prayer service at Mother
Emanuel AME Church in Charleston, South Carolina, were gunned
down by Dylann Roof, a white supremacist. Two days after the shooting, attention turned from Roof and white supremacist violence in the
US to testimonies of forgiveness by family members of the murdered
and survivors of the shooting. Their words were lauded as a model for
the nation. One reporter during an interview asked survivors of the
shooting who forgave Roof, "Do you ever get tired of always being
strong?" The women responded, "All the time, all the time." Throughout the arraignment and trial, Roof showed no remorse, writing in his
journal while imprisoned that the shootings and his loss of freedom
were worth it. He wrote, "I would like to make it crystal clear I do not
regret what I did. I am not sorry. I have not shed a tear for the innocent
people I killed."[59]

On September 6, 2018, Botham Jean, a twenty-six-year-old Black
man, was sitting in his Dallas, Texas, apartment eating ice cream
around 10:00 p.m. Amber Guyger, a thirty-year-old white female off-
duty police officer, entered his home, believing it was her apartment
just one floor below. Guyger, alarmed by his presence (what she called a
"large silhouette"), fired two shots, striking Botham fatally in the chest.
After turning on the lights, Guyger realized she was in the wrong apartment and called 911. Botham died shortly after at the hospital.

Ronnie "Bunny" Babbs, a twenty-nine-year-old Black woman residing in the apartment complex, posted her video of the incident on social
media after reading and hearing contradictory statements that Guyger
and other officials made about the shooting. Babbs indicated that after
she heard two shots, a man yelled, "Oh my God! Why did you do that?"[60]
Guyger then appeared frantic, pacing outside the apartment on her cell
phone. She admitted that she did not administer CPR properly.[61] The
Dallas Police Department placed Guyger on administrative leave with
pay, and three days later, she was charged with manslaughter. Within
two months, Guyger was charged with murder and pled not guilty. At
her trial in October 2019, her defense presented a picture of a model
officer, a white woman in distress who mistakenly entered the wrong
apartment after working a long shift. Guyger testified, saying in part, "I
was scared whoever was inside my apartment was gonna kill me and I'm
sorry."[62] Guyger's lawyers argued that Botham's death was the result of
an "unfortunate set of circumstances." The opposing counsel followed
with witnesses and a succession of incendiary and racist social media
posts and text messages authored by Guyger. Within five hours of deliberations, the jury convicted Guyger of murder. She received a sentence of
ten years in prison, far less than the ninety-nine-year maximum.

Botham's younger brother, Brandt Jean, asked Judge Tammy Kemp
if he could speak. Brandt, visibly moved, publicly forgave Guyger, telling her he loved her, he wanted the best for her, and he did not want
her to go to jail. Then Brandt asked permission to hug Guyger. The two
embraced for nearly one minute, exchanging words and tears. The Black
female bailiff stroked Guyger's hair. Guyger turned to the judge, a
Black woman, and asked her for a hug. Judge Kemp replied, "Ms. Guyger, Mr. Jean has forgiven you. Please forgive yourself so that you can
have a purposeful life."[63] Guyger asked the judge, "Do you think God
will forgive me?"[64] Judge Kemp replied yes. She then proceeded to her
office, returned holding her personal Bible, and handed it to Guyger,
saying, "This is the one I use every day."[65]

This scene began saturating the airwaves of media outlets. The
stories placed the spotlight on Brandt, Judge Kemp, and the bailiff's
acts of kindness. True to form, the nation's attention and conversation
shifted immediately from police violence against Black-bodied people
and racial disparities in America to Black people's display of forgiveness

and grace. No fewer than two months after the conviction, on December 3, 2019, the Institute for Law Enforcement Administration honored Brandt Jean at the institute's annual ceremony in Plano, Texas. After replaying his courtroom apology video, the institute presented Brandt the 2019 Ethical Courage Award for his public display of empathy and forgiveness toward Amber Guyger. After a standing ovation, Brandt accepted the award. No words were spoken at the ceremony about Botham's senseless death and police accountability. Two weeks after her conviction, Guyger filed a notice to appeal her conviction, citing insufficient evidence to convict her of murder and requesting an acquittal of the murder charge and a new hearing.

On March 13, 2020, Breonna Taylor, a twenty-six-year-old Black female full-time emergency room technician, was asleep in her bed inside her apartment on the south end of Louisville, Kentucky. Taylor and her boyfriend, Kenneth Walker, were startled by a loud pounding at the door shortly before 1:00 a.m. Taylor yelled out, "Who is it?" No response. Then the pounding continued, and Taylor again asked, "Who is it?"[66] But there was still no response. Suddenly, there was a loud bang, and the door was pushed off its hinges. Walker immediately fired one shot to protect Breonna and himself and was met by a succession of firepower, which one neighbor described as sounding "like the OK Corral."[67] Another neighbor exclaimed, "They just unloaded."[68] The intruders were plainclothes police officers serving a signed no-knock search warrant as part of a narcotics investigation. They used a battering ram to break down the door and enter the apartment. Walker's one shot at the door struck Sgt. Jonathan Mattingly in the leg, and the return fire from Officer Brett Hankison's and Detective Myles Cosgrove's guns—more than twenty rounds—entered Taylor and Walker's home and neighboring apartments. After multiple rounds struck Taylor, she fell to the floor, bleeding in the hallway of her home.

Walker was immediately taken into custody and charged with assault and the attempted murder of a police officer, even though he had a right to carry a firearm under Kentucky law. The Louisville Metropolitan Police Department (LMPD) placed the three officers on administrative reassignment with pay. Six days after her shooting, Taylor's family held a prayer vigil in downtown Louisville. Two weeks later, Walker was released and placed under house arrest. On April 27, Taylor's mother,

Tamika Palmer, sued the officers for excessive force and gross negligence. Taylor had committed no crime, posed no immediate threat, and did not resist or attempt to evade officers. Yet the officers unloaded a succession of bullets into her home from various angles, breaking objects, destroying property, endangering neighbors, and ultimately killing Taylor.

Public protests and petitions demanding answers and investigations intensified, and a clearer picture around the Breonna Taylor shooting began to emerge. Five clear points caused significant pause. First, Breonna Taylor was not a suspect. Her home was a "soft target" and not central to an ongoing narcotics investigation. The main target, Taylor's ex-boyfriend, Jamarkcus Glover, a known drug dealer, was already in police custody on the day of the shooting. Second, weeks after the shooting, word leaked that Glover was offered a plea deal if Glover named Taylor as a codefendant in his case, an apparent cleanup and cover-up attempt by the police. Glover denied such allegations and refused the plea deal. Third, Louisville police sought to name Taylor's home as a known location where Glover received mailed packages to traffic narcotics but has yet to substantiate the allegation. Fourth, Amy Hess, the Louisville chief of public safety, publicly acknowledged that mistakes were made in the case. Fifth, the City of Louisville settled the Taylor family's civil suit, awarding them $12 million along with notable policy changes and reforms.

However, the criminal case against the officers presented to the grand jury by Kentucky attorney general Daniel Cameron fell flat. Cameron, a Black man, concluded Taylor's shooting was tragic but not a crime. "Ultimately, our judgment," Cameron said, "is that the charge that we could prove at trial beyond a reasonable doubt was for wanton endangerment against Mr. Hankison" for shooting into the neighbors' homes.[69] Cameron concluded that the officers shooting at Walker and Taylor was justifiable because Walker fired first. He also maintained that he presented all of the evidence and a thorough and complete case to the grand jury.[70] But one juror later filed a suit calling for complete transparency, and three others called for Cameron's impeachment.

In the end, a Black woman who had been asleep in her bed was now dead on her floor, lying in a pool of her blood. She remained on the floor for over thirteen hours as the men walked around her as though her life had no meaning, no significance. Neither the officers nor Cameron assumed responsibility for any aspect of the death of Breonna Taylor. Officer Hankison pleaded not guilty to three counts of wanton endangerment for shooting into Taylor's neighbors' apartments. Sgt. Mattingly emailed his LMPD colleagues, saying, "I know we did the legal, moral, and ethical thing that night."[71]

All of these troubling and violent stories are a mere snapshot of Americans' public disregard for Black life and the rush for absolution without accountability. These stories, like Freedmen's Memorial, speak directly to the complexities of Black people's generosity, graciousness, and forgiveness. They simultaneously speak to white-bodied people and their allies' lack of remorse, acceptance, and accountability for their injury to Black-bodied people. The work of formerly enslaved and free Black people to establish a memorial in honor of Lincoln and freedom, despite the brutality and ongoing institutionalized terror they encountered, demonstrates their kindhearted nature and willingness to work together. Americans have often used and co-opted this kindness by publicly parading Black people's forgiving spirit to deflect attention away from their culpability in acts of violence against Black people. Governments, institutions, corporations, and media outlets also play a role by failing to call out and properly hold accountable those who inflict harm. As a society, we can no longer hug away or seem oblivious to racism, white supremacy, white fragility and fear, and injury to others, especially injury that leads to loss of life. Cruelty is not patriotic, and patriots are not cowards. We as a society can no longer expect forgiveness without also demanding justice and accountability. Forgiveness does not absolve America of its responsibility to redress slavery, institutionalized racism, human harm, and murder.

Freedmen's Memorial conveys a story, from a dominant culture's perspective, of formerly enslaved Black people giving their meager monies to give thanks to Lincoln and the nation. And in the end, we witness a half-naked, bent Black man with his hand out as the man standing erect over him offers no hint of contrition or shame. Generosity, graciousness, forgiveness, and, most of all, equality and fairness should be what we all strive to achieve. However, these virtues are meaningless when they are not mutually given and received within the human community. These virtues are meaningless without a society holding accountable, in systemic and tangible ways, those who inflict, incite, support, and perpetuate acts of racial injustice and violence. We need new models, new memorials, new monuments, and fresh voices working together to dismantle the hierarchy of human value in America, fresh voices, old and young, with diverse perspectives, courageous enough to reimagine and construct a more inclusive history.

## Conclusion

In some sense, Freedmen's Memorial preserves and upholds the myth of whiteness and its association with heroism, benevolence, and racial superiority. It seeks to tell a story of American exceptionalism and freedom absent of American hypocrisy and slavery. America did hold Black-bodied people in bondage as part of a more extensive European network to cement its presence and advancement in the world. From its inception, the young nation was and continues to be intentionally cruel to Black and Native American people. From 1619 to the present, Black people have not been "the special object of consideration" of Europeans, early American colonists, and the nation's Founding Fathers. Slavery was the economic engine that ushered in the young nation. At its peak, "slavery was a $3 billion-plus industry and a major engine of the US economy" and a significant contributor to European countries' growth.[72] The early founders and their descendants did not readily turn their backs on the institution because "slavery's profitability far outweighed the moral outrage it engendered."[73] Douglass captured this reality in his speech, and Ball and the other men chose to conceal it in Freedmen's Memorial.

A monument's power rests not in its ability to shy away from truths but in honoring the full scope or a more nuanced depiction of an individual, group, and historical moment. A monument's power lies in its ability to prioritize and remain open to different stories and cultural contexts that contradict or complement dominant narratives in hopes of a more life-giving shared outcome. Accurate depictions of an individual, group, or event seek to convey all sides of the story—the harmful and the heroic, the distasteful and the healing, the white and the Black, the bent and the privileged. We sense this in Douglass's speech as he both takes issue with Lincoln and celebrates his actions.

Freedmen's Memorial falls short because it provides us a one-sided, biased, and inaccurate account grounded in the myth of American exceptionalism. It tells us a story of American freedom absent of American tyranny. It tells us a story of Lincoln's heroism while excluding Lincoln's practices of oppression. The memorial neglected to include the voices and capture the full scope of those Black people who played a role in its erection and should have been the main focus of its design. They, too, are patriots. The monument's failure is not an aberration. The same holds for many markers on the National Mall and across the country. Such monuments of selective memory and willful omission told from the dominant culture's perspective signify another form of institutionalized racism and white privilege.

We must be diligent in telling a more inclusive story of America, our Founding Fathers, and the white men we revere while also being intentional about honoring those early essential laborers who have made sacrifices for the good of this nation. We must do so by telling the full story of their lives and contributions. The full breadth of their stories and the key events from their perspectives and their descendants' perspectives are essential to the historical narrative. When we arch toward these aims, we do, as Douglass says, "highest honors to ourselves and those who come after us . . . we defend ourselves from a blighting scandal." We, as a nation, have yet to embrace the outcome of what we have done. History calls us to do so because America's role in the institution of slavery and the violent exploitation of Black-bodied people reaches far and wide beyond our shores. America is just one piece of the more extensive network that traumatically altered Black-bodied people's destinies and dreams. America must accept its blighted and destructive past. Only in doing so will its history be accurately reflected in its monuments and memory.

# CHAPTER SEVEN

# Black Memory
## Black Market, and the
## Transatlantic Slave Trade

*The inescapable fact that stuck in my craw, was: my people had sold me and the white people had bought me. . . . It impressed upon me the universal nature of greed and glory.*

—ZORA NEAL HURSTON, *Dust Tracks on a Road*

*When we see that our problem is so complicated and so all-encompassing in its intent and content, then we realize that it is no longer a Negro problem, confined only to the American Negro; that it is no longer an American problem, confined only to America, but it is a problem for humanity.*

—MALCOLM X

There is no adequate account of American history without the inclusion of American slavery. The institution of slavery in the United States is a fundamental part of American and world history. Millions of enslaved Black-bodied people and their descendants were instrumental in shaping the New World, a world that ultimately enriched European families, companies, and institutions.

Without question, the United States did not operate alone in the violent subjugation of Black people. Early mainland North American colonists continued the practices of human trafficking they inherited from their European forebears and carried them over to the New World. During the fifteenth century and before the US was conceived, ships left Portugal and headed to Africa to secure human cargo. Portugal was soon joined by Spain, followed by the Netherlands, Denmark, France, and Britain. By the early seventeenth century, all six countries had a hand in buying, kidnapping, and selling Black people for the purpose of free labor, capital gain, and expansion beyond Europe.

This international network in the trafficking of Black people became known as the transatlantic slave trade. Portugal, Spain, the Netherlands, Denmark, France, Britain, and other European countries were also the primary players in colonizing territories throughout the New World and parts of Africa. The persecution of Black people was not just an American reality but a global one. Without question, the transatlantic slave trade was a global legalized violation of Black-bodied people. The trade set the standards for Black people's disenfranchisement and racial disparagement in labor and social location in the US and across the Americas, the West Indies, and Europe. The oceanic trade was also an intentional and brutal mass displacement of millions of Black- and Brown-bodied people with no thought of their welfare or well-being.

Given this, it is important for societies—and here specifically, the US—not to gloss over stories of American slavery with stories of emancipation. There is little nobility in freeing, by an act of compromise or war, a group of people held in bondage over 250 years and continue to disenfranchise, disparage, and displace today. There is also little nobility in a nation's selective memory and the memorialization of white male figures on the National Mall and the omission of millions of essential Black laborers who helped forge the US into existence.

The horror of perpetual chattel slavery begins with the United States' founding crime—racism—and the unrepentant greed that it fueled. For over 250 years, the United States was a willing and active participant in the institution of slavery and the transatlantic slave trade. Acknowledging such a role shines a light on America's past, which provides us with warning signs to curtail and confront economic greed and systemic and present-day acts of racism and targeted harm toward vulnerable groups in the US. How did this global network, buttressed by greed and consumption and sustained by racist practices, work?

# The Transatlantic Slave Trade:
# A Global Network of Human Harm

The transatlantic slave trade, commonly referred to as the Atlantic slave trade, occurred between early sixteenth and late nineteenth centuries and was the largest transoceanic transplantation and trade in human beings in world history. The forced migration of millions of Black people involved a triangular trade route between three major regions—Europe, Africa, and the New World (the Americas and the West Indies). On the first leg of the triangular trade, European slave ships set sail from Europe toward West and West-Central Africa carrying manufactured goods—cloth, trinkets, beads, guns, iron, beer, and so on—for sale and trade. After selling or trading these items, some European vessels left African ports and returned to Europe with a cargo of gold, ivory, spices, hardwoods, and other natural resources from Africa. African people were also aboard these vessels for trade or labor in Europe.

Other European ships took a different route. They set sail from Africa carrying cargos of Black people across the Atlantic Ocean to the New World. This second leg of the journey, from Africa to the Americas and West Indies, was known as the Middle Passage, the most brutal part of the triangular trade. African women, men, and children were trapped in hand and leg irons and packed tight like sardines in the hull of the ship. Those who survived this leg of the journey often did so by lying in each other's feces and existing on very limited food and water. On occasion, women and girls roamed the main deck, making them accessible to the crewmen. Before disembarking in the New World or immediately upon arrival, some Africans were cleaned with gunpowder, lemon juice, and palm oil, a mixture rubbed into their skin and then polished with a brush like leather shoes to make them glisten in preparation for sale.

In the New World, they produced a variety of raw materials beneficial to world economies. We discussed tobacco, rice, sugar, and cotton in chapter 1, but among the other commodities were indigo, silk, whale oil, lumber, wood, furs, rum, iron, gunpowder, and tools. Enslaved laborers also helped build roads, buildings, and infrastructures. Some raw materials were produced first by laborers in South America and the West Indies. By the turn of the seventeenth century, Europeans enlarged their commerce and colonization enterprises to regions beyond South America and the West Indies to territories within North America.

At the completion of the second leg of the journey, enslaved laborers drained, scrubbed, and cleaned the ships and loaded them with raw materials for sale and distribution primarily in Europe. The journey from the New World back to Europe was the third and final leg of the ship's transatlantic journey. The transatlantic slave trade, the selling and loading of Black bodies onto slave ships and importing them in slave markets throughout Europe and the New World, was the first open and collective commodification of Black people and public statement that Black people's lives did not matter. Black people possessed no intrinsic value. Black people were racialized and thingified as insignificant not-quite-humans, whose value rested in the money their Black hands and bodies could produce. American racism and the blatant disregard of Black people's contribution did not happen in a vacuum.

## Black Market for Black Labor

As of today, the Slave Voyages website's Trans-Atlantic Slave Trade Database estimates that between 1514 and 1866, there were thirty-six thousand individual slaving expeditions by Europeans and Americans from the African continent that made their way across the Atlantic Ocean, transporting between 11.9 and 12.5+ million Black-bodied people to a life of perpetual bondage.[1] Some scholars articulate a much higher number of expeditions crossing the Atlantic and Africans taken from their homeland. The current and widely used number is often based on shipping manifestos, censuses, diaries, merchant receipts, and other data. Of the total number of Africans taken, an estimated 9.6 to 10.8+ million Black-bodied people were transplanted to the Americas and West Indies, with approximately 500,000 imported into the mainland North American colonies.

The total number of Black people taken, however, does not account for those taken into slavery before 1514. The number also does not account for those uprooted from different parts of Africa and forced to labor in colonized regions within Africa and throughout the world. The number also fails to accurately account for those who were murdered or died in anguish from malnutrition, sickness, heartbreak and sadness, suicide, and other complications, as well as those smuggled illegally into Europe, the US, and throughout the New World after the transatlantic trade was banned. Not only are the voices of those who labored marginalized and muted, so too are the voices of those who remain uncounted.

Moreover, when considering the total number of those enslaved in the New World and across Europe, it is important to take into consideration the millions more born into slavery on North and South American, West Indian, European, and African soil. As noted, in the mainland North American colonies alone, for example, approximately five hundred thousand Black-bodied captives arrived from Africa, but when slavery ended, over four million Black people were freed. This underscores the role that human breeding and childbearing, and the integration of enslaved laborers from the West Indies into the US labor force played in the building of this nation. It also lays bare the weight of racism and the lasting effects the institution of slavery has on the lives of Black people across the globe. How can one ever know the actual number of lives lost and affected when numbers are often either unrecorded or misrepresented and manipulated to serve an individual's or institution's interests?

Though the cumulative number is still open to debate, indisputable is the fact that European countries turned to Africa, the cradle of civilization, to enslave Black people to enrich their European way of life. Europeans were driven by a strong sense of superiority and entitlement and fueled by greed, power, biblically guided notions of divine providence, and an appetite for expansion. Such hunger laid the groundwork for the justification and legalization of inhumane acts against Black people, most of which were sanctioned by the government or monarch and by the pope and the Catholic and Protestant Churches. Most often Europeans did not operate without the aid of African chiefs and middlemen. African countries participated as well. European nations benefited. Without question, "from the middle of the 15th century, Africa entered into a unique relationship with Europe," but the result "led to the devastation and depopulation of Africa" that "contributed to the wealth and development of Europe."[2]

Yet Black people were not the only precious resources taken from Africa. During and after the transatlantic slave trade, European nations stole thousands of manuscripts and ethnographic collections, cultural artifacts, artwork, natural resources, precious jewels, indigenous sacred ceremonial masks, divination boards, and royal thrones, scepters, and statues from Africa. A vast amount of these stolen African cultural and spiritual artifacts is currently housed in European and US institutions, museums, and private homes, with the most significant number housed in the British Museum in London, the Musée du Quai Branly in Paris, the Ethnologische Museum in Berlin, the Metropolitan Museum of Art in New York, and the Boston Museum of Fine Arts. It is estimated that "up to 90% of Sub-Saharan Africa's material cultural legacy is outside of the continent."[3]

Chart 7.1 provides a snapshot of the European nations' involvement in the transatlantic slave trade. It shows the European country involved in the trade, the estimated number of Black-bodied people taken into captivity by the European country, the regions of importation in the New World, and the commodities that enslaved laborers produced. The chart is not an exhaustive account of the trade but rather provides a window into this global network in the exploitation of Black people violently tasked with building a New World that advanced Europeans' presence and wealth in the world.

Portugal, Spain, the Netherlands, Denmark, France, and Britain's involvement in the transatlantic slave trade commenced and ended at various points between the fifteenth and nineteenth centuries. Of the six nations, Portugal and Britain were the most efficacious slave-trading nations, accounting for over three-fourths of all African people taken and displaced from their African homeland. Portugal and Britain's surge to the top at different junctures of the trade is most evident in their exportation numbers. The combined estimated total of enslaved Africans taken against their will by Portugal and Britain is over 9.1 million people. In some sense, in terms of the numbers, Portugal and Britain, the two leading competitors in the trade, serve as bookends, with Spain, the Netherlands, Denmark, and France situated between them.

Chart 7.1 reflects a staggering number of Black-bodied people uprooted from their families and homeland. But numbers do not tell the full picture of their sacrifice and labor and the cost of human life. The numbers do not speak to the anguish, emotional toil, and unprecedented stress, the feelings of loneliness and isolation and a deep yearning for home. The numbers do not show us the lengths to which Europeans went to acquire Black people and force them across rough waters into a life of

## Chart 7.1. Europe's role in the slave trade between the sixteenth and nineteenth centuries

| Country | Estimated Africans stolen | Region of importation | Commodities produced |
|---|---|---|---|
| Portugal | 5,848,266 Black-bodied people | Africa, Europe, Dutch and Spanish Americas, Brazil, the British and French Caribbean, and mainland North America In 1619, Portuguese slavers captured and traded Africans with Spain, but an English ship, the *White Lion*, overtook the Spaniards. Twenty captives taken aboard the *White Lion* arrived in Point Comfort, serving as a marker for the start of slavery in the US. | sugarcane, sugar, tobacco, cotton, coffee, dye, and gold from mining |
| Spain | 1,061,524 Black-bodied people | Africa, Europe, Dutch and Spanish Americas, Brazil, the British and French Caribbean, the Danish West Indies, and mainland North America Under Spanish colonization, New Mexico had a few enslaved Black laborers. | sugarcane; sugar; tobacco; cacao; potatoes; corn; peanuts; bulbs; seeds; plants; tomatoes; pineapples; silver, diamonds, and gold from mining; and fortifications and other structures |
| The Netherlands | 554,336 Black-bodied people | Africa, Europe, Dutch and Spanish Americas, Brazil, the British and French Caribbean, the Danish West Indies, and mainland North America In the seventeenth century, the Dutch Republic established a colony on the east coast called New Netherland. The area included territories within New York, New Jersey, Delaware, and Connecticut, with outposts in Pennsylvania and Rhode Island. The colony was established by the Dutch West India Company. | furs (Native Americans), timber, tobacco, and food The Dutch West India Company also used enslaved laborers to clear lands, mill lumber, cut logs, and build wharves, roads, fortifications, and other structures |
| Denmark | 111,040 Black-bodied people (some sources estimate 120,000) | Africa, Europe, Dutch and Spanish Americas, Brazil, the British and French Caribbean, the Danish West Indies, and mainland North America | sugarcane, sugar, tobacco, cotton, rum, molasses, dyewood, mahogany, and fortifications and other structures |
| France | 1,381,404 Black-bodied people | Africa, Europe, Dutch and Spanish Americas, Brazil, the British and French Caribbean, the Danish West Indies, mainland North America, and Canada | sugarcane, sugar, tobacco, coffee, cattle farming, spices, fishing, and indigo |

## Chart 7.1. Europe's role in the slave trade between the sixteenth and nineteenth centuries (*continued*)

| Country | Estimated Africans stolen | Region of importation | Commodities produced |
|---|---|---|---|
| Great Britain | 3,259,441 Black-bodied people | Africa, Europe, Dutch and Spanish Americas, Brazil, the British and French Caribbean, the Danish West Indies, mainland North America, and Canada | sugarcane, sugar, tobacco, cotton, molasses, rum, coffee, wheat, hemp, corn, fish, lumber, wine, olive oil, bar iron, glassware, and industrial plants |

servitude. They do not tell us how Black people resisted bondage, how they pushed back, and how they weathered unimaginable storms while fashioning with their hands a New World.

Numbers have a numbing effect. When we focus on the numbers and gloss over the atrocities of slavery and Black people's contributions, we rob ourselves of dignity and the invitation to repent and evolve as a society. We also rob ourselves of the dignity that comes with honoring and valuing those essential workers worth remembering and memorializing. We lose sight of the value of their lives and become desensitized to the historical trauma—the dreadful act of buying and selling human beings. Once desensitized, we learn to speak of slavery as one among many other past events, permitting us to conceive of Black people as necessary by-products of European and US prominence and economic growth. Such is evident when Black people are told to "get over it" because today's America bears no connection or responsibility to the enslaved past and the enslaved people's descendants suffering from generational inequality. As a consequence, we either turn away, remain silent, or downplay or normalize the barbaric and brutal treatment of Black people from the time of American slavery to the present. This is why we need not only the stories of Black people's triumph over adversity but also their pain. We need to be reminded. We need to hear the stories of their capture as well as their contribution. We need to memorialize these stories in our souls and in the public square and own the full breadth of their lives because this is how we heal. They are calling us to sit with their stories until their stories take a hold of us and move us to act in grace, gratitude, and honor on their behalf. We owe them this, and we owe this to ourselves.

Each one of the millions taken from Africa represents a person: a mother and father, a son and daughter, a little girl playing by the coast who never saw the storm coming, a little boy standing at the water's edge and suddenly taken into the cold and damp castle, and a builder, an innovator, an artist loaded onto the dreaded ship. Each number represents the intentional dismantling of a civilization, of ethnic ties and tribal units, of religious rites and cultural traditions, of market women and tribal councils, of social networks and political systems, of communities and villages, of townships and cities, of families and homes, of precious minerals and ancient people and legacies, of civilizations long admired and ransacked at will, of people who wept as they boarded the ship and lost sight of their homeland, and of others who jumped overboard, resisted captivity, and survived enslavement in the New World. Many of their children also gave birth to children, born into slavery, throughout the Americas, the West Indies, Europe, and other colonized regions.

Numbers absent of a fuller historical record can lull us into a deep sleep about the United States' origins and the role Black people played in its development. Such omissions can cause us to question the necessity of a memorial for those who, against their will, gave their lives and made possible a world that would not have existed, quite literally, without their blood, sweat, and tears. Numbers alone hide the metanarrative that plunged them into slavery, the narrative that drove the slave trade, commandeered the slave ships, filled the slave markets, and lined the pockets of people in power.

The metanarrative of slavery's impact upon Black-bodied people reveals the interrelationship of hedonistic greed, consumption, racism, and unremorseful violence inflicted upon Black-bodied people by the slaveholding society in America until the late nineteenth century. Seven countries—Portugal, Spain, the Netherlands, Denmark, France, Britain, and the United States—saw each captive as a number and the numbers as sources of profit. Without consideration for Black life, they sent ships bearing the flags of their respective slaveholding countries to Africa and traumatically altered the well-being of Black people for generations to come.

We pause now, just for a moment, to reflect, to see, hear, feel, taste, and smell the weight of this global pandemic, this legalized racist violation in the US, whose roots spread throughout Europe. We pause to sit with those who labored or died before they ever reached New World soil. We also do so to acknowledge the importance of their lives and all that they built. We do so to connect with the density of their experiences and the influence of their sacrifice. We do so to feel the weight of their battered wings as they lived, labored, and protested for their right to the tree of life. Today, pieces of each of them are ingrained in the wood of the ships that carried them across the waters. Their spirits and their DNA—in blood, sweat, feces, and tears—still imbue the lumber of those ships lost, shipwrecked, stored in museums, abandoned, demolished over time, and forgotten.

The ships upon the Atlantic waters put in full view the demarcation between them, the captured and colonized lying at the bottom of the ship, and the colonizer above deck taking in the morning sun after a successful capture. We pause for a moment to feel the weight of the ships on the waters carrying Black people's souls and dreams to a world that intended to harm them. We do so with ritual intent, hoping to awaken us, to shock our system into awareness, because numbers only tell a fraction of a story and must never stand alone. This is the kind of work of naming we must do to open our hearts and open dialogues of truth that lead to repair and healing. Perhaps it is also a truth that leads to empathy, to accountability, and, ultimately, to the memorialization of those stolen and made to build the world we now inhabit.

## Portugal

In the late fall of 1794, Portuguese crewmen loaded 512 enslaved women, men, and children onto the *São José-Paquete de Africa* (also referred to as *São José-Paquete de Africa*), a small 340-ton slave ship owned by the Pereiras, a prominent Portuguese family. Earlier that year, on April 27, the vessel captained by Manuel João Pereira headed toward Mozambique, a coastal region colonized by Portugal in the southeast of Africa. The ship's name designation, *São José-Paquete de Africa* (translated as "Saint Jose[ph]—a Package from Africa"), suggests that the owners believed Saint Joseph, the patron of the worker and protector of the Catholic Church, blessed their expedition and gifted Portugal with involuntary laborers.

Though most of the enslaved Africans taken into captivity during the transatlantic slave trade came from West and West-Central Africa, Mozambique and Madagascar played a small role, making up less than 1 percent of the trade. Both regions became important to Europeans seeking to expand and monopolize trade along the African coastline. In particular, the Portuguese often traveled between Mozambique and Angola—namely, Luanda, another Portuguese colony and major slave port.

On December 3, the *São José Paquete Africa* began its seven-thousand-mile voyage from Mozambique to the New World, with its captives securely shackled in the dark and dismal hull. It was clear from the ship's overcrowded conditions that the captain and crewmen purchased and grabbed all the Africans they could muster. Within days of their capture, the Africans on board transitioned from being everyday people with dreams to commodities for profit. They were now the property of Portugal, entering a lifetime of free labor on sugar plantations throughout Maranhão, a Portuguese colony in northeastern Brazil situated along the Atlantic Ocean. It was an unimaginable new normal.

As Portugal's property, it is unclear whether or not these particular captives were branded with scorching-hot irons into their flesh before their departure. The Portuguese were the first to engage in the practice of branding. As early as the fifteenth century, they branded enslaved Africans to signify ownership—that the person was the property of the king of Portugal, a merchant, an explorer, a slave trader, a family, or whomever. Branding on the arm, chest, shoulder, or other parts of the body varied from nation to nation, and the branding symbols were typically initials or emblems of the monarch or individual proprietors or Christian icons like a cross—regardless of whether the enslaved was an adherent of that faith.

Branded or not, little could change the course of those aboard the *São José Paquete Africa*. On December 27, just twenty-four days into its journey to the New World, strong winds began tossing the ship to and fro as it rounded the Cape of Good Hope. Hours later, as the waves increased in ferocity, the captain sent distress signals to the distant shoreline using repeated cannon fire. Within minutes, a Dutch barge began making its way toward them. Some onboard began making chords out of rope and cloth to help crew and captives disembark onto the barge. But as the *São José Paquete Africa* approached Camps Bay and Clifton Beach near Cape Town, South Africa, it crashed on rocks and was caught between two reefs. It was too late. The Portuguese slave ship was torn asunder. Though the captain and crew tried to save as many enslaved women, men, and children as they could, some were still chained to the ship's hull, and their fates were clear.

Approximately 212 African women, men, and children still in shackles sank with the *São José Paquete Africa* beneath the violent waves. The others made it to the shoreline. The captain and his crew survived. Before the surviving enslaved women, men, and children could catch their breaths from the tragedy, they were resold two months later at a slave market in Western Cape, a region colonized by the Dutch and then overtaken by the British. The *São José Paquete Africa*'s failure to complete the second and third legs of its transatlantic journey did not deter the captain, the crew, and the Pereira family from continuing their involvement in the slave-trading business.

Though the Portuguese may have lost the *São José Paquete Africa* and 212 of its human cargo, it was clear they both were replaceable. Portugal was the forerunner of the transatlantic slave trade and some argue the nation that profited most from it. At its inception, Portugal, a small European country that runs the length of the western coast of the Iberian Peninsula, was the initiator and leading competitor in the early part of the transatlantic slave trade.[4]

With the support of the Crown and papal bulls (decrees from the pope), Portugal also claimed rights to lands occupied by the Indigenous peoples.[5] During the fifteenth century, Portugal colonized African territories such as present-day Guinea-Bissau, Angola, Mozambique, Cape Verde, São Tomé, and Príncipe, as well as New World territories like Uruguay, Guanare, Venezuela, Colónia do Sacramento, and present-day Brazil, where enslaved workers were transported in large numbers to work the Portuguese sugar plantations. Portugal's ties to the US were also far reaching.

Between the fifteenth and eighteenth centuries, Portugal's capture of 235 Black-bodied people increased to an estimated 5.8 million African women, men, and children. Portugal's presence in the trade eventually waned. However, the country gained considerable wealth from colonization, conquests, commerce, sugar production, and other commodities. Though slavery declined in Portugal, Portuguese maritime and slave trading continued, aiding the Dutch, French, and English in their shipment and selling of African people and material commodities throughout the Americas and West Indies.

## Spain

In the fall of 1819, the *Antelope*, a Spanish ship registered in Cadiz, Spain, and owned by prominent Spanish slave trader Santiago de la Cuesta y Manzanal, left the coast of Havana, Cuba, and headed to Africa. Before the *Antelope*'s 1819 expedition, the ship had made four trips under Spain's flag to and from West and West-Central Africa, carrying a cargo of human laborers to Cuba. Cuba and other parts of the West Indies and the Americas were within New Spain, regions conquered, colonized, occupied, or claimed by Spain. Havana was a key Spanish port in the trade. On this particular journey, the *Antelope*, under the command of Vicente de Llovio and his thirty-three crewmen, was en route to Cabinda, a small province of Angola colonized by Portugal.

By March 1820, the crewmen had loaded 331 enslaved Africans, mostly scared and defenseless children, in the ship's hull. Their terrifying journey to the New World had just begun. On March 23, the *Antelope*, anchored along the Cabinda coast, was unexpectedly overtaken by a privateer. John Smith, captain of *Columbia* (later *Arraganta*) and his US crewmen, had set sail from Baltimore months earlier with a mission to seize and pillage Spanish and Portuguese ships and their human cargo. Smith was carrying papers granting him rights to do so as an act of war on behalf of the Uruguayan revolutionary leader José Gervasio Artigas. Before the *Antelope*'s capture, Smith and his men, with the flags of Artigas and the US waving from *Columbia*'s deck, had conducted surprise attacks on other vessels on the high seas. As soon as the crewmen stormed the *Antelope* and opened the hull's door, they realized they had hit a gold mine: the largest number of Africans captured on their journey thus far, and 65 percent of them were children, a guaranteed dividend. It was clear the *Antelope* was not going to Cuba, as Smith and his men steered both vessels toward other parts of the New World in search of slave markets. Smith, however, had trouble selling all of his captives. The US, France, Britain, and the Netherlands had banned international slave trade by this point, and enforcement agents were roaming the waters searching for illegal vessels. Though some agents turned a blind eye, others were more vigilant. It was a throw of the dice, but Smith persisted.

Unlike the *São José Paquete Africa*, it seemed more apparent that the *Antelope* and *Columbia* would arrive at their final destination—until the *Columbia* shipwrecked. Smith, still determined, transferred the human cargo, crewmen, and goods from the *Columbia* to the *Antelope*. After assuming control, he renamed it the *General Ramirez*. But the overcrowding and the long journey were detrimental to Smith's mission. Children were dying and suffering from sadness, hunger, and dehydration.

One day while anchored among the Sea Islands in Spanish Florida, karma visited Smith and his men. US customs officers aboard the US Revenue Cutter Service ship *Dallas* spotted the *Antelope* and went aboard. The ship, captained by John Jackson, was one of ten vessels commissioned by the US Congress to intercept ships illegally importing enslaved Africans into the US. After investigating, Jackson and his men immediately seized the *Antelope* and the enslaved. They also took into custody Smith and his crew, charging them with piracy. The ships headed to Georgia, a mainland North American colony named after King George and founded by the English, specifically James Oglethorpe, a landowner and army officer of King George. Though Georgia's officials prohibited slavery for a short period in Georgia, enslaved laborers were instrumental in building the colony before the ban and eradication.

On July 24, 1820, the *Antelope* arrived at Bolton's Wharf docks in Savannah, Georgia, for adjudication. In the hull were 258 children who had survived the awful 122-day expedition from their homeland to the New World. The voyage had begun with 331 kinspeople; nearly one-fourth had died during the long and arduous Middle Passage. Those who survived were children under the age of fourteen, roughly half of them between five and ten years old. As each of their small frames touched the Southern air, you could see the journey's weight on their Black bodies. They disembarked on US soil fragile and afraid—and the majority without their mothers or fathers. Most were too sick and weak to parade across the town to the slave market, a customary practice in the US from ship to market. What would come of them, and who would care?

No doubt a legal battle ensued, with the US, Spain, and Portugal each claiming their right to the bounty. Were the children the property of any nation, or should they be freed due to their illegal importation? The men placed the children in an enslaved encampment, a makeshift prison, to await their fate, not knowing a day would turn into a month and a month into several and several into seven years. Though facing trial for three charges of piracy, Smith filed suit for ownership of the *Antelope*. He and his men were not imprisoned while awaiting trial.

During their seven-year encampment, Savannah city officials and local proprietors capitalized on the lengthy legal appeals and the surplus of potential laborers. They forced the fittest children to work under brutal conditions throughout the city, picking up debris, cleaning public spaces, and leveling fortifications for the city's expansion. Some slaveholders were able to triple their profits by receiving payments from the city for taking in children, forcing those same children to labor on their properties, and outsourcing them to other planters.

The lower courts acquitted Smith and his men of all charges. But by 1825, the fate of the young survivors rested in the hands of the US Supreme Court. United States senator John Berrien (Georgia) represented the vice-consul of Spain, and Jared Ingersoll, former Pennsylvania delegate and signer of the US Constitution, represented Portugal. Attorney General William Wirt and Francis Scott Key, author of the national anthem and member of the American Colonization Society, served as counsel for the US. The Supreme Court would also hear arguments regarding the ownership of the *Antelope*.

In the end, the Supreme Court, with Chief Justice John Marshall at the helm, dismissed Smith's claim to the *Antelope*. The court ruled in favor of the US, Spain, and Portugal. The men and nations won, and the children aboard the *Antelope* lost their battle in an American courtroom, which never chose to hear their pleas of pain and separation and now also of toil and bondage. They were not the children of the chief justice nor the children of the men who captured them and argued against them in court. They were the children of Africa with no rights a white man was bound to respect. The three nations received compensation for the children, whether through payment or enslavement. Over one hundred children were returned to Africa, a gesture motivated not by goodwill but rather by US occupation. The children were free (but not really). The US sent them to New Georgia, a township founded by the American Colonization Society in Montserrado County, Liberia, to help build up the US-funded region on African soil, as mentioned in earlier chapters. Imagine how it must have felt on the continent of your birth, so close but still miles away from home.

As for the others, the non-Africans? Those men went about their daily lives, profiting in the trafficking of children and enriching themselves at the cost of human tragedy. The loss of human life and his ship, the *Antelope*, seemed to be of no consequence to Santiago de la Cuesta y Manzanal. He and Spain had more Black bodies and vessels at their disposal. In 1820 alone, the year the *Antelope* anchored in Savannah, Georgia, over seventy-five ships flying the Spanish flag traveled the high seas to Africa for human cargo.

Spain was the second European country to set sail to parts unknown during the Age of Discovery.[6] Both Portugal and Spain shared the same monarch until 1640 and were pioneers of the transatlantic slave trade. Before 1640, Spain and Portugal accounted for 97 percent of the European slave voyages.[7] Eventually, tensions and wars ensued between Spain and Portugal. Early treaties and papal bulls during the Age of Discovery set lines of demarcation between the two countries. Spain was authorized to engage in the slave trade and colonize lands but was limited in its access to the trade along the West African coastline. That did not stop Spain.

Spain not only managed to export nearly five hundred thousand African captives, including those aboard the *Antelope*, on ships bearing their flag but also found an economically savvy way to import enslaved Africans into New Spain. Between 1543 and 1834, Spain granted licenses (*asiento*) to other countries traveling to the West African coastline to sell, trade, or furnish enslaved laborers to New Spain, making Spain a principal colonial power broker in the transatlantic slave trade and one of Europe's wealthiest countries.[8] The country's influence across the New World reached far and wide, with territories colonized, claimed, or occupied within mainland North America that included Florida, Alabama, Mississippi, Louisiana, and Texas, along with present-day Mexico and New Mexico, California, Nevada, Colorado, Utah, Arizona, Oregon, and Washington and parts of Idaho, Montana, Wyoming, Kansas, and Oklahoma and the southwestern part of Canada.[9] Though Spain's economy declined at some point during the transatlantic slave trade, Spanish America was a significant market for intra-American slave trading. Spanish individuals and companies profited tremendously from sugar production and land occupation.

## The Netherlands

In the fall of 1737, seven hundred enslaved women, men, and children held in the dungeon of Elmina Castle on the western coast of Africa crossed through the Door of No Return, the last door the enslaved passed through, signifying their departure from Africa, never to return. From there they made their way to the dreaded slave ship. Men with guns herded the seven hundred from the castle into the dark hull of the Dutch ship. The *Leusden* (pronounced *listen*), a Dutch West India Company vessel, was on its final voyage across the Atlantic headed to Suriname, a small country in the New World on the northeastern coast of South America under Dutch colonial rule. The captives aboard the *Leusden* were en route to a trading post for sale and subsequent labor on sugar plantations.

After weeks at sea, the vessel encountered an unexpected storm near Suriname at the Marowin River's mouth. In haste to save himself and his men, the ship's captain brought fourteen or so enslaved Africans from the hull to assist above deck. Rather than rescue those remaining below, the captain, in fear of an uprising, ordered the hatch doors nailed shut. The women, men, and children tried to escape from the hull, but to no avail.

As the *Leusden* began its descent, the crewmen struggled to protect it from its demise but, realizing their own impending fate, jumped overboard, taking with them a large chest filled with gold. The enslaved assisting them followed suit and jumped into the sea. As the survivors made their way to dry land, the *Leusden* sank quickly into the depths, taking the remaining Black souls left in the hull of the ship. A small number somehow managed to break free from the hull and swim toward dry land, where men with guns were waiting. Breathless and feeble, they collapsed onshore and were taken immediately with the others to the slave market. By the end of the ordeal, over 650 Black people had died of suffocation or drowning.

During the investigation, the captain testified he had nailed the hull door shut because he feared for his life and the crew's safety. The captain was acquitted, and his crew received an award and public recognition from the Dutch West India Company for saving the gold. The number of the enslaved lost at sea was recorded with no words of remorse spoken. Their death, however, was classified as the single largest such loss of life in the transatlantic slave trade.

Between 1596 and 1829, the Dutch were actively involved in the transatlantic slave trade. Early on, the *Leusden* was one of fifteen such slave ships owned by the Dutch West India Company, an Amsterdam-based trading company with offices in Rotterdam, Hoorn, Middelburg, and Groningen and financed by Amsterdam bankers and slavers. By 1629, the Dutch company had acquired more than one hundred armed slave ships and a fifteen-thousand-man army of soldiers and sailors. The company had also made a substantial profit after raiding Spanish ships containing silver.

Ships owned or sponsored by the Dutch West India Company along with those of other Dutch maritime merchants transported Black bodies to toil on sugar and coffee plantations in Suriname, the Dutch Antilles, Aruba, and other locales. The Society of Suriname, an organization established to run Suriname's sugar plantation complex, was formed by the city of Amsterdam in partnership with the Dutch West India Company and the Van Aerssen van Sommelsdijck, a family with strong ties to the institution of slavery. On most occasions, the commodities produced by enslaved hands throughout these and other regions arrived for refinement, distribution, and sale in Amsterdam. The Netherlands, and specifically the city of Amsterdam, experienced an economic boom from the production of food, timber, tobacco, and also the slave trade and enslaved laborers.

For a short period during the transatlantic slave trade, the Netherlands' construction and seizure of slave castles and fortresses in West Africa and the US as well as their advanced naval operations and sugar plantation complex made them a noteworthy challenger in a slave trade dominated by Portugal and Spain. The revenue acquired from commodities—sugar, coffee, wheat, and so on—produced by Black hands financed much of the Netherlands' golden age, a period of economic growth and an age known for its artistic, literary, scientific, and philosophical achievements between the sixteenth and seventeenth centuries. The revenue also contributed to the creation of Amsterdam's striking canals and city center. In the US, the Netherlands' maritime industry, commercial ventures, and significant fur- and slave-trading posts along the Hudson, Delaware, and Connecticut Rivers also helped that region become a leading economic powerhouse.[10]

By the end of the transatlantic slave trade, the Dutch had transported over a half million women, men, and children from Africa into captivity. Approximately one in ten enslaved people in Suriname managed to flee captivity and seek refuge with other fugitive enslaved women, men, and children living in formerly enslaved Maroon communities in the Surinamese bush. Those captured stood on display in the country's city center as public spectacles for six months.

### Denmark

In the fall of 1786, the *Christiansborg*, a Danish vessel bearing the flag of Denmark, left the Gold Coast and headed toward the New World. The *Christiansborg* began its journey from København (Copenhagen) years prior and was now harbored along the western coast of Africa, awaiting its departure for St. Croix in the Virgin Islands and then onward to the mainland North American colonies. Before leaving the Gold Coast, Captain Jens Jensen Berg and his crewmen stopped at the Windward and Ivory Coasts and the Bright of Benin to purchase African people. On October 10, 1786, the *Christiansborg* disembarked, carrying 452 captives shackled in the hull and various other areas of the ship. Of these 452 Africans taken from their homeland and loved ones, 39.4 percent were men, 23.6 percent were women, 21.2 percent were boys, and 15.8 percent were girls.

Paul Erdmann Isert, a Danish chief surgeon and merchant, was the last to board the ship before its departure. Upon arrival, he immediately took note of the overcrowded conditions and weariness of those captured, writing in his journal,

> Imagine the sight of such a multitude of miserable people—some who were by chance born to slave parents; some who were captured in war; some who were stolen and innocent of any crime; some who, for other casual reasons, were sold to the Europeans—all of them now about to be transported in heavy chains from their fatherland to another country which they do not know. Their future cannot possibly hold anything good in store for them when the Europeans use such violent means to secure them. In their own country they have themselves heard such

dreadful tales of how the slaves are treated . . . they give no credence to all the assurances from the Europeans that they are going to be taken to a beautiful country. . . . On the contrary . . . they fear death far less than slavery.

The *Christiansborg* was on its thirteenth transatlantic voyage at the time of its departure. Cannons were placed strategically throughout the ship to protect the captain and crew from privateers and slave insurrections. On this leg of the journey, the crew walked about the top and bottom decks carrying guns (muskets and bayonets), keeping a watchful eye on the captives' every move. At night, they fired their guns and cannons to keep the women, men, and children in a perpetual state of fear. Isert observed the fear on their faces as the cannons fired and they sat chained together in gendered pairs. It was clear some had lost hope of ever seeing their homeland and loved ones again, while others sat determined, quiet, and resolute, as if to say, *I will determine my fate, not the European.*

At daybreak, the men and boys went above deck for short periods to stretch and catch a glimpse of daylight and fresh air. Isert joined them. After two days passed, they became familiar with the routine, stopping to observe the ship's operations and converse occasionally with one another through hand signs and gestures, until the guards herded them back into the hull, unaware that they were plotting a rebellion. One morning, they rose to carry out their plan.

They seized control of the top deck, grabbing Isert, beating him, and slashing his face with a knife. Then they made their way to the weapons at the stern of the ship but were met by other crewmen who began attacking them with bayonets. A fight ensued. The men and boys—and the women and girls who joined them—kept fighting without weapons, determined to take control of the ship and return home. But it soon proved that their hands were no match for guns and cannons. The crewmen began firing the weapons, causing the men to withdraw. Some captives managed to release their iron chains, while others remained chained in pairs. The crewmen grabbed as many as they could, threatening them all with guns. But the captives kept fighting. Several minutes later, the crewmen managed to return some to the hull. It was a delicate balance between protecting themselves and not killing the human commodities whose buyers were standing on the shores of St. Croix, awaiting their arrival. At some point, some Africans broke free of the crewmen and others, still chained in pairs; ran hurriedly to the ship's edge; and jumped overboard. The crewmen hoisted ropes, urging them to climb aboard, but some refused the lifeline and went down into the waters. Others grabbed hold, climbed up, and went back into the hull. The revolt lasted two hours. Thirty-four enslaved Africans died. The captain and crewmen all survived. For weeks, Isert lay in a makeshift bed clinging to life under the care of two enslaved women. The men had beaten him so severely because they thought he was the slave owner and the cause of their bondage. On December 18, 1786, the *Christiansborg* arrived in St. Croix with 406 of its originally 452 captives. The majority worked on plantations throughout the West Indies, and a small percentage endured another harsh journey to the mainland North American colonies. Isert wrote a book condemning the practice of slave trading.

The insurrection was the second to occur aboard the *Christiansborg*. The two insurrections sent a clear message through the Danish markets that enslaved African women, men, and children were not passive recipients of captivity. The insurrections did not stand alone. From the seventeenth to the early nineteenth century, there were an estimated 485 recorded slave revolts involving ten or more persons aboard slave ships waiting on the shoreline or en route to the New World.[11] These reports are recorded in captains' logbooks, diaries, and ship manifestos. Yet this number does not account for the unrecorded revolts or the number of times individual Africans revolted in protest against white terror. Each revolt on the slave ships crossing the deep waters signified that Black people understood they were not meant to be enslaved and they were willing to fight back and die as a testament to their humanity. Their African forebears and violent European captors would one day pay a soul price for selling, enslaving, and harming them.

 Despite the warnings, the *Christiansborg* continued its slave voyages under the Denmark flag, making over fifteen trips to the shores of Africa. It was one of many vessels chartered by Danish and Norwegian trading companies, wealthy merchants, clergypersons, government officials, and the Danish Crown. Between 1671 and 1807, Denmark made nearly three thousand voyages carrying enslaved Africans to the Caribbean alone.[12]

Since the mid-seventeenth century, Denmark-Norway was an active participant in the trafficking of human beings for free labor, becoming the seventh-largest slave-trading nation, with colonized regions throughout the New World and Africa. Both Danish and Norwegian individuals and businesses were represented in all aspects of the trade and benefited from the enterprise. Enslaved labor and sugar become the leading commodities that sustained and advanced Danish economies. Denmark played a significant role well into the eighteenth century, supplying enslaved laborers to specific planters and regions throughout the West Indies and the Americas.

But Denmark's and Norway's involvement in the trade extended well beyond acquiring enslaved laborers; they also built or acquired factories and fortifications, most notably Fort Christiansborg, Frederiksborg, and Osu Castle, and colonized regions in the New World and Africa. The Danish Crown became enriched by the production of sugarcane and rum.[13]

In 1867, the Danish government, recognizing that the Danish West Indies—St. Thomas, St. Jan (St. John), and St. Croix—was in economic decline, decided to sell the Danish West Indies to the US. On March 31, 1917, the Danish and US governments signed the Treaty of the Danish West Indies. The US purchased the region for $25 million in gold coin and changed its name to the Virgin Islands of the United States. By the end of the transatlantic slave trade, Denmark had transported a total of 111,040 women, men, and children from Africa into captivity. Some sources estimate that number as being as high as 120,000.

### France

In the fall of 1773, the *Soleil*, a French slave ship under the command of Captain Louis Mosnier and his thirty-eight-man crew, began its routine transatlantic journey from Nantes, France. The *Soleil*, along with other French vessels, played a role in shipping commodities to and from the American colonies, the West Indies, and France. At the time, the *Soleil*, a 180-ton ship, was on its second voyage from Nantes to Apa, a small town in the Badagry region of Lagos, Nigeria. On March 23, 1774, after trade negotiations ended and the human cargo was loaded, the *Soleil* departed the region with 374 African women, men, and children and headed toward Saint-Marc, a town colonized by the French in the western portion of present-day Haiti.

As with most slave voyages, the enslaved were kept just beneath the deck, but on occasion, women were made to roam the main deck to make them accessible to the crewmen. At some point during *Soleil*'s eighty-five-day journey from Africa to its docking at Saint-Marc on June 16, 1774, fourteen Black women decided they would not be subjected to either the crewmen or a life of bondage. While at sea, the women decided that when summoned up deck, they would choose their own fate. They devised a plan and waited for the moment. Captain Mosnier, in anguish, recorded the loss of a portion of his cargo in his daily logbook, saying, "They threw themselves into the sea, 14 black women, all together, all at the same time, in a single motion—what diligence they had, the waves were very large and rough, the winds blowing with torment. The sharks had already eaten many before it was possible to launch a boat so that we could only save seven of them of which one died."[14] The fourteen Black women plunged to their deaths to resist European tyranny. Some have since called their act suicide. Others have called it courageous—these fierce Black women flying like blackbirds, above the ship and over the bloody Atlantic waters, denying the European his self-prescribed right to own their bodies. Together, like a flock of birds bound to one cause alone, they lifted off the ship and jumped to freedom.

Their jump in defiance was not an aberration. Throughout the transatlantic slave trade, many enslaved Africans jumped from French, Portuguese, Spanish, Dutch, Danish, British, and US ships and into shark-infested waters. They were not interested in the "better life" in the Europeans' New World. They knew a horrible destiny awaited them, and they dreaded the arrival of ships that left European ports and waited for them along the African shoreline.

For France, Nantes was the first and primary starting point for most French-led transatlantic slave voyages. The bustling Nantes port, especially during the eighteenth century, helped Nantes become one of the leading European trading regions. The French profited from slave labor and sugar production in Saint-Domingue (present-day Haiti), Louisiana, and other parts of the New World. The shipping industry in Nantes and free labor and commercial and agricultural production were pivotal in France's rise to economic prominence. During the transatlantic slave trade period, the wealth Haiti produced was so substantial that western Haiti became known as the Paris of the Antilles. Haiti was the wealthiest French colony in the West Indies, and Louisiana became one of the most prosperous French territories in the US.

Both Haiti and Louisiana were important inflection points for the flow of goods, products, and enslaved laborers to and from France and Europe and, in some cases, the Americas and West Indies. Sugar plantations in Haiti and Louisiana were wellsprings of prosperity for France and domestic and foreign proprietors and merchants. The income and taxations of sugar production alone were significant sources of the French budget and generated enormous wealth for the French government. The production of cotton and indigo in Louisiana and coffee and indigo in Haiti also engendered wealth for France, beginning one of the wealthiest colonies in the New World.[15] By the end of the transatlantic slave trade, France had transported over 1.4 million women, men, and children into captivity.

## Britain

In the winter of March 1781, the *Zong*, a British slave ship, departed from Liverpool, England, and sailed toward Africa. Upon docking off the western coast, the ship's captains, Luke Collingwood and Edward Howard, and their twenty-men crew set out to purchase and also kidnap African people from three areas in Ghana—the Gold Coast, a region on the Gulf of Guinea; Cape Coast Castle, a large commercial fort (slave castle) on the Gold Coast; and Anomabu (also spelled Anomabo and Annamaboe), a town on the coast of Mfantsiman.

On September 6, after obtaining supplies in São Tomé, the *Zong* disembarked, carrying approximately 440 Africans into captivity. The *Zong*'s owners, members of the Gregson slave-trading syndicate, insured each of the enslaved and ship for £8,000 with Lloyd's of London. Today, the corporation, founded by Edward Lloyd in 1686, is the oldest insurance and reinsurance marketplace in the world. The corporation is protected by the Lloyd's Act and subsequent acts of Parliament.

With their insurance policy secured, the captains and crew sailed toward the New World. While en route to Black River, Jamaica, Captain Collingwood, the crew members, and several enslaved Africans became ill. Within weeks, sixty-two captives had died. As the *Zong* drew closer to the shoreline, about one hundred enslaved Africans were still holding on but sick. The captain and crew, however, aware of the conditions of the insurance policy, unanimously decided to throw the sick Africans into the sea over a seven-day period. On November 29, fifty-four women and children were hurled through cabin windows and into the waters. Two days later, forty-two men were thrown overboard, followed by thirty-six more a few days later.

The captains and crew knew that the owners would have no right to the insurance claims if the Africans died onshore or of natural causes aboard the ship. But if it became necessary for a ship's captain to jettison part of his cargo to save the rest due to an unexpected storm, fire, or any imminent peril and apparent danger at sea, an insurance claim could be filed under what is known as a general average clause (an ancient maritime law). Knowing this, the captain and crew threw the women, men, and children into the sea to collect the insurance. The crew's actions infuriated the enslaved, who watched in horror. They pleaded to the men, insisting on their willingness to neither eat nor drink water to preserve the rations. But their pleas fell on deaf ears. In defiance of their captors' cruelty, ten jumped into the waters in solidarity with their fellow captives.

On December 28, 1781, the *Zong* docked at Black River, Jamaica. The owners immediately filed a claim to cover their losses. But after reviewing the claim, the insurers refused payment. The owners took the insurers to court (*Gregson v. Gilbert* [1783] 3 Doug. KB 232), and a series of trials ensued. Before the first trial began on March 6, 1783, the *Zong* logbook went missing. At trial, the crew maintained they had no choice but to commit the act for the welfare of the remaining enslaved captives and fellow crewmen. They maintained their actions were necessary after discovering a navigational error. Once they turned the ship back on course, they realized they did not have enough food and water to sustain the crewmen and enslaved captives. Inevitably, they had to throw some overboard to preserve the others. The court ruled in the owners' and crewmen's favor.

But at a later appeal hearing in May 1783, the judges ruled against the owners as new evidence emerged. Upon hearing of the incident, Olaudah Equiano, a formerly enslaved man, alerted white antislavery advocate Granville Sharp to the incident and the crew's deliberate attempt to kill Black people to collect insurance. The incident went public and was posted in newspapers, emboldening abolitionists during the eighteenth and nineteenth centuries. Sharp pushed for the owners and crewmen to be prosecuted for the senseless murders, but to no avail.

In 1788, Parliament passed the Slave Trade Act, the first legislation regulating Britain's role in the transatlantic slave trade and the maximum number of enslaved African captives permitted on British ships. This law, however, did nothing to curtail the illegal transportation of enslaved Africans, even after the subsequent act was passed in 1807. By 1791, Parliament had also banned insurance from paying claims on slaves who were "thrown overboard." In 2007, a monument was erected at Black River, Jamaica, dedicated to the murdered slaves on the *Zong*.

The *Zong* departed Africa with 440 Africans, but only 208 arrived at the Black River port. The records indicate that 232 Africans died while at sea (62 of sicknesses, 130 to 132 thrown overboard, and 10 in solidarity). How shall we account for the remaining 28 to 30 enslaved persons? What happened to them? What were the names of all these lives lost? Do they not matter? The *Zong* concluded its transatlantic journey with a mortality rate of 53 percent. Over half of the Black lives had ended before they even reached the New World. The *Zong* was one of many slave ships bearing the flag of Great Britain that traveled across the Atlantic waters carrying enslaved women, men, and children. By the 1690s, Britain was the forerunner in transporting enslaved Africans from West and West-Central Africa. It is estimated that Great Britain, an island consisting of three territories—England, Scotland, and Wales in the North Atlantic Ocean off the northwest coast of Europe—made over ten thousand such voyages to Africa between 1562 and 1807 alone. In the eighteenth century, Britain surpassed all five of the aforementioned European nations, becoming the largest slave trader and the country with the most substantial ties and control of the mainland North American colonies.[16] The British Empire grew most notably from its colonization enterprise, its reach stretching to parts of the West Indies, the US and Canada, South America, Africa, and Europe. Britain acquired great wealth from all aspects of the trade, especially in commodity production and exportation.[17]

In the US, Britain's biggest cash crop was cotton. During the first half of the nineteenth century, cotton accounted for over half of all exports in the US. Both the British and the US economies were dependent on cotton production. Seventy-five percent of the cotton picked by enslaved

Black-bodied people came from the Deep South. Britain received cotton from American plantations for processing in their cotton mills. Forty percent of Britain's exports were textiles produced from cotton. The British economy flourished from the slave trade, enslaved labor, maritime operations, commodity production, land acquisition, and colonialization.

By the end of the transatlantic slave trade, Great Britain had transported over 3.3 million women, men, and children from Africa into captivity, accounting for 40 percent of the total number of Black-bodied people taken from Africa. The British benefited tremendously from the slave trade, purchasing elaborate mansions and investing their fortunes in British enterprises. English people also established banks and funded new industries with the proceeds. The transatlantic slave trade bolstered Britain's economy and created jobs and opportunities for ordinary British people. Ship owners, slave traders, plantation owners, bankers, gun makers, clergymen, missionaries, politicians, and the royal family all benefitted from slavery.

## The United States

In the spring of 1860, a renovated two-masted schooner named the *Clotilda* set sail under the dark of night from Mobile Bay, Alabama. Captain William Foster and his eleven-man crew were headed to Whydah, a village in the Kingdom of Dahomey (present-day Benin) to purchase Africans for labor in the Deep South. Timothy Meaher, a wealthy Irish landowner and shipping merchant from Maine, financed the expedition with the knowledge that the mission was a crime. The *Clotilda* was no different than Spain's *Antelope*. It was illegal to export and import enslaved Africans from Africa to the US. But Foster and Meaher did not care about the 1807 Act Prohibiting Importation of Slaves. They could profit from the trade because slavery was still legal in the US and parts of the Americas and West Indies. The Deep South was in dire need of enslaved Africans to work the cotton and sugar fields. In fair weather, the schooner made its way through swampy waters past Cuba, evading the authorities. Thirteen days into the journey, just outside of Bermuda, a hurricane interrupted the voyage, damaging the *Clotilda*. While docking for repairs, the crewmen grew anxious, demanding more pay or threatening to reveal the ship's plan to authorities. Foster agreed to pay the bribe, and the *Clotilda* was back on the waters, arriving along the western coast of Africa two months later.

Foster met with the prince of Whydah and gave him $9,000 in gold and merchandise to purchase 125 African women, men, and children, mostly believed to be Yoruba and Fon peoples. After they reached an agreement, the prince took Foster to the slave castle to select 125 Africans and brand them if needed. Among those selected was Kazzoola (a Yoruba name also spelled Kossola; in the American colonies, he was called Cudjo or Cudjoe Lewis), a nineteen-year-old young man from Attako. His village under King Akia'on found itself in an unexpected battle with the Kingdom of Dahomey. In the dark of night, Dahomey forces destroyed the wall protecting Cudjo's town because King Akia'on refused to give Dahomey soldiers the people's crops. Cudjo and his people, alarmed by their presence, went running to the bushes. They killed the king and went after the people. Many years later, Cudjo, in an interview with anthropologist and folklorist Zora Neale Hurston, recalled his flight, saying,

> Soon as I out de gate dey grabee me. . . . I beg dem, please lemme go back to my mama, but dey don't pay whut I say no 'tenshun. Dey tie me wid de rest . . . dey march us to esoku (the sea) . . . den we come in de place call Dwhydah. (It is called Whydah by the whites.) . . . When we git in de place dey put us in a barracoon behind a big white house. . . . We stay dere in de barracoon three weeks. We see many ships in de sea. . . .
>
> When we dere three weeks a white man come in de barracoon wid two men of de Dahomey. One man, he a chief of Dahomey and de udder one his word-changer. Dey make everybody stand in a ring—'bout ten folkses in each ring. De men by dey self, de women by dey self. Den de white man lookee and lookee. He lookee hard at de skin and de feet and de legs and in de mouth. Den he choose. Every time he choose a man he choose a woman. Every time he take a woman he take a man, too. Derefore, you unnerstand me, he take one hunnard and thirty. Sixty-five men wid a woman for each man. Dass right. Den de white man go 'way. I think he go back in de white house. But de people of Dahomey come bring us lot of grub for us to eatee 'cause dey say we goin' leave dere. We eatee de big feast. Den we cry, we sad 'cause we doan want to leave the rest of our people in de barracoon. We all lonesome for our home. We doan know whut goin' become of us, we doan want to be put apart from one 'nother. But dey come and tie us in de line and lead us round de big white house.[18]

The next day, Foster and his men began loading Cudjo and the others onto the *Clotilda* and tossed the barrels of gold and goods overboard for the king's men. While boarding successfully, Cudjo and seventy-four others were alarmed to see a steamer fast approaching. In haste, the crewmen rushed to load more Africans. They managed to get thirty more on board and sailed away with 110 captives toward Mobile, Alabama, to the white men waiting. The fate of the fifteen to twenty Africans left onshore is unknown. Cudjo began crying. Before the men came, he had had a full life and was preparing for marriage. Now all was gone. After being betrayed by the king of Dahomey and his people, he and the others were entering the belly of a different beast. Cudjo stated,

> Soon we git in de ship dey make us lay down in de dark. . . . Dey doan give us much to eat. Me so thirst! Dey give us a little bit of water twice a day. Oh Lor', Lor', we so thirst! . . . On de thirteenth day dey fetchee us on de deck. We so weak we ain' able to walk ourselves, so de crew take each one and walk 'round de deck till we git so we kin walk ourselves. We lookee and lookee and lookee and lookee and we doan see nothin' but water. Where we come from we doan know. Where we goin, we doan know. De boat we on called de *Clotilde*.[19]

After evading authorities, the *Clotilda* made its way to Petit Bois Island in Mississippi and anchored in the cover of night off Point of Pines in Grand Bay, Mississippi, on July 9. Cudjo recalled his final hours on board, saying, "We Afficans know we 'bout finish de journey. We been on de water seventy days and we spend some time layin' down in de ship till we tired. . . . Nobody ain' sick and nobody ain' dead. Dey tell us to keep quiet."[20] Foster went ashore for a horse and buggy and headed toward Mobile for a steam tug to tow the *Clotilda* "up [the] Spanish river into the Alabama River at Twelve Mile Island."[21] Cudjo recalled how the crewmen "towed de ship up de Spanish Creek to Twelve-Mile Island. Dey tookee us off de ship and we git on another ship" to hide them in the canebrake.[22] Foster stayed behind and "burned [the] schr. [*Clotilda*] at the water's edge and sunk her" to destroy any evidence of its illegal transport.[23] Cudjo recalled the *Clotilda* burning, saying, "Dey burn de *Clotilde* 'cause dey skeered de gov'ment goin' rest dem for fetchin' us 'way from Affica soil."[24] Afterward, Foster paid the crewmen and sent them to Northern states, telling them to never speak of what had happened.

Cudjo and his enslaved comrades, fifty-five women and fifty-four men hidden in the canebrake, were taken and hidden on John Dabney's plantation, a friend of the Meaher brothers. On the eleventh day, Cudjo and the others received clothes in preparation for distribution to those who invested in the *Clotilda*'s voyage. Some enslaved Black people remained with Dabney, while the majority were divided up between the Meaher brothers, Tim, Burns, and Jim. Foster received ten for his time and efforts. Others continued on their journey aboard another steamer for sale on the Black market in Selma and beyond.

But the authorities became aware of the plot. By 1861, Meaher and Foster were indicted for the illegal transportation of enslaved Africans into the US. The case was dismissed for lack of evidence—There was no ship, manifesto, or enslaved Africans on record. Cudjo and the others labored for five years on the Meaher brothers', the Burneses', Dabney's, Foster's, and other buyers' properties until the Civil War.

As soon as word reached Cudjo and the others on Timothy Meaher's plantation that they were free, they immediately wanted to go back to Africa. They believed their people were waiting for them and pleaded with Meaher to send them back. But Meaher called them fools. They also petitioned the government for restitution for their illegal capture, but their request was denied. Before the *Clotilda* came, they had beautiful land in Africa, and now they had nothing. They asked Meaher for a small plot of land as restitution, as reparation for their enslavement. But Meaher called them fools. Instead, he permitted them to sharecrop on his land, and they agreed. What else could they do? Where else could they go? So they worked and worked and worked. They planted, harvested, and sold produce. They worked day and night in the fields, at the local shipyards and mills, and in homes as domestics. Even though many were cheated of their earnings, they kept working regardless, until collectively they had saved enough to buy land from Meaher.

In 1866, Cudjo and thirty-one formerly enslaved Africans established Africatown. They built it from the ground up, including a store, church, school, graveyard, and homes. They carved out a slice of their homeland by re-creating their West African village three miles north of Mobile, Alabama. They selected a chief and a judicial system, enacted laws, and appointed two judges to govern the community. They appointed a medicine man and woman, herbalists who tended to the community's well-being, and a teacher for the school. They incorporated the rhythms, colors, songs, and dances of their native village. They integrated all the native customs, tongues, traditions, ceremonies, foods, rituals, and cultural idioms they could remember on the small plot of land they had purchased from the man who called them fools. They were free, and he remained a criminal.

Some of the interviewers and others who came to visit Africatown listened with skepticism to Cudjo and the others as they told the story about their arrival on "the last known slave ship to come to the US."[25] But the residents of Africatown continued to share their story with each succeeding generation. As one descendant, Gail Woods, said, "My grandmother would tell us the story so we wouldn't forget and so that we could continue to tell the story . . . so many people said that it didn't really happen that way, that we made the story up."[26] Where was the proof? Where was this mysterious ship named *Clotilda*? The formerly enslaved Africans of Africatown and their descendants knew that their experience, their pain, and their perseverance in America were real. They knew what they had planted. They know what they had built. They knew that the African soil and the ship that had robbed them of their hopes, dreams, and sorrows, sunk in the nearby bay, were real.

In 1935, Cudjo "Kossola" Lewis died. His story lives on through Zora Neale Hurston's book *Barracoon* (2018). Hurston believed him, but publishers spent years diminishing her account. As a result, it took ninety years for her interviews with Cudjo in 1927 to see the light of day. Decades later, the public spotlight was placed on other founders of Africatown. Among them were Redoshi (Sally) Smith, Matilda McCrear, Maggie, Gumpa (Peter Lee), Jaba Shade, Ossa Keeby, Abache, and Charles (Oluale). Their story lives on through the town they built, designated as a national historic site in 2012 and recorded in the National Registry. Their story lives on through their descendants and the monument placed in front of the community church they built. But most of all, their story lives on through the recovery of the *Clotilda*. On May 22, 2019, the Alabama Historical Society officially announced that the *Clotilda*, the last known slave ship that had carried Cudjo and the 109 other Africans to the US, had been found in a remote branch of Alabama's Mobile River. Cudjo and the founders of Africatown now have some resolution, but more importantly, they now have a public say in the matter.

Unfortunately, the story of Cudjo and the other Africans on the *Clotilda* is not unique. After the passage of the Slave Trade Act of 1794 and the Act Prohibiting the Importation of Slaves in 1807, the *Clotilda* was one among hundreds of US vessels engaged in the illegal trafficking of African people between 1808 and 1860. During the first half of the nineteenth century, it is estimated that approximately 1.2 million Black-bodied people were imported illegally from Africa into the US.[27] This estimation stands in stark contrast to the total number of enslaved Africans (500,000) said to have arrived "legally" into the US via the transatlantic slave trade or the Middle Passage slave trade.

Chapter 1 spoke of the United States' and Britain's connectedness in the institution of slavery. As we saw, Britain was not the only European country with deep ties to the US and to the New World. Portugal, Spain, the Netherlands, Denmark, and France all had ties to the US in some form or another via the transatlantic slave trade. All seven countries had a hand in altering the lives of Black people during the transatlantic slave trade and for generations to come. Stories of the *Clotilda* and all the other European ships carrying the soul force and yearnings of Black-bodied people give us a deeper look at the people who were taken and the countries that took them.

Europeans' entanglement in slavery, its blatant disregard of all that was familiar and sacred to Black people (homeland, customs, loved ones, kinship ties, religious rites, and cultural traditions), and its nonrecognition for their labors and sacrifice undergird systemic racism throughout the globe. The racial divide was most prevalent during the transatlantic slave trade with the violent kidnapping of millions of African people from their homelands and a public demarcation between Europeans and Black-bodied people aboard slave ships. In the US, the racial divide continued with the subsequent institutionalization of racial disparity. The institution of slavery placed Europeans and the nations they represented on the path to expansion and economic growth, solidifying their presence in the New World and the prominence of and the partiality toward whiteness. Such partiality pollutes race relations in America today and hinders our progress toward justice, fairness, and freedom for all and respect for those Black-bodied people of the past. Some European countries, aware of their role in the human tragedy, have offered public apologies, while others remain silent.

The United States' involvement and subsequent gains from the transatlantic slave trade connect us directly to where this book began. The commodification, traumatization, and involuntary labor of Black-bodied people for European advancement made the US a powerful and prosperous independent nation. Chapter 1 and the chapters that follow provide evidence of how the American South and North benefited economically and politically from the sale and trade of Black people and the commodities produced by them in the US. Their labors and ingenuity also contributed to building this nation. There is no doubt that the United States' origins and existence are rooted in the disdain for but the necessary presence of Black people.

During the transatlantic slave trade, Black-bodied people were relegated to the dark, dingy, damp bottoms of slave ships. Those who survived this traumatic journey were forcibly made to labor against their will to help fashion a New World with little to no protections or consideration for their humanity. There is no real American greatness unless we own this reality, because it is this reality that lingers behind and within the pages of the US Constitution, the Declaration of Independence, the Emancipation Proclamation, the Immigration Act of 1790, and treaties. This reality drives how America sees, feels, hears, and thinks of Black people since they arrived in the New World. And this is why white supremacists are killing Black people. They choose not to see us. As white people continue to kill us, year after year, decade after decade, century after century, they are slowly killing themselves and the country they love. Our death is their death, and if we continue on this path, it shall be America's death too—that is, what we believe America can be will never be what we desire it to become. Democracy will die if white supremacy continues to live.

Revisiting the history of the enslavement of African people in America is our responsibility to see America and its cherished myth of whiteness as it truly is. Now America must see and own the roots of systemic racism, the roots of white America's burden—greed and power at the expense of those whom they have devalued and othered. America's ownership of slavery is our freedom. And the elevation, respect, and commemoration of Black bodies are our redemption. Facing this head-on is our passageway to something more life-giving and meaningful. We must do the work honestly and with integrity to create a *more perfect union.*

We turn our attention in the final chapter to ways of moving forward through onus, remembrance, and healing by honoring those who have sacrificed their lives on our behalf. They are the bulwarks of American greatness, and when we honor them, we, in a sense, honor ourselves—our character, our patriotism, and our nation.

# CONCLUSION

# Black Blues Rising

## Calling for a National Reckoning

*There is no place you or I can go to think about or not think about, to summon the presences of or recollect the absences of slaves; nothing that reminds us of the ones who made the journey and of those who did not make it. There is no suitable memorial or plaque or wreath or wall or park, or skyscraper lobby. There is no three-hundred-foot tower. There's no small bench by the road.*

—Toni Morrison

In 1993, Toni Morrison stood before a crowded room of royalty and other distinguished guests seated at the Swedish Academy in Stockholm, Sweden. Morrison, in poised poetic beauty, graced the podium and opened her Nobel Prize in Literature acceptance speech by saying,

> I entered this hall pleasantly haunted by those who have entered it before me. That company of Laureates is both daunting and welcoming, for among its lists are names of persons whose work has made whole worlds available to me. The sweep and specificity of their art have sometimes broken my heart with the courage and clarity of its vision. The astonishing brilliance with which they practiced their craft has challenged and nurtured my own. My debt to them rivals the profound one I owe to the Swedish Academy for having selected me to join that distinguished alumnae.[1]

As I listened to Morrison pause to acknowledge her predecessors, I thought about us as a human community, where we have missed the mark in our care and acknowledgment of enslaved laborers. I thought about how we have failed to pause and focus our gaze on the work of their hands, brick by brick, soul by soul, keenly aware that one cannot honor those one does not value. As Morrison's voice echoed throughout the hall that celebrates human achievement, contributions, and sacrifice, I was transported to structures throughout the world built by Black hands, ever mindful of how daunting it is to traverse those spaces that carry Black people's labors and dreams but seldom mention their names or acknowledge their contribution. I think about the wealth that was generated from their labors and how individuals, corporations, institutions, and the seat of our national government have profited from their labors.

I think now of the places we have journeyed together in this book: the deep rich soils we tread that were once tilled by Black bodies, the breath of places to which we have gone, from countries to villages to colonies to cities; from slave castles to slave ships to slave pens; from slave markets to plantations to industries and corporations; from Mount Vernon to towns and taverns to the White House, the US Capitol, and other federal buildings; from courtrooms and church houses to universities and libraries; and from parks and ports to canals and harbors to the Potomac and other rivers, outlets, and oceans that carried Black people to the New World. Within the nation's capital and cities throughout the US, there is no place one can tread without encountering some reminder of American slavery: the stone and rock excavated and all the tobacco, sugar, wheat, rice, and corn sown and harvested by Black hands; the textiles, the masonry, and the mills; the whale oil, the lumber, and the furs; the silk, indigo, and the molasses; the rum, gunpowder, iron, and tools; the ships, paved roads, railroads, and carriages; the baskets, the quilts, and all that cotton—good Lord, the bales and bales of cotton—the structures, the mansions, the estates, and the cathedrals; the blueprints, the inventions, and the innovations. All of this fashioned by Black hands. Black-bodied people deemed insignificant and unworthy built and served and sacrificed to help make possible the world we inhabit today.

Yet as Morrison says, there is no "suitable memorial or plaque or wreath or wall or park, or skyscraper lobby . . . three-hundred-foot tower," not even a "small bench by the road." In her work, Morrison is clear: "suitable" means powerful. Though memorials have been erected throughout the US since Morrison made this assertion, there still remains no monument on the National Mall and few throughout the nation's capital on sites significant to American slavery that speak powerfully of the enslaved past. The weakness of the existing stand-alone monument in the epicenter of democracy, such as Freedmen's Memorial and the stone marker in Emancipation Hall of the US Capitol, is attributable to their failure to capture the broad range and depth of the enslaved experience and their contributions to this nation—and to the United States' role in Black people's subjugation. The few monuments that do exist show us neither the depth of the human atrocity perpetrated (and continue to perpetrate) against Black people nor the extraordinary labors and creativity of Black people.

As Morrison stood in that Swedish hall, I thought about the US and all the European countries involved in the slave trade. What grand markers had these European countries erected in their respective capital cities to honor the Black bodies captured and transported to build their empires and expand their imprint on the world? I thought about Morrison in Sweden: the country celebrating her "visionary force and poetic import" of Black life was the same country that manufactured the iron that European nations used to shackle Black bodies. As Morrison spoke, all these worlds were colliding and coexisting. And therein lie the beauty and power of Morrison: her ability to travel within and between worlds, opening us to a lived reality both beautiful and shameful, life-giving and soul damning. Slavery is just as real as freedom, and we cannot hug it away. What the US and global countries have done to Black-bodied people cannot be prayed away, glossed over, or whitewashed, and what Black people have given and continue to give to this country and to the world can no longer be denied or ignored.

Morrison's voice that night from the academy in Stockholm carried the fluidity and certainty, the humility and yearning of a deep and ancient river. As in all of her literary works, Morrison's voice is clear, prophetic, and awakening. Her spiritual sight captivates and pulls us into the deep reservoir of Black life to awaken, baptize, and connect us to a past that is our present. Through her literary skills, she calls us to shift our gaze to a Black world that needs no explanation and makes no apologies for its existence. Black people are more than "enslaved" and would have been much more if they had not been stolen. Even with bent backs, they built. This does not make them magical or resiliently superhuman. It makes America horrid.

Morrison continued her speech, saying,

> Once upon a time there was an old woman. Blind. Wise. In the version I know the woman is the daughter of slaves, black, American, and lives alone in a small house outside of town. Her reputation for wisdom is without peer and without question. Among her people she is both the law and its transgression. The honor she is paid and the awe in which she is held reach beyond her neighborhood to places far away; to the city where the intelligence of rural prophets is the source of much amusement.
>
> One day the woman is visited by some young people who seem to be bent on disproving her clairvoyance and showing her up for the fraud they believe she is. Their plan is simple: they enter her house and ask the one question the answer to which rides solely on her difference from them, a difference they regard as a profound disability: her blindness. They stand before her, and one of them says, "Old woman, I hold in my hand a bird. Tell me whether it is living or dead."
>
> She does not answer, and the question is repeated. "Is the bird I am holding living or dead?" Still she doesn't answer. She is blind and cannot see her visitors, let alone what is in their hands. She does not know their color, gender or homeland. She only knows their motive. The old woman's silence is so long, the young people have trouble holding their laughter. Finally, she speaks, and her voice is soft but stern. "I don't know," she says. "I don't know whether the bird you are holding is dead or alive, but what I do know is that it is in your hands. It is in your hands."[2]

The bird in the young people's hands can metaphorically speak to several realities in our world today. Morrison sees the bird in all our hands as language. For the remainder of her speech, she draws from the story to talk about the power of language. For Morrison, language, like the bird, is "susceptible to death, erasure; certainly, imperiled and salvageable only by an effort of the will. She [the old woman] believes that if the bird in the hands of her visitors is dead, the custodians are responsible for the corpse."[3]

As I come to a close in this book, I understand the bird in our hands to be Black-bodied people. We, American citizens, have the power, responsibility, and moral obligation to determine how Black people are treated, honored, and remembered. We possess the compassion to acknowledge our mistreatment of them, honor their sacrifice and labors, and set them free. We decide by our actions to support either their well-being or their death. If Black-bodied people, like the bird, "die [in this country] out of carelessness, disuse, indifference and absence of esteem, or killed by fiat," those who "parade their power" at the bird's expense and others who remain silent and complicit are "accountable for [a Black person's] demise."[4] Bird-watching: the voyeuristic gazing upon Black people's disenfranchisement and pain is not a spectator sport. It is real and dangerous and costs lives every day.

My hope in this work is to open our eyes to the lives that labored against their will and contributed to the formation of early America both fiscally and physically—the toil, the sacrifice, the cost. Historically, we have not done well by them. We have dishonored the bird in our hands. One of America's greatest sins is capturing and caging Black people without their permission and forcing them into a life of servitude. From the arrival of the first slave ship, which docked on stolen indigenous soil, early settlers later called Americans were relentlessly cruel to Black people. The nation's Founding Fathers and other early colonists used the Black population for their national and self-interests. Black people served as a means to an end.

It was only toward the close of these white men's lives, when death seemed imminent and they believed that their souls would be in the hands of a merciful God, that some turned their gaze toward the evils of slavery. The final versions of their founding documents remained silent on the issue of slavery. These men and the colonizing nation around them continued holding Black people in captivity until they reached their death and had little strength and vitality to demand their labors. The innumerable sins and harms the Founding Fathers and other early colonists committed against Black people were not foremost on their minds while profiting economically, socially, and politically from the institution of slavery. Upon death, but usually, only then, some freed their enslaved Black women, men, and children, while others willed Black people to their children. It took a civil war and constitutional amendment to force white colonizers, their descendants, and other proslavery advocates to let go of the bird in their hands.

But even when freedom came after America's Founding Fathers and early colonists died, future generations of bird haters found other means to clip Black people's wings, impairing their flight in the vilest ways and under the most horrid conditions. The disenfranchisement of Black people did not begin and end during American slavery. Emancipation did not shield Black people from violence nor free them from economic inequality, political suppression, racial disparity in the US criminal justice system, and social oppression. After the Civil War, the Reconstruction era was well on its way to becoming one of the most violent and disenfranchising periods in American history for Black people. The successes that a small percentage of Black people achieved during this period paled in comparison to the economic, political, and social barriers that crippled or disadvantaged them. Even after Reconstruction, Black people never really had a chance in an American system that intentionally and disproportionately impeded Black people's quality of life.

America was built on the backs of Black and Brown people who were never intended to reap the full benefits the New World economy and social systems afforded, and this is a reckoning the US must face. No doubt there are some pivotal moments since slavery at which Black people's wage-earning power increased. However, such wage-earning power has yet to translate into collective and sustained economic bargaining in the US. When white people arrived in the New World, most had access to or opportunities to acquire land, housing, and loans. Most received paid employment, material resources, and financial assets, which many passed down to their children. The same cannot be said of the vast majority of Black people who arrived or were born on American soil and labored against their will without pay. More often than not, when Black people have made significant economic advancements, they have been defrauded or approached with hostility and violently dispossessed of their financial and material gains.

Recall in chapter 5, the Freedman's Savings Bank scandal and how Black people were swindled from their capital on the heels of emancipation. Alternatively, explore more deeply the 1921 Black Wall Street (Greenwood massacre) in Tulsa, Oklahoma, where a Black town was bombed and burned to the ground by an angry white mob whom white city officials not only deputized but gave weapons because they feared

Black economic and social advancement. They scorched 100 Black-owned businesses, including schools, churches, libraries, hospitals, hotels, and stores. They also set fire to over 1,250 homes and looted over 200 other Black residences, leaving more than 1,000 Black people homeless. In the end, they killed approximately 300 Black people. Imagine, after American slavery, descendants of former enslaved and free Black people, putting their resources together to build a town they could call their own. Imagine the pride they must have felt only to see it burn to the ground by whites who feared their presence. The burning of Tulsa was not an aberration. In 1919, two years before Tulsa, whites took to the streets in cities throughout the US, scorching Black neighborhoods, businesses, and towns from January to December, a period known as the Red Summer. Black people living in Alabama, Arkansas, Arizona, Connecticut, Delaware, Kentucky, Florida, Georgia, Illinois, Indiana, Maryland, Mississippi, Nebraska, New York, Oklahoma, Pennsylvania, South Carolina, Texas, Tennessee, Virginia, West Virginia, and Washington, DC, were catching hell and faced massive losses.

The Freedman's Savings Bank scandal, the Greenwood (Black Wall Street) massacre, and the Red Summer riots are just three among a multitude of concerted efforts to keep Black people in their place and thwart any strides toward financial solvency. America has exploited Black labor and also swindled and deprived Black people since slavery of their quality of life and equal economic participation in the American dream.

Another reckoning the US must face is that America was built on the backs of Black and Brown people who were never intended to have political power in America. Black people were not seen as fully human and systematically prevented from fully participating in American democracy. Recall Jefferson, Lincoln, and other white men's words about Black people's inferiority in previous chapters. Though Black people were granted citizenship with the ratification of the Fourteenth Amendment in 1868, they were not given full protection under the law, which confined them to second-class citizens' status for nearly one hundred years after the law was signed. During Reconstruction, a record number of Black people held public office. However, within time, white supremacist violence and blatant acts of racial discrimination and voter suppression diminished these gains. Whites feared "Negro rule" and

Black people's political influence and power, which would threaten their entitlements, privileges, and long-standing status and power.

Take, for example, the early founding documents of our nation discussed in chapters 1–4 and how these documents redefined Black people's humanity and their entitlement to citizenship or excluded them altogether from the decision-making process. Also consider the tensions that arose during Reconstruction between white Democrats, seeking to preserve slavery, and white Republicans, seeking equality for Black people. In the early 1870s, for example, tensions peaked during the highly contentious Louisiana gubernatorial battle between Republican William Pitt Kellogg and Democrat John McEnery. Kellogg won the election with Black voters' help. McEnery and his supporters immediately cried foul, saying the Republicans stole the election. White supremacist groups and other McEnery supporters, hoping to preserve the Old South, heightened their protest efforts throughout Louisiana, and some terrorized the region. Residents of Grant Parish, a predominately Black township, grew concerned that local white supremacist groups—the KKK and the White League (a.k.a. the White Man's League)—would seek to control the town. Blacks and whites gathered to protect the neighborhoods and the local courthouse in Colfax. After surrounding the courthouse, they were met and outnumbered by heavily armed white male supremacist militia. Among the militia were politicians, city officials, clergymen, police officers, and military veterans. The white insurrectionists fired a cannon at the courthouse, and then both groups battled until the Blacks and their white allies surrendered. Upon surrendering, the militia murdered nearly 150 Black men and three whites in public view. They intentionally created a public spectacle by riddling bodies with bullets while hanging and violently beating others. Then they threw the bodies into the nearby Red River. President Grant dispatched federal troops and officially declared Kellogg the winner. Louisiana courts indicted ninety-seven white supremacist group members, but the US Supreme Court overturned the case in 1876. Ultimately, "legal loopholes and corrupt officials" acquitted the men and paved the way for yet more public and private slayings of Black people in America.[5]

Nearly twenty-five years after Colfax, whites fearing "Negro rule" outlined a plan in their *Democratic Handbook of 1898* to suppress Black voting and thwart their chances of winning elections in Wilmington, North Carolina. Suppression tactics ranged from posting negative ads to empowering white militia groups, such as the Red Shirts to serve as poll watchers to beating and intimidating voters. The tactics proved futile when some Blacks won their elections.[6] Determined to take matters into their own hands, nearly two thousand whites led by Southern Democratic officials overthrew the local government, forcing the mayor and the city's board of aldermen out of office. At the time, it was considered the only coup d'état on American soil. The white supremacist group destroyed the local Black printing press and other Black businesses and residences. They carried out planned attacks on Black residents, killing nearly one hundred.

These are just a few examples of the myriad of violent and debilitating measures used to stifle Black people after American slavery. Incidents like these and many others continued well into the civil rights period and persisted into the new millennium. Slavery was the starting point. Repeatedly in America's past, political parties have employed tactics aimed at fomenting racial animus and nullifying Black political power. The era of Trumpian republicanism is the latest manifestation of such tactics. What is troubling is that throughout history, among those involved in inciting, participating, and legalizing political suppression and violence are politicians, judges, sheriffs, and other members of law enforcement and the military. Their involvement helped lay bare the glaring racial disparities in the US. This point leads me to another reckoning the US must face.

Without question, America was built on the backs of Black and Brown people who have been unduly criminalized by a racially biased criminal justice system. This system reinforces a plantation model of criminalization, subjugation, and terror to legally control Black people and privilege, preserve, and protect the welfare of white people. Recall the plight of Black people in the previous chapters and how they were subjected to white terror and white fragility. The criminal justice system's three major institutions—law enforcement, courts, and corrections—have historically and discriminatorily targeted Black people.

Early on, colonists established slave patrols to regulate Black people's mobility and curtail Black protest and uprisings in response to white terrorism and racial injustice. Slave patrols led by the local sheriff, law enforcement, white citizens, and local white militia set out to publicly humiliate and intimidate Black people. Public beatings, hog-tying, dehumanizing arrests, hangings, and floggings at whipping posts on courthouse grounds and other sites served to paralyze and instill fear in the Black community to maintain white control and safety. When slavery ended, Black people continued and still continue to fall prey to violence at law enforcement's hands. Many of these incidents result in death by the police. From 2013 to 2020, Black "people were 3.5 times more likely to be shot fatally by police than a white person, and this ratio increases substantially according to state and neighborhood."[7] During this period, "98.3% of killings by police have not resulted in officers being charged with a crime."[8]

Early on, it was also clear that an exclusionary all-white male court system would favor white men. White colonists often appealed to the Supreme Court and lower federal, state, and city courts because the courts' makeup represented their interests and more often than not ruled in colonists' favor. The courts' guiding documents—the US Constitution, Black Codes, Jim Crow laws, and local and state laws—also served their interests, protected their property rights, and ensured their security. The laws primarily protected white Christian men—namely, wealthy landowners and early white immigrants and settlers. Since slavery to the present, seldom have the laws of this country been applied equally to all its people, creating two justice systems in America—one that meted out considerably less justice than the other.

As a result, the incarceration rates among Black and Brown people are also higher than any other racialized group in US history. From slave pens to modern-day US prisons, Black people continue to be the demographic most often imprisoned and given longer sentences for nonfelony offenses. The "racial and ethnic makeup of US prisons continues to look substantially different from the demographics of the country as a whole."[9] In 2019, Black people made up less than 15 percent of the US population, but their numbers in the US prison system are far higher than any other racialized group. Today's prison system also mimics slavery through its exploitive labor practices sanctioned by the Thirteenth Amendment. The amendment prohibited slavery in the US "except as punishment for a crime whereof the party shall have been duly convicted." Such a clause allowed slavery to continue in the prison system, resulting in incarcerated persons becoming slaves of the state and working against their will. The prison industrial complex continues to oppress Black and Brown people and poverty-stricken whites by paying them pennies on the dollar to mass-produce goods for Americans' consumption. State governments also exploit incarcerated persons by requiring them to work on state-sanctioned projects. For many Americans, the US criminal justice system is, as often described, "slavery by another name."

There has long been plenty of unequivocal historical evidence of America's criminalization of Black people. The modern-day public lynching and flogging of Ahmaud Marquez Arbery, Breonna Taylor, and George Perry Floyd Jr. within months of each other in 2020 harkens back to slavery and points to Americans' depraved indifference toward Black life. Arbery, jogging throughout his residential neighborhood, was taunted and senselessly gunned down by white men in a truck. Taylor, sleeping in her bed, was awakened and killed in a botched police raid by plainclothes white male officers who shot into her home and left her bleeding to death on the floor of her apartment. Floyd, shopping and suspected of using a counterfeit $20 bill, suffocated to death after a white police officer pressed his knee into Floyd's neck for nearly ten minutes. During the ordeal, the officer, chilling with his hands in his pockets, ignored Floyd's pleas that he could not breathe.

While some Black people continue to battle racial disparities in the criminal justice system, others are challenged by failing social structures that place them, Native Americans, and low-income communities at higher risk. Undoubtedly, one final reckoning the US must face is that America was built on the backs of poor Black and Brown people whose descendants and other essential workers still feel the weight of social oppression in America. Since the Reconstruction era, low-income Black and Native American communities have continued to struggle with poverty, hunger, displacement, homelessness, wage inequality, affordable health care, adequate education, fair and decent housing, land ownership, voting rights, clean water, employment, bank loans, small business ownership, mental health care, and safe, environmentally friendly, and nontoxic neighborhoods. Yet they do not stand alone. White people are among America's poor.

All of these and other systemic economic, political, criminal-justice, social, and environmental barriers are clear evidence that since the arrival of the first slave ship on stolen soil, Americans have not done right by Black people. Enslaved and free Black people helped build this country and continued giving to this nation after emancipation. Yet despite their sacrifice and care, many Black people awake each morning under the threat of systemic racialized injustice and death. Many are still living the economic, political, social, and racialized disparities instituted since American slavery. Americans have deeply bruised and sometimes severed Black people's wings while still damning them to fly, to fetch and catch commodities and other resources for Americans' guilty pleasure. Then without hesitation, Americans have arrogantly blamed the bird that they caged and whose wings they clipped for its own condition. Americans' disdain and carelessness for Black people today do not occur in a vacuum; they have been real and potent since slavery.

## A Litany for Black Lives: "We Are In Your Hands"

The challenge before us is to truly see Black people, to move their plight to the forefront of our consciousness and connect to the depths of their historical trauma and contribution to this nation, and to do so with a more profound sense of urgency and reverence for Black people's lives and well-being. For as we see them, we sense their vibrations in our hearts, souls, and minds, calling out to us, saying, "We are in your hands."

> We, the over four million Black people of the United States of America, made to work against our will and upon whose backs Americans now benefit and rest, are in your hands.
>
> We, the enslaved Black laborers, the essential workers who built this nation and its wealth from sunup to sundown under the threat of ridicule and death without pay and rights to citizenship, literacy, voting rights, education, and freedom of religion, are in your hands.
>
> We, the Black field hands, forced to till America's fields, clear the roads, fashion the infrastructure, and lay out the streets and railroads, are in your hands.
>
> We, the Black domestics, made to clean Americans' homes, cook their meals, and nurse their babies, are in your hands.

We, the Black voters, beaten and murdered while fighting for voting rights and against voter suppression in pursuit of free and fair elections, are in your hands.

We, the Black depositors in Freedman's Bank and all those who worked hard and struggled to get their financial footing in America, are in your hands.

We, the Black gatekeepers of our cities, the seekers of peace and rest, lynched, burned, raped, beaten, and left to die during the Red Summer and beyond, are in your hands.

We, the Black residents of Black Wall Street and all the Black people who fashioned towns and watched white people riot in them, set them ablaze, and burn them to the ground, are in your hands.

We, the Black troops of the Fifty-Seventh, Sixty-Third, and Seventieth US Colored Infantry and all the Black regiments who served in the Civil War and buried in unnamed graves in Arlington Cemetery, are in your hands.

We, the Black soldiers of the Sixth US Colored Heavy Artillery and all the Black men and women who took and fired a blow for freedom, are in your hands.

As we continue to see them, we feel the vibrations of their stories, name by name, soul by soul, sacrifice after sacrifice, calling out to us saying,

I, Frederick Douglass and all the Black, white, and Native American abolitionists, protestors, and activists who risk our lives daily and work tirelessly for justice, fairness, and peace in America are in your hands.

We, Hercules Posey, Charlotte Scott, and all the poor, unseen, and exploited Black domestic servants and minimum wage workers who rise every morning and serve for pennies on the dollar with slim chance of living the American Dream are in your hands.

I, Sally Hemings and all the Black women raped, trafficked, and forced to bear children fathered by America's Founding Fathers, early colonists, their sons and friends are in your hands.

We, Mary and Emily Edmonson, Ona "Oney" Maria Judge and all the Black women who summon up the courage to walk out the front door of houses of bondage and never look back are in your hands.

We, Benjamin Banneker, Solomon Galleon Brown, and all the unsung Black scientists, writers, and intellectuals whose revolutionary findings, ideas, and research are dismissed or downplayed are in your hands.

We, Philip Reid, Laura "Dolly" Johnson, and all the Black essential workers who repair, serve, clean, and secure the White House, US Capitol, and other federal buildings and landmarks are in your hands.

I, Henry Highland Garnet and all America's religious leaders and politicians, unmoved by dangling carrots and who courageously and publicly stand against the forces of racism, white supremacy, and injustice are in your hands.

We, Mary Edmonia Lewis, John Hemmings, and all the Black artists, poets, and inventors who never got a chance to express the full beauty of our imaginations are in your hands.

We, Denise McNair, Addie Mae Collins, Cynthia Wesley, Carole Robertson, and all the Black children killed or missing whose names never made the headlines are in your hands.

We, The Charleston 9: Clementa C. Pinckney, Cynthia Marie Graham Hurd, Susie Jackson, Ethel Lee Lance, Depayne Middleton-Doctor, Tywanza Sanders, Daniel L. Simmons, Sharonda Coleman-Singleton, and Myra Thompson, and all those gunned down in an American church, mosque, or synagogue are in your hands.

I, Botham Jean and all the Black men and boys killed by frightened white women or brutally murdered for allegedly looking at one are in your hands.

I, Ahmaud Marquez Arbery and all the mothers and fathers mourning the loss of their sons and daughters murdered and lynched by white supremacists are in your hands.

I, George Perry Floyd Jr. and all the unarmed Black men and women killed by police or who died unlawfully in their custody are in your hands.

I, Breonna Taylor, abruptly awakened by police and shot without cause eight times in my home, and all the Black women whose deaths are trivialized or treated as an unfortunate tragedy are in your hands.

They are our reminder that we, as a nation, cannot address our current maladies without addressing the root of America's first malignancy—slavery. They are calling out to us, breaking open ugly truths so we can move forward with empathy and with the knowledge that what is behind us is before us. They, like the old woman and the children in Morrison's Nobel Prize speech, are our teachers, for they had lived and died once upon a time in a real-world America that severed their wings.

But now, with the past as prologue, we can do better. How we memorialize and honor enslaved Black people and their contribution lies within our reach. We can chart a different course in empathy and knowledge, taking their labors and presence seriously. We can choose to walk upon the earth in grace and gratitude, knowing the places we tread are the same places on which these elders toiled, tilled, laughed, and wept. These same places where they once lived and in which they are buried, we have erected modern-day buildings. We can choose to memorialize the full breadth of what enslaved and free Black people gave to this country, who they were, and what they built and sacrificed. We can mark their time and place in the world as we have marked other noble and patriotic Americans. As we honor them, we bring honor to ourselves.

We can also pay respect to those who recently died too soon—those murdered on the streets and in their homes and others who died due to systemic inequities and white supremacy violence. As a society propelling into the future, we can no longer ignore or whitewash the fact that America's ethos and institutions are welded deeply in a peculiar orientation that is hostile and depriving toward Black people. We can no longer afford to be bird-watchers of this truth. We can chart a bold, new course of action that takes the realities of inequality and racism seriously in a manner that gives us great pause and deeper reflection on our individual and societal treatment of Black people in America, the kind of reflection that leads to accountability and change, a reflection that takes Black people's wounds and feelings of hurt, anger, pride, resilience, helplessness, optimism, and hope seriously. These wounds and feelings are real and deep and should never be taken lightly. A society cannot keep injuring a people in the same place, century after century, and remain oblivious to both the blow and the wound.

We can forge a new course of action in truth and honesty, acknowledging and accepting the full breadth of America's origins and its ongoing threat to Black existence. We can forge a new course of action by refusing to accept any killing, wrongful death, or disenfranchisement of Black people. We can continue to make this known through voting, policy changes, public protest, rallies, marches, reform, publications, speaking out, and other long-standing and innovatively new means.

Each of us must do our part. Their fate lies in each of our hands, and the future will pay, as Morrison goes on to say, "close attention to what [we] have done as well as to what [we] have said."[10] They will take note of the "barrier [we] have erected between generosity and wisdom."[11] I close this book with a feeling of reflective grace and joy, a sense of sobering humility and possibility when thinking about how everyday people, held in bondage, built this country. How each day they rose to build on stolen colonized lands that soon stretched into rural towns, then spread wider into cities and, in some cases, into a state. Day after day, year after year, decade after decade, generation after generation, they kept building, brick by brick, state by state, soul by soul, until finally, a young nation with a capital city, a new republic, a leading democracy. This is their nation, and it is to them we are indebted. We are their caretakers, and I hear them calling, "See me, free me."

## Blackbirds Flying: The National Sanctuary Memorial to Enslaved Black Laborers

Nearly six years after seeing Freedmen's Memorial for the first time, my soul felt a sigh of profound pride when I sat at the unveiling ceremony of the permanent home of the Smithsonian National Museum of African American History and Culture on the National Mall in September 2016. Even today, I still feel a profound sense of pride when I walk through the national museum. Though important, I am calling for something beyond being archived, collected, preserved, and displayed as past life forces and animated objects of artistic, cultural, intellectual, and scientific significance to educate and inform us. I am calling for an outdoor installation located centrally on, or very close to, the National Mall that complements and extends beyond the experiential encounter of the African American museum. I envision a National Sanctuary Memorial to Enslaved Black Laborers to publicly honor, educate, and affirm the pivotal role enslaved Black people played in laying the foundations of the nation's capital.

The enslaved women, men, and children who built this country, brick by brick, state by state, soul by soul, need a plot of land designated as their own, a place not to be enclosed but rather to be set free. They need a place where they can spread their wings and we, the human community, may feel summoned to join them; a place where they can rest and be memorialized and we sit and reflect among them, honoring their presence and contribution; a place for the human community to gather to honor the work of their hands, feel the weight of their sacrifice, and hopefully with a willingness face our ugly truths, in accountability and repentance, of a past and present, which many among us economically, socially, and politically still benefit. They need a gathering place to weep, celebrate, and release the wrongs and laments we inflicted upon them, a place where we all can value their gifts and the sacred truth that Black people are children of God and, therefore, that without question, Black lives matter.

A place is needed where we come to grips with our connection to people, events, and places beyond our private homes, communities, towns, and cities. We soul-note the wisdom of the COVID pandemic, telling us that what affects us personally can affect others locally, nationally, and globally and vice versa. We could hold this place as sacred and return to the world we inhabit with renewed minds and a sense of action, commitment, and knowledge.

The National Sanctuary Memorial to Enslaved Black Laborers would include two primary components: an open-air space, which served as a national sanctuary for gathering, ceremony, rest, and reflection so crucial to realizing this specific benchmark in American history, and a permanent monument dedicated to those who helped build this country. In addition to these primary components, space would also be designated within the sanctuary in memorandum to Black lives past and present.

### The National Sanctuary Memorial

Often when we think of sanctuary, we think of a church—a sacred building where we worship. I am pointing to something beyond that image. I envision this sanctuary as an immersive, dynamic, and designated sacred space within nature that emotes a feeling of connection to the past and everything around us, a space wherein we gain a deeper awareness and appreciation of those enslaved women, men, and children who worked, lived, and died. Essential elements within the open-air sanctuary would be greenery and shrubby from or representative of the eight principal African regions enslaved Africans were taken into slavery—Senegambia, Sierra Leone, the Gold Coast, the Bight of Benin, the Bight of Biafra, West-Central Africa, Mozambique, and Madagascar.

A labyrinth representing enslaved Black people's transatlantic journey from Africa to the New World and their struggles negotiating new terrains is also central to the National Sanctuary Memorial. Visitors interested in walking the labyrinth within the sanctuary would embark on their journey that ultimately leads them to the center of the sanctuary, where a fixed monument and an impermanent installation to enslaved laborers rest. The labyrinth would also extend beyond the sanctuary and into the city. Visitors seeking more exploration and discovery can take the labyrinth bus tour into the city to discover places built by or impacted by enslaved labor. This tour takes visitors to smaller memorials or installations located on key sites—churches, businesses, federal buildings, libraries, schools, and other landmarks—that were once central to slavery in the district. This network of designated landmarks within the city would constitute a bus, or if desired, walking trail of sites, terminating at the sanctuary's center point. Interpretation along this trail could be modeled on the fine work published by Cultural Tourism DC in its trail guides.

Four other elements central to the sanctuary are a water feature or fountain for prayer, libations, and rituals; benches and grassy areas for quiet reflection, rest, and reading; grassy areas for communing, sharing a meal, or conducting outdoor meditations or yoga; and a small meeting area or amphitheater to hold public discussions and debates.

When standing and walking within the sanctuary, I hope we also gain a deeper awareness of a more expansive American history that broadens existing normative narratives. As we reflect, we are welcome to weep and ponder the realities of a history untold and devalued. We are permitted, without judgment, to free our outrage and shame and seek forgiveness and responsibility for a violent history and its toxicity that have met us in the present.

## A Monument within the Sanctuary Memorial

At the center of the National Sanctuary Memorial would stand a federally funded, stand-alone monument dedicated solely to those enslaved laborers who helped build this country. A monument is essential because it creates a different kind of consciousness, one that redefines and challenges old and long-standing notions of what it means to be an American and a democratic nation. The monument can serve as a powerful tribute that speaks insistently of the enslaved past and reminds us, as a nation, to be better caretakers and stewards of the bird in our hands so as not to repeat the ills of the past. Space would also be designated

adjacent to the fixed monument for revolving impermanent installations. Contemporary artists would be invited to create installations to
spark a dialogue between the fixed monument and the current moment.
In this way, the memorial offers a nuanced historical event as well as
dynamic engagement with the social movements of the time.

The power of the fixed monument, installations, and smaller memorial is their collective power to open new doors of knowledge, raise
consciousness, and inspire action and healing. Even Senator Blanche
Lambert Lincoln (Democrat, Arkansas), Senator Edward Spencer Abraham (Republican, Michigan), and Congressman John Lewis (Democrat, Georgia) understood the significance of powerful markers. When
walking past the *Statue of Freedom* that stands in Emancipation Hall,
Lincoln pointed to its power of captivation, saying, "As you walk into
Emancipation Hall and you see this huge statue . . . the *Statue of Freedom*,
what an unbelievable feeling it gives, not just to schoolchildren, but to
any American who walks in there." Yet Congressman Lewis points us
to how some memorials miss the mark. During the unveiling ceremony
of a small stone and two plaques honoring the enslaved laborers who
worked on the US Capitol, Lewis said,

> Imagine constructing this nation's Capitol building with your own
> two hands . . . to toil under the sun without the help of a crane, a lift,
> without any of the modern tools that we have today; imagine in Wash-
> ington's oppressive summer heat and humidity, to chisel and pull mas-
> sive stones out of a snake and mosquito-infested quarry. Just imagine.
> Imagine, having to fight through the bone-chilling winter in rags and
> sometimes without shoes. Just imagine, the United States government,
> our government, paying your owner, not you, but your owner $5 a
> month for your labor. This Capitol, the most recognizable symbol of
> our democracy, was not built overnight, it was not built by machines. It
> was built through the backbreaking work of laborers and slave laborers
> [who] struggled to erect this massive building brick by brick, stone by
> stone.[12]

After speaking these words, the stone and plaques were unveiled,
neither of which spoke to the enormous weight of Black people's presence and contribution. Neither were powerful enough symbols to help
us, as Congressman Lewis espouses, "see . . . feel, and . . . communicate
the back-breaking labor that slaves completed to help construct our

Capitol."[13] I am advocating for a powerful monument that catches our gaze and draws us in, one that activates our imagination; touches our core; causes us to pause, reflect, remember; and leaves us with a desire to know more about its context and story. The enslaved constructed the nation's capital and other US regions not because they wanted to but because they were forced to do so. The US government remained complicit in the practice of slavery in the US well into the Civil War.

## An Area within the Sanctuary in Memoriam to Black Lives Lost

Important in this sanctuary is also a designated section that serves as a memorial, a place of refuge and protection, for those birds who died too soon. America's role in slavery, its toxicity, and its denial of the human atrocity have spilled into its institutions and the consciousness of those in powerful and authoritative positions. As a result, Black women, men, and children in America have senselessly lost their lives due to inequities and lack of accountability in the criminal justice system, health care, and other facets of society. They have also lost their lives to white supremacist violence and hate crimes. A designated area within the sanctuary in memoriam to those who died too soon, particularly within the new millennium, should include a memorial wall and libation area for placing flowers, posting pictures, and affirming words or names in remembrance of those Black people or groups lost to police misconduct, white supremacist violence or societal inequality in the US. Such a memorial may allow us, as a human community, to make connections to the past to inform our present.

## A Sacred Reflective Place for the Human Community to Gather

The sanctuary becomes an important place for the human community to connect within. The stories in this book remind us that the human community can be painfully cruel and also quite resilient and beautiful. When we lose sight of our resiliency and beauty, the sanctuary can serve as a safe space for each of us to reconnect to ourselves, the past, nature, the earth, and one another. The sanctuary may provide us an opportunity to gather ourselves, regain our value, and reenter our homes, work spaces, and communities with a renewed appreciation for each other, the ancestors, and all life forces around us—nature, the earth, animals, and our ancestors.

The sanctuary, the monument, and the installations throughout the nation's capital city can serve as *the clearing*, a passageway to affirming our collective humanity and existence and, hopefully, feel and demonstrate a sense of reverence to those people and things from whence we come. Historically, *the clearing* for Black people has served as a space of freedom and profound connection to the divine, nature and life forces seen and unseen. Slavery and bondage cannot touch us there. We are embraced by a cloud of witnesses that love on us and remind us of the resiliency and beauty of our humanity.[14]

Over time, the National Sanctuary Memorial can offer us, the human community, a space to empty ourselves, a space to shift our gaze and free ourselves of expectations, norms, prejudices, religious and white supremacist dogma, and artificial trappings that sometimes bind and deaden us. In the process, we come to see that that which we despise is not our true selves but rather our socialization and indoctrination. This does not happen overnight. It takes time, care, self-assessment, and dialogue. Our commitment can help us reach the place where the baggage and debris in our lives and society clear, and we become *woke* and connected to an inner and external sanctuary that reminds us that we matter. We learn here and accept that Black lives, historically and in the present, do matter. We also open ourselves to a deeper connection and awareness of our responsibility to the earth, the world around us, and one another. If willing, we see that we are all images of something infinite, resilient, beautiful, and divine that connects us to a past that lives among us to teach us. When we reach this place, we have done something wonderful with the bird that is no longer in our hands; as Morrison says in the closing of her Nobel Prize speech, we have "truly caught it."[15] Then Morrison affirms this act by saying, "How lovely it is, this thing we have done—together."[16]

A national site of freedom and respite is fitting for a people who worked the land under the threat of death and bondage. A national enslaved labor sanctuary memorial encompassing a federally funded, stand-alone monument with intentionality toward national and individual reckoning creates the possibility for us, as a human community, to face our past, see and reflect upon the plight of Black people in America, accept responsibility, and seek long-term means to repair the breaches. In so doing, we can then move forward with a different kind of consciousness and historical memory and narrative, a consciousness that redefines and challenges old and long-standing notions of what it means to be an American and a democratic nation.

*    *    *

The National Sanctuary Memorial to Enslaved Black Laborers can become a powerful inspiration to the human community, especially those Black lives around us still seeking a just and fair nation. The memorial can also serve as a powerful tribute to those Black women, men, and children who helped build this country, brick by brick, soul by soul. It is their labors, and their dreams that call us to action. We owe them. We owe ourselves. I close with this Ogbo Ato, a Yoruba ancestral prayer in the Ifa tradition, in honor of the work of enslaved Black people on American soil and throughout the world. I invite them to bless the work that lies ahead as we, the human community, seek ways to own and heal from our historical past, and work together to build with our hands, hearts, and minds a memorial in their honor:

> *Egungun kiki egungun*
> *Praise to the mediums of the Ancestors,*
> *Egun iku ranran fe awo ku opipi*
> *Ancestors who have preserved the mystery of featherless flight.*
> *O da so bo fun le wo*
> *You create the words of reverence and power.*
> *Egun iku bata bango egun de*
> *The drums of the Ancestors announce the arrival of the Ancestors.*
> *Bi aba f'atori na le egun a se de*
> *On the strong mat you spread your power, the Ancestors are here.*
> *Ase*
> *May it be so.*
>
>                                          —EGUN PRAYER

# Notes

## Introduction

1. Toni Morrison, "Nobel Lecture" (lecture, Nobel Prize in Literature, December 7, 1993), accessed September 28, 2020, https://www.nobelprize.org/prizes/literature/1993/morrison/lecture/.
2. Sara Lee, "We Will Not Give Up on London Memorial," *BBC News*, June 10, 2020, accessed October 19, 2020, https://www.bbc.com/news/uk-england-london-52995586.

## Chapter One

1. Verner W. Crane, "The Origin of the Name of the Creek Indians," *Mississippi Valley Historical Review* 5, no. 3 (December 1918): 340, accessed August 6, 2017, http://www.jstor.org/stable/1888814.
2. Pauline Maier, ed., *The Declaration of Independence and the Constitution of the United States* (New York: Bantam Classics, 2008), 8.
3. Maier, 8.
4. John W. Blassingame, ed., *The Frederick Douglass Papers: Correspondences of Frederick Douglass*, vol. 1, *1842–1852* (New Haven, CT: Yale University Press, 2009), 370.
5. Blassingame, 375.
6. Ned and Constance Sublette, *The American Slave Coast: A History of the Slave-Breeding Industry* (Chicago: Lawrence Hill Books, 2016), 28.
7. Dorothy Sterling, ed., *We Are Your Sisters* (New York: W. W. Norton, 1997), 31–32. For an expanded analysis, see also Renee K. Harrison, *Enslaved Women and the Art of Resistance in Antebellum America* (New York: Palgrave Macmillan, 2009), chap. 4.

8  "From Thomas Jefferson to John Wayles Eppes, 30 June 1820," *Founders Online*, National Archives, https://founders.archives.gov/documents/Jefferson/98-01 -02-1352.

9  Harriet Beecher Stowe, *A Key to Uncle Tom's Cabin; Presenting the Original Facts and Documents upon Which the Story Is Founded. Together with Corroborative Statements Verifying the Truth of the Work*, vol. 1 (London: Clarke, Beeton, 1853), 326–49.

10  Blassingame, *Frederick Douglass Papers*, 371–72.

11  Edward E. Baptist, *The Half Has Never Been Told: Slavery and the Making of American Capitalism* (New York: Basic Books, 2014), xxiii.

12  Blassingame, *Frederick Douglass Papers*, 372.

13  Eric Williams, *Capitalism and Slavery* (Chapel Hill: University of North Carolina Press, 1944), preface.

14  For further insight on the role cotton and sugar played in buttressing the American economy, see R. W. Fogel and S. L. Engerman, *Time on the Cross: The Economics of American Negro Slavery* (New York: W. W. Norton, 1974). See also Baptist, *Half Has Never Been Told*.

15  Williams, *Capitalism and Slavery*, 23.

16  Historian David Eltis notes that it was the size of the labor pool of the mainland North American colonies that distinguished the English system from others—Dutch, Danish, Portuguese, and Spanish. See David Eltis, *The Rise of African Slavery in the Americas* (Cambridge: Cambridge University Press, 2000), 195.

17  Thomas Hariot, *A Brief and True Report of the New Found Land of Virginia (1588)*, Electronic Texts in American Studies 20, ed. Paul Royster (Lincoln: University of Nebraska–Lincoln, 1588), https://digitalcommons.unl.edu/ etas/20.

18  "Britain in the New World," U.S. History, accessed August 6, 2017, http://www .ushistory.org/us/2d.asp.

19  "Indentured Servants in the U.S.," *History Detectives: Special Investigations*, PBS, accessed August 6, 2017, http://www.pbs.org/opb/historydetectives/feature/ indentured-servants-in-the-us/.

20  "Indentured Servants."

21  Gary Nash, Julie Roy Jeffrey, John R. Howe, Allan M. Winkler, Allen F. Davis, Charlene Mires, Peter J. Frederick, and Carla Gardina Pestana, *The American People: Creating a Nation and Society*, Concise Edition, Volume 1, Edition 8, (Boston: Pearson, 2016), 43.

22  Nash et al., *American People*, 43.

23  Baptist, *Half Has Never Been Told*, 3.

24  "Tobacco Farming the Old Way," Anchor: A North Carolina History Online Resource, NCPEDIA, Anchor, accessed August 6, 2017, https://www.ncpedia .org/anchor/tobacco-farming-old-way.

25  Davey, "European Tobacco." See also Nash et al., *American People*, 32, 40–44, 47.

26  Nash et al., *American People*, 79.

27 Emily Jones Salmon and John Salmon, "Tobacco in Colonial Virginia," Encyclopedia Virginia, accessed August 6, 2017, https://www.encyclopediavirginia.org/Tobacco_in_Colonial_Virginia#start_entry.

28 Gar Olson, *Blood Spilled for Freedom: America's Struggle for Survival 1776–1815* (Bloomington, IN: Author House, 2014), 53. See also "New Tastes, New Trades," On the Water, Smithsonian National Museum of American History, accessed August 6, 2017, http://americanhistory.si.edu/onthewater/exhibition/1_3.html.

29 W. W. Sellers, Esq., *A History of Marion County, South Carolina: From Its Earliest Times to Present* (Columbia, SC: R. L. Bryan, 1902), 19.

30 Peter A. Coclainis, "Rice," New Georgia Encyclopedia, October 31, 2016, accessed August 20, 2017, http://www.georgiaencyclopedia.org/articles/business-economy/rice.

31 Kwesi DeGraft-Hanson, "Unearthing the Weeping Time: Savannah's Ten Broeck Race Course and 1859 Slave Sale," *Southern Spaces*, February 18, 2010, accessed August 12, 2017, https://southernspaces.org/2010/unearthing-weeping-time-savannahs-ten-broeck-race-course-and-1859-slave-sale/.

32 William Dusinberre, *Them Dark Days: Slavery in the American Rice Swamps* (Athens: University of Georgia Press, 2000), ix.

33 Greg Timmons, "How Slavery Became the Economic Engine of the South," History, March 6, 2018, accessed August 12, 2018, https://www.history.com/news/slavery-profitable-southern-economy.

34 Iron Gray (a.k.a. Abel Charles Thomas), *The Gospel of Slavery: A Primer of Freedom* (New York: T. W. Strong, 1864), 3.

35 Paul Buchheit, "Slavery Has Had Four Eras in the United States, and Its Abominable Impact Continues Today," Buzzflash, April 14, 2014, accessed August 12, 2017, http://www.truth-out.org/buzzflash/commentary/slavery-has-had-four-eras-in-the-united-states-and-its-abominable-impact-continues-today.

36 Gene Dattel, *Cotton and Race in the Making of America: The Human Costs of Economic Power* (Lanham, MD: Rowman and Littlefield, 2009), xi.

37 Howard Dodson, ed., *Jubilee: The Emergence of African American Culture by the Schomburg Center for Research in Black Culture* (Washington, DC: National Geographic Society, 2003), accessed August 7, 2017, http://news.nationalgeographic.com/news/2003/01/0131_030203_jubilee2_2.html.

38 Ned and Constance Sublette, *American Slave Coast*, 408.

39 Edward E. Baptist, "Picking Cotton under the Pushing System," *Slate*, August 24, 2015, accessed August 12, 2017, http://www.slate.com/articles/life/the_history_of_american_slavery/2015/08/slavery_under_the_pushing_system_why_systematic_violence_became_a_necessity.html.

40 Baptist, "Picking Cotton." See also Baptist, *Half Has Never Been Told*.

41 George P. Rawick, ed., *The American Slave: A Composite Autobiography*, vol. 4, *Texas Narratives, Parts 1 and 2* (Westport, CT: Greenwood, 1941), 35–36.

42 For a synopsis of Acklen's life, see Jennifer Watts, "Aelicia Acklen: The Lady of Belmont," Tennessee State Museum, March 16, 2021, accessed March 31, 2021, https://tnmuseum.org/junior-curators/posts/adelicia-acklen-the-lady-of-belmont. See also "Adelicia Acklen," History of American Women: Colonial Women, 18th–19th Century Women, *Women History Blog*, July 2014, accessed

August 30, 2017, http://www.womenhistoryblog.com/2014/07/adelicia-acklen.html.

43 Eugene R. Dattel, "Cotton and the Civil War," Mississippi History Now, accessed August 20, 2017, http://mshistorynow.mdah.state.ms.us/articles/291/cotton-and-the-civil-war.

44 Henry Louis Gates Jr., "Why Was Cotton King?," Root, February 4, 2013, accessed August 20, 2017, https://www.theroot.com/why-was-cotton-king-1790895124. See also Henry Louis Gates Jr., "100 Amazing Facts about the Negro: Why Was Cotton 'King'?," African Americans: Many Rivers to Cross, PBS, accessed August 20, 2017, http://www.pbs.org/wnet/african-americans-many-rivers-to-cross/history/why-was-cotton-king/.

45 James Griffiths, "Healthy Eating, Roman Style: Ancient Pompeiians Had Surprisingly Good Teeth," CNN, accessed August 25, 2017, http://edition.cnn.com/2015/10/04/health/roman-sugar-healthy-teeth/index.html.

46 See Harrison, Enslaved Women, 15, 239.

47 Jon L. Wakelyn, ed., America's Founding Charters: Primary Documents of Colonial and Revolutionary Era Governance, vol. 1 (Westport, CT: Greenwood, 2006), 232.

48 Mary Battle, "African Passages, Lowcountry Adaptations," Lowcountry Digital History Initiative, accessed August 19, 2017, http://ldhi.library.cofc.edu/exhibits/show/africanpassageslowcountryadapt/sectionii_introduction/barbadians_in_carolina.

49 Battle.

50 W. C. C. Claiborne, Official Letter Books of W. C. C. Claiborne, 1801–1816, vol. 3, ed. Dunbar Rowland (Jackson, MI: State Department of Archives and History, 1917), accessed August 11, 2017, https://archive.org/stream/officialletterbo03claiiala/officialletterbo03claiiala_djvu.txt.

51 Claiborne.

52 Claiborne.

53 Alice Bayne Windham Webb, ed., Mistress of Evergreen Plantation: Rachel O'Connor's Legacy of Letters 1823–1845 (Albany: State University of New York Press, 1984), xviii.

54 Windham Webb, xviii.

55 Eltis, Rise of African Slavery, 195.

56 Exactly one month before the signing of the document, Congress had accepted a resolution put forward by Richard Henry Lee that stated, "Resolved: That these United Colonies are, and of right ought to be, free and independent States, that they are absolved from all allegiance to the British Crown, and that all political connection between them and the State of Great Britain is, and ought to be, totally dissolved." See "This Day in History, August 02: Delegates Sign Declaration of Independence," History, accessed September 4, 2017, http://www.history.com/this-day-in-history/delegates-sign-declaration-of-independence.

57 "Thomas Jefferson and Slavery," Thomas Jefferson Foundation, accessed August 18, 2017, https://www.monticello.org/site/plantation-and-slavery/thomas-jefferson-and-slavery.

58  "To George Washington from John Hancock, 6 July 1776," *Founders Online*, National Archives, https://founders.archives.gov/documents/Washington/03 -05-02-0153.

59  "To Washington from Hancock, 6 July 1776."

60  "General Orders, 9 July 1776," *Founders Online*, National Archives, http:// founders.archives.gov/documents/Washington/03-05-02-0176.

# Chapter Two

1  "European Immigration to America," Emmigration.info, accessed April 30, 2018, http://www.emmigration.info/european-immigration-to-america.htm.

2  "British Involvement in the Transatlantic Slave Trade," Abolition Project, accessed June 19, 2018, http://abolition.e2bn.org/slavery.html.

3  "British Involvement."

4  Shiho Imai, "Naturalization Act of 1790," Densho Encyclopedia, March 19, 2013, accessed June 18, 2018, https://encyclopedia.densho.org/Naturalization %20Act%20of%201790/.

5  Matt Novak, "Britain Sent Thousands of Its Convicts to America, Not Just Australia," Gizmodo, May 29, 2015, accessed June 18, 2018, https://paleofuture .gizmodo.com/britain-sent-thousands-of-its-convicts-to-america-not -1707458418.

6  Journalist Matt Novak notes, "Even before the Transportation Act of 1718 really opened the doors for Britain's dumping of undesirables in America, some colonies tried to pass laws that would prohibit the practice." Both Virginia and Pennsylvania, for example, tried to prohibit the practice but were overruled by Britain's king. See Novak, "Britain Sent Thousands."

7  Edward D. Neill, John Washington, and Robert Orme, "The Ancestry and Earlier Life of George Washington," *Pennsylvania Magazine of History and Biography* 16, no. 3 (October 1892): 262, accessed March 11, 2017, http://www.jstor .org/stable/20083489. See also Willard Sterne Randall, *George Washington: A Life* (Houston, TX: New Word City, 2014).

8  Randall, *George Washington*, loc. 242.

9  Johannah Cornblatt, "'Town Destroyer' versus the Iroquois Indian," *US News*, June 27, 2008, accessed March 11, 2018, https://www.usnews.com/news/ national/articles/2008/06/27/town-destroyer-versus-the-iroquois-indians. See also Charles Edwin Congdon, *Allegany Oxbow: A History of Allegany State Park and the Allegany Reserve of the Seneca Nation* (Salamanca, NY: Salamanca Area Museum Association, 1997); and "Conotocarious," Mount Vernon Digital Library, MountVernon.org, accessed March 11, 2018, http://www.mountvernon .org/research-collections/digital-encyclopedia/article/conotocarious/.

10  "This Day in Virginia History, Virginia Memory, Library of Virginia, Sept 04, 1661, John Washington Patented Land with Twenty-Four Headrights," Virginia memory.com, accessed August 6, 2017, http://www.virginiamemory.com/reading _room/this_day_in_virginia_history/september/04.

11  *Epsewasson* was sometimes spelled *Eppsewasson* and *Ipsewason*.

12  Randall, *George Washington*, loc. 256.

13  Randall, loc. 256. Also note the term *patent* is a direct quote. A land patent is an exclusive land grant made by a sovereign entity with respect to a particular tract of land. To make such a grant "patent," a sovereign (proprietary land-owner) must document the land grant, securely sign and seal the document (patent), and openly publish the documents for the public to see. An official land patent is the highest evidence of right, title, and interest to a defined area. It is usually granted by a central, federal, or state government to an individual or to a private company.

14  Randall, loc. 256.

15  Randall, loc. 248–49.

16  Worthington Chauncey Ford, ed., *Wills of George Washington and His Immediate Ancestors* (Brooklyn, NY: Historical Printing Club, 1891). See also Historical Genealogical Society, *The New England Historical and Genealogical Register*, vol. 44 (Boston: New England Historic Genealogical Society, 1890), 79.

17  Charles H. Callahan and the Federalist Papers Project, *George Washington: The Man and the Mason* (Washington, DC: Memorial Temple Committee of the George Washington Masonic National Memorial Association, 1913), 28.

18  Ford, *Wills of George Washington*.

19  Ford.

20  W. Gillingham and George Washington, *Map of George Washington's Land at Mount Vernon, Fairfax Coy., Virginia, as It Was & as It Is. Laid down from Old Maps Made by G. Washington and from Actual Surveys*, 1859, map, Library of Congress Geography and Map Division, accessed April 9, 2018, https://www.loc.gov/resource/g3882m.ct002394/.

21  "[Diary Entry: 19 February 1760]," *Founders Online*, National Archives, http://founders.archives.gov/documents/Washington/01-01-02-0005-0002-0019.

22  "Cash Accounts, 1761," *Founders Online*, National Archives, http://founders.archives.gov/documents/Washington/02-07-02-0001. See also "From George Washington to Lund Washington, 24–26 February 1779," *Founders Online*, National Archives, http://founders.archives.gov/documents/Washington/03-19-02-0279.

23  "From Washington to Washington, 24–26 February 1779."

24  "From George Washington to John Posey, 11 June 1769," *Founders Online*, National Archives, http://founders.archives.gov/documents/Washington/02-08-02-0147.

25  "To George Washington from John West, Jr., 26 April 1769," *Founders Online*, National Archives, http://founders.archives.gov/documents/Washington/02-08-02-0136. See also "From George Washington to Lund Washington, 15 August 1778," *Founders Online*, National Archives, http://founders.archives.gov/documents/Washington/03-16-02-0342.

26  "To George Washington from Thomas Hanson Marshall, 18 June 1769," *Founders Online*, National Archives, http://founders.archives.gov/documents/Washington/02-08-02-0150. See footnote 1, which reads, in part,

> GW's letter to Marshall has not been found. Shortly after he came into possession of Mount Vernon in 1754 GW began acquiring other tracts

on the neck between Dogue and Little Hunting creeks and kept at it until in 1786 with the acquisition of the French parcels he owned the entire neck and several contiguous tracts as well. See "The Growth of Mount Vernon, 1754–1786," in *Diaries*, 1:240–42. Thomas Hanson Marshall, who lived across the Potomac in Charles County, Md., owned nearly five hundred acres bordering, to the west, the Mount Vernon tract. As early as 1760, GW began angling for Marshall's Virginia land (see Marshall to GW, 21 June 1760). It was not until 1779, however, that the Marshall tract of 480½ acres became a part of GW's Mount Vernon (see GW to Lund Washington, 15 Aug., 17 and 18 Dec. 1778, DLC:GW, and Lund Washington to GW, 2 Sept. 1778, ViMtvL). As this letter of 18 June indicates, GW in 1769 began negotiating with Marshall to make an exchange of Marshall's land at Mount Vernon for a tract of land neighboring Marshall's plantation in Maryland, which GW proposed to acquire from his neighbor Robert Alexander. Alexander agreed on 22 June to sell to GW a portion of this Maryland land inherited by his young wife, Mariamne Stoddert Alexander.

27 "From Washington to Washington, 15 August 1778."
28 "From Washington to Washington, 15 August 1778."
29 "To Washington from Marshall, 18 June 1769." See footnote 1.
30 "Expansion of Mount Vernon's Mansion," George Washington's Mount Vernon, accessed April 6, 2018, http://www.mountvernon.org/the-estate-gardens/the-mansion/expansion-of-mount-vernons-mansion/.
31 "The Mansion," George Washington's Mount Vernon, accessed April 6, 2018, http://www.mountvernon.org/the-estate-gardens/the-mansion/.
32 "From George Washington to Lund Washington, 26 November 1775," *Founders Online*, National Archives, http://founders.archives.gov/documents/Washington/03-02-02-0396.
33 "Ten Facts about the Mansion," George Washington's Mount Vernon, accessed April 7, 2018, http://www.mountvernon.org/the-estate-gardens/the-mansion/ten-facts-about-the-mansion/.
34 "Ten Facts about the Mansion."
35 For greater detail, see Andrea Wulf, *Founding Gardeners: The Revolutionary Generation, Nature, and the Shaping of the American Nation* (New York: Vintage, 2011).
36 "Expansion of Mount Vernon's Mansion."
37 Robert F. Dalzell Jr. and Lee Baldwin Dalzell, *George Washington's Mount Vernon* (Oxford: Oxford University Press, 1998), 209. See also "Washington and the New Agriculture," Library of Congress Digital Collections, accessed April 8, 2018, https://www.loc.gov/collections/george-washington-papers/articles-and-essays/introduction-to-the-diaries-of-george-washington/washington-and-the-new-agriculture/.
38 "[January 1760]," *Founders Online*, National Archives, http://founders.archives.gov/documents/Washington/01-01-02-0005-0001.
39 Because Mrs. Washington's first husband died without a will, his property was divided according to English common law, which allowed the widow

one-third of the property for her life only (called her right of dower), after which it would revert to their children or their descendants. Upon her marriage to GW, all of Martha's property came under his control during her lifetime, including her share of the slaves from the Custis estate. One of her "dower slaves" who was transferred to Mount Vernon by GW was Morris (born ca. 1730), who worked as a carpenter (1760–63), a tradesman (1764–65), and overseer of GW's Dogue Run plantation (1766–94). Morris's wife was Hannah, who, with a child, had been purchased by GW from William Cloptan on June 16, 1759, for £80 (General Ledger A, folio 56). Morris and Hannah were married circa 1765 when both were transferred to the Dogue Run plantation. Like most large planters, GW referred to his plantation workers collectively either as his people or his family. For more info on dower, see "Appendix F. List of Dower Slaves, 1760–61," *Founders Online*, National Archives, https://founders.archives.gov/documents/Washington/02-06-02-0164-0028.

40 "From George Washington to Robert Cary & Company, 20 September 1759," *Founders Online*, National Archives, http://founders.archives.gov/documents/Washington/02-06-02-0189-0001.

41 Lavern Y. Smith, "Tobacco," Mount Vernon Digital Library, MountVernon.org, accessed April 9, 2018, http://www.mountvernon.org/digital-encyclopedia/article/tobacco/. See also Allan Kulikoff, *Tobacco and Slaves: The Development of Southern Cultures in the Chesapeake 1680–1800* (Chapel Hill: University of North Carolina Press, 1986), 45–76.

42 Susan Deford, "Tobacco," *Washington Post*, May 14, 1997, accessed April 9, 2018, https://www.washingtonpost.com/archive/1997/05/14/tobacco/89b1e1e6-3d24-41fd-b3ef-9ca45bb0bf62/?utm_term=.71d79e1f5ca9.

43 Smith, "Tobacco."

44 Smith. See also Salmon and Salmon, "Tobacco in Colonial Virginia"; and Walter Hening, *The Statutes at Large Being a Collection of All the Laws of Virginia from the First Session of the Legislature in the Year 1619*, vol. 2 (New York: R. & W. & G. Bartow, 1823), 9–20, 48.

45 "From George Washington to Thomas Knox, 26 December 1757," *Founders Online*, National Archives, http://founders.archives.gov/documents/Washington/02-05-02-0044.

46 "From Washington to Cary & Company, 20 September 1759." See also "From George Washington to Robert Cary & Company, 20 September 1765," *Founders Online*, National Archives, http://founders.archives.gov/documents/Washington/02-07-02-0252-0001.

47 Don Higginbotham, ed., *George Washington Reconsidered* (Charlottesville: University Press of Virginia, 2001), 69.

48 This rough estimate figure is taken from the approximate total sum of hogsheads listed in Washington's cash accounts from 1754 to 1761. It was common during this time for hogsheads to weigh between 1,000 and 1,500 pounds. In 1759 alone, Washington's enslaved laborers produced 23,427 pounds of tobacco. See "Tobacco and Staple Agriculture," Virginia Places, accessed April 9, 2018, http://www.virginiaplaces.org/agriculture/tobaccostaple.html#four.

49  "To George Washington from Humphrey Knight, 2 September 1758," *Founders Online*, National Archives, http://founders.archives.gov/documents/Washington/02-05-02-0361.

50  "Cash Accounts, 1761," *Founders Online*, National Archives, http://founders.archives.gov/documents/Washington/02-07-02-0001. See also "Invoice from Robert Cary & Company, 6 August 1759," *Founders Online*, National Archives, http://founders.archives.gov/documents/Washington/02-06-02-0178.

51  Andrew G. Gardner, "How Did Washington Make His Millions?," Colonial Williamsburg: That the Future May Learn from the Past, Winter 2013, accessed April 9, 2018, http://www.history.org/foundation/journal/winter13/washington.cfm.

52  "From Washington to Cary & Company, 20 September 1765."

53  Colin G. Calloway, *The Indian World of George Washington* (New York: Oxford University Press, 2018).

54  "From Washington to Cary & Company, 20 September 1759."

55  "Washington and Wheat," George Washington's Mount Vernon, accessed June 3, 2018, http://www.mountvernon.org/george-washington/farming/washingtons-crops/washington-and-wheat/.

56  John R. Maass, *George Washington's Virginia* (Charleston, SC: History, 2017), 196.

57  "From George Washington to William Pearce, 10 May 1795," *Founders Online*, National Archives, http://founders.archives.gov/documents/Washington/05-18-02-0098.

58  "Ten Facts about the Gristmill," George Washington's Mount Vernon, accessed June 3, 2018, http://www.mountvernon.org/the-estate-gardens/gristmill/ten-facts-about-the-gristmill/.

59  "Ten Facts about the Gristmill."

60  Maass, *George Washington's Virginia*, 196–98.

61  "George Washington's Fishing Operations at Mount Vernon," George Washington's Mount Vernon, accessed June 3, 2018, http://www.mountvernon.org/the-estate-gardens/historic-trades/fisheries/fishing-operations/.

62  "[Diary Entry: 11 April 1769]," *Founders Online*, National Archives, http://founders.archives.gov/documents/Washington/01-02-02-0004-0012-0003.

63  "Ten Facts about the Gristmill."

64  "Gristmill Pics," George Washington's Mount Vernon, accessed June 3, 2018, https://millpictures.com/mills.php?millid=1291.

65  "Ten Facts about the Gristmill."

66  "Ten Facts about the Gristmill." Also note that my estimation of the final figure is based on the US inflation rate from 1799 to 2018. According to the Bureau of Labor Statistics' consumer price index, the dollar experienced an average inflation rate of 1.36 percent per year. Prices in 2018 are 1838.4 percent higher than prices in 1799. In other words, $7,500 in the year 1799 is equivalent in purchasing power to $145,379.79 in 2018, a difference of $137,879.79 over 219 years. The amount of $460 in the year 1799 is equivalent in purchasing power to $8,916.63 in 2018, a difference of $8,456.63 over 219 years.

67 "Amid Controversy, Scholastic Pulls Picture Book about Washington's Slave," NPR, January 18, 2016, accessed June 11, 2018, https://www.npr.org/sections/ thetwo-way/2016/01/18/463488364/amid-controversy-scholastic-pulls -picture-book-about-washingtons-slave.

68 Stephen McLeod, ed., *Dining with the Washingtons: Historic Recipes, Entertaining, and Hospitality from Mount Vernon* (Chapel Hill: University of North Carolina Press, 2011), 25.

69 Adrian Miller, "The Man Who Fed the First President—and Hungered for Freedom," *Washington Post*, February 25, 2017, accessed June 2, 2018, https://www .washingtonpost.com/lifestyle/food/the-man-who-fed-the-first-president-and -hungered-for-freedom/2017/02/24/7897d572-f475-11e6-b9c9-e83fce42fb61 _story.html. See also Adrian Miller, *The President's Kitchen Cabinet: The Story of the African Americans Who Have Fed Our First Families, from the Washingtons to the Obamas* (Chapel Hill: University of North Carolina Press, 2017).

70 "From George Washington to George Lewis, 13 November 1797," *Founders Online*, National Archives, http://founders.archives.gov/documents/Washington/06-01 -02-0419.

71 Karl Marx and A. J. Dragstedt, *Value: Studies by Karl Marx* (London: New Park, 1976).

72 "[Diary Entry: 18 February 1786]," *Founders Online*, National Archives, https:// founders.archives.gov/documents/Washington/01-04-02-0003-0002-0018.

73 "[Diary Entry: 18 February 1786]."

74 "From Washington to Pearce, 10 May 1795."

75 Eric W. Nye, "Pounds Sterling to Dollars: Historical Conversion of Currency," University of Wyoming, accessed June 4, 2018, http://www.uwyo.edu/numimage/ currency.htm.

76 Dalzell and Dalzell, *George Washington's Mount Vernon*, xvi.

77 Dalzell and Dalzell, xvi.

78 Ira Berlin, Marc Favreau, and Steven F. Miller, eds., *Remembering Slavery: African Americans Talk about Their Personal Experiences of Slavery and Emancipation* (New York: New Press, 1996), 73–75.

79 "Ten Facts about Washington & Slavery," George Washington's Mount Vernon, accessed June 14, 2018, http://www.mountvernon.org/george-washington/ slavery/ten-facts-about-washington-slavery/.

80 "Slave Labor," Fred W. Smith National Library for the Study of George Washington Digital Archives, accessed June 5, 2018, https://www.mountvernon.org/ library/digitalhistory/digital-encyclopedia/article/slave-labor/. See also Dennis J. Pogue, "Archaeology of Plantation Life: Another Perspective on George Washington's Mount Vernon," *Virginia Cavalcade*, Autumn 1991, 79.

81 "Spinning and Weaving Records, 1768," *Founders Online*, National Archives, http://founders.archives.gov/documents/Washington/02-08-02-0118. See also Erin Allen, "George Washington and the Weaving of American History," *Library of Congress Blog*, March 10, 2015, accessed June 15, 2018.

82 "Spinning and Weaving." See also Allen, "George Washington."

83 "Slave Labor." See also Pogue, "Archaeology of Plantation Life," 79.

84 The lists have been printed in the *Papers of George Washington*, Colonial Series. These lists name slaves living at Mount Vernon but do not include

children under the age of sixteen and a few elderly slaves who were not tithed. The lists of tithables also include the names of indentured white servants and other whites living on the farms, including George Washington's overseers and managers. For further information on Washington's enslaved laborers, see "From George Washington to William Triplett, 25 September 1786," *Founders Online*, National Archives, https://founders.archives.gov/documents/Washington/04-04-02-0247. See also "Memorandum Division of Slaves, 1762," *Founders Online*, National Archives, https://founders.archives.gov/documents/Washington/02-07-02-0107. See George Washington, *The Diaries of George Washington*, ed. George Washington, Donald Jackson, and Dorothy Twohig (Charlottesville: University Press of Virginia, 1979), 4:277–83, https://www.loc.gov/item/75041365/.

85   "Slave Labor." See also Pogue, "Archaeology of Plantation Life," 79.
86   Daina Ramey Berry, *The Price for Their Pound of Flesh* (Boston: Beacon, 2017), 3.
87   See Harrison's previous work, *Enslaved Women*, 169.

# Chapter Three

1   Foundational to the written document, unlike its predecessor, the Articles of Confederation, the US Constitution laid out not only the establishment of a national government with representatives from each of the states but a federal government with three branches (legislative, executive, and judicial). Also central to the Constitution was identifying the function, purpose, scope, limits, and duties of the national government, along with a system of checks and balances to control potential abuse of power among its branches. In its preamble, the document established five basic principles for this new republic: (1) justice, (2) domestic tranquility, (3) common defense (protection), (4) promoting general welfare, and (5) securing the blessings of liberty.

2   In hopes of having the nation's capital in their region, Maryland and Virginia delegates proposed two bills ceding land for the construction of a national city. In December 1788, the Maryland General Assembly passed a bill entitled An Act to Cede to Congress a District of Ten Miles Square in This State for the Seat of the Government of the United States. One year later, the Virginia General Assembly passed a similar act, entitled An Act for the Cession of Ten Miles Square, or Any Lesser Quantity of Territory within This State, to the United States, in Congress Assembled, for the Permanent Seat of the General Government.

3   "From Thomas Jefferson to James Monroe, 20 June 1790," *Founders Online*, National Archives, https://founders.archives.gov/documents/Jefferson/01-16-02-0312.

4   "From Jefferson to Monroe, 20 June 1790." See also "Editorial Note," *Founders Online*, National Archives, https://founders.archives.gov/documents/Washington/05-07-02-0090-0001.

5   The Funding or Assumption Act of 1790, known originally as An Act Making Provision for the [payment of the] Debt of the United States, was approved on August 4, 1790. One month prior, on July 1, 1790, the Senate had passed the

Residence Act bill, known originally as An Act for Establishing the Temporary and Permanent Seat of Government of the United States. On July 9, 1790, the House of Representatives approved the bill, and President Washington signed the bill into law on July 16, 1790.

6 "Richmond on the James," WordPress, accessed August 25, 2018, https://rotj .wordpress.com/2011/01/27/george-washingtons-vision-at-canal-walk/.

7 "From George Washington to the United States Senate and House of Representatives, 24 January 1791," *Founders Online*, National Archives, last modified June 13, 2018, http://founders.archives.gov/documents/Washington/05-07 -02-0152. Original source: *Papers of George Washington*, Presidential Series, 7:277–78.

8 Washington based his selection on the site of the new Federal City on five factors: First, the lands along the Potomac River and below and adjacent to Georgetown on the eastside of Rock Creek were accessible to commerce, and their proximity was advantageous to "the country's principal north-south overland transportation route." Second, because the Potomac stretched all the way to the Ohio River Valley, Washington "conceived of the Potomac valley as a major transportation corridor that could unite the eastern seaboard with the interior of the continent." Third, Washington saw the Potomac's distance from the Atlantic Ocean as a security advantage, protecting the new government from invasion and combatants. Fourth, Washington was guided by the beauty of the region; situating the new seat of the empire along "rolling riverside terrain of old tobacco fields" created a picturesque scene. Fifth and finally, Washington believed that placing the new metropolis in this region would increase Georgetown's property values. See "From George Washington to William Deakins, Jr., and Benjamin Stoddert, 3 February 1791," *Founders Online*, National Archives, https://founders.archives.gov/documents/Washington/05 -07-02-0179. See "Presidents and the Potomac," White House History, June 2, 1997, accessed August 24, 2018, https://www.whitehousehistory.org/presidents -and-the-potomac. See "To George Washington from Thomas Jefferson, 15 March 1784," *Founders Online*, National Archives, https://founders.archives .gov/documents/Washington/04-01-02-0160. See also Beth Daley, "Draining the Swamp: A Guide for Outsiders and Career Politicians," The Conversation, March 8, 2017, accessed August 26, 2018, http://theconversation.com/draining -the-swamp-a-guide-for-outsiders-and-career-politicians-73422.

9 Ernest F. M. Faehtz, F. W. Pratt, S. R. Seibert, and Joseph M. Toner, *Sketch of Washington in Embryo: Viz., Previous to Its Survey by Major L'Enfant, 1792*, map, Library of Congress Geography and Map Division, accessed August 27, 2018, https://www.loc.gov/item/87694248/.

10 "From Washington to Deakins and Stoddert, 3 February 1791."

11 "From Washington to Deakins." See also "Editorial Note."

12 "Agreement of the Proprietors of the Federal District, 30 March 1791," *Founders Online*, National Archives, http://founders.archives.gov/documents/Washington/ 05-08-02-0016.

13 "Agreement of the Proprietors." See also "March 1791," *Founders Online*, National Archives, http://founders.archives.gov/documents/Washington/01-06-02-0002 -0002.

14 "Agreement of the Proprietors."

15 "Washington, DC—Founding of the Nation's Capital," Visiting Washington DC Online, accessed August 27, 2018, https://www.visitwashingtondconline .com/washington_dc_history7.htm.

16 "March 1791."

17 Catharine Van Cortlandt Mathews, *Andrew Ellicott: His Life and Letters* (New York: Grafton, 1908), 90.

18 "To George Washington from Pierre L'Enfant, 11 September 1789," *Founders Online*, National Archives, https://founders.archives.gov/documents/Washington/ 05-04-02-0010.

19 L'Enfant envisioned transforming the terrain into a bustling city "advanta- geously situated" with "publique Edifices" capturing picturesque views of "three grand Streems." From the height of these structures, "every Grand building would rear with a majistick aspect over the Country all round and advantageously seen From twenty miles off." L'Enfant also proposed "a majes- tick Colum or a grand Pyramid being Erected," which later became the Wash- ington Monument. The plan included bridges and "a Grand Navigation of the potowmack." In the city center, he imagined "a direct & large Avenue midle way paved for heavy Carriage and walks on eachside planted with double Rows of trees, a Street Laid out on a dimention proportioned to the Greatnes, which the Capital of a powerfull Empire ought to manifest." He allotted space on the Capitol grounds for a bronze equestrian statue of George Washington in Roman dress holding a truncheon in his right hand, per Congress's resolution (August 7, 1783). "Memorandum of Pierre-Charles L'Enfant, 26 March 1791," *Founders Online*, National Archives, http://founders.archives.gov/documents/ Washington/05-08-02-0005.

20 "To George Washington from Pierre-Charles L'Enfant, 22 June 1791," *Found- ers Online*, National Archives, last modified June 13, 2018, http://founders .archives.gov/documents/Washington/05-08-02-0199.

21 "To Washington from L'Enfant, 22 June 1791." See footnote 2.

22 "To Washington from L'Enfant, 22 June 1791."

23 "To George Washington from Pierre-Charles L'Enfant, 19 August 1791," *Founders Online*, National Archives http://founders.archives.gov/documents/Washington/ 05-08-02-0307.

24 Historic American Buildings Survey, *L'Enfant-McMillan Plan of Washington, DC (The Federal City)* (Washington, DC: National Park Service, Department of the Interior, 1933), 5.

25 "To Washington from L'Enfant, 19 August 1791."

26 On August 26, 1791, Jefferson messaged Madison saying, "The President left L'Enfant's plan, with a wish that you & I would examine it together immediately, as to certain matters, & let him know the result. As the plan is very large, will you walk up & examine it here?" "To James Madison from Thomas Jefferson, 26 August 1791," *Founders Online*, National Archives, http://founders.archives .gov/documents/Madison/01-14-02-0069. See also "Memorandum for Thomas Jefferson, 27 August 1791," *Founders Online*, National Archives, http://founders .archives.gov/documents/Washington/05-08-02-0321.

27  The following is a list of questions Washington had for Jefferson to review with
the commissioners:

> Will circumstances render a postponement of the Sale of Lots in the
> Federal city advisable? If not Where ought they to be made
>     Will it in that case, or even without it, be necessary or prudent to
> attempt to borrow money to carry on the difft works in the City?
>     Whether ought the building of a bridge over the Eastern branch to be
> attempted—the Canal set about—and Mr Peter's proposion with respect
> to wharves gone into now—or postponed until our funds are better ascer-
> tained & become productive?
>     At what time can the several Proprietors claim, with propriety, pay-
> ment for the public squares wch is marked upon their respective tracts?
>     Ought there to be any wood houses in the town?
>     What sort of Brick or Stone [Houses] should be built—& of wht
> height—especially on the principal Streets or Avenues?
>     When ought the public buildings to be begun, & in what manner had
> the materials best be provided?
>     How ought they to be promulgated, so as to draw plans from skilful
> Architects? and what would be the best mode of carrying on the Work?
>     Ought not Stoups & projections of every sort & kind into the Streets to
> be prohibited absolutely?
>     What compromise can be made with the Lot holders in Hamburgh &
> Carrollsburgh by which the plan of the Federal city may be preserved?
>     Ought not the several Land holders to be called upon to ascertain their
> respective boundaries previous to the Sale of Lots?
>     Would it not be advisable to have the Federal district as laid out, (com-
> prehending the plan of the Town) engraved in one piece?

28  Jonathan Elliot, *Historical Sketches of the Ten Miles Square Forming the District
of Columbia with a Picture of Washington Describing Objects of General Interest
or Curiosity at the Metropolis of the Union* (Washington, DC: Booksellers in the
District of Columbia, 1830). See also John Stewart, "Early Maps and Surveyors
of the City of Washington, D.C.," *Records of the Columbia Historical Society,
Washington, D.C.* 2 (1899): 53, accessed September 12, 2019, https://www.jstor
.org/stable/40066723; and "From George Washington to Tobias Lear, 2 October 1791," *Founders Online*, National Archives, http://founders.archives.gov/
documents/Washington/05-09-02-0020.

29  During this period, *territory* and *district* were used interchangeably. *District*
became more widely used among citizens of the new republic and eventually
replaced the term *territory* in the city's name once the US Capitol was incorporated in 1871. Among the other names considered for the new city were Virgin
Capital, City of His Love (*His* capitalized signifying God), and Second Rome.
Naming regions (states, cities, towns) and buildings and erecting memorials
in the US in honor of white American public figures or European immigrants
and cities were not uncommon. The United States, in essence, was emerging
as a smaller representation of European countries, exemplified in the names of

its states, cities, municipalities, counties, buildings, and the erection of statues and monuments. Essentially, Europe was being replicated in the US.

30 "Proclamation, 17 October 1791," *Founders Online*, National Archives, http://founders.archives.gov/documents/Washington/05-09-02-0052.

31 "Proclamation, 17 October 1791."

32 "Proclamation, 17 October 1791."

33 Washington responded to the commissioners on November 20, sharing their grave concern and noting that he had been surprised by "such perverseness in Major L'Enfant's . . . conduct." Washington advised the commissioners that he had appointed L'Enfant because "he was better qualified than any one in the US" but that L'Enfant's "refusal [to provide copies of] the Map, at the Sale, [gave] him to understd through a direct channel, though not an official one, as yet (further than what casually passed between us, previous to the Sale, at Mount Vernon[)], that he must, in future, look to the Commissioners for directions." See "From George Washington to David Stuart, 20 November 1791," *Founders Online*, National Archives, http://founders.archives.gov/documents/Washington/05-09-02-0118.

34 "From George Washington to Daniel Carroll of Duddington, 28 November 1791," *Founders Online*, National Archives, http://founders.archives.gov/documents/Washington/05-09-02-0134.

35 "Enclosure II: George Washington to Pierre Charles L'Enfant, 1 December 1791," *Founders Online*, National Archives, http://founders.archives.gov/documents/Jefferson/01-22-02-0329.

36 See "From George Washington to Daniel Carroll of Duddington, 2 December 1791," *Founders Online*, National Archives, http://founders.archives.gov/documents/Washington/05-09-02-0145. See also "To George Washington from Pierre L'Enfant, 7 December 1791," *Founders Online*, National Archives, http://founders.archives.gov/documents/Washington/05-09-02-0157. See "To George Washington from the Commissioners for the District of Columbia, 21 December 1791," *Founders Online*, National Archives, http://founders.archives.gov/documents/Washington/05-09-02-0189.

37 See *The Papers of George Washington Digital Edition* (Charlottesville: University of Virginia Press, Rotunda, 2008), accessed September 13, 2018, http://rotunda.upress.virginia.edu/founders/GEWN-05-09-02-0365.

38 "Thomas Jefferson to Pierre Charles L'Enfant, [27 February 1792]," *Founders Online*, National Archives, http://founders.archives.gov/documents/Hamilton/01-11-02-0061.

39 "To George Washington from Pierre L'Enfant, 27 February 1792," *Founders Online*, National Archives, http://founders.archives.gov/documents/Washington/05-09-02-0367.

40 "From George Washington to David Stuart, 8 March 1792," *Founders Online*, National Archives, http://founders.archives.gov/documents/Washington/05-10-02-0036. Washington considered offering L'Enfant "from $2,500 to $3,000 for his services" (the equivalent of between $65,000 and $75,000 in 2019).

41 "To George Washington from David Stuart, 18 April 1792," *Founders Online*, National Archives, http://founders.archives.gov/documents/Washington/05-10-02-0173.

42 James Dudley Morgan, "The Reinterment of Major Pierre Charles L'Enfant," *Records of the Columbia Historical Society, Washington, D.C.* 13 (1910): 121, accessed September 13, 2018, https://www.jstor.org/stable/40067014.

43 Pierre Charles L'Enfant, *Plan of the City of Washington*, 1792, map, Library of Congress Geography and Map Division, accessed August 15, 2018, https://www.loc.gov/resource/g3850.ct000509/.

44 Van Cortlandt Mathews, *Andrew Ellicott*, 85–86.

45 "From Washington to Stuart, 8 March 1792."

46 "From George Washington to Thomas Jefferson, 4 March 1792," *Founders Online*, National Archives, http://founders.archives.gov/documents/Washington/05-10-02-0012. See also "Thomas Jefferson to Washington, D.C., Commissioners, March 6, with Statements," March 6, 1792, manuscript, Thomas Jefferson Papers at the Library of Congress, https://www.loc.gov/item/mtjbib005962/.

47 James Reed Dermott (ca. 1756–1803), a native of Ireland who did some teaching at academies in northern Virginia, produced a map of Alexandria by 1791. Employed from March 1792 in the surveying and platting of the federal district, he prepared a comprehensive "Appropriation Map" that showed the city's lots and documented the form that L'Enfant's design was taking on the ground. His criticism of Andrew Ellicott, who was carrying out the field surveys, contributed to the dismissal of Ellicott and his assistants. They and others decried Dermott in turn as a troublesome, ill-tempered sot, and in January 1798, he too was discharged. For more insight, see the editor's notes to "To Thomas Jefferson from James Reed Dermott, 7 March 1801," *Founders Online*, National Archives, http://founders.archives.gov/documents/Jefferson/01-33-02-0163. See also "To George Washington from the Commissioners for the District of Columbia, 23 March 1794," *Founders Online*, National Archives, http://founders.archives.gov/documents/Washington/05-15-02-0332.

48 Bob Arnebeck, *Through a Fiery Trial: Building Washington, 1790–1800* (Lanham, MD: Madison Books, 1991), 150. See also "To Washington from the Commissioners, 23 March 1794."

49 For greater context on the ongoing dispute, allegations, and termination, see "From George Washington to the Commissioners for the District of Columbia, 3 April 1793," *Founders Online*, National Archives, http://founders.archives.gov/documents/Washington/05-12-02-0324. See also "To George Washington from Andrew Ellicott, 16 March 1793," *Founders Online*, National Archives, http://founders.archives.gov/documents/Washington/05-12-02-0254; Lorna Hainesworth, *America's Premier Surveyor: The Life and Times of Andrew Ellicott* (Randallstown, MD: Lornament, 2012), 5.

50 "To George Washington from David Stuart, 10 December 1792," *Founders Online*, National Archives, June 13, 2018, http://founders.archives.gov/documents/Washington/05-11-02-0295.

51 Van Cortlandt Mathews, *Andrew Ellicott*, 94–95.

52 "To Washington from Stuart, 10 December 1792." See also "To George Washington from the Commissioners for the District of Columbia, 5 January 1793," *Founders Online*, National Archives, http://founders.archives.gov/documents/Washington/05-11-02-0371.

53 "To Washington from the Commissioners, 5 January 1793." See also Van Cortlandt Mathews, *Andrew Ellicott*, 96–97.

54 "To Washington from the Commissioners, 5 January 1793." See also "To George Washington from the Commissioners for the District of Columbia, 9 January 1793," *Founders Online*, National Archives, http://founders.archives .gov/documents/Washington/05-11-02-0384. See also "To George Washington from the Commissioners for the District of Columbia, 8 February 1793," *Founders Online*, National Archives, http://founders.archives.gov/documents/ Washington/05-12-02-0074.

55 "Enclosure: From Thomas Jefferson to the United States Senate and House of Representatives, 18 February 1793," *Founders Online*, National Archives, last modified June 13, 2018, http://founders.archives.gov/documents/Washington/ 05-12-02-0120-0002. Original source: *Papers of George Washington*, Presidential Series, 12:167–68.

56 The commissioners' letter to Ellicott read in part, "We received information of many Inaccuracies in the returns of work done in the City, and of several Squares certified and divided which had not been measured or marked on the Ground. . . . We now desire you will not proceed." "To George Washington from the Commissioners for the District of Columbia, 11–12 March 1793," *Founders Online*, National Archives, http://founders.archives.gov/documents/ Washington/05-12-02-0230.

57 "Washington to Carroll, 2 December 1791."

58 Silvio A. Bedini, *The Life of Benjamin Banneker: The First African-American Man of Science*, 2nd ed. (Baltimore: Maryland Historical Society, 1999), 144.

59 "To George Washington from Andrew Ellicott, 28 February 1794," *Founders Online*, National Archives, http://founders.archives.gov/documents/Washington/ 05-15-02-0227.

60 "Andrew Ellicott," BillionGraves, accessed October 28, 2018, https://billiongraves .com/grave/Andrew-Ellicott/4784287.

61 For further references, see Bedini, *Life of Benjamin Banneker*; George Ely Russell, "Molly Welsh: Alleged Grandmother of Benjamin Banneker," *National Genealogical Society Quarterly* 94 (2006): 305–14; Martha E. Tyson, *Banneker, the Afric-America Astronomer, from the Posthumous Papers of Martha E. Tyson, Edited by Her Daughter* (Philadelphia: Friend's Book Association, 1884); Martha E. Tyson, *A Sketch of the Life of Benjamin Banneker, from Notes Taken in 1836* (Baltimore, MD: John D. Toy, 1854); James Davie Butler, "British Convicts Shipped to American Colonies," *American Historical Review* 2 (1897): 12–33; and David F. Musto, "Review: Barriers and Achievements," *Science* 178, no. 4057 (1972): 151–52, accessed August 27, 2018, https://www.jstor .org/stable/1734865.

62 Ron Eglash, "The African Heritage of Benjamin Banneker," *Social Studies of Science* 27 (1997): 307–15, accessed December 20, 2018, https://www.academia .edu/8007571/The_African_Heritage_of_Benjamin_Banneker?auto= download.

63 For free Blacks, such a felony offense was punishable by flogging and imprisonment, and whites were often expelled from the colonies. In 1691, Virginia

became the first colony to criminalize marriages between whites and free Blacks, followed by Maryland in 1691.

64 For further insight, see Russell, "Molly Welsh," 305–14; and Ellen E. Swartz, "Removing the Master Script: Benjamin Banneker 'Re-membered,'" *Journal of Black Studies* 44, no. 1 (January 2013): 31–49, accessed August 27, 2018, https:// www.jstor.org/stable/23414702. See also John H. B. Latrobe, Esq., "Memoir of Benjamin Banneker," *African Repository and Colonial Journal* 21, no. 11 (December 31, 1845): 326–27; Benjamin Banneker, *Benjamin Banneker's Pennsylvania, Delaware, Maryland and Virginia Almanack and Ephemeris for the Year of Our Lord 1792* (Baltimore, MD: William Goddard and James Angel, 1792), accessed October 5, 2018, https://memory.loc.gov/cgi-bin/ampage ?collId=ody_rbcmisc&fileName=ody/ody0214/ody0214page.db&recNum=1& itemLink=r?ammem/AMALL:@field(NUMBER+@band(rbcmisc+ody0214)) &linkText=0; Benjamin Banneker, *Banneker's Almanack and Ephemeris for the Year of Our Lord 1793* (Philadelphia: J. Crukshank, 1793); and Benjamin Banneker, *The Virginia Almanack, for the Year of Our Lord 1794. Being the Second after Leap Year and the Eighteenth of American Independence. Calculated by the Ingenious, Self Taught Astronomer, Benjamin Banneker, a Black Man* (Petersburg, VA: William Prentis, 1794).

65 For further references, see Bedini, *Life of Benjamin Banneker*; Eglash, "African Heritage," 309; Charles A. Cerami, *Benjamin Banneker: Surveyor, Astronomer, Publisher, Patriot* (Hoboken, NJ: John Wiley & Sons, 2002), app. 1, 217–19; Lionel Fanthorpe and Patricia Fanthorpe, *Mysteries and Secrets of Numerology* (Toronto: Dundurn, 2013), 115–16; Laird Scranton, *The Science of the Dogon: Decoding the African Mystery Tradition* (Rochester, VT: Inner Traditions, 2006); Banneker, *Benjamin Banneker's Pennsylvania*, 2; John H. B. Latrobe, "Memoir of Benjamin Banneker: Read before the Historical Society of Maryland," *Maryland Colonization Journal* 2, no. 23 (May 1845): 353–64; Phillip LePhillips, "The Negro, Benjamin Banneker: Astronomer and Mathematician, Plea for Universal Peace," *Records of the Columbia Historical Society* 20 (1917): 114–20; and "From Thomas Jefferson to Condorcet, 30 August 1791," *Founders Online*, National Archives, http://founders.archives.gov/ documents/Jefferson/01-22-02-0092. Presently, some of Banneker's original almanacs are housed at George Washington University's Gelman Library in Washington, DC.

66 Michael A. Gomez, *Exchanging Our Country Marks: The Transformation of African Identities in the Colonial and Antebellum South* (Chapel Hill: University of North Carolina Press, 1998), 47.

67 Cerami, *Benjamin Banneker*, 217–19.

68 See Swartz, "Removing the Master Script," 40. See also Cerami, *Benjamin Banneker*, 115–16; and Scranton, *Science of the Dogon*.

69 Cerami, *Benjamin Banneker*, 217–19. See also Swartz, "Removing the Master Script," 40; Fanthorpe and Fanthorpe, *Mysteries and Secrets*, 115–16; and Scranton, *Science of the Dogon*.

70 Cerami, *Benjamin Banneker*, 217–19. See also Swartz, "Removing the Master Script," 40; Fanthorpe and Fanthorpe, *Mysteries and Secrets*, 115–16; and Scranton, *Science of the Dogon*.

71  Oella is a small mill town in western Baltimore County along the Patapsco River.

72  Banneker, *Benjamin Banneker's Pennsylvania*. Also note drawing from original printings of Banneker's almanacs housed in George Washington University's Gelman Library in Washington, DC.

73  Silvio A. Bedini, "Benjamin Banneker and the Survey of the District of Columbia, 1791," *Records of the Columbia Historical Society* 69/70 (1969): 24, accessed May 9, 2018, https://www.jstor.org/stable/40067703.

74  Tyson, *Sketch*, 11–12.

75  "From Jefferson to Condorcet, 30 August 1791."

76  "From Jefferson to Condorcet, 30 August 1791."

77  "From Jefferson to Condorcet, 30 August 1791."

78  "To Thomas Jefferson from Benjamin Banneker, 19 August 1791," *Founders Online*, National Archives, http://founders.archives.gov/documents/Jefferson/01-22-02-0049.

79  Jefferson's views about Black people were widely known in his *Notes on the State of Virginia*. Sir Augustus John Foster, a British diplomat and politician, remarked during his US visit with Jefferson,

> Mr. Jefferson told me of a Negro named Bannister [Banneker] who died in the year 1806, at Baltimore, being a perfect Black, the son of an African . . . annually published an almanack, but the President asserted that in other Respects he appeared to little advantage, particularly in his Letters, he having received several from him, which were very childish and trivial. He told me, also, that the negroes have, in general, so little foresight. . . . Jefferson's opinions in regard to the Mental Qualities of the Negro Race were certainly not favourable for he considered them to be as far inferior to the Rest of Mankind as the mule is to the Horse, and as made to carry Burthens, while he augured but little good as likely to result from their Emancipation . . . scouting any body that opposes them [for example, Founding Fathers] and he quoted Laws South Sea Scheme, the Tea Tax on America and appeared to think that we should only render the Negroes' fate more miserable by our Perseverance in endeavouring to abolish the Trade.

See Margaret Bailey Tinkcom, "Caviar along the Potomac: Sir Augustus John Foster's 'Notes on the United States,'" *William and Mary Quarterly* 8, no. 1 (1951): 102, accessed January 12, 2018, https://www.jstor.org/stable/1920734.

80  Onesimus explained, "People take Juice of *Small-Pox* and cutty-skin, and putt in a Drop; then by'nd by a little *sicky, sicky*; then very few little things like *Small-Pox*; and no body die of it; and no body have Small-Pox anymore." Onesimus's remedy was incorporated. See Kenneth Silverman, *The Life and Times of Cotton Mather* (New York: Welcome Rain, 2011), 339.

81  It is important to note that enslaved and free Black women were also pioneering. However, because in most states Black and white women were considered subordinate to men, most of their inventions went unrecorded or unrecognized by the larger public during Jefferson's lifetime. Judy W. Reed, who invented a "dough

kneader and roller," was the first Black woman to receive a US patent (1884). Her invention improved upon existing dough kneaders by mixing more evenly and protecting the dough from dust and other debris during the kneading process. Reed's patent number, 305,474, was entered into the official US Patent record.

82 "To Washington from the Commissioners, 5 January 1793," footnote 2.

83 Fred E. Woodward, *Chart Showing the Original Boundary Milestones of the District of Columbia*, 1906, map, Library of Congress Geography and Map Division, accessed September 5, 2018, https://www.loc.gov/resource/g3851f .ct004223/.

84 "Boundary Stones of the District of Columbia," Boundary Stones, accessed October 30, 2018, http://www.boundarystones.org/.

85 Bedini, "Benjamin Banneker and the Survey." The excerpt is taken from the *Columbia Centinel*, May 7, 1791. It is a reprint of an article that first appeared in the *Alexandria Gazette* on April 21, 1791, and the *Gazette of the United States* on April 30, 1791.

86 Bedini.

87 Latrobe, "Memoir," 326–27.

88 Benjamin Banneker's obituary from October 28, 1806, *Federal Gazette* and *Baltimore Daily Advertiser.* This obituary shares pages with advertisements offering rewards for runaway slaves; see "The Dreams of Benjamin Banneker," Maryland Center for History and Culture, accessed December 26, 2018, https://www .mdhistory.org/the-dreams-of-benjamin-banneker/.

89 Silvio A. Bedini, ed., *Early American Scientific Instruments and Their Makers* (Washington, DC: Museum of History and Technology, Smithsonian Institution, 1964), 22, accessed October 30, 2018, http://www.scientificlib.com/en/ Technology/Literature/SilvioABedini/EarlyAmericanScientificInstruments .html#Footnote_11_11. See also Latrobe, "Memoir"; and LePhillips, "Negro, Benjamin Banneker."

90 Department of Commerce, Bureau of the Census, *Negro Population 1790–1915* (Washington, DC: Government Printing Office, 1918), 29, accessed November 11, 2018, https://www.census.gov/library/publications/1918/dec/negro-population -1790-1915.html.

91 Department of Commerce and Labor, Bureau of the Census, *1790 Census: Heads of Families at the First Census of the United States Taken in the Year 1790, Records of the State Enumerations: 1782 to 1785, Virginia* (Washington, DC: Government Printing Office, 1908), 8, accessed November 11, 2018, https:// www.census.gov/library/publications/1907/dec/heads-of-families.html.

92 Alexander Lane, "The Legend of the Slaves Building the Capitol Is Correct," PolitiFact, January 19, 2009, accessed November 11, 2018, https://www.politifact .com/truth-o-meter/statements/2009/jan/19/nancy-pelosi/legend-slaves -building-capitol-correct/. For more insight, see also Danny Lewis, "The White House Was in Fact, Built by Slaves: Along with the Capitol and Other Iconic Buildings in Washington, D.C.," *Smithsonian*, July 26, 2016, accessed November 11, 2018, https://www.smithsonianmag.com/smart-news/white-house-was -fact-built-slaves-180959916/#dK4U75hbhGGWz74C.99.

93 Mrs. Abby Gunn Baker, "The Erection of the White House," *Records of the Columbia Historical Society* 16 (1913): 12.

94  "To Thomas Jefferson from the Commissioners of the Federal District, 5 January 1793," *Founders Online*, National Archives, http://founders.archives.gov/documents/Jefferson/01-25-02-0022.

95  See notes in "To Jefferson from the Commissioners, 5 January 1793."

96  See notes in "To Jefferson from the Commissioners, 5 January 1793."

97  155 Cong. Rec. 17602 (daily ed. July 14, 2009) (statement of Senate Saxby Chambliss).

98  Arnebeck, *Through a Fiery Trial*, 233.

99  "Broadside: Sale of Lots in the Federal City, 8 October 1792," *Founders Online*, National Archives, http://founders.archives.gov/documents/Washington/05-11-02-0108.

100  "From George Washington to Tobias Lear, 12 April 1791," *Founders Online*, National Archives, http://founders.archives.gov/documents/Washington/05-08-02-0062.

101  T. H. Adams, "Washington's Runaway Slave, and How Portsmouth Freed Her," *Granite (NH) Freeman*, May 22, 1845, reprinted in Frank W. Miller, *Portsmouth New Hampshire Weekly*, June 2, 1877. See also Thomas H. Archibald, "Washington's Runaway Slave," *Liberator*, August 22, 1845, Encyclopedia Virginia, accessed December 16, 2018, https://encyclopediavirginia.org/entries/washingtons-runaway-slave-the-liberator-august-22-1845/.

102  Frederick Kitt, "Advertisement for the Capture of Oney Judge," *Philadelphia Gazette*, May 24, 1796, Encyclopedia Virginia, accessed December 16, 2018, https://www.encyclopediavirginia.org/Advertisement_for_the_Capture_of_Oney_Judge_Philadelphia_Gazette_May_24_1796.

103  Adams, "Article Reporting Interview."

104  Adams.

105  Adams.

## Chapter Four

1  Daniel Drayton, *Personal Memoir of Daniel Drayton, for Four Years and Four Months a Prisoner (for Charity's Sake) in Washington Jail, Including a Narrative of the Voyage and Capture of the Schooner Pearl* (New York: American and Foreign Anti-slavery Society, 1855), accessed August 14, 2018, https://www.loc.gov/resource/llst.008.

2  William Tindall, *Standard History of the City of Washington from a Study of the Original Sources* (Knoxville, TN: H. W. Crew, 1914), 463.

3  Edward Strutt Abdy, *Journal of a Residence and Tour in the United States of North America: From April 1833, to October 1834*, vol. 2 (London: J. Murray, 1835), 96–98.

4  Fredrika Bremer, *The Homes of the New World: Impressions of America*, vol. 2, trans. Mary Howitt (London: Arthur Hall, Virtue, 1853), 98, 99.

5  Solomon Northup, *Twelve Years a Slave: Narrative of Solomon Northup, a Citizen of New-York, Kidnapped in Washington City in 1841, and Rescued in 1853* (1853; repr., New York: 37 INK, Atria, 2013), 23.

6  For further insight, see David Fiske, Clifford W. Brown, and Rachel Seligman, *The Complete Story of the Author of Twelve Years a Slave* (Santa Barbara, CA:

Praeger, 2013); Frederick Gutheim and Antoinette J. Lee, *Worthy of the Nation: Washington, DC, from L'Enfant to the National Capital Planning Commission*, 2nd ed. (Baltimore, MD: Johns Hopkins University Press, 2006), 50–52; and Tingba Apidta, *The Hidden History of Washington, DC: A Guide for Black Folks*, rev. ed. (Washington, DC: Tingba Apidta, 2005), 16–24.

7 *Slave Pen, Alexandria, Va.*, ca. 1861–65, photograph, Library of Congress Prints and Photographs Division, accessed January 31, 2019, https://www.loc.gov/item/2013651888/.

8 *Slave Pen, Alexandria, Va.*

9 Some attribute its official name—the White House—to Theodore Roosevelt, who used the name formally on official presidential letterhead. Some suggest the name emerged after the new Executive Mansion's gray-sandstone exterior was painted white after the British, following the War of 1812, torched it. Others suggest the name was influenced by Martha Washington's reference to Mount Vernon as the "White House Plantation."

10 "From Abigail Smith Adams to Cotton Tufts, 28 November 1800," *Founders Online*, National Archives, http://founders.archives.gov/documents/Adams/99-03-02-0799.

11 "Slaves Built the White House and Capitol—See the Record," National Archives, December 10, 2008, accessed November 28, 2018, https://www.archives.gov/press/press-releases/2009/nr09-28-images.html.

12 Among them were Georgetown merchant and the treasurer of Federal City commissioner's board, William Deakins, and James Dermott and Middleton Belt, slave owners who were hired to oversee the enslaved labor force at some of the surveying and construction sites. Two of the city's commissioners, Gustavus Scott and William Thornton, as well as wealthy developer Thomas Law, whose wife, Elizabeth Parke Custis, was George and Martha Washington's granddaughter, profited also from hiring out their laborers. Thornton was later commissioned to design the US Capitol. Architect James Hoban brought with him to the city several of his enslaved carpenters to aid him in constructing the President's House.

13 "From George Washington to Tobias Lear, 30 July 1792," *Founders Online*, National Archives, https://founders.archives.gov/documents/Washington/05-10-02-0405. See also "From George Washington to the Commissioners for the District of Columbia, 8 June 1792," *Founders Online*, National Archives, https://founders.archives.gov/documents/Washington/05-10-02-0289. See also "To George Washington from the Commissioners for the District of Columbia, 19 July 1792," *Founders Online*, National Archives, https://founders.archives.gov/documents/Washington/05-10-02-0385. Original source: *Papers of George Washington*, Presidential Series, 10:551–52.

14 "From Washington to Lear, 30 July 1792."

15 According to Washington's correspondences and diaries, Washington's use of the word *hands* in his writings was in direct reference to enslaved laborers.

16 Hoban's inspiration for the White House design was the Leinster House in Dublin, Ireland, an Irish structure that currently serves as the seat of the Irish parliament. For more info, see Clarence Lusane, *Black History of the White House* (San Francisco: Open Media Series / City Lights Books, 2011), 108, 109.

17  *Monthly Payroll for Carpenters and Joiners at the President's House*, National Archives, RG 217, Records of the Commissioners of the City of Washington, accessed November 28, 2018, https://www.archives.gov/press/press-releases/2009/nr09-28-images.html.

18  Chris Myers Asch and George Derek Musgrove, *Chocolate City: A History of Race and Democracy in the Nation's Capital* (Chapel Hill: University of North Carolina Press, 2003), 33.

19  Asch and Musgrove, 33.

20  Lusane, *Black History*, 108, 109.

21  *White House, [Washington, D.C.]*, 1918, glass negative, National Photo Company Collection, Library of Congress, accessed February 13, 2019, https://www.loc.gov/item/2016819382/.

22  James Fisher, "Narrative of James Fisher," in *Slave Testimony: Two Centuries of Letters, Speeches, Interviews, and Autobiographies*, ed. John Blassingame (Baton Rouge: Louisiana State University, 1977), 234.

23  "From John Adams to George Churchman, 24 January 1801," *Founders Online*, National Archives, https://founders.archives.gov/documents/Adams/99-02-02-4766.

24  Linda Mann, "Slavery and French Cuisine in Jefferson's Working White House," White House Historical Society, accessed February 13, 2019, https://www.whitehousehistory.org/slavery-and-french-cuisine-in-jeffersons-working-white-house.

25  "The Emancipation Proclamation," National Archives, accessed February 5, 2019, https://www.archives.gov/exhibits/featured-documents/emancipation-proclamation.

26  "To Washington from L'Enfant, 22 June 1791."

27  "From George Washington to the Commissioners for the District of Columbia, 2 April 1793," *Founders Online*, National Archives, https://founders.archives.gov/documents/Washington/05-12-02-0323. See also "From George Washington to the Commissioners for the District of Columbia, 31 January 1793," *Founders Online*, National Archives, https://founders.archives.gov/documents/Washington/05-12-02-0044; and "From Thomas Jefferson to Daniel Carroll, 1 February 1793," *Founders Online*, National Archives, https://founders.archives.gov/documents/Jefferson/01-25-02-0116.

28  "From Washington to the Commissioners, 31 January 1793." See also "From George Washington to David Stuart, 30 November 1792," *Founders Online*, National Archives, https://founders.archives.gov/documents/Washington/05-11-02-0264. See also "To Washington from the Commissioners, 19 July 1792," footnote 1.

29  In 1795, George Hadfield (1763–1826) designed the first office buildings for cabinet departments, but his refusal to relinquish the plans resulted in his termination by the commissioners in 1798. The commissioners then turned to James Hoban (1758–1831), designer of the White House, now charged with supervising the construction of the White House and the Capitol. Hoban provided oversight on the Senate Chamber (north wing) completion and designing its interior. He remained with the project until shortly after the unfinished Capitol opened its doors in 1800. English immigrant Benjamin

Henry Boneval Latrobe (1764–1820) followed Hoban and oversaw the final construction stages, completing the House Chamber (south wing) in 1807. But work on the Capitol seemed futile when it nearly burned to the ground during the War of 1812. Latrobe assumed a new role becoming the second architect of the Capitol in 1815. He made touches to the interior by placing tobacco leaves (symbolizing the young nation's wealth) and corncobs (representing the young nation's bounty) on columns and border walls throughout House and Senate Chambers and designing the neoclassical-style Supreme Court Chamber. Charles Bulfinch (1763–1844), a Boston native and the Capitol's third chief architect, rebuilt and renovated, after the war, the northern and southern wings; the western portico, grounds, and landscape; and the center section, which included the addition of a low wooden dome. Bulfinch also designed the Library of Congress, temporarily housed in the Capitol. While working on the Capitol, Bulfinch also created the Federal Penitentiary in Washington, DC, between 1827 and 1828. In 1829, the US Capitol building was complete, nearly thirty-six years after its construction began. See "Dr. William Thornton," Architect of the Capitol, accessed May 17, 2019, https://www.aoc.gov/architect-of-the-capitol/dr-william-thornton. See also "History of the US Capitol Building," Architect of the Capitol, accessed May 17, 2019, https://www.aoc.gov/explore-capitol-campus/buildings-grounds/capitol -building/history; "American Architecture Series, Charles Bulfinch: Biography of American Architect, Neoclassical Federal Style," Visual Arts Cork, accessed May 17, 2019, http://www.visual-arts-cork.com/architecture/charles -bulfinch.htm; and "The Statue of Freedom," Architect of the Capitol, accessed May 18, 2019, https://www.aoc.gov/art/other-statues/statue-freedom.

30 The listing was compiled by US Congress's Slave Labor Task Force and available in the National Archives' records of the Office of Public Buildings and Public Parks of the National Capital. For more information, see "Record Group 42— Records of the Office of Public Buildings and Public Parks of the National Capital," National Archives, accessed May 18, 2019, https://www.archives.gov/ research/african-americans/record-groups/rg-042-public-buildings.

31 Vivien Green Fryd, "Lifting the Veil of Race at the U.S. Capitol: Thomas Crawford's *Statue of Freedom*," *Common-Place: The Interactive Journal of Early American Life* 10, no. 4 (July 2010), accessed May 18, 2019, http://commonplace .online/article/lifting-veil-race-u-s-capitol/.

32 Crawford's third design was a woman with hair flowing from a military helmet encircled by nine stars. At the crest of the helmet was an eagle's head and feathers. A large brooch with the letters "US" (United States) inscribed was clasped to her dress just below her breast line. The woman was draped in a ceremonial robe, carrying in the handle of a sword hilt of a sheathed sword wrapped in a scarf. In her left hand, she carried a laurel wreath of victory and a shield of the US with thirteen stripes, representing the original thirteen American colonies.

33 Mills had garnered a reputation for his works—namely, his equestrian statue of former president Andrew Jackson unveiled in President's Park (i.e., Lafayette Square) in 1853. His Jackson statue was the first equestrian sculpture made in the US. The government offered to rent Mills's foundry and pay him $400 a month for materials and compensation to cast the *Statue of Freedom*.

34 "Philip Reid and the *Statue of Freedom*," United States Senate, accessed May 17, 2019, https://www.senate.gov/artandhistory/history/common/generic/Civil_War _ReidPhilip_StatueofFreedom.htm.

35 Wikipedia, s.v. "Philip Reid," accessed May 19, 2019, https://en.wikipedia.org/ wiki/Philip_Reid.

36 "Philip Reid."

37 "The Civil War: The Senate's Story: Philip Reid and the *Statue of Freedom*," United States Senate, accessed May 17, 2019, https://www.senate.gov/ artandhistory/history/common/generic/Civil_War_ReidPhilip_Statueof Freedom.htm.

# Chapter Five

1 Frederick Douglass, "We Have Decided to Stay," *North Star*, June 2, 1848.

2 Richard Doyle, "The Land of Liberty: Recommended to the Consideration of Brother Jonathan," *Punch Magazine*, December 4, 1847. See also Frederick Douglass, "The Land of Liberty," *North Star*, January 14, 1848.

3 Douglass, "We Have Decided to Stay."

4 On September 2, 1789, Congress passed An Act to Establish the Treasury Department.

5 Hamilton had served under Washington during the American Revolution. History has often touted Hamilton as a nonslave owner and abolitionist due to his writings and involvement in the Society for the Promotion of the Manumission of Slaves. But the author of fifty-one of the eighty-five *Federalist Papers* authored no antislavery or equal protection laws, treatises, or pamphlets for the welfare and freedom of enslaved and free Black peoples.

6 Hamilton's system consisted of three major parts: (1) assuming the states' debts incurred by the American Revolutionary War by issuing interest-bearing bonds, (2) instituting tariffs for importing goods to raise federal revenue and help domestic businesses, and (3) establishing a national bank and national currency as a means to hold funds and use securities as capital to encourage future growth. "The US Financial System and Hamilton," Town Square Business Resource Center, accessed April 1, 2019, https://squareup.com/townsquare/the-us-financial -system-and-alexander-hamilton.

7 Those who deposited their earnings could have their monies "invested in stocks, bonds, Treasury notes, or other securities of the United States" if desired. Depositors profited from the interest on their investment, creating a win-win for former enslaved women and men and war veterans.

8 Walter Lynwood Fleming, *The Freedmen's Saving Bank: A Chapter in the Economic History of the Negro Race* (Chapel Hill: University of North Carolina Press, 1927). Note that this was an expansion of his paper, "The Freedmen's Saving Bank: A Paper," published in the *Yale Review* 15, nos. 1–2 (May–August 1906): 40–146.

9 "Black History Month, Freedman's Savings and Trust Company," Oxford University Press's Academic Insights for the Thinking World, accessed April 2, 2019, https://blog.oup.com/2007/02/Black_history_m2/.

10  "Freedman's Bank," Encyclopedia of African-America Culture and History, accessed April 2, 2019, https://www.encyclopedia.com/history/encyclopedias-almanacs-transcripts-and-maps/freedmans-bank.

11  "Freedman's Bank."

12  Freedman's Savings Bank, accessed April 3, 2019, http://freedmansbank.org/.

13  Virgil M. Harris, "Will of Salmon P. Chase," in *Ancient Curious and Famous Wills* (Boston: Little, Brown, 1911), 344.

14  Fleming, *Freedmen's Saving Bank.*

15  "The Freedman's Savings Bank: Good Intentions Were Not Enough; A Noble Experiment Goes Awry," Office of the Comptroller of the Currency, accessed April 3, 2019, https://www.occ.treas.gov/about/who-we-are/history/1863-1865/1863-1865-freedmans-savings-bank.html.

16  "Lasting Impact of Freedman's Bank," US Department of the Treasury, accessed April 3, 2019, https://home.treasury.gov/about/history/freedmans-bank-building/lasting-impact-of-freedmans-bank#:~:text=Lew%2C%20noted%20that%20%E2%80%9CThe%20legacy,benefits%20of%20our%20growing%20economy.%E2%80%9D.

17  Although the exact location of the pen is unknown, a common conclusion among researchers is Williams's slave pen was located on the Smithsonian grounds between Seventh and Eighth Streets, just south of the institution. Slave owner Jefferson Finis Davis, who later became president of the Confederate States from 1861 to 1865, confirms the pen's proximity to the institution during his tours of the region, writing, "It is the house by which all must go who wish to reach the building of the Smithsonian Institution." For more insight, see Mark Auslander, "Enslaved Labor and Building the Smithsonian: Reading the Stones," *Southern Spaces*, December 12, 2012, accessed April 4, 2019, https://southernspaces.org/2012/enslaved-labor-and-building-smithsonian-reading-stones.

18  Smithson was born in Paris, France, in 1765. Because his parents were not married, his mother, Elizabeth Hungerford Keate Macie, the widow of James Macie, gave birth to Smithson in secret and named her son Jacques-Louis Macie. His father, Hugh Percy, the First Duke of Northumberland, was married, at the time, to Lady Elizabeth (Percy) Seymour, Duchess of Northumberland, a member of the leading landowning families in England in 1740. Hugh changed his surname from Smithson to Percy when he married Elizabeth. His son Jacques-Louis Macie, on the other hand, upon his parents' death, changed his surname from Macie to Smithson. In college, he studied chemistry—namely, the composition of minerals and other aspects of science. He went on to give lectureships at the Royal Society and embarked on geological expeditions throughout Europe with noted scientists.

19  "James Smithson Makes His Will," Smithsonian Institution Archives, accessed April 4, 2019, https://siarchives.si.edu/collections/siris_sic_638.

20  Auslander, "Enslaved Labor."

21  Auslander.

22  Pamela M. Henson, "The Smithsonian Castle Construction Begins," Smithsonian Institution Archives, March 19, 2019, accessed April 8, 2019, https://siarchives.si.edu/blog/smithsonian-castle-construction-begins.

23 Henson.

24 Henson.

25 Garrett Peck, *The Smithsonian Castle and the Seneca Quarry* (Charleston, SC: History, 2013), 51–52, Kindle.

26 "Convert Perch to Square Foot—Conversion of Measurement Units," Convert-Units, accessed April 9, 2019, https://www.convertunits.com/from/perch/to/square+foot.

27 Peck, *Smithsonian Castle*.

28 *The Smithsonian Institution*, ca. 1840–70, photograph, Library of Congress Prints and Photographs Division, accessed April 4, 2019, https://www.loc.gov/item/2014649278/.

29 Brown also completed writings of his own, published poems, and presented his research to churches, community groups, and civic organizations. As an educator and activist, Brown served on the board of trustees of various DC public schools and Wilberforce University. He founded the Pioneer Sabbath School in DC and, in 1866, served as president of the DC chapter of the National Union League, a political organization for African American advancement. From 1871 to 1874, Brown was a member of the House of Delegates for Washington, DC.

30 "African American Groundbreakers at the Smithsonian: Challenges and Achievements," Smithsonian Institution Archives, accessed April 4, 2019, https://siarchives.si.edu/history/featured-topics/African-Americans/solomon-brown.

31 Henson, "Smithsonian Castle Construction Begins."

32 "From George Washington to the United States Senate and House of Representatives, 25 October 1791," *Founders Online*, National Archives, https://founders.archives.gov/documents/Washington/05-09-02-0062.

33 "To George Washington from John Carroll, 20 March 1792," *Founders Online*, National Archives, https://founders.archives.gov/documents/Washington/05-10-02-0079. Original source: *Papers of George Washington*, Presidential Series, 10:135–36.

34 Robert Emmett Curran, SJ, *The Bicentennial History of Georgetown University from Academy to University, 1789–1889*, vol. 1 (Washington, DC: Georgetown University Press, 1993), xv.

35 "The College Hires Sukey, 1792–1797," Georgetown Slavery Archive, accessed August 3, 2019, https://slaveryarchive.georgetown.edu/items/show/70.

36 "The College Hires Sukey and Becky, 1800–1803," Georgetown Slavery Archive, accessed August 3, 2019, http://slaveryarchive.georgetown.edu/items/show/102.

37 Maryland Province Archives, "The Purchase of Mary and Her Children, February 1792," Georgetown Slavery Archive, accessed August 3, 2019, https://slaveryarchive.georgetown.edu/items/show/272.

38 "The College Hires 'Nat Negro,' 1792–1795," Georgetown Slavery Archive, accessed August 3, 2019, https://slaveryarchive.georgetown.edu/items/show/105.

39 "Clem Hill Defrays Sons' College Expenses through the Labor and Sale of Enslaved Persons, 1792–1793," Georgetown Slavery Archive, accessed August 3, 2019, https://slaveryarchive.georgetown.edu/items/show/119.

40 Matthew Quallen, "Quallen: Jesuit Ideals Facing the Slave Trade," *Hoya*, January 16, 2015, accessed August 7, 2019, https://www.thehoya.com/jesuit-ideals-facing-slave-trade/.

41 Rachel L. Swarns, "272 Slaves Were Sold to Save Georgetown. What Does It Owe Their Descendants?," *New York Times*, April 16, 2016, accessed August 7, 2019, https://www.nytimes.com/2016/04/17/us/georgetown-university-search-for-slave-descendants.html.

42 Detroit Publishing, *Georgetown University, Washington, DC*, ca. 1904, dry plate negatives, Library of Congress Prints and Photographs Division, accessed March 27, 2019, https://www.loc.gov/item/2016803882/.

43 Alex Gangitano, "The Long, Accident-Prone History of Getting the Library of Congress Out of the Capitol," Roll Call, accessed March 27, 2019, https://www.rollcall.com/2017/08/08/the-long-accident-prone-history-of-getting-the-library-of-congress-out-of-the-capitol/.

44 "Thomas Jefferson to Samuel H. Smith, 21 September 1814," *Founders Online*, National Archives, https://founders.archives.gov/documents/Jefferson/03-07-02-0484-0003.

45 "Thomas Jefferson to John Vaughan, 1 March 1815," *Founders Online*, National Archives, https://founders.archives.gov/documents/Jefferson/03-08-02-0241. See also "Jefferson to Smith, 21 September 1814."

46 "Samuel H. Smith to Thomas Jefferson, 7 October 1814," *Founders Online*, National Archives, https://founders.archives.gov/documents/Jefferson/03-08-02-0008.

47 "Samuel H. Smith to Thomas Jefferson, 19 October 1814," *Founders Online*, National Archives, https://founders.archives.gov/documents/Jefferson/03-08-02-0029.

48 "Thomas Jefferson to Samuel H. Smith, 27 February 1815," *Founders Online*, National Archives, https://founders.archives.gov/documents/Jefferson/03-08-02-0234. See also "Samuel H. Smith to Thomas Jefferson, 21 March 1815," *Founders Online*, National Archives, https://founders.archives.gov/documents/Jefferson/03-08-02-0290.

49 "Samuel H. Smith to Thomas Jefferson, 11 March 1815," *Founders Online*, National Archives, https://founders.archives.gov/documents/Jefferson/03-08-02-0266. See also "Joseph Dougherty to Thomas Jefferson, 15 February 1815," *Founders Online*, National Archives, https://founders.archives.gov/documents/Jefferson/03-08-02-0211; and "To Thomas Jefferson from Joseph Dougherty, [on or before 25 April 1802]," *Founders Online*, National Archives, https://founders.archives.gov/documents/Jefferson/01-37-02-0262.

50 "Editorial Note," *Founders Online*, National Archives, https://founders.archives.gov/documents/Jefferson/03-07-02-0484-0001.

51 "Thomas Jefferson's Library," Rare Books and Special Collections Reading Room, Library of Congress, accessed March 27, 2019, https://www.loc.gov/rr/rarebook/coll/130.html.

52 "The Memoirs of Israel Jefferson," *PBS Frontline*, accessed March 27, 2019, https://www.pbs.org/wgbh/pages/frontline/shows/jefferson/cron/1873israel.html. See also Isaac Jefferson, *Memoirs of a Monticello Slave: As Dictated to Charles Campbell in the 1840's by Isaac, One of Thomas Jefferson's Slaves*, ed. Rayford W. Logan (Charlottesville: University of Virginia Press, 1951), accessed March 29, 2019, https://babel.hathitrust.org/cgi/pt?id=ucl.$b534612&view=1up&seq=11.

53 Mitchell Owens, "Slaves' Contribution to Monticello Style," *New York Times*, February 13, 1997, accessed March 27, 2019, https://www.nytimes.com/1997/02/13/garden/slaves-contribution-to-monticello-style.html.

54 Endrina Tay, "'Unquestionably the Choicest Collection of Books in the U.S.': The 1815 Sale of Thomas Jefferson's Library to the Nation," *Commonplace: The Journal of Early American Life* 16, no. 4 (2016), accessed March 27, 2019, https://www.monticello.org/site/blog-and-community/posts/1815-book-sale.

55 Kurt S. Maier, *The Library of Congress: A Tour in Words and Pictures* (New York: Gramercy, 2000), 19.

56 Erin Allen, "Inquiring Minds: Exploring Jefferson's Universe," *Library of Congress Blog*, accessed March 27, 2019, https://blogs.loc.gov/loc/2013/02/inquiring-minds-exploring-jeffersons-universe/.

57 Maier, *Library of Congress*, 32.

58 Maier, 33.

59 Henry Highland Garnet, "An Address to the Slaves of the United States of America," PBS, August 21, 1843, accessed July 3, 2019, https://www.pbs.org/wgbh/aia/part4/4h2937t.html.

60 Henry Highland Garnet, "Let the Monster Perish," BlackPast, January 28, 2007, accessed July 9, 2019, https://www.blackpast.org/african-american-history/1865-henry-highland-garnet-let-monster-perish/. See also Rev. Henry Highland Garnet, *A Memorial Discourse Delivered in the Hall of the House of Representatives, Washington, D.C. on Sabbath, February 12, 1865, with an Introduction by James McCune Smith* (Philadelphia: Joseph M. Wilson, 1865), 69–91.

61 Garnet, "Let the Monster Perish." See also Garnet, *Memorial Discourse*, 69–91.

62 Garnet, "Let the Monster Perish." See also Garnet, *Memorial Discourse*, 69–91.

63 Garnet, "Let the Monster Perish." See also Garnet, *Memorial Discourse*, 69–91.

64 Garnet, "Let the Monster Perish." See also Garnet, *Memorial Discourse*, 69–91.

65 Garnet, "Let the Monster Perish." See also Garnet, *Memorial Discourse*, 69–91.

66 Garnet, "Let the Monster Perish." See also Garnet, *Memorial Discourse*, 69–91.

67 Garnet, "Let the Monster Perish." See also Garnet, *Memorial Discourse*, 69–91.

68 Garnet, "Let the Monster Perish." See also Garnet, *Memorial Discourse*, 69–91.

69 Garnet, "Let the Monster Perish." See also Garnet, *Memorial Discourse*, 69–91.

70 Garnet, "Let the Monster Perish." See also Garnet, *Memorial Discourse*, 69–91.

71 Garnet, "Let the Monster Perish." See also Garnet, *Memorial Discourse*, 69–91.

## Chapter Six

1 Ruth Hairston Early, *Campbell Chronicles and Family Sketches: Embracing the History of Campbell County, Virginia 1782–1926* (1994; repr., Baltimore, MD: Genealogical, 2003), 494.

2 Early, 492.

3 *Genealogies of Virginia Families: From "Tyler's Quarterly Historical and Genealogical Magazine,"* vol. 1 (Baltimore, MD: Clearfield, 2007), 265–66.

4 Wm. P. Rucker to Mr. James E. Yeatman, Marietta, Ohio, June 29, 1865, in *Final Report of the Western Sanitary Commission from May 9th, 1864 to Dec. 31st, 1865*, ed. Western Sanitary Commission (Saint Louis, MO: R. P. Studley, 1866), 132–33, accessed December 21, 2019, http://hdl.handle.net/2027/uiug.30112049382978.

5 Rucker to Yeatman, 133.

6  C. D. Battelle to Mr. J. E. Yeatman, Marietta, Ohio, June 29, 1865, in Western Sanitary Commission, *Final Report*, 133–34.

7  The St. Louis Western Sanitary Commission was founded in 1861 by General John C. Frémont's General Order 159. The members included influential philanthropists. William Greenleaf Eliot, a Unitarian minister and founder of Washington University, provided the oversight of the commission and brought Yeatman on board to serve as its president. Eliot saw the need to form a sanitary commission in the West as a separate entity from the US Sanitary Commission. Frémont, Eliot, and Yeatman had a vested interest in providing field hospitals in the West and improving the St. Louis sewer system. By 1863, the commission was instrumental in providing medical treatments and homes for soldiers and aid to newly freed persons, white refugees from the South, and Union prisoners of war.

8  Battelle to Yeatman, 134.

9  Rucker to Yeatman, 132–33.

10  Rucker to Yeatman, 133.

11  Kirk Savage, *Standing Soldiers, Kneeling Slaves: Race, War, and Monument in Nineteenth-Century America* (Princeton, NJ: Princeton University Press, 1997), 91.

12  Savage, 91.

13  Mr. James E. Yeatman to the Editors of the *Democrat*, in Western Sanitary Commission, *Final Report*, 131.

14  Yeatman to the Editors, 130.

15  W. C. Lupton to Mr. James E. Yeatman, Marietta, Ohio, June 15, 1865, in Western Sanitary Commission, *Final Report*, 136.

16  Lupton to Yeatman, 137.

17  Lupton to Yeatman, 137–38.

18  Savage, *Standing Soldiers*, 92.

19  Savage, 92.

20  Freeman Henry Morris Murray, *Emancipation and the Freed in American Sculpture: A Study in Interpretation* (Washington, DC: Freeman H. M. Murray, 1916), 202.

21  Henry James, *William Wetmore Story and His Friends: From Letters, Diaries, and Recollections* (Whitefish, MT: Kessinger, 2007), 83.

22  It is quite possible that Ball's revised sculpture was inspired not only by the emblem, Alexander, and the commission's suggestions but also by other existing analogous works. Among them were a lithographic named *Freedom to the Slaves*, distributed between 1863 and 1870 by American printmaking firm Currier and Ives; the engraved graphic *Glorification of the American Union*, by Jean-Baptiste P. Michiels and published in 1873; and the marble sculpture *The Greek Slave*, carved by Hiram Powers in 1846. Given these and other works, it is clear that Ball did not conceptualize in a vacuum.

23  "Lincoln Park," National Park Service, accessed December 30, 2019, https://www.nps.gov/nr/travel/wash/dc87.htm#:~:text=The%20name%20apparently%20stuck%20and,site%20to%20bear%20his%20name (URL inactive).

24  "Lincoln Park."

25  "Lincoln Park."

26  Frederick Douglass, *Inaugural Ceremonies of the Freedmen's Memorial Monument to Abraham Lincoln, Washington City, April 14, 1876* (St. Louis, MO:

Levison and Blythe, 1876); see also Ana Lucia Araujo, *Shadows of the Slave Past: Memory, Heritage, Slavery* (New York: Routledge, 2014), 157.

27 Douglass, *Inaugural Ceremonies.*

28 Douglass.

29 Douglass.

30 Douglass.

31 Thomas Ball, *Lincoln Statue, Lincoln Park, [Washington, D.C.],* ca. 1918–20, glass negative, National Photo Company Collection, Library of Congress, accessed March 17, 2019, https://www.loc.gov/item/2016819395/.

32 Douglass, *Inaugural Ceremonies.*

33 Douglass.

34 Douglass.

35 "How a Statue of a Freed Slave Kneeling at Lincoln's Feet Missed the Point," *Root,* June 17, 2014, accessed March 17, 2020, https://www.theroot.com/how-a -statue-of-a-freed-slave-kneeling-at-lincoln-s-fee-1790876027.

36 Murray, *Emancipation,* 199.

37 Thomas Ball, *My Threescore Years and Ten: An Autobiography,* 2nd ed. (Boston: Roberts Brothers, 1892), 298–99.

38 Murray, *Emancipation,* 27–28.

39 For expanded insight, see Rayford W. Logan, *The Negro in American Life and Thought: The Nadir, 1877–1901* (New York: Dial, 1954).

40 Fisher, "Narrative of James Fisher," 234.

41 *Federal Writers' Project: Slave Narrative Project, Vol. 4, Georgia, Part 1, Adams-Furr,* 1936, United States Work Projects Administration, https://www.loc.gov/ item/mesn041/.

42 *Federal Writers' Project: Slave Narrative Project, Vol. 2, Arkansas, Part 6, Quinn-Tuttle,* 1936, United States Work Projects Administration, https://www .loc.gov/item/mesn026/.

43 "Statement of Lonnie Bunch," in *The Construction of the United States Capitol: Recognizing the Contributions of Slave Labor,* 110th Congr., Washington, DC, November 7, 2007 (Washington, DC: US Government Printing Office, 2008), accessed May 25, 2020, https://www.govinfo.gov/content/pkg/CHRG-110hhrg41186/ html/CHRG-110hhrg41186.htm.

44 David Brion Davis, "Free at Last: The Enduring Legacy of the South's Civil War Victory," *New York Times,* August 26, 2001, accessed March 26, 2020, https://www.nytimes.com/2001/08/26/weekinreview/free-at-last-the -enduring-legacy-of-the-south-s-civil-war-victory.html#:~:text=American %20slaves%20represented%20more%20capital,in%20manufacturing %20or%20railroads%20nationwide; and Henry Wiencek, "The Dark Side of Thomas Jefferson: A New Portrait of the Founding Father Challenges the Long-Held Perception of Thomas Jefferson as a Benevolent Slaveholder," *Smithsonian,* October 2012, accessed March 26, 2020, https:// www.smithsonianmag.com/history/the-dark-side-of-thomas-jefferson -35976004/.

45 Wiencek, "Dark Side."

46 Douglass, *Inaugural Ceremonies.*

47 Abraham Lincoln, "First Inaugural Address" (delivered March 4, 1861, Washington, DC), accessed March 27, 2020, http://www.abrahamlincolnonline.org/lincoln/speeches/1inaug.htm.

48 Abraham Lincoln, "Stephen Douglas and Slavery," Digital History ID 369 (1858), Digital History: Using New Technologies to Enhance Teaching and Research, accessed March 27, 2020, https://www.digitalhistory.uh.edu/disp_textbook.cfm?smtID=3&psid=369.

49 Alexander Stephens, "Cornerstone" (speech delivered March 21, 1861, Savannah, Georgia), Teaching American History, accessed March 28, 2020, https://teachingamericanhistory.org/library/document/cornerstone-speech/.

50 Derrick Bell, *Faces at the Bottom of the Well: The Permanence of Racism* (New York: Basic Books, 1993).

51 Rt. Rev. Stephen Elliott, DD, *Our Cause in Harmony with the Purposes of God in Christ Jesus. A Sermon Preached in Christ Church, Savannah, on Thursday, September 18th, 1862, Being the Day Set Forth by the President of the Confederate States, as a Day of Prayer and Thanksgiving, for our Manifold Victories, and Especially for the Fields of Manassas and Richmond, Ky.* (Savannah: Power Press of John M. Cooper, 1862), 21–22, accessed March 27, 2020, https://docsouth.unc.edu/imls/elliott5/elliott5.html. Also note that many early Americans used the curse in Genesis 9 to support their claim that God predestined Black people to a life of servanthood. In the Genesis account, Noah damned Ham's descendants to a life of servanthood because Ham, his son of a darker hue, dishonored and sinned against him. Over time, notions of darkness, Blackness, servitude, and racial hierarchy and supremacy interpreted from the Genesis account became interwoven with American's assumptions about slavery and race. The Genesis account, often referred to as the "Hamite Curse," along with other biblical passages supporting slavery and caste systems, emboldened slave owners and other proslavery advocates during the antebellum period and precipitated well beyond slavery in the US.

52 "Speech of Alexander H. Stephens, to the Georgia Legislature, November 14, 1860," Civil War Causes, accessed March 27, 2020, https://civilwarcauses.org/steph2.htm.

53 Elliott, *Our Cause*, 21–22.

54 Douglass, *Inaugural Ceremonies*.

55 Ariel Worthy, "Sarah Collins Rudolph Revisits 16th Street Baptist Church and Recalls the Moment the Bomb Went Off," *Birmingham Times*, September 14, 2017, accessed March 27, 2020, https://www.birminghamtimes.com/2017/09/sarah-collins-rudolph-revisits-16th-street-baptist-church-and-recalls-the-moment-the-bomb-went-off.

56 Worthy.

57 Worthy.

58 "Gov. Ivey Apologizes after Attorney, 16th Street Baptist Church Bombing Victim Ask for Apology and Compensation," WBRC, September 30, 2020, accessed October 12, 2020, https://www.wbrc.com/2020/09/30/gov-ivey-apologizes-after-attorney-th-street-baptist-church-bombing-victim-ask-apology-compensation/.

59 Catherine E. Shoichet and Khushbu Shah, "Dylann Roof Diary: 'I Do Not Regret What I Did. I Am Not Sorry,'" CNN, January 5, 2017, accessed April 6, 2020, https://www.cnn.com/2017/01/05/us/dylann-roof-trial.

60 Jennifer Emily, "Is a Witness in the Botham Jean Case Less Credible after Raising $30k on GoFundMe?," *Dallas News*, February 18, 2019, accessed April 6, 2020, https://www.dallasnews.com/news/crime/2019/02/18/is-a-witness-in-the-botham-jean-case-less-credible-after-raising-30k-on-gofundme/. Babbs also indicated Botham's door could not have been ajar as Guyger claimed because each apartment's front entrance is a fire safety door and therefore shuts automatically. Babbs was faced with criticism when she made the ethical decision to courageously step forward to shed more light on the shooting. Upon surfing the web, persons located her place of work, a pharmaceutical company, and urged the company to terminate her, saying she was a "radical," "antipolice," and "a Black extremist." Babbs was fired and had difficulty finding employment. She accused the company of blacklisting her credentials in the state of Texas.

61 "Accused Former Dallas Police Officer Amber Guyger Takes the Stand," CBS DFW, September 27, 2019, accessed April 6, 2020, https://dfw.cbslocal.com/2019/09/27/accused-former-dallas-police-officer-amber-guyger-takes-the-stand/.

62 "Accused Former Dallas Police Officer."

63 Ed Lavandera, Holly Yan, and Ashley Killough, "This Judge Came under Fire for a Hug and a Bible. Now Tammy Kemp Explains Her Actions after the Amber Guyger Trial," CNN, October 8, 2019, accessed April 6, 2020, https://www.cnn.com/2019/10/08/us/judge-tammy-kemp-interview-amber-guyger-trial.

64 Lavandera et al.

65 Lavandera et al.

66 Darcy Costello and Tessa Duvall, "Minute by Minute: What Happened the Night Louisville Police Fatally Shot Breonna Taylor," *Louisville Courier-Journal*, May 14, 2020, accessed June 10, 2020, https://www.courier-journal.com/story/news/2020/05/14/minute-minute-account-breonna-taylor-fatal-shooting-louisville-police/5182824002/.

67 Dylan Lovan, "3rd Breonna Taylor Grand Juror: Cops 'Got Slap on the Wrist,'" Associated Press, November 16, 2020, accessed November 30, 2020, https://apnews.com/article/shootings-archive-louisville-breonna-taylor-005f99347b202b3add4baca340a54820.

68 Darcy Costello and Tessa Duvall, "911 Call from Breonna Taylor Shooting: 'Somebody Kicked in the Door and Shot My Girlfriend,'" *Louisville Courier-Journal*, May 28, 2020, accessed June 7, 2020, https://www.courier-journal.com/story/news/local/2020/05/28/breonna-taylor-shooting-911-call-details-aftermath-police-raid/5277489002/.

69 Daniel Trotta, "Kentucky AG Says He Did Not Recommend Charges against Two Breonna Taylor Officers," Reuters, September 30, 2020, accessed October 1, 2020, https://www.reuters.com/article/global-race-usa-louisville-idINKBN26L1XP.

70 Darcy Costello, "Key Takeaways from AG Daniel Cameron's Investigation on the Breonna Taylor Case," *Louisville Courier-Journal*, September 23, 2020, accessed September 30, 2020, https://www.courier-journal.com/story/news/local/breonna-taylor/2020/09/23/breonna-taylor-decision-takeaways-camerons-investigation/3508067001/.

71 Janelle Griffith, "Wounded Officer in Breonna Taylor Shooting: 'I Know We Did the Legal, Moral and Ethical Thing,'" NBC News, accessed September 22,

2020, accessed September 30, 2020, https://www.nbcnews.com/news/us-news/
wounded-officer-breonna-taylor-shooting-i-know-we-did-legal-n1240732.

72  "The Mere Distinction of Colour," James Madison's Montpelier, accessed
March 29, 2020, https://www.montpelier.org/learn/6-ways-that-understanding
-slavery-will-change-how-you-understand-american-freedom.

73  "Mere Distinction."

## Chapter Seven

1  For more insight, see the Trans-Atlantic Slave Trade Database, https://www
.slavevoyages.org.

2  Hakim Adi, "Africa and the Transatlantic Slave Trade," *BBC History*, October 5,
2012, accessed May 18, 2020, http://www.bbc.co.uk/history/british/abolition/
africa_article_01.shtml.

3  Ciku Kimeria, "The Battle to Get Europe to Return Thousands of Africa's Stolen
Artifacts Is Getting Complicated," *Quartz Africa*, November 29, 2019, accessed
June 13, 2020, https://qz.com/africa/1758619/europes-museums-are-fighting-to
-keep-africas-stolen-artifacts/.

4  Portugal's trafficking in Africa dates as far back as the Middle Ages, when the
Moors ruled the Iberian Peninsula. The country's link to Africa was most notable
during Europe's Age of Discovery, or Age of Exploration, between the early fifteenth and late eighteenth centuries. In the early fifteenth century, Prince Henry,
the navigator and son of King John I, sponsored explorations from Portugal to
western Africa in search of gold, Christian allies and networks, and a water route
to Asia. He convened cartographers, navigators, and shipbuilders to create navigation technology to reach areas in present-day Africa, India, China, and the
Americas. Portugal's growing navigational knowledge and ingenuity in maritime operations ushered in the Age of Discovery and, in some ways, ignited the
transatlantic slave trade. In 1441, the first enslaved Africans arrived in Portugal
gifted to Prince Henry by Portuguese explorer Antão Gonçalves after his raid on
African villages. The following year, additional explorers set sail with the flag of
Portugal hoisted and a banner that read, "Order of Christ." Within weeks, Portuguese slave ships flooded the region, conducting more predawn raids on African
villages. The predawn raids were on Nair Island, Tidra Island, and the Serenni
peninsula. When the battles ended, the men "praised God . . . for their victory"
and returned to Portugal with 235 captives, the largest number since Portugal's
involvement in slave trading. For further insight, see Gomes Eannes de Azur-
ara, *The Chronicle of the Discovery and Conquest of Guinea*, vol. 1, ed. Charles
Raymond Beazley and Edgar Prestage (New York: Burt Franklin, 2011), 65–66,
accessed May 21, 2020, https://www.gutenberg.org/files/35738/35738-h/35738-h
.htm.

5  Portugal's pursuits were strengthened by papal bulls—in particular, the *Dum
Diversas*, the *Doctrine of Discovery* (June 18, 1452), and the *Romanus Pontifex*
(January 5, 1455) issued by Pope Nicholas V (Tommaso Parentucelli). These
two bulls granted Portugal monopoly of the trade and also established Portugal's rights to exploration, the conquering of lands, and the enslavement of

non-Christian Europeans. The latter bull solidified Portugal's role and also set forth boundaries for other European nations, especially in relation to Africa.

6  In 1470, despite the bulls issued to Portugal, Spanish merchants were eager to capitalize on the trade. Tensions heightened between Portugal and Spain. Both countries wanted access to Africa's riches and were willing to inflict harm to achieve that aim. By 1475 the two regions were at war.

7  In 1476, Spanish explorer Carlos de Valera of Castile traveled to Africa and returned with gold and nearly four hundred enslaved Africans, the largest number captured by Spain. Other ships followed. In 1518 alone, Spanish ships imported four thousand Black-bodied people into New Spain.

8  "Spain Case Study," Understanding Slavery Initiative, accessed May 21, 2020, http://www.understandingslavery.com/index.php-option=com_content& view=article&id=366&Itemid=219.html.

9  Spain also claimed the South American countries of Guatemala, Belize, Costa Rica, El Salvador, Honduras, Nicaragua, and Chiapas, as well as Cuba, Dominican Republic, Puerto Rico, and Trinidad and Tobago in the West Indies.

10  Dutch entrepreneurs established New Netherland, located along the Hudson Valley River, creating trading posts, towns, and forts up and down the river with the aid of enslaved laborers. Among the establishments were Fort Orange (present-day Albany), New Amsterdam City (present-day New York City), and Wiltwyck (present-day Kingston). The Netherlands controlled the area between 1609 and 1664.

11  David Richardson, "Shipboard Revolts, African Authority, and the Atlantic Slave Trade," *William and Mary Quarterly* 58, no. 1 (2001): 78.

12  Erik Gøbel, "Transatlantic Slave Trade Shipping," in *The Danish Slave Trade and Its Abolition* (Leiden: Brill, 2016), 24.

13  In 1733, for example, the Danish West India Company, a slave-trading enterprise, purchased St. Croix from France. Within a year the Moravians settled in St. Croix and established missions, and nearly nine years later, the Danish Crown assumed control of the region, making St. Croix a major slave-trading port. Copenhagen, in particular, experienced a sustained period of prosperity, resulting in growth, including the building of elegant houses, manors, and the castle that to this day can be found in the Frederiksstaden district.

14  Alissa J. Rubin, "They Threw Themselves into the Sea, 14 Black Women, All Together," *New York Times*, October 20, 2018, https://www.nytimes.com/2018/ 10/30/world/europe/france-nantes-slave-trade-museum-memorial.html.

15  The country's production of raw sugar and coffee estimated in the millions each year between 1789 and 1797. The country was also a large producer of indigo and cotton. By 1780, 40 percent of all sugar and 60 percent of all coffee from Haiti was purchased and consumed in Europe.

16  Great Britain was the predominant trafficker of human beings. Britain's dominance in the transatlantic slave trade was between 1640 and 1807.

17  In some sense, Britain was a master of all commodities—tobacco, sugar, rice, wheat, lumber, cotton, and so forth. The East India Company of England gained dominance over the Netherlands in the spice trade, and tobacco products in the British American colonies brought great wealth to King James I. By the eighteenth century, Britain had exported four million pounds of sugar from its sugar

plantations in the West Indies. British businesses, maritime operations and ports, factories, corporations, the textile industry, and industrial plants benefited from slavery.

18  Zora Neale Hurston, *Barracoon: The Story of the Last "Black Cargo"* (New York: Amistad, 2018), 3, 46, 52–55.

19  Hurston, 55.

20  Hurston, 56.

21  Captain William Foster, "Last Slaver from U.S. to Africa A.D. 1860," Mobile Public Library Digital Collections, accessed May 6, 2020, http://digital .mobilepubliclibrary.org/items/show/1802.

22  Hurston, *Barracoon*, 56.

23  Foster, "Last Slaver."

24  Hurston, *Barracoon*, 56.

25  Sandra E. Garcia and Matthew Haag, "Descendants' Stories of the *Clotilda* Slave Ship Drew Doubts: Now Some See Validation," *New York Times*, January 25, 2018, accessed September 3, 2020, https://www.nytimes.com/2018/01/25/us/ slave-ship-alabama-descendants.html.

26  Garcia and Haag, "Descendants' Stories."

27  National Archives and Records Administration Southeast Region, Atlanta, *The African Slave Trade: A Selection of Cases from the Records of the U.S. District Courts in the States of Alabama, Georgia, North Carolina, and South Carolina* (Morrow, GA: National Archives and Records Administration, 2008), accessed May 15, 2020, https://www.archives.gov/files/atlanta/finding-aids/ african-slave-trade.pdf.

# Conclusion

1  Morrison, "Nobel Lecture."

2  Morrison.

3  Morrison.

4  Morrison.

5  Danny Lewis, "The 1873 Colfax Massacre Crippled the Reconstruction Era," *Smithsonian*, April 13, 2016, accessed October 10, 2020, https://www.smithsonianmag .com/smart-news/1873-colfax-massacre-crippled-reconstruction-180958746/.

6  Whites opposing the election published a manifesto entitled "The White Declaration of Independence," whose opening reads as follows:

> Believing that the Constitution of the United States contemplated a government to be carried on by an enlightened people; Believing that its framers did not anticipate the enfranchisement of an ignorant population of African origin, and believing that those men of the State of North Carolina, who joined in forming the Union, did not contemplate for their descendants' subjection to an inferior race: We, the undersigned citizens of the City of Wilmington and County of New Hanover, do hereby declare that we will no longer be ruled, and will never again be ruled by men of African origin.

The declaration included a series of demands, such as a refusal to be governed by or share power with newly elected Black men, for jobs presently occupied by Black people, and to live in peace and protection from Black people.

7  Michael Siegel, Rebecca Sherman, Cindy Li, and Anita Knopov, "The Relationship between Racial Residential Segregation and Black-White Disparities in Fatal Police Shootings at the City Level, 2013–2017," *Journal of the National Medical Association* 111, no. 6 (December 2019): 580–87, accessed October 8, 2020, https://doi.org/10.1016/j.jnma.2019.06.003. See also "Police Violence Map," Mapping Police Violence, accessed October 8, 2020, https://mappingpolice violence.org/.

8  "Police Violence Map."

9  John Gramlich, "Black Imprisonment Rate in the U.S. Has Fallen by a Third since 2006," Pew Research Center, May 6, 2020, accessed July 25, 2020, https://www.pewresearch.org/fact-tank/2020/05/06/Black-imprisonment-rate-in-the-u-s-has-fallen-by-a-third-since-2006/.

10  Morrison, "Nobel Lecture."

11  Morrison.

12  Lewis expresses the same sentiment on two separate occasions with a few minor additions to one event versus another. For fuller insight into Lewis's excerpt, see *Construction of the United States Capitol*.

13  *Construction of the United States Capitol*.

14  For Black people, in particular, burdened with the historical and present weight of living in America, Morrison's Baby Suggs (Beloved) sends them a gentle reminder in the clearing to love themselves home every day, to retreat to their true selves, and to live free. She enters the clearing, and "after situating herself on a huge flat-sided rock," she "bows her head and prays silently." Then lifts her head and says,

Here . . . in this here place, we flesh; flesh that weeps, laughs; flesh that dances on bare feet in grass. Love it. Love it hard. Yonder they do not love your flesh. They despise it. They don't love your eyes; they'd just as soon pick em out. No more do they love the skin on your back. Yonder they flay it. And O my people they do not love your hands. Those they only use, tie, bind, chop off and leave empty. Love your hands! Love them. Raise they up and kiss them. Touch others with them, pat them together, stroke them on your face 'cause they don't love that eaither. You got to love it, you. And no, they aint in love with your mouth. Yonder, out there, they will see it broken and break it again. What you say out of it they will not heed. What you scream from it they do not hear. What you put into it to nourish your body they will snatch away and give you leavins instead. No, they do't love your mouth. You got to love it. This is flesh I'm talking abou there. Flesh that needs to be loved. Feet that need to rest and to dance; backs that need support; shoulders that need arms, strong arms I'm telling you. And O my people, out yonder, hear me, they do not love your neck unnoosed and straight. So love your neck; put a hand on it, grace it, stroke it and hold it up. And all your inside parts that they'd just as soon slop for hogs, you got to love them. The dark, dark liver—love it, love it, and the beat and beating heart, love that too. More than eyes or feet. More than lungs that have yet to draw free air. More than your life-holding womb and your life-giving private parts, hear me now, love your heart. For this is the prize.

Baby Suggs "did not tell them to clean up their lives or go and sin no more. She did not tell them they were the blessed of the earth, its inheriting meek or its glorybound pure." She used her words to celebrate the beauty of their Black lives and blackness. Baby Suggs, holy, told them in *the clearing* to remember "the only grace they could have was the grace they could imagine. That if they could not see it, they would not have it." See Toni Morrison, *Beloved* (New York: Vintage, 2004), 102–3.

15  Morrison, "Nobel Lecture."
16  Morrison.

# Index

Page numbers followed by *f* and *t* refer to figures and tables, respectively.